TRAVELS IN VICTORIAN DEVON

*The Illustrated Journals
and Sketchbooks of*

PETER ORLANDO HUTCHINSON

DEVON ANTIQUARY 1810 – 1897

Entitled: *Peter Orlando Hutchinson, aetatis 38.*
(Not dated)   (DRO, Z19/2/8D/99)

COMPILED AND EDITED BY
JEREMY BUTLER

DEVON BOOKS

First published in 2000 by Devon Books
Text © 2000 Jeremy Butler

ISBN 1 85522 755 X

British Library Cataloguing-in-Publication-Data
A CIP data record for this book is available from the British Library

DEVON BOOKS
Official Publisher to Devon County Council
Halsgrove House
Lower Moor Way
Tiverton EX16 6SS
T: 01884 243242
F: 01884 243325
www.halsgrove.com

Printed and bound in by Centro Grafico Ambrosiano, Italy

CONTENTS

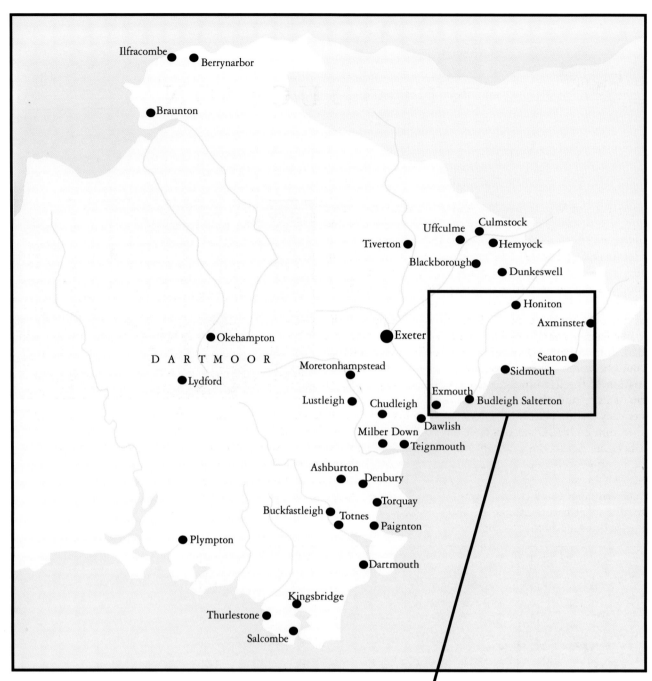

Ilfracombe
Berrynarbor

Braunton

Okehampton
D A R T M O O R
Lydford

Moretonhampstead

Lustleigh
Chudleigh
Milber Down
Dawlish
Teignmouth

Exeter

Tiverton

Uffculme
Culmstock
Hemyock
Blackborough

Dunkeswell

Honiton
Axminster

Seaton
Sidmouth

Exmouth
Budleigh Salterton

Ashburton
Denbury
Torquay
Buckfastleigh
Totnes
Paignton

Plympton

Dartmouth

Kingsbridge
Thurlestone
Salcombe

**PLACES MENTIONED
AND ILLUSTRATED
IN THE DIARIES**

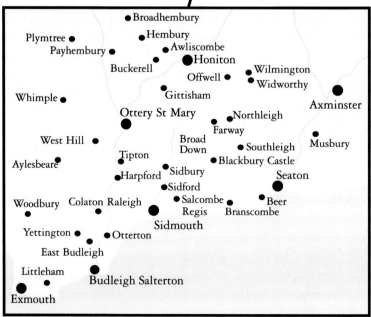

Broadhembury
Plymtree
Hembury
Payhembury
Awliscombe
Buckerell
Honiton
Offwell
Wilmington
Widworthy
Gittisham
Whimple
Axminster
Ottery St Mary
Northleigh
Farway
West Hill
Broad
Down
Southleigh
Musbury
Tipton
Blackbury Castle
Aylesbeare
Harpford
Sidbury
Seaton
Sidford
Woodbury
Colaton Raleigh
Salcombe
Beer
Regis
Branscombe
Yettington
Sidmouth
Otterton
East Budleigh
Littleham
Budleigh Salterton
Exmouth

INTRODUCTION

I was born at Winchester November 17, 1810, my father at that time being physician to Winchester Hospital, as he before had been to Exeter Hospital, and I was baptised at Heavitree October 22, 1811. My earliest recollection of life is when, I believe, I was about three, sitting on my mother's lap in a carriage driving down Peters Street, Tiverton. I first saw the sea at Dawlish, and I now see it as if it were but yesterday. There was a little ripple on the water from a gentle on-shore wind, and the sea was of a dark blue colour. I could scarcely believe that all that could be water. When I was about seven I got an inflammation of the left hip joint from a chill or something of that nature, and went through the pains of a 'hip-case' and kept my bed for sixteen months. My parents removed to Teignmouth with their then four children, and I in time got about again. When I was about ten, I was taken one day to the studio of Luny, the painter, and saw him at work. To the best of my recollection he had no hands or fingers but only round stumps, and he held his brush between the two stumps. I think also, he was deformed in his feet and went about in a chair. I was too young to be a judge of his paintings, but I recall a great naturalness about his coast scenes near Teignmouth, with the pack-horses bringing home red rock for building.

Entitled: *Sketch near Dawlish, Devon. May 1836.*
(DRO, Z19/2/8A/126)

Entitled: *House in St. Peter's Street, Tiverton, Devon, adjoining St. Peter's churchyard, bought about 1813 by Andrew Hutchinson, M.D., F.R.S., and sold by him to John Heathcoat Esq., M.P., 1825.* (Not dated)
(DRO, Z19/2/8D/2)

My brother was put into the Royal Navy where my mother's interest lay, her father having been one of Sir John Jervis's admirals. *He* brought up five sail of the line and added them to Sir John's fleet just before the Battle of St. Vincent on the 4th of February 1797 and contributed much to the success of the battle, after which he was made a Baronet and Sir John Jervis Earl St. Vincent. He made between eighty and ninety thousand pounds in prize money before he died, of which my mother had nine thousand and her three children who grew up, three each. Thus does money soon get cut up and divided.

About 1822, my father left Teignmouth and returned to his house in Tiverton. It was the last house on the left at the top of Peter Street and the grounds ran over

Entitled: *Anne Hutchinson, daughter of Sir William Parker of Harburn, co. Warwick, Bart. Ego feci 1848, - P.O.H.* (DRO, Z19/2/8D/95)

Entitled: *Andrew Hutchinson, M.D., Member of the Royal College of Physicians, F.R.S.* (Not dated) (DRO, Z19/2/8D/97)

Entitled: *Tiverton Bridge, from Collipriest, Devon.* (DRO, Z19/2/8A/128)

to the tower and down to the river below the churchyard. Three years after he sold it to Mr. Heathcoat of the lace factory, who converted the house into two as it was very large, and in January 1825 he took his family to Sidmouth where he bought a house and grounds which I now have beside the Old Chancel, which I built.

My brother left the Navy, went to South Australia, bought land near Port Elliot, came back, married, went out again, died in 1870 and left a widow with four children well provided for. I had a section out there myself near Port Victor, which cost £100 and I recently sold it for £1000. My sister married the eldest son of General Rumley of Arcot House near Sidmouth, and eventually they also went to Australia and bought land near Salisbury, where she still survives. My unfortunate lameness prevented my going out in the world and running the race of life with other boys, but I went to day schools and had foreign teachers of languages and had tutors at home, Italian, French and dead languages, but never went to college. My father was of Catherine Hall, Cambridge. He was a capital French scholar with a good pronunciation for he had sojourned in France in his youth, and I used to read a good deal with him.

Arrived at man's estate, I found myself without a profession, and if a young man allows the right age for a commencement to slip by, he loses the chance and will never get into the right groove afterwards. But I was now strong and well except for occasional violent rheumatic or neuralgic pains in my legs that quite disabled me at times. But I determined to 'walk it off' and try a change of air. I consumed a whole summer walking through north and south Wales, the pain rather bad at intervals. Upon this I published a book, which was a very childish affair. Another year, I tried to 'walk it off' again by going all round Scotland, and coming back I passed through Gretna Green. And here I heard such a multitude of sensational stories about runaway matches and all that kind of nonsense, that I committed them to paper in two volumes, of which Bentley bought the copyright. A silly work, only to be ashamed of in maturer years. But I was 'young and foolish' and the work suited foolish readers. And a five act tragedy founded on early American history, and a five act comedy on the occasion of some literary competition thirty or forty years ago when Mrs. Gore, then a popular writer, ran off with the prize of fifty pounds; and sundry poems in verse and rhyme of several fyttes each, all of which were never sent to the printer any more than my History of Sidmouth; and one or two three-volume novels the manuscripts of which I threw aside and know not what has become of them; and an amount of trash printed in newspapers and magazines that are only remembered to be laughed at and condemned.

And then I made a very pleasant tour to Boston and the northern States of America, Canada, the Great Lakes and Niagara. *I* took a good look at places where my ancestors had lived from 1634 till 1776 and was shown the spot near North Square, Boston, where Governor Hutchinson's house had stood which the mob destroyed in August 1765, and one of his country estates six miles out at Milton which the new American government confiscated and sold to its own advantage for thirty-eight thousand pounds lawful paper money, as I see in my great-grandfather's diary. Then, when Washington was bombarding Boston in March 1776, they had to clear out in a hurry and my father was born on the ship coming to England and was baptised at Kensington. And then I made a walking tour through the midland counties of England, and another year I took the eastern counties, and paid two or three visits to the Continent.

My first lesson in music was given me on the top of my father's house at Tiverton by the mason's boy who pulled a fife out of his pocket and from that time I was mad to learn music, so I was put under a master. In after years I used to take French horn or flute parts at the concerts of the Oratorio Society in Exeter, Michael Rice being leader, and at the public and private concerts in Sidmouth. Many the invitation and many the pleasant evening I owe to music.

I was always fond of carpentry and resolved that if all trades failed, I would turn carpenter. My admiration for gothic architecture originated at Blurton and Normancot in Staffordshire, the vicarages of my cousins, but especially at Lichfield when my cousin the late Canon Hutchinson was in residence and the Cathedral was so long under the care of Sir Gilbert Scott. This line of study probably suggested the building of the Old Chancel at Sidmouth, the first part of which having been made out of the rejected portions of the old chancel of the parish church, pulled down and rebuilt in 1860. Of the new or added part, I do not think there is a moulding or mullion or window label but what I can give authority for as late Third Pointed. My oak carving (very pleasant work) in the oak room and other places from necessity merged sometimes into the Jacobean. What drawing I know, I first picked up with Charles Frederick Williams, a boy of my own age *and* only child of a Welsh harper who had been on the permanent staff of musicians to Lord Courtenay at Powderham, and lived at the Castle. After returning from Powderham, Mr. Williams, the father, took a house at Sidmouth near my father's, and as young Williams was brought up to be a professional artist in watercolour, owing to our intimacy, I was much associated with him in sketching. Was there ever such a jumble of studies? Truly, a jack of all trades is master of none. One half the labour that I turned my energies to would have accomplished greater results if directed to a single object. In December 1846 I lost my father, and as my brother and sister were in Australia, I stayed at home with my mother. When I was a boy, my young mind had been opened to the wonders of geology by a niece of my mother's, a very clever person indeed, who died a few years after. I had supposed that the round world was merely a mass of earth and rocks pressed together like a snowball, but when she explained to me the regular succession of strata and the great facts involved in their deposition, a new field of research was opened up to me which has never lost its interest. I studied the great section of the Red Marl of the Triassic on the Sidmouth cliffs when bathing.

I bathed often in the summer for enjoyment and for health, and to cure me of the rheumatism in my leg as I hoped, and in this I succeeded only not exactly in the way I had intended. In the autumn of 1850, I bathed on into October when the water was cold and there was a piercing north-easter blowing, 'enough to cut a snipe in two' as the sportsmen say, and I thought it would harden me but I overdid the dose. I was chilled through, and the effect flew to the weak points, *so* I was laid up for a month with a most terrible succession of rheumatic pains. Then an abscess near the hip began to develop, and the month after another on the fleshy part of the leg, and a month *later* another until I was nearly drained to death's door. Then I went upon crutches for six months whilst I was recovering. But the effect of all this upon me was wonderful. It cleansed my system of all impurities and cured my rheumatism, and for thirty years afterwards I enjoyed a spell of continued health with scarcely an ache or a pain or an hours illness of any kind. Of course, I lived a temperate and regular life. There is no health to anybody without that. I rarely touched wine and never smoked from choice, *and* neither did my father or brother. I take no merit for this. It was choice. It is he who has a weakness for these things and resists them on principle *who* deserves the praise.

In 1855 I lost my mother and, as my brother and sister were in Australia, it would take the best part of a twelvemonth to settle her affairs and account to them; so I let the house for a year and having put things in train, went a second time to Normandy and Paris to make researches for my History of Sidmouth. In 1856 I returned and settled down, and then the ladies began to say that of course I should get married directly. Well, I always intended to get married some day, only I preferred doing it my own way. I wanted, not a housekeeper, but a well-educated person with tastes like my own as a congenial companion. A single man is generally a prey to dishonest servants. I had not kept house long before I found out that no man's house is complete or well looked after unless there is a lady at the head of the establishment. And then when they rallied me again over my dilatoriness, I said in my excuse that ladies had got so many fingers on both hands, I couldn't find out which was the right one to put the ring on, and that I was too shy to ask questions. One must say something.

In 1857 the first edition of my little Sidmouth Guide came out, *which* I gave to the bookseller. I joined the Volunteer Artillery and was several years a lieutenant in it. In 1868, I joined the Devonshire Association and occasionally read a paper. The meetings were always very agreeable. In 1870, I was having a third spell at building the Old Chancel, just as I could spare pocket money. At the age of sixty-five I was still like a boy, with all the activity and buoyancy and feeling usually ascribed to twenty-five, and too fond of fun and joking for a person who ought to have come to the years of discretion. At sixty-eight I began to suspect that I was not quite so supple in my limbs as I had been, so I named this period 'the beginning of downhill'. By 1880 we had had those severe winters in succession, but I was out every day regardless of ice and snow. However, in February 1881, from want of care, I got a cold and an attack in the throat of the nature of bronchitis or something of that sort, from the effects of which I have never quite recovered. But still, dating from 1850 to 1880 I have completed thirty years of good health, and for this long continued blessing I feel truly thankful to the Giver of all Good. (*Diary: Thursday November 17, 1881*).

So writes Peter Orlando Hutchinson in his Diary, looking back on his life on his seventy-first birthday. It is however, far too modest a self-assessment by an extraordinarily gifted man, remarkable even by Victorian standards of energy and enterprise. Had he been less of a jack-of-all-trades, as he describes himself, and directed his pursuits more narrowly, his talents and originality would surely have propelled him to a distinguished place amongst his contemporaries. As it was, as a gentleman of leisure with just sufficient funds at his disposal to avoid the strict necessity of following a profession, he chose to pursue an astonishingly wide variety of interests, and these with more than ordinary competence. He seems to have been equally at home with such crafts as embroidery, needle and leatherwork as he was in embellishing the easternmost piers of the parish church with decorative plasterwork or undertaking the stone carving round the vestry door. He loved music and was a good enough instrumentalist on the flute and French horn to take part in public performances at Exeter and elsewhere, and naturally was much in demand for musical soirees in the houses of other Sidmouth gentry. He eventually became less enamoured of participating in these events though ('my flute doesn't dine out') complaining after one such evening's entertainment that the press of the audience left him with barely enough room to stand. He was justly proud of his abilities as a wood carver but he was also a very fine engraver, illustrating many of his own publications and, as was the fashion amongst both men and women in an age when no great gulf separated the arts and sciences, he conducted various scientific experiments with his friends on such subjects as astronomy, magnetism, defraction, etc. The seemingly casual invention of various mechanical devices recorded in the Diaries was almost routine at the time, but one particular line of enquiry pursued over several years was rather more idiosyncratic. With the start of the Crimean campaign in April 1854, Hutchinson expresses his surprise at finding the country at war and, rather naively as it turned out, his disappointment at being too old to take an active part in it. Nevertheless, determined to do what he could, as 'a man may serve his country sometimes without fighting', he was soon in contact with the government about an iron-clad gunboat he had designed and a new type of artillery shell filled with a particularly unpleasant explosive. The latter at least seems to have been considered seriously enough by the authorities to warrant a brief description in the Illustrated London News. His interest in artillery increased when he was given a brass gun captured from pirates off Borneo by his cousin John Roberton, a naval officer, which he had re-bored and mounted on a carriage. This he took around town to show to his friends and amuse, he says, the residents by firing it out to sea from the esplanade. It was however, a toy compared to the iron gun four feet eight inches at the breech he had made in Birmingham a few years later. Apart from the quixotic intention of defending Sidmouth single-handedly in the event of a French invasion, he did have a serious purpose in mind. The superiority of rifled ordnance had been recognised and he was attempting to design a fluted shot for use in the many smooth bore pieces then still in service. He had various types of casing manufactured to his own design and at his own expense and tested them out at targets on Sidmouth beach, publishing the results in the newspapers and eventually in a small book. Occasionally a 'bruised' shot would go wildly off course but the townspeople apparently took a remarkably tolerant attitude to this periodic bombardment of their surroundings, even cheering when he appeared with limber and gun. He was much in demand for starting the regatta races and other sporting events. Hutchinson's military ambitions seem to have been fulfilled when he was persuaded to join the newly-formed Volunteer Artillery Corps as a lieutenant, and though hesitant at first because of his lameness and the possible expense, his amateur experiments made him the most experienced man in the unit.

These however, were little more than pastimes and Hutchinson's considerable claims to attention lie in other directions. His magnificent 'History of Sidmouth', a local history unsurpassed and rarely equalled for any town in the country, is well if not widely known, mainly because it has never been published in its entirety. Nor was it ever intended to be, as Hutchinson estimated that a single volume along with a dozen plates would cost £200 and he doubted whether he could ever sell enough copies to recover even that sum. However, excluding the final volume of old prints, rather more than half a version of the text eventually appeared in print, often improved upon and re-written as miscellaneous articles in various West Country journals. Over thirty years were spent in gathering materials, including copying and translating the medieval Latin manuscripts held in the monastic libraries of northern France and in the London Record Office. He taught himself to become a competent enough medieval scholar to receive the approbation of that most severe critic Dr. Oliver of 'Monasticon' fame, and was one of the members responsible for the Devonshire Association's Domesday translation. The volumes of the 'History' are beautifully illustrated with his own watercolours, many of which are included in this edition. He seems to have made little of his gifts as an artist, but these coloured sketches and the hundreds more in the five sketchbooks left to Exeter Museum include some exquisite images. Not only are they miniature masterpieces, often amusing, but they have become valuable records of scenes now gone, as Hutchinson's antiquarian conscience took seriously the duty of an artist to depict objects faithfully and he was highly critical of the 'artistic licence' assumed by others. For a short period he experimented with oil painting, carefully recording the amount of time he spent on each picture, but he regarded it as an indulgence and confined himself thereafter to watercolours. Though the 'History of Sidmouth', Hutchinson's magnum opus, was to remain in manuscript, the list of his published works on a great variety of subjects was formidable as a glance at the bibliography at the end of Volume One shows. He also wrote numerous articles and letters on the topics of the day to local and national newspapers, some issues containing two or even three contributions by him signed with different variations of his name.

A more tangible memorial, and one that visitors to the town soon become aware of, is the house he built off Coburg Terrace, the Old Chancel. He might well have continued to live on in his parent's home next door but for the decision in 1858 radically to restore the parish church, involving the demolition of its medieval chancel. Hutchinson decided to save what he could of the ancient fabric, and for a small sum had it re-erected in miniature on his grounds. At first he intended it merely as a workroom and library and somewhere to put his growing collection of odds and ends, but when more stone became available with the restoration of Awliscombe church a few years later the idea grew of enlarging the building and eventually converting it into a residence. From then on the building was periodically enlarged in a medieval style as money could be spared, Hutchinson himself undertaking the plasterwork and wood carving decorating the quirky interior. Not surprisingly considering the piecemeal and unplanned additions, Hutchinson confided to his Diary his dissatisfaction with the final result, contrary to the opinion of some of his friends who apparently considered it a matter of preference: 'One of his characteristics was that he had no idea of what other people call 'comfort'. His house was cold and gloomy; he never had a good fire or a comfortable chair, and this peculiarity remained with him to the last as was shown in his refusal to have any proper nursing'. (Letter from J. Kennet Were to Perceval dated October 17, 1897, soon after Hutchinson's death). Cold and gloomy perhaps, but also an extraordinary monument to one of Sidmouth's most notable citizens.

THE ANTIQUARY *Hutchinson mentions geology as an abiding interest from his boyhood having been introduced to the subject by a cousin, and he was fortunate to live in such a geologically varied area. In his younger days he published a small book on his pioneering work on the cliffs and exposures of south-east Devon and was still lecturing on the subject to small audiences into old age. Perhaps his most valuable legacy however, is one not mentioned in his autobiography at all, his contribution to Devon's archaeology. By the middle of the nineteenth century most counties of England had a written history containing a section devoted to the earthworks and other ancient structures in their regions, though it was often little more than a list with approximate dimensions. Devon was fortunate that in addition to the two fair foundations laid down by Polwhele and Lysons, there were a number of local archaeological studies as well, such as Rowe's Perambulation of Dartmoor, Davidson on the earthworks of east Devon, Shortt on the Exeter region and Woolcombe's unpublished manuscript on the hillforts, and there were also occasional reports in local and national journals. For a time Devon had been at the centre of intensive archaeological attention following the important series of bone cave excavations by McEnery, Pengelly, Buckland and others, the latter assisted at Chudleigh by one of Hutchinson's cousins, but by mid-century few individuals were actively engaged in the subject. Gentlemen still had their cabinets of curiosities, as indeed did Hutchinson, which might contain objects of local antiquarian interest. Hutchinson was known to collect such things and was the first to be approached in the hope of reward when boys discovered something unusual on the beach after a gale or farmers dug up some object in their fields. He acquired a reputation amongst local people as an expert on more or less any subject and his opinion was sought on the identification of anything from a 'petrified orange filled with diamonds' to a fishermen's unusual catch. Most of the Sidmouth mammoth teeth, eroded apparently from some source in the Sid valley, ended up in the Old Chancel museum, as did many of the coins found locally. These were of wide provenance and date and included a rare Bactrian specimen and enough Roman examples to suggest a limited presence. Some objects Hutchinson actively sought out like the peck of tesserae from Holcombe Roman villa bought at a Musbury auction, whilst others such as an old cracked jug bought from a townswoman for 6d, were preserved for their local associations. More exotic objects, like a marble ram's head from the Cyrene excavations or a Sanskrit writing set, were given by friends with sons serving the Empire abroad, or were left to him on the death of a friend. He inherited Heineken's geological specimens after his death in 1883 and an interesting collection of fossil bones from Buckland's cave exploration at Chudleigh from his cousin Anne Roberton. At the heart of the museum however, was the comprehensive collection of fossils, geological specimens and flint implements Hutchinson himself had picked up on the cliffs and hills around Sidmouth. Over the years the best objects were presented to the public museum at Exeter, and in the early days of its foundation he proudly remarks on the brave show his and Heineken's donations made to the fledgling displays. Some of his specimens, recognisable from his careful drawings, are still on show there, whilst others have returned to Sidmouth, on view in the cabinets of its excellent museum.*

Hutchinson's growing interest in archaeology can be followed quite closely in his Diary. Returning from Ladram Bay over High Peak Hill one day (September 13, 1848) the appearance of the earthworks surrounding the 'old camp' on the summit struck him more forcibly than before and he determined 'to examine it more closely'. Over the following few weeks he returned many times with compass and tape 'to set it out fair' and eventually wrote it up for an article in the Gentleman's Magazine. After investigating other camps in the area, Hutchinson and his friend Heineken returned to High Peak armed with a kitchen poker and a spade, wrapped up in brown paper to escape notice 'for we had no permission', to dig into an apparent tumulus between the ramparts. It was an amateurish start, not enhanced by Heineken's attempt to salt the mound with a Roman coin, but Hutchinson soon realised the potential of archaeological research if done properly. Some years later he correctly anticipated recent conclusions at this complicated site by paying close attention to the stratification of objects within the layers (see September 18, 1871). Unlike many of his better-known contemporaries, he developed a remarkably modern attitude towards the responsibilities of an excavator, digging primarily only those monuments that were actively being damaged such as the Lovehayne tumulus, or on sites which had already been destroyed. This was rescue archaeology, but he also had a research agenda with specific enquiries in mind. Excavations were undertaken to determine whether the flint mounds near Bury Camp were indeed burial tumuli, to attempt to settle the argument over whether Ancient Britons used the sling by careful excavation of the barrows on Salcombe Hill, to determine the nature of the foundations revealed on Sidmouth beach after a storm, and whether the underwater tree stumps off the coast were in their original position. He realised that techniques were likely to improve in the future 'and I am aware that too free handling of the tool may destroy valuable historical evidence'. He was both impressed and influenced by Bateman's 'Ten Years Digging' (1861) into the midland barrows, summarising the book's conclusions and copying some of the illustrations into the Diary, and at a later date by Evans' 'Rude Stone Implements' (1872). Noticing a remark by Evans that with the exception of the bone caves 'no palaeolithic implements have as yet been found further west in Britain' than the Axe valley, Hutchinson enthusiastically embarked on this new field of archaeological research, spending many days walking the newly ploughed fields in the vicinity and building up a fine collection of worked flint. His growing reputation resulted in the Society of Antiquaries appointing him their Local Secretary for Devonshire in 1865, much to his surprise, a post he held for twenty-four years. He joined the Devonshire Association in 1868, attended most of the annual meetings and usually read at least one paper on some aspect of history or archaeology. He was on friendly terms with many of the archaeologically inclined members such as Pengelly, Brooking Rowe and Ormerod and corresponded with others further afield, including Perceval the Somerset antiquary, Charles Warne of Dorset barrow fame and Franks of the British Museum, who visited him at home when touring into the West Country.

In declining to tackle such easy targets as the large Broad Down tumuli with the possibility of spectacular finds, Hutchinson sacrificed a more prominent place in Devon's archaeological record. These barrows and High Peak Camp were to be dug into in 1859-61 by the Rev. Kirwan, rector of Gittisham, an antiquary of the old school whose idea of excavation was to direct the labourers to the spot with instructions to save anything of interest. He was a busy man with many calls on his time and felt it was only necessary to be on hand when an interment was likely to be reached. Hutchinson disapproved of such methods and took it upon himself to attend the diggings if possible, and if not, to search through the discarded debris afterwards. He also deplored the fact that Kirwan had been given permission to 'dig over as many barrows as zeal may invite', remarking that care and deliberation spent on a single tumulus would give far more satisfactory results. Perhaps though, Kirwan was right to proceed as he did however rudimentary his technique, considering the damage since inflicted on those once magnificent Bronze Age monuments, many of which have now been destroyed. Fortunately Hutchinson spent many days mapping and measuring the tumuli of south-east Devon when the area was much less enclosed, his comprehensive account appearing as the second report of the Barrow Committee of the Devonshire Association. He also deserves much credit for his efforts to preserve the prehistoric antiquities of Dartmoor through a public petition and appeals to the Duchy through the Society of Antiquaries of London. The maps, plans of Iron Age camps and other earthworks and the barrow sections in the Diaries and elsewhere are included in this edition, as are the many beautiful sketches of archaeological finds.

THE ILLUSTRATIONS *Amongst the artistic treasures in the custody of the Devon Record Office are the six volumes of Hutchinson's superlative watercolour sketches. Of over seven hundred and fifty individual drawings, about a third have a Devon association and practically all these are reproduced in the present volumes. Most of the remainder illustrate his walking tours through Wales and the Midlands (1833-5), his journey to America (1837-8), to Belgium and Scotland in 1838 and to France and the Channel Islands in 1852 and 1855. Other watercolours are taken from the manuscript History of Sidmouth, from the Diaries, or are archaeological illustrations sent to the Society of Antiquaries of*

London, whilst the black and white sketches are mostly from the Diaries. His choice of subjects was as idiosyncratic as might be expected, since he found everything of interest from the extraordinary to the commonplace. Most of them are illustrative, one of the few exceptions being the amusing sketch poking fun at the local clergy exorcising the neighbourhood ghost. He was a superb figure artist, capturing the appearance of a New York chimney sweep, a Maori chief visiting London or nuns in a Normandy procession quite as naturally as the more intimate portraits of his parents. He was though, disappointingly reticent about sketching the many friends and acquaintances mentioned in the Diaries, very few of whom appear. Dramatic current events are depicted, like the aftermath of the Dowlands landslip and the vessels periodically stranded or wrecked in the vicinity of Sidmouth after a particularly vicious storm, as are ephemeral subjects such as the Yeomanry exercising on Salcombe Hill. Particularly valuable for their historical interest are such scenes as Brunel's short-lived atmospheric railway and those seaside views depicting coastal features long since eroded out of all recognition. Like the cliffs above the Chit Rocks at Sidmouth and the stacks and arches in Ladram Bay, Hutchinson periodically returned to sketch the picturesque Elephant Rock near Dawlish, chronicling its slowly disintegrating profile over twenty years. The elephant, and even the name itself, has long gone from the characterless promontory of Langstone Point visible today. Most of his landscape views however, were chosen more for their geological or curiosity value rather than for their scenic qualities. Faults and quarry sections, springs and boggy pools predominate over the usual pastoral subjects, but even here onlookers often enliven the scene adding colour and movement to the composition. Also of interest are the architectural sketches, though it was often the smaller buildings or even just the decorative details rather than the grand houses that appealed most to Hutchinson. Interestingly, many of the buildings he describes as on the verge of collapse, like the terrace on School Street in Sidford, Manston Farm and Lydford Castle, not only still exist but are now in far better condition than when he sketched them. Sadly, others such a Garnsey's tower have indeed collapsed or been entirely swept away as he predicted.

THE TEXT *The text of the present volumes is based primarily on Hutchinson's five-volume Diary kept in the Devon Record Office. Where no Diary entry accompanies an illustration in the sketchbooks the text is augmented with extracts from his other manuscripts, letters, etc., or as a last resort, his published writings, listed in the bibliography at the end of volume one. The text accompanying the Dowlands landslip pictures for instance, comes from the small book he wrote about it at the time since those Diary years no longer survive. He was a prolific writer of articles and letters to the Exeter and other provincial newspapers, and interesting or amusing extracts from some of these have also been included on occasions since they are not easily accessible. The Diaries were never intended for publication nor, originally, for anyone's eyes but his own. Indeed, he burnt earlier years on two separate occasions and contemplated destroying the remainder more than once. It seems it was only when assembling the information for his long article on the Broad Down barrows (1880) based on his personal recollections that he recognised their value to himself and perhaps to others. When it came to designing and constructing the elaborate bookcase he was to present to the Exeter Museum to hold his literary works, a section was reserved to take them, and it seems likely that it was at this stage that the prospect of public scrutiny prompted the discreet removal of a number of pages.*

Hutchinson commenced his Diary in 1832 at the age of twenty-one and kept it up more or less continuously for sixty-two years, until shortly before his death. It thus originally covered practically the whole of Queen Victoria's reign, though as already mentioned Hutchinson regrettably decided that the first two decades were too childish to retain. Consequently, though a few of those earlier pages have survived, apparently accidentally, the remaining portion only really starts half way through the year 1848. It is not a day to day record however, entries often being separated by days or even weeks, as he put down his thoughts and the events he found of interest. Entries such as weddings and funerals, social gatherings, picnics in the country, local gossip, etc., jostle alongside notes on archaeological and geological expeditions with his friend Heineken, scientific experiments and other matters reflecting the wide range of his interests. The closely but clearly written pages contain well over half a million words however, so only a selection of entries could be encompassed within these two volumes, the criterion for inclusion being principally those entries with a Devon connection or setting. Some aspects of his historical and archaeological studies have already been touched on, but there are also fascinating details of local customs that had not then quite died out and his valuable accounts and sketches of churches as yet to undergo drastic

Victorian remodelling. Of no little interest is the surprisingly large number of ships wrecked on the coast in the vicinity of Sidmouth to which Huchinson was an eyewitness, many of them not recorded elsewhere, even in the provincial newspapers. The History of Sidmouth reveals that the late summer of 1838 was a particularly unfortunate period: 'Around August four vessels were wrecked and all on the beach together'. In 1841 'a Guernsey schooner was driven against the west end of the sea wall and wrecked. About this period a two masted vessel was wrecked against the point of the cliff just beyond the mouth of the Sid. I remember the event but have no note of the date'. On June 7, 1843, 'a ship was driven on shore at Budleigh Salterton' and from 1848 onwards the Diaries record a whole catalogue of shipping disasters, occasionally illustrated by some of Hutchinson's most accomplished watercolours.

Also included are many entries reflecting on Hutchinson's personality and character, such as his views on women. Despite his fondness for the ladies, and his feelings were reciprocated judging by the number of Valentine cards he received each year and happily totted up in his journal, Hutchinson never married. Appreciative comments sprinkle the pages, as when he wondered whether 'the prettiest flowers were not walking about' at an Exeter horticultural show. Occasionally names are mentioned with more than a hint of interest, such as Amelia Elphinstone whom he dreamt of after meeting her one evening at Lime Park. Nothing came of it however, despite their friends seating them together on social occasions. He was disappointed when Heineken's nieces returned to Yorkshire, and a cryptic note 'don't tell anyone' suggests he was smitten by the Ermen girls staying next door at Dawlish. Discretion ruled however, even in the Diary, as these entries are little more than factual records and if he ever confided his deeper feelings to the pages it must have been on those neatly cut out at the margin. One slightly more candid entry is a copy of an amusing poem he wrote when in his sixties, addressed to an unknown lady complaining that he had forgotten the shape of her nose, but there is no hint of any further developments. Having returned to Coburg Terrace after a spell in France following his mother's death the pressure was on, but even the formidable urgings of the elder matrons of the town still with daughters to dispose of only brought forth rather feeble excuses. The trouble was that there was no real necessity. Apart from his talents and good nature, Hutchinson's natural charm ensured that he was a welcome guest at any evening's entertainment and he took full advantage of it. With so many interests and amusements he was probably reluctant to sacrifice his freedom, and there was also perhaps the fear that without a profession he was not wealthy enough to afford a wife let alone a family, women being 'such costly people'. Once age had placed him clear of any danger of entanglement however, Hutchinson could safely indulge a bachelor's lament for lost opportunities, concluding 'on the whole it is better for people to marry'.

One especially likeable side of Hutchinson's character was his affinity with animals and concern for their welfare, particularly at a time when such feelings were far from being universal. The few occasions in the Diaries where he vents his feelings in stronger language mostly refer to incidents of animal suffering, such as when he came across the hind leg of a rabbit trapped in a gin on High Peak Hill. He waxes indignant at the way horses were sometimes worked till they dropped and shamed the local carpenter into releasing a blackbird he had rescued from winter starvation once the warmer weather arrived by enquiring 'what crime has it committed that it should be sentenced like a felon to imprisonment for life'. He took great care of his pets, ensuring his drake Mr. Tommy witnessed the burial of 'his wife' so he would know what had become of her for instance, and constructing rope ladders outside various windows in order that his old cat could come and go as he pleased. He enjoyed visiting the travelling zoos when they came to town, as it was the only way stay-at-homes could see exotic animals, but remarks that he would rather see them perform out of love for their keepers. When a neighbour rushed in to inform him that circus elephants were demolishing his hedge and grubbing up the garden turf, he merely went out to watch their antics with amusement. Birds were his particular concern in winter. He provided them with as much food 'as would have kept a person alive', recognised them individually and worried when a familiar character did not appear at feeding time.

Some of the more bizarre events, such as Captain Boyton's attempt to cross the channel with the aid of a small sail attached to his bathing suit or the plans for a boat train designed to carry complete ships across Devon from coast to coast, have been retained, as have a few of the 'penny dreadful' incidents appearing in the newspapers which Hutchinson thought worth recording. Routine events that any diarist might jot down however, such as where he dined that day, are generally left out of this edition, as are most entries on national and international politics and the activities of the Royal Family, both of them subjects in which Hutchinson took a great interest. Also excluded are long sections recording his travels around the country and abroad, journeys illustrated by hundreds more superb watercolours in the sketchbooks.

It seems probable that the entries were written straight into the Diary with little preparation and few corrections, yet the text even with its unpolished imperfections is remarkably readable. A few minor alterations have been made, mainly to simplify the punctuation. Some commas have been deleted for instance, or substituted for semi-colons or dashes, strings of shorter or note-like sentences have occasionally been combined where indicated by italics, a few repetitions have been ignored and in one or two places an obvious afterthought has been relocated.

THE MISSING DIARY YEARS *An entry in the Diary for March 7, 1871 records that Hutchinson destroyed his diary up to February 1849, though before April 27, 1848 would be more accurate. However, a few earlier leaves survive at the beginning of the first volume recounting part of the voyage back from America in 1838 and also giving an account of his father's death in 1846. Rather oddly, a number of pages also survive interleaved with the drawings in the sketchbooks, including the rest of the return voyage from America. Together with the dated sketches, later boyhood reminiscences and what he tells us in his autobiography, a general picture of Hutchinson's earlier years can be pieced together.*

Much of his early adult life was dominated by the painful affliction to his leg and his periodic endeavours to cure it by arduous exercise. Health (as it is called, that is, the want of it) has been a chain that has linked me almost constantly at home, like Andromeda to the rock, but with feelings very different. *His first attempt to 'walk off' his lameness was made in 1833 at the age of twenty-two with a tour through Wales, becoming the subject of an amusing book 'A Pedestrian Tour of one Thousand Three Hundred and Forty-seven Miles through Wales and England, by Pedestres and Sir Clavileno Woodenpeg, Knight of Snowden'. Taking only a knapsack containing a sketchbook, a volume of Shakespeare and his wry-knecked flute, a hat fitted up inside as a flybook and a trusty walking stick Clavileno Woodenpeg, which he knighted after a successful defence in a fracas outside an inn, Hutchinson was justly proud of having walked more or less every step of the way from his home in Sidmouth and back again. At first he found the going hard:* During the first week after this departure, it is impossible that I can attempt to describe the feelings of loneliness and abandonment that haunted me at every step on the road, and at every instant of the day. *But this is one of the few sober remarks in the book, and what seemed to the writer to be* a very childish affair *is to the reader a highly entertaining account of Pedestres' Welsh adventure, who would* always rather be virtuous than sinful, where it can be done without sacrifice. *His itinerary from south to north and back through the Midlands can also easily be followed from the wonderfully detailed dated sketches of Welsh castles and costumes, amongst the most accomplished of all his compositions. Much taken with the scenery of the Peak District, he was back again two years later, walking and sketching in Derbyshire and Staffordshire. Hutchinson's most ambitious journey took place in 1837 with a voyage to America to look up the estates of his ancestors in an uncommon reversal of the usual flow. The very considerable property of his great-grandfather, the Governor of Massachusetts at the time of the War of Independence, had been confiscated by the new American government and the impoverishment of his branch of the Hutchinson family seems to have generated a mild but lifelong phobia towards the citizens of that country.* I have no great reason to admire what comes from the other side of the water; we Hutchinsons not having quite recovered yet from the riot, destruction and confiscation of a hundred years ago. *(Letter to Perceval dated October 13, 1888). After landing in New York, Hutchinson travelled to Boston and then on to Quebec, journeying up the St. Lawrence to Niagara Falls and returning through New York state. He accomplished over a hundred sketches of the people and scenery but on this occasion apparently with no book in contemplation.*

Hutchinson returned to England in February 1838 having been away just over a year but was soon travelling again, this time to Flanders, staying at Ostend and Bruges for two months. By August however, he had landed at Greenock in Scotland, apparently on a private yacht, to undertake another curative walking tour this time around the Highlands. He must have spent some time on Iona carefully copying the many grave slabs on the island, and from Argyll he went on to Inverness and then down the east cost to Dundee, sketching and keeping a separate journal of his travels. After what must have been an exhausting fifty-seven days he was back at Greenock. For some reason he decided to return to England overland through Gretna Green where he acquired enough material to write 'The Chronicles of Gretna Green', published in London in 1844. Despite the subject, the book is a rather ponderous history and in later life Hutchinson was ashamed to admit it as his own. When a friend noticed a copy advertised in a booksellers catalogue he wrote back: Hast thou found me, oh mine enemy? All my life I have been studiously concealing that childish production from your notice, but nothing escapes your vigilant eyes. What must the taste for reading be when I say it sold better than all my sober disquisitions. *(Letter to Perceval dated September 23, 1881). Hutchinson relates how he came to write it:* It so befell for our pleasant recreation, we had been making a peregrination round the Highlands, and were returning homewards towards the dew-dropping south – ay, and had even crossed the Debatable Land and arrived in the ancient city of Carlisle. By another chance also, we here became acquainted with a funny, laughing specimen of humanity, who had himself taken a wife to his bosom at Gretna, and who was full of anecdote touching the adventure so soon as he saw how curious and amused we were. He eloquently narrated how impatiently his lady-love and himself sped over the border in the carriage and never saw one bit of Solway Moss or the country, for the reason before given – how he found 'the blacksmith' so called, infinitely drunk and fast asleep; how he shook him by the shoulders to arouse him to life and to duty imperative – how the said blacksmith rubbed his maudlin eyes and cried out for another noggin; - and how he could have been married for a shilling only he came in a chaise, and so he paid half a guinea. Such words were not without their effect; the man was stirred up within us; we repented of our sin and incontinently girding up our loins for the journey, we forthwith hastened back over the Sark and took up our lodgement in the mansion hard by the Green. *(Chronicles of Gretna Green).*

Hutchinson arrived back at Sidmouth on November 17, his twenty-eighth birthday, but his travels for the year were not quite done: we only remained there two days – saw no one save my father and mother – and did not go outside the house. Determined to go to Mallow in Ireland to see my godmother Mrs. Jephson and her son Denham Norreys. *How long he stayed in Ireland is not known, but he was in Sidmouth by the end of the following year, at liberty to sketch and chronicle the great Dowland landslip. This cataclysmic occurrence is probably the most remarkable such event ever to have been recorded in this country and his illustrated and apparently first hand account was published in The Saturday Magazine for February 8, 1840. A fuller version published as a small guidebook appeared later in the year, as by this time the extraordinary scenic results of the landslide had become a popular tourist attraction.* It was about three o'clock in the morning of Tuesday 24th December, 1839, that the family of Mr. Chappell, who occupies Dowlands Farm, was suddenly disturbed out of their sleep by a strange and unaccountable noise resembling the rumbling of thunder or the distant roar of artillery. Not being able to account for it at the time however, and the sounds gradually ceasing, the alarm passed off and nothing more occurred for more than twenty-four hours – that is, about the same time the following night, when the great catastrophe began. There is a terrace or

Entitled: *View of the ruined cottage in the landslip. January 14, 1840.* (DRO, Z19/2/8C/172)

Entitled: *View of the landslip near Axmouth, Devon. Looking towards the west. January 14, 1840. Published in the Penny Magazine No. 505.*
(DRO, Z19/2/8C/170)

undercliff extending about a quarter of a mile broad and sloping down towards the sea, running along immediately under the perpendicular face of the cliff, and on this comparatively level stage stood two cottages surrounded by their gardens. It was about three o'clock then, on the morning of Christmas Day, that the occupier of one of these was aroused by noises so loud and terrific that he got up in order if possible to ascertain the cause. On coming down stairs he discovered that the floors were thrown out of their original level and that his dwelling was tottering as if ready to fall. The door was so wrenched and distorted that he was unable to open it without the assistance of a crowbar. The garden and the surrounding district were sliding on their foundations, large fissures were opening in the earth and it was subsiding in terraces towards the sea. He instantly set about getting his family out before they should be buried in the ruins. *The cottages* are both totally destroyed so far that they can never be inhabited again; the one has had its walls rent from top to bottom, whilst the other is nothing but a heap of stones.

During the whole of Christmas Day, a great subsidence took place, the ground slowly and majestically sliding away. The tract which sank down extends more than a mile in length, and measures on average some four hundred feet in width. The depth is variously stated. In the accounts that have appeared it is called more than two hundred feet... . This gigantic furrow cuts off a portion of the once united mainland... . On the upper soil of this detached part may still be seen the

Entitled: *View of the landslip, looking towards the east. Published in the Saturday Magazine, Feb.8, 1840.* (Not dated) (DRO, Z19/2/8C/173)

others. But since the erection of the new church, burials are not allowed to take place, not even in the old vaults. In common graves about twelve yards west of the north-west corner of the churchyard, close against the wall that bounds the lane, in a cluster are Thomas Hutchinson, son of the judge, William his younger brother, formerly curate of this parish, Louisa, William's wife, and Henrietta their child. At William's feet lies Thomas's son, William, but without a monument. It was my wish that my father should be near them, but two days before his death he said he might as well be buried at Sidmouth. (Diary). *The family memorials in Heavitree churchyard did not survive for much longer. On later visits he noticed the graves deteriorating and eventually found the tombstones removed altogether and propped up against the wall.*

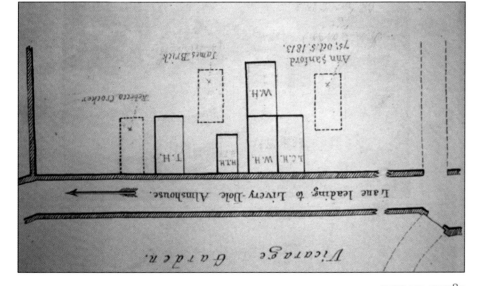

46/12/26-2. Plan of the north-west corner of Heavitree church-yard, Devon, January 26, 1847. (DRO, Z19/2/8D/5).

The first five surviving pages of the diary are an account of Hutchinson's journey back from New York to England in 1838, an uneventful voyage apart from an attack of sea-sickness on the second day out. The ship left New York on February 1 and arrived at St Katherine Docks in London on March 1.

Next entry: 'Remnants from the earlier part of my diary. Perhaps I might with advantage have saved such portions as preserved the records of actual facts; but as there was so much in it that was childish I threw it indiscriminately into the fire'.

Hutchinson destroyed some further years on March 7, 1871, so that the next entry reads: 'All my diary for fifteen years previous to this I have burnt as being useless'. *(That is, before December 25, 1846). This now seems particularly regrettable since over 450 of his early sketches are without any corresponding Diary text. Few of these are of Devonshire subjects however.*

A sad Christmas. December 25. Hutchinson was in London when he received some melancholy news. Christmas Day. Received the following letter from my brother. 'Sidmouth, December 24, 1846. My dear Peter. Your father died yester-day at 6PM and it is my mother's particular wish that you come down to the funeral which is to take place here on Tuesday if possible. You and my mother are named executor and executrix, and £500 are left to you as well as half of section 10 (at Alexandrina, South Australia, being the plot of 134 acres bounded on the east by the river Hindermarsh and on the south by the sea). As I am bothered with business and have many letters to write, it is not necessary to say more, as we expect to see you soon. I am your affectionate brother, Brigham Hutchinson'.

On the receipt of the above I made immediate preparations for the journey. I excused myself from Mr. Green's Xmas party, but without alleging the reason, and went to the Paddington Station to enquire about the departure of the trains. (*Diary*).

Saturday December 26. Got on the rail at Paddington at a quarter before ten and was taken by the express train to Exeter in four and a half hours, distance I think 194 miles. As I had two or three hours to spare, I walked out to Heavitree where my uncles and cousins have been buried, to enquire the particulars in case my father should be buried there, as I was disposed to wish for. Learnt from the Mr. Atherley the vicar, that in the vault in the church my grandfather Judge Hutchinson and his wife were buried, but I forget whether there were any

4/6/12/26-1. North-west corner of Heavitree churchyard, Devon. January 26, 1847.

1 (DRO, Z19/2/8D/7)

1846

portrait of his manner: *'how typical an antiquary in aspect, in face and figure, in character and demeanour, Mr. Hutchinson was. His very handwriting was a copy from the
antique, carefully, slowly and elaborately executed; his utterance and diction were equally
deliberate'*. Another account by A.E.Chandler, 'The Old Chancel and its Designer',
concentrating particularly on the building and Hutchinson's part in the church restoration
dispute, appeared in the 1950's published by the Sid Vale Association. A more rounded
biography is 'Peter Orlando Hutchinson of Sidmouth, Devon', published in 1983 by the
author Catherine Lineham whose index for the Diaries is kept in the Record Office. These
comparatively brief accounts can, however, barely do justice to such a remarkable polymath
and amiable companion. More than a century after his death in 1897, it is perhaps time
for Hutchinson to tell his own story.

ACKNOWLEDGEMENTS

*Many librarians gave generously of their time is assisting with the compilation of these
volumes, in particular John Draisey, County Archivist and the staff of the Devon Record
Office, and Ian Maxted, County Local Studies Librarian, who kindly gave permission for
the watercolours in the sketchbooks and the History of Sidmouth to be reproduced. Bernard
Nurse, FSA did the same for those held in the library of the Society of Antiquaries of
London, identified in their archives by Jane Marchand, Dartmoor National Park archae-
ologist. Also of great assistance were the staff of the West Country Studies Library in
Exeter, Adrian James of the Society of Antiquaries in London, Judith Harrison of the
British Library, James Turner and Pamela Wooton of the Devon and Exeter Institution
and, by no means least, Rosemary Whitfield, curator, and Maureen Church, archivist of
Sidmouth Museum.*

Entitled: *Chimney of the new Preventive
Coastguard Station, built by the engineer of the
South Devon Railway.   Sketched October 3, 1847.*
(DRO, Z19/2/8D/141)

turnips and young wheat which were sown there last autumn... The most notable objects which arrest the eye in the midst of the wildest parts of this wilderness are vast towers and pinnacles of chalk, which jut up from the bottom of the chasm... assuming the most picturesque and fantastic forms imaginable... There is another feature which is no less remarkable; the rising of a reef of rocks from the bottom of the sea and the formation of a harbour or enclosed bay in consequence... It is composed of clay, blue earth and rocks, and ranges irregularly along the coast for a mile... When the reef first showed itself, it stood forty feet above the water, but it has been gradually sinking and is now not more than half that height. (A Guide to the Landslip, near Axmouth, Devonshire). This event no doubt furthered Hutchinson's interest in the local rock formations, for in 1843 'The Geology of Sidmouth and South Eastern Devon' was published, a pioneering work on the district but one, like his other early writings, he was later to deride.

Later in the year and in the one following, 1841, Hutchinson was back wandering around the Welsh borderlands, but no amount of exercise seems to have been able to cure his leg. He was still suffering some years later, as an entry for September 19, 1846 shows. Returned a galvanic-electric apparatus which I have been making use of for the rheumatism in my left leg, caught a couple of months ago on Hampstead Heath. I have tried it a fortnight and done myself immense benefit. There are comparatively few sketches illustrating these later tours, and indeed he seems to have lost interest in the paint-box for a while. 1846 finds him enjoying the social life in London, regularly attending the Marquis of Northampton's soirees for instance, and it was at a party on Christmas Day that he received the baleful news of his father's death. He promptly went home for the funeral (see December 25, 1846) and shortly afterwards seems to have returned to Sidmouth permanently, to live with his widowed mother at No. 4 Coburg Terrace. No doubt be found the seaside town a small world, but it gave him the opportunity to take a closer interest in the neighbourhood and it is from this period that the Diary and the long series of Devonshire sketches really starts.

FURTHER READING   *Several monographs have been written about Peter Orlando Hutchinson. Some six years after his death, the Rev. H. Clements, vicar of Sidmouth, delivered a rather superficial account of his life in an address to the Devonshire Association ('A Local Antiquary', 1903) portraying him as little more than a talented eccentric, a perception that has to some extent persisted. Although they were acquainted and on friendly terms for more than forty years, Clements seems to have had little intimate knowledge of his neighbour, possibly because Hutchinson did not entirely trust the clergy after his disagreeable experience over the restoration of the parish church. As the Diaries show, that unpleasant interlude was hardly 'the only burst of active enterprise that interrupted the even tenor of a singularly calm and uneventful life'. Clements does however provide a credible pen*

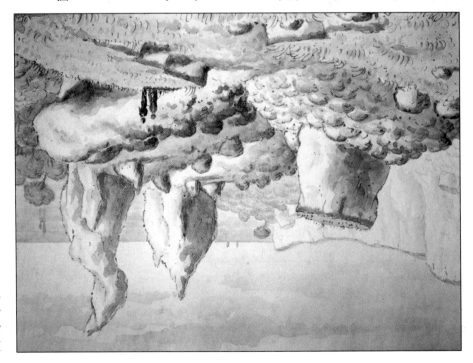

Entitled: *View of part of the landslip near Axmouth, Devon – looking east, January 14, 1840.*
(DRO, Z19/2/8C/171)

1848

There now follows a further gap in the Diary, though some of Hutchinson's activities over the next few months, walking, sketching, etc., can be inferred from the dated watercolours in the sketchbooks. Whilst living with his mother in Sidmouth, he paid extended visits to some of his relations in the area, to his cousin's family in Uffculme where the Rev. Jones was master at the grammar school, to another cousin Mary Roberton in Chudleigh and to Dawlish. On October 2, 1847, he went over to the Dart, perhaps going via Brunel's atmospheric railway and travelling on the newly introduced 'atmospheric train'. The rare contemporary illustration of its mechanism in the accompanying sketch shows the cast-iron pipe between the rails at the eastern entrance to Kennaway tunnel at Boat Cove, Dawlish with the 'Old Maid' and 'Parson and Clerk' behind. At last we catch up with the continuous Diary record with an entry on April 27, 1848 simply recording a letter sent to Alexandrina, South Australia, followed by another family death:

Death of Aunt Mary Roberton. *Tuesday May 9.* Went to Tiverton to attend the funeral of Aunt Mary Roberton, my mother's sister, who died last Thursday the 4th instant at 10 PM, from an affection in the left breast caused by a violent

48/5/2-3. *Cedar of Lebanon on the lawn of Heightley Cottage, near Chudleigh. Coloured from nature May 15, 1848.* (DRO, Z19/2/8D/113)

48/5/2-1. *Tunnel through the South Cliff of the South Devon Atmospheric Railway and the electric telegraph. Coloured on the spot October 2, 1847.* (DRO, Z19/2/8D/63)

48/5/2-2. *Chudleigh Rock from the south, near Lewel House. Coloured on the spot 1848.*
(DRO, Z19/2/8D/121)

48/5/2-5 *Bridge over the brook below Chudleigh Rock. Coloured on the spot June 26, 1848.*
(DRO, Z19/2/8D/131)

48/5/2-6. *James Crouch's bridge over the River Teign, two miles below Chudleigh. Done there June 28, 1848.*
(DRO, Z19/2/8D/133)

blow which she received in her youth.   Met her son-in-law the Rev. J. Jones at the Tiverton Road Station and we went on together. (*Diary*). *Hutchinson then returned to Heightley Cottage, Chudleigh, and whilst there sketched various scenes in the vicinity.*

Ramble near Chudleigh.   *Friday July 7.   Hutchinson was staying at Heightley Cottage, Chudleigh in July 1848.*   Rambled over the hills in the neighbourhood of the Hennock Road. (*Diary*).

Chudleigh Quarry. *Saturday July 8.*   The hay not quite made enough to house, but very nearly.   Took a walk to the quarry and made a sketch of it. Came home with rheumatism in my lame leg.   What a plague that leg is!
> If you should chance to get a lame leg
> You will find it a terrible plague. (*Diary*).

48/5/2-7. *Organ in Chudleigh church.   Coloured on the spot May 21, 1848.*
(DRO, Z19/2/8D/111

48/7/8. *New Quarry, east of Chudleigh Rock, and the Palace kiln.   Coloured on the spot July 8, 1848.*
(DRO, Z19/2/8D/143)

Hay making.   *Sunday July 9.*   It rained constantly all day.   Alas for the hay!
> Young ducks will thrive on a rainy day,
> But rain is a grievous thing for hay,
> That truth to this conclusion brings,
> That ducks and hay are different things. (*Diary*).

Heightley Cottage.   *Tuesday July 11.* Made two sketches of Heightley Cottage. (*Diary*).

48/7/11-1. *Heightley Cottage near Chudleigh.   Coloured out of doors July 1848.   Since burnt down.* (*DRO, Z19/2/8D/149*)

48/7/11-2. *Heightley Cottage from the greenhouse. Coloured on the spot July 1848.*   (DRO, Z19/2/8D/151)

48/7/13-1. *Uffculme grammer school. October 1847.* (DRO, Z19/2/8D/53)

48/7/13-2. *Playground of Uffculme school. October 1847.* (DRO, Z19/2/8D/51)

Leaving Heightley. *Thursday July 13.* Left Heightley for Uffculme. Went to Exeter in the carriage, then took rail to Tiverton Road Station and then a fly to Uffculme, where we arrived safe. (*Diary*). *Hutchinson paid frequent visits to his Uffculme cousin Marianne Jones and her husband Rev. Francis Jones, master of Uffculme Grammar School. From later passages in the Diary it seems that the children especially looked forward to his visits, particularly his god-daughter Agnes.*

Whetstone Hills. *Saturday July 15, 1848.* Made two drawings for the little Joneses and in the evening took a walk with them on Uffculme Down – No! I took a walk with them yesterday evening. I went up there this afternoon alone, and made a drawing of the Whetstone Hills. (*Diary*).

Return to Sidmouth. *Monday July 17.* My mother and myself left Uffculme and returned home to Coburg Terrace, Sidmouth, from which I had been absent some two months. (*Diary*).

Arson. *Wednesday July 19.* About an hour after midnight when I was in bed but not asleep, my attention was arrested by a bright glare of light shining into my room. I jumped out of bed, opened the window and looked out. There was a

48/7/15. *The Whetstone Hills, where whetstones, scythe stones, grindstones, etc., are quarried, as seen from Uffculme Down, Devon. Coloured on the spot July 15, 1848.* (DRO, Z19/2/8D/153)

large blaze of fire, the flames of which were rising over the roofs of the houses in the direction of the marsh. The next morning I heard that it was a fire in the timber yard of Charles Farrant, upholsterer, and that about a hundred pounds worth of timber was destroyed. It is supposed to have been the work of an incendiary. Farrant is not very popular. A fire occurred in the same spot some months ago, and it seems a spite exists owing to his having stopped up a thoroughfare in that neighbourhood. (*Diary*).

Coburg Terrace. *Thursday July 27. No Diary entry records Hutchinson's sketch of the gothic facades along Coburg Terrace. At this time he was living at Number 4, the end building on the right, along with his mother, brother Bingham and Captain and Mrs. Rumley his sister and brother-in-law.*

48/7/27. *Coburg Terrace, Sidmouth. July 27,1848.* (DRO, Z19/2/8D/155)

South Australia. *Friday July 28.* Made a coloured drawing. *Hutchinson was occupying himself with woodworking, sketching, etc. This southerly view of the town is the first of a series of Sidmouth sketches as seen from Hutchinson's home in Coburg Terrace (see also February 1849). Due to the legacy of 134 acres of land at Alexandrina left to him by his father, he began to take an interest in Australia.* The colony of South Australia has now been founded eleven years and a half, contains upwards of 25,000 inhabitants and is in a most flourishing state. I almost wish I were out there looking

48/7/28. View from No.4 Coburg Terrace, looking south. Coloured from nature July 28, 1848. (DRO, Z19/2/8D/157)

after my land at Alexandrina. The plan which has been adopted with respect to this colony has answered well, namely that the money expended on the purchase of land from the crown is devoted to the purpose of sending out respectable emigrants, on the principle that land is of no use without labourers to till it. The moral condition of the colony too, has been much promoted by the care that has been taken in only sending out persons of good and steady character, both men and women. (*Diary*).

48/7/29. View from No.4 Coburg Terrace, looking south-east. Amyat Place and the church tower. Coloured from the original July 29, 1848. (DRO, Z19/2/8D/159)

Amyat Place, Sidmouth. *Saturday July 29.* Had an industrious day at drawing. Did a coloured sketch of Amyat Place. (*Diary*).

Sketches from Coburg Terrace. *Tuesday August 1.* Passed most of the day sketching. (*Diary*).

Wednesday August 2. Ditto. (*Diary*).

Thursday August 3. Ditto. (*Diary*).

Walk over Peak Hill. *Sunday August 6.* After church took a walk over Peak Hill. Met Mrs. James Jenkins and her two daughters on the top of the hill and

48/8/1-1. View from No.4 Coburg Terrace, looking south-east by east. The new churchyard, etc. Coloured on the spot August 1, 1848. (DRO, Z19/2/8D/161)

48/8/1-2. View from No.4 Coburg Terrace, looking east. Coloured from nature August 3, 1848. (DRO, Z19/2/8D/163)

48/8/6. Coming down Peak Hill – near the top. Coloured on the spot, July 30, 1847. (DRO, Z19/2/8D/33)

saw Miss Catherine Cunningham as I was coming down. (*Diary*). *Hutchinson's annexed sketch of the steep ascent of Peak Hill from Sidmouth was done the previous year.*

Lithograph of the interior of Sidmouth Church. *Monday August 7.* Commenced my lithographic drawing of the new organ in Sidmouth Church upon the stone. It is sundry long years since I dabbled in this work and I feel quite out of practise. I hope soon to do a map of the town and parish reduced from the large map executed according to the provisions of the Tithe Commutation Act, now in the keeping of the church-wardens, so I do this drawing to get my hand in. (*Diary*).

Tuesday August 8. Six hours at lithography and two hours yesterday, making eight. Spent the evening at Lime Park, where besides the Walkers I met Captain Elphinstone and his eldest daughter and Mrs. FitzGerald and two daughters. Captain Elphinstone is the lineal descendant of the Lord Balmerino who was beheaded for his share in the rebellion of 1745. He is too poor or too

48/8/11-1. *Nave of Sidmouth church, Devon. Coloured on the spot November 22, 1847.* (DRO, Z19/2/8D/89)

48/8/11-2. *New organ, erected in Sidmouth church December 1847. Sketched January 1848.* (DRO, Z19/2/8D/91)

indifferent to prosecute this claim to the title. (*Diary*).

Work completed. *Friday August 11.* Six hours at lithography and finished the work. This makes twenty-four hours that the work has taken me to do. I have made it a close copy of my drawing of the new organ in my sketchbook, with the only difference the addition of a group of figures. (*Diary*). *The original sketch of the organ was done in January 1848, shortly after it was put in. An earlier sketch shows the old organ as it was in November 22, 1847.*

Saturday August 12. Handed the lithographic stone over to Harvey, the bookseller, and he will send it to Risdons, 25, High Street, Exeter, to get a proof taken and see how it turns out. (*Diary*).

Monday August 14. Bingham's birthday. He is 42. Received a proof inscription of my lithographic drawing. The grain of the stone is too coarse for a good effect. They get these things up better in London. I spent the evening at Mr. Heineken's, chiefly at music. (*Diary*). *As there was no satisfactory remedy, Hutchinson eventually decided to do the work over again.*

Sidmouth regatta. *Wednesday August 16.* A regatta took place at Sidmouth today. It was a dead calm, and owing to the heat a dense mist covered everything on the water, but soon after noon the mist cleared away. The sun was bright and extremely hot and the sea as glassy and smooth as a fish-pond. Some boats started but they only crept along at a snail's pace and the three cutter yachts that came lay with their sails motionless and did not move at all. Three steamers arrived, including a large one from Weymouth, and since the tide was high and the water so smooth, she ran her bow aground on the beach so that the passengers could walk ashore. The calm however, was favourable for the rowing matches and these were very good, but the best fun was to see the boys try to walk along a horizontal pole fixed to the stern of the committee boat to win a leg of mutton, or to fall into the water. I hired a small boat and rowed about for five hours (*Diary*).

Walk to Ladram Bay. *Wednesday September 13.* Walked to Ladram Bay along the beach and returned over the hills. I have not taken this walk for six or seven years. It is rather a rough one on

48/9/13-1. *The arches at Ladram Bay, near Sidmouth. Coloured on the spot September 13, 1848.* (DRO, Z19/2/8D/181)

the beach and in order to get through the arch at Ladram Bay, one must calculate the time so as to be there at low water at spring tide, for at neap tide it is not low enough to walk through. Today the moon was full and I arrived there at twenty minutes before twelve and found the tide very low. I can see some alterations in the cliff face since I was here last. When I was on the sands in Ladram Bay, I fell in with a gentleman who had that morning rambled over from Sidmouth. But he had gone over Peak hill, the way I meant to return, and I directed him how he could go back the way I had come, which at first he was afraid to do for fear of being caught by the tide. In the course of our conversation he talked on the subject of geology, and observed that he had been reading a book called *'The Geology of Sidmouth and South-Eastern Devon'* written by a Mr. Peter Orlando Hutchinson. I could scarcely contain my countenance, but remarked with all the gravity I could assume that I remembered having read it some years ago. We then separated and I climbed to the top of High Peak. On the way up I made a

48/9/13-2. *Natural arch, Ladram Bay near Sidmouth, Devon.* (Not dated) (DRO, Z19/2/8A/116)

48/9/13-3. *Natural arch, Ladram Bay, near Sidmouth, Devon.* (Not dated) (DRO, Z19/2/8D/11)

coloured sketch of Ladram Bay. I gave myself half an hour to examine the remains of the earthworks of the old camp, for I have not the least doubt that is what it is. On examining the escarpment of the cliff next the sea, where the hill has been abraded away, in two places I remarked a stratum of ashes and charcoal, one about three feet below the surface down to which I could not reach. But the other was in a more accessible place and not above a foot below the surface. These fires appear to have been made on the ridge of the agger or earthwork, but whether for signal or culinary purposes is not certain. It appears then, that the earthwork was subsequently heightened and the remains of the fire buried, but the wearing away of the hill has laid the ashes bare and showed the appearance of the black stratum. I collected several pieces of charcoal and brought them home. On being held over a candle flame, they reddened like a piece of charcoal recently made. I must make another visit to the hill and examine it more closely. (*Diary*). *The two undated sketches of the natural arch at Ladram Bay were probably done some years earlier.*

Lost week's work. *Friday September 15.* Oh horror! I have just heard from the lithographic printer of Exeter that the stone on which I had executed for the second time my view of the interior of Sidmouth Church has broken into two halves under the weight of the press! Here is another week's work gone. The first time a flaw in the stone, the second time the stone cracked in two! 'The third time', says the proverb 'is always lucky'. He said however, that as the accident happened under his hands, he would make it good to me and that he would draw it himself, but if he does it won't be <u>my</u> doing and I want the lithograph to be <u>my own work</u>. After a little vexation, I resolved to have courage to do it again, and sent for another stone. (*Diary*).

Return to High Peak. *Saturday September 16.* Superb weather! We shall apparently have a fine autumn after all and I have resolved to make the most of it out of doors. Today I planned another examination of High Peak Hill *and* started after breakfast. Made a coloured sketch of the hill from Peak Hill, which took me two hours, discussed my lunch and then walked to the summit of High Peak. Erected a little flagstaff on which I fixed an old cambric pocket handkerchief as a signal to Mr. Heineken in Sidmouth. Then erected an upright staff four feet long having two cross pieces three feet apart. By means of this Mr. Heineken will measure the distance of the summit of the hill from his house in the High Street with the micrometer of his large telescope. Then examined the worn away face of the cliff and dug out some charcoal, which I carried home. Found nothing there in the antiquarian way, but several imperfect geological specimens of the Greensand, which were not worth taking. Returned home, after being out six

48/9/16-1. *High Peak Hill from Peak Hill. Coloured from nature September 16, 1848.* (DRO, Z19/2/8D/183)

hours. (*Diary*). *The second, undated, view of High Peak from the cliffs below Peak Hill was probably done the previous year.*

Mr. Fish's house. *Monday September 18.* Went to see Mr. Fish's cottage. I believe it must be some eight or ten years since I was there last. What an exhibition to be sure! There is a profusion of everything that costs money (except books) but we look in vain for anything that bespeaks talent, good breeding, science or mind. (*Diary*).

Day sketching. Tuesday September 19. *There is no Diary entry but Hutchinson spent much of the day sketching two aspects of his house and garden in Coburg Terrace with the coach house and stable behind.*

Sidbury Castle Hill. *Thursday September 21.* The splendid weather still continues. Took advantage of it by making an examination of the old British, Saxon or Danish camp on the summit of Silbury Castle Hill. Started after breakfast and ascended the south end of the hill, but it was a most difficult scramble and I had great difficulty in getting up. Since I was here last (about six years ago) the thorns, brambles, heather, fern, trees and brushwood have grown so high and close that it required considerable effort to get through. The best places to get up are either from the north-west or the south-east. The hill is about five hundred feet high, the summit oval in form and two aggers enclose it. I measured the two diameters of the inner agger with a ten foot rod which I cut coming up, and made the longest 1450 feet, being somewhat more than a quarter of a mile, whilst the short diameter was 430 feet. Examined the whole of the top of the hill all round the entrenchments, but the coppice and bushes in some parts were so thick that I found great difficulty in tracing the works with certainty. At the north-west point where it joins Ottery Hill there appeared to be a deep entrenchment between two parallel earthworks thrown up like hedges, as if a flanked and protected entrance road existed here, but the trees were so thick that it was difficult to trace it far. Independent however, of the fact that this hill is conical and isolated, the remarkable circumstance of two springs of water rising out of the ground on the summit within the circumvallation must have rendered it a notable site for a stronghold. And whilst there are ponds of

48/9/16-2. *High Peak Hill, near Sidmouth.* (Not dated) (DRO, Z19/2/8D/43)

48/9/19-1. *Coburg Terrace, Sidmouth, from the higher end. Coloured from nature September 19, 1848.* (DRO, Z19/2/8D/177)

48/9/19-2. No.4 Coburg
Terrace, from the garden.
Coloured on the spot September 19,
1848. (DRO, Z19/2/8D/179)

good water on the surface at this height, the well at Buscombe Farm in the valley
below is seventy feet deep.

Some antiquaries, in their endeavours to find the 'Lost Station' have, without
sufficient grounds, pointed to this hill as the probable site, but which I am more
disposed, and strongly disposed, to assign to High Peak Hill. The distance of
the 'Lost Station' from Isca, or Exeter, in the Itinerary of Antonine is set down as
fifteen Roman miles and this agrees with the distance of High Peak. General
Simcoe, in writing on this subject, because he could not make any of the known
camps in the neighbourhood agree with the required distance, suggested that the
Roman was wrong and had made a mistake in his figures! This was a new way
of settling the question.

48/9/21. Sidmouth, from the
summit of Sidbury Castle Hill.
(Date cut off).
(DRO, Z19/2/8D/187)

Having completed my measurements and observations on the top of the hill,
discussed my luncheon and made a rough drawing of Sidmouth as seen from
thence, I commenced my rough descent and walked home. (*Diary*).

Geology west of Sidmouth and High Peak camp. *Thursday September 28.* Yesterday the moon was new and I took the opportunity of the spring tides to make another series of observations along the beach to Ladram Bay. Started after ten AM, and as I went on I made a sketch of the features of the cliff all the way, especially marking the faults or dislocations, of which there are several. Not taking those between Sidmouth and the limekilns (which I must take another day) I began at the limekilns and went westwards. There appears to have been a slight perpendicular crack at the 'First Roosings', so-called, as the strata from the limekilns thereto (about a furlong) dips downwards towards the west, but afterwards rise towards the west according to the general course along this coast. All along under Peak Hill there is no disruption, but I am not sure whether there is not a dislocation at the beginning of High Peak Hill, just after the second of two little points of the cliff jut out on the sand. A few hundred yards beyond this where there is a cavern, there is a crack, and then a few hundred yards further, a little beyond the isolated tall mass of rock, is another crack and small cavern. Just beyond this we come to the first of the masses of rock on the beach having a volcanic appearance, *and* this and the crack last mentioned are spoken of in my *Geology of Sidmouth.* The next marked locality we come to is the projecting point of High Peak Hill, off which stands the isolated rock called 'Picket Rock', which I believe means Peak-ed Rock or sharp rock, from its shape. Further off in the sea and never left quite dry even at the lowest tides, is a smaller and flatter rock. On the small extent of beach immediately to the west of this point of the hill are found globular nodules of ironstone, from the size of a pea to that of an apple. In the next cove there are two dislocations meeting at the top like the letter A, *and* a few yards further westwards we come to an arch through a slightly projecting point. I recollect when there was no arch there, perhaps about twenty years ago. In this cove stands a large isolated rock, once of course united to the mainland. By the bye, the eastern point of this last cove looks as if it will soon be detached from the mainland. It is planted with potatoes on the top and

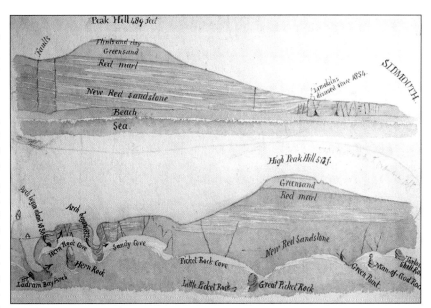

48/9/28-1. *Geological sketch of the coast from Sidmouth to Ladram Bay.* (Not dated) (DRO, Z19/2/8D/191)

48/9/28-2. *Rocks under High Peak Hill.* (Not dated) (DRO, Z19/2/8C/203)

48/9/28-3. *Distant view of Sidmouth, Devon, from the rocks under Peak Hill. 'Man of God' Rock, so-called by the sailors.* (Not dated) (DRO, Z19/2/8C/202)

48/9/28-4. *Rocks under High Peak Hill.* (Not dated) (DRO, Z19/2/8C/204)

this plot of garden can only be reached by a narrow footpath. Lastly we come to the celebrated natural arch, and having passed this, which can only be done at low water spring tides, we are in Ladram Bay. Two curious isolated rocks stand in this bay. *The accompanying coloured sketches, undated but probably done the previous year, show the various geological features from Peak Hill westwards to Ladram Bay.*

Having completed my observations geological I climbed to the summit of High Peak to make some observations antiquarian. On the way I had a great feast of blackberries and these I enjoyed with a crust of bread and some apples I had in my pocket. The more I look at and consider the remains on the summit, the more I am convinced that a station of great vastness and strength once existed there. I examined it again today and contemplated its entrenchments. The form of the work appears to have been egg-shaped, the smaller end pointing towards Peak Hill and tending in its long diameter north-east and south-west.

48/9/28-5. *Sidmouth from the top of the natural arch, Ladram Bay.* (Not dated) (DRO, Z19/2/8D/15)

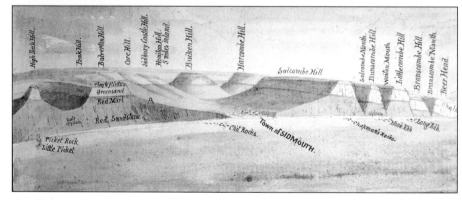

48/9/28-6. *Geological view of Sidmouth, Devon.* (Hist. of Sid. I,11)

On the north-east side, where it was probably most easily approached, the works are stronger *and* there are indications of three aggers on this side. I again examined the strata of charcoal and today I managed to reach lower down the sea face of the cliff than before, and whilst lying flat and with my arm at full stretch, I managed to get out a piece of charcoal as big as an egg, being part of a knotty joint in a large branch of a tree. This I brought it away, as it was the largest I had found. The grain and texture resemble oak. As these fires were made on the top of the earthwork in an exposed situation, I am disposed to think that they were signal fires and not used for dressing food. I will shortly write a letter on the subject of the hill and the Roman roads through this neighbourhood to Woolner's Gazette, for something more ought to be said about them, and I will record in print the result of my observations. (*Diary*).

Survey of High Peak Camp. *Friday October 6.* Made arrangements to survey the top of High Peak Hill. The remains of the ancient stronghold on this hill have occupied my attention a good deal lately. I had been thinking of writing a letter to one of the Exeter papers on the subject of Moridunum and pointing out High Peak as the possible site, but the matter grows and I am disposed to think that it would be a suitable article for the Gentleman's Magazine. Indeed, I have some notion now of embodying my investigations in the form of a book, for I find that I shall have material enough. When I was returning home yesterday week over Peak Hill, the idea suggested itself that the track across the Common about forty yards from the edge of the cliff on the summit, descending on the western side and still used as the pathway, might be the remains of the old British road from Sidbury Castle Hill to High Peak. It is not impossible but it may have been a branch of Ikenild Street. It appears to come from Bulverton Hill inland, all along the crown of Peak Hill towards the sea, turns to the westward at about a hundred yards from the cliff and then points directly to High Peak. The end abuts out over cliff where the land has fallen away between the two hills, Peak and High Peak. We come to the other end at the base of the cone of High Peak, where it continues on to Otterton *and* it may then have gone on to Woodbury Castle and Exeter.

Today the summit of High Peak was enveloped in thick sea fog, but I commenced my survey and carried it through. It was terribly wet driving straight lines through the furze and long grass, *and* the fog prevented my making some distant observations with the spyglass and compass as I had intended. I was more than six hours out and returned rather fagged. (*Diary*).

Saturday October 7. Received a proof impression of my last lithographic effort. This is more like what I desired *and* I think it will do. So much for perseverance. Plotted yesterday's survey on another piece of paper so as to set it out fair. The fog prevented my making it perfect in several places *so* I must go there again soon - though I will take care to choose a clear day. (*Diary*).

Tuesday October 10. As my survey last Friday was very unsatisfactory, I went up again today. The atmosphere was clear but it blew a hurricane from the north. There was a man cutting furze on the hill but some of the bundles were blown away over the cliff as if they had been feathers. I was afraid to go near the edge of the cliff myself. In spite of this I laid out my survey lines and angles, though I think I must come up again to perfect the business. I managed it much more agreeably today than last Friday. (*Diary*).

Wednesday October 11. Plotted out on a fair sheet of paper my rough notes of yesterday. (*Diary*).

Thursday October 12. A mild, quiet morning but a somewhat hazy atmosphere. I went however, to High Peak to take some bearings and perfect my survey. Was out seven hours and discussed my crust on the summit and washed it down with blackberries. It is surprising with what gusto one enjoys dry bread when out on such expeditions. Took the bearings of many of the points in my survey, went over some of my measurements again and corrected my angles. I hope that it is now tolerably correct, allowance being made for the absence of theodolite and chain. On looking over the cliff, I put up a covey of eight partridges, which I have done several times before. Curious place for partridges. (*Diary*).

Friday October 13. Plotted out my plan of Peak and High Peak Hills. Mr. Heineken spent the evening with me and I showed *him* my model of a safety valve for steam boilers contrived six or seven years ago, which I term a 'piston valve'. The idea and principle he thinks are new and therefore he urges me to communicate it to the 'Mechanic's Magazine'. I will think about this (*see October 19, 1848*). (*Diary*).

Cliff east of Sidmouth. *Saturday October 14.* After breakfast I went down to the mouth of the River Sid and made a coloured sketch of the cliff, being the western

48/10/14. *Geological view of
the cliff east of Sidmouth.
Coloured on the spot.*
(Not dated).
(DRO, Z19/2/8D/193)

point of Salcombe Hill rising immediately above the river. Two faults or dislocations are visible here and to the geologist are worth noting. (*Diary*). The River Sid falls into the sea on the eastern side of the town but it is only after heavy rain that the mouth is open, as at other times it is usually barred by a bank of gravel. One summer evening when I was a boy, about six o'clock at high water spring tide, I recollect in company with a playmate rowing from the sea into the mouth of the river. We passed up some distance, turned about and rowed out to sea again, *but* this can only be done on rare occasions. The sea face of the point of the hill on the east side of the river is dislocated by two faults rising westwards. The white beds are not often visible, as the rain washes the red earth charged with peroxide of iron over them. The point of the cliff above them is capped by a bed of alluvium. On comparing these white beds with those that appear in the cliff opposite Chit Rocks on the west side of the river, there seems to be a strong resemblance between them. (*History of Sidmouth, I, 12*).

Sent my essay entitled *What is the Present National Spirit of our Literature, and to what is it Tending* to the editor of Woolner's Exeter Gazette according to his request. (*Diary*).

Arrival of cholera. *Monday October 16.* There is now no question about the Asiatic cholera having arrived amongst us. For some weeks past several doubtful cases have occurred in London and elsewhere, but now there is no longer doubt. There have been between thirty and forty decided cases in London, about as many in Edinburgh and a few in other places on the eastern side of the Country. The deaths have been from two thirds to three quarters of the persons attacked. It was stated a short time ago by Dr. Shapter, the Mayor of Exeter at a public meeting, when the subject of precautionary measures was discussed, that the disease travels westwards at the rate of about 280 miles a month, *or* nearly 10 miles a day. There appears to be much less alarm in the Country at the arrival of this terrible visitant than there was in 1832. Indeed it seems to excite few apprehensions and people go on with their ordinary occupations and amusements as usual. We may expect it in Devonshire shortly. (*Diary*). *Dr. Shapter, author of 'The History of the Cholera in Exeter', was one of the leading authorities of the day on the disease and its possible causes.*

Safety valve. *Thursday October 19.* Sent to the 'Mechanics Magazine' my invention of a safety valve for steam boilers, which I name the 'piston valve',. The notion was struck out some seven years ago but has been laid aside till now. Spent the evening with Mr. Heineken doing experiments in galvanism. (*Diary*).

Test for cholera. *Tuesday October 24.* The papers mention that the recent cold weather has arrested the progress of the cholera in London. Since the disease appeared in England a few weeks ago there have been about two hundred cases. This includes London, Woolwich, Leith, Edinburgh, etc., where most cases have occurred, and these are all on the eastern side of the Country. It is now however reported that one case occurred the other day at Portland and one at Plymouth. This is taking a long step westwards *and* if this is the case Exeter will not long escape. It was said some time ago in the reports we received from Russia, that in those places where the epidemic was raging, magnets lost their power and the electric telegraphs became useless. As the peculiar state of the atmosphere which is apparently the cause of this scourge, or accompanies it, may be looked for in Great Britain since the disease is among us, I have a wish to test this by experiment. I have hung up a small magnet in my room which, by having a small bucket attached to the piece of steel placed against the ends of the horseshoe, will support about a pound and a quarter. Should the same phenomena appear in England as remarked on the Continent, I shall be able to observe whether the magnet loses its power of supporting the weight now hanging to it, that is, by the by, if the cholera will allow me to do so. (*Diary*).

Strange parcel. *Thursday October 26.* This morning at breakfast time a parcel was brought to the house addressed to the Hon. Mr. Hutchinson. For some time we hesitated to open it, but not knowing of any person of our name in the place, at last we did so. To our amazement we discovered six dozen toothbrushes!

Much puzzled, we made enquiries and it came out that a Mr. Hutchinson had recently arrived with his wife and the parcel was intended for him. We have found out that he has come here for the winter, and he is apparently descended from the same parent as ourselves. (*Diary*). *They called on* Mr. Hutchinson-of-the-toothbrushes, *as Peter called him in the Diaries, the next day, and indeed on a number of occasions throughout the winter.*

Cliff west of Sidmouth. *Saturday October 28.* Made two drawings of the cliff west of Sidmouth in order to show the faults or dislocations, of which there are several opposite the Chit Rocks. (*Diary*). These sections *of the cliff* were taken by me in October 28,

48/10/28-1. *Geological view of the cliff west of Sidmouth. Coloured on the spot October 28, 1848. The view is compressed in its horizontal dimensions.* (DRO, Z19/2/8D/195)

48/10/28-2. *Geological view of the cliff west of Sidmouth. Coloured on the spot October 28, 1848. This view, like the former, is compressed in its horizontal dimensions. It unites with the former at its east end.* (DRO, Z19/2/8D/197)

1848. They are interesting as showing the great changes that have taken place since. The road from the old limekilns down to the beach was finally washed away about 1853 *and* soon afterwards a portion of the cliff on which the limekilns stood fell into the sea, carrying part of the building with it. (*History of Sidmouth, 1*)

Article on Moridunum. *Monday October 30.* Occupied for some hours in writing the rough draft of a paper on the subject of the old camp on High Peak Hill and a consideration of the probable site if Moridunum. (*Diary*).

Walk on Peak Hill. *Saturday November 4.* The day fine and clear but the north-west wind cold. Took my mother a walk up Peak Hill, *but* she can't climb hills as well as she used to do. A passing cloud brought down a sprinkling of snow. This is too soon. (*Diary*).

'Old Popes' Day 1848. *Sunday November 5.* At church this morning with my mother and received the sacrament. Being 'Gunpowder Plot' day, the appropriate prayers were read *and* the Act of Parliament also that requires these prayers to be read was given us in full. (*Diary*).

Article completed. *Monday November 6.* Finished my *Dissertation on the Site of Moridunum*, which I wish to have printed in the 'Gentleman's Magazine'. This evening sundry 'Old Popes' visited us, well illuminated by blazing tar barrels. (*Diary*). *The article on Moridunum and a plan of High Peak camp and its surroundings appeared in the February 1849 issue of the Gentleman's Magazine.*

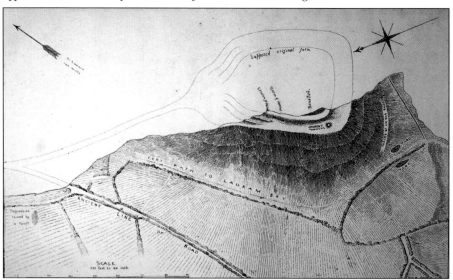

48/11/6. *Plan of the summit of High Peak Hill.* (Hist. of Sid. I, 29a)

Unofficial prints. *Friday November 10.* There is a curious law case reported in the Times of the 7th instant, entered 'Prince Albert versus Strange'. It seems that the Queen and Prince Albert, for the last seven or eight years, have been amusing themselves with etching on copper various subjects, some original, some copies, and having impressions for their own private use taken off by a copper-plate printer called Brown in Windsor. Brown's journeyman had surreptitiously taken off a number of impressions which he first kept to himself, but now has made arrangements for publishing and selling them. With this view, a catalogue of sixty-three subjects, among which are about ten portraits of the Princess Royal done by the Queen, has been issued. In order to get a better sale they have been avowed as the works of Her Majesty and her Consort. Mr. Strange of Paternoster Row is the ostensible publisher and the Prince has applied for an injunction to restrain this appropriation of private property. The case has excited a good deal of amusement. (*Diary*).

Knocked knee. *Sunday November 12.* At church. My knee that I hit in the dark last Monday evening hurts me so much that I will lay up and nurse it. (*Diary*).

Still housebound. *Wednesday November 15.* Coloured three views of my lithographs of the inside of Sidmouth Church. This makes ten. Having kept house since Sunday my knee feels better, *but* it is very tiresome as I wanted to go to the top of High Peak Hill, especially as the weather is fine and dry. (*Diary*). *Hutchinson had been housebound since damaging his knee over a week ago and was to remain so for the next two months.*

Articles published. *Saturday November 18.* The first half of my essay entitled *What is the present national spirit of our literature, and to what is it tending* appears today in Woolmer's Exeter and Plymouth Gazette. The rest of it is promised next week, for it was too long to print all at once. In the Mechanic's Magazine of today appears my communication, with the illustrations, relative to my so-called 'piston-valve', which I forwarded to the editor on the 19th of October. (*Diary*).

Housebound. *Tuesday November 21.* The weather today is superb and I long to be once more ferreting about on the top of Moridunum – I mean High Peak hill.

I am very glad I did not knock my knee and disable myself until after I made my survey and completed the article for the 'Gentleman's Magazine'. (*Diary*).

Shortcomings. *Wednesday November 22.* In the '*Western Luminary*', Exeter paper, of today there is one of a series of articles entitled '*The Nooks and Corners of Devon*', or something to that effect. In the one today there is some antiquarian notice of the camps in the neighbourhood of Sidmouth. The article is subscribed by the initials W.P.S., *and* I imagine this must be W.J.P.Shortt of Heavitree, the author of '*Sylva Antiqua Iscana*' and '*Collectanea Curiosa Antiqua Dumnonia*'. He was ignorant of a fortress on High Peak Hill when he published his books, but three years ago he issued a prospectus to obtain subscribers for another work, and I then directed his attention to this fact by means of a letter in Woolner's Paper. As his book has not come out I suppose he could not get enough subscribers and he is now possibly bringing out his materials without cost to himself through the medium of a journal. I remember promising to become a subscriber. In the '*Western Luminary*' he mentions a station on 'Peak Hill' meaning High Peak, the summit of which he never seems to have visited. He remarks on it merely incidentally and evidently he is not aware either of the size or importance of that station. Some of his other remarks are made with his usual carelessness. He writes in such a haphazard manner and often speaks with great positiveness when he is quite wrong, that it is impossible to rely on his assertions. (*Diary*).

Troublesome knee. *Monday November 27.* The blow to my knee still feeling uneasy, I applied six leeches to it, as advised by Dr. Cullen. I ought to keep quiet for a while, but this is very trying when one feels the desire to be rambling over the hills. (*Diary*).

Electric light. *Tuesday December 12.* In the newspapers an appalling accident, or rather an act of culpable carelessness, has recently been mentioned, in which seventy-three persons were suffocated by being shut down in the fore cabin of a steamer off the north coast of Ireland during a storm. They put into Londonderry when it was discovered. The captain is in custody.

The last new invention is the production of light by the use of electricity. The most brilliant effects have been produced in London by erecting the apparatus in Trafalgar Square, on the summit of the Duke of York's column and other commanding situations. It is said that the gas lamps are quite eclipsed. A company has been formed and the public is invited to take shares. It is thought that this light will supersede gas and is quite well adapted for streets, squares, large buildings, light houses and the like. (*Diary*).

Piano practice. *Wednesday December 13.* Practised an hour and a half on the pianoforte, a thing I never did before, but everybody was out and I had it all to myself. I shall however, never make a pianoforte player. One must begin young to play that instrument well. There are so many notes at a time to read and the work of the two hands is so isolated by which the practical management of this instrument is so unlike that of most others, the flute, violin, clarinet, etc., that nothing but commencing early will enable a person to overcome its difficulties and peculiarities. But owing to the handful of chords and combinations of sounds that can be produced on it by which the intricacies of counter point, thorough bass and modulation can be studied and surveyed, it is an instrument that every really musical person should learn to become master of. The practical part of the science of harmony cannot be properly gone into and handled on any other, unless the organ, but this is in a manner the same thing. I now regret I did not begin the pianoforte when I began the flute, when I was somewhere about ten years old. Many vexations and disappointments however, which have come upon me during the last five years, have much cooled my love of music, and I may add poetry. The stern realities of life are grievous coolers of youthful sentiment. (*Diary*).

Burlesque. *Saturday December 16.* The first fytte of my burlesque in the style of an ancient poem entitled *Ye Merrie Geste of Exancester* is printed in Woolmer's paper. They have made a mistake in the last line of the eighth stanza by printing the word 'concentrated' instead of 'concenter'd', so that although the sense remains the same the iambics will not scan. *(Diary)*. *The burlesque, an old poem which has only recently been brought to light, autographed by Petrus de Sidemew, was a lampoon on the election of a successor to Courtenay who had recently resigned as a member for the Southern Division of Devonshire. Further verses by 'Petrus de Sidemew' were shortly to be 'discovered' at opportune times (see December 25,1849 and December 31, 1850).*

Cold morning. *Sunday December 24.* Could not go to church. Wind north-east and as cold as ever. When I stole a glance out of bed across the room, I saw my bottle of hair oil on my dressing table looking like lard. This serves me for a thermometer at that distance and I leave it in sight in order to see the state of affairs when I open my eyes of a winter's morning. The real thermometer stood at 38 degrees. When I drew my razor strop out of its case, it was all over white hoar frost, the frost of oil. *(Diary)*.

48/5/2-4. 'Addison's Oak', Ugbrook Park.
Coloured on the spot May 30, 1848. The
tradition says that Addison wrote several papers
for the Spectator under the tree. It measures 25
feet in circumference.
(DRO, Z19/2/8D/117)

1849

New leaf. *Monday January 1.* New Years Day! Now then, I mean to turn over a new leaf. (*Diary*).

Californian gold rush. *Tuesday January 2.* The gold mines in Upper California have sent America mad. The ground is on the banks of the Sacramento and the San Joachin, not far from the port of San Francisco. No sooner does a ship touch there than the sailors desert and run away to the gold fields. All the servants have left their masters, clerks their employers and soldiers their garrisons. With a spade and a basin they wash the gravel and collect gold worth from five to ten pounds each person a day. Everything is neglected for gold, and the necessities of life are getting very scarce. (*Diary*).

Mrs. Fellowes meditations. *Sunday January 7.* Finished reading *Scattered Jems: or Weekly Meditations by a Lady.* This lady is Mrs. Fellowes, wife of the vicar of the adjoining parish of Sidbury. 'Sweet are the roses of adversity' says Shakespeare *and* this volume is the fruit of adversity. The Fellowes were once of some affluence but reckless living and the depreciation of West India property owing to the emancipation of the slaves, and recently the extraordinary determination of the Whigs not to do anything to rescue the West Indies planters from destruction though they encourage the importation of slave grown sugar from Cuba and other places, these things suddenly brought an amiable family to great straits. When it was proposed to publish this book by subscription, people liberally came forward, many taking six or eight copies and paying for them but only actually receiving one, a generous ruse to favour the author. Mrs. F. put £100 in her pocket by this book. Thus pleased with her success she has since brought out another, but her friends were tired of paying more than once for copies and only taking one, so that her second has not gone off as the first did. Many of the copies still hang on hand, and I rarely see her, but she asks my advice as to how she can get a sale for them. (*Diary*).

49/2/?-1. View from No.4 Coburg Terrace, looking north-east. Sketched February 1849. (DRO, Z19/2/8D/165)

49/2/?-2. *View from No.4 Coburg Terrace, looking north by east. Coloured from nature.* (Date cut off). (DRO, Z19/2/8D/167)

Progress of cholera. *Friday February 2.* I have been watching the progress of the cholera for some weeks, intending to make a memorandum as soon as the number of cases should attain 10 000, towards which it has been tending. By the Times newspaper of the 31st ultimo, the following return appears:

> Number of cases in Great Britain - 10 195
> Deaths - 4512
> Recoveries - 2572
> Under treatment or result not known – 3054

On turning back the pages of my Diary, I see that the cholera made its appearance in this Country in the beginning of last October, so that we have had above 10 000 cases in four months. It is probable that on the approach of spring the disease may manifest itself even more strongly. (*Diary*).

Californian gold. *Saturday February 3. For several weeks past news of the gold rush to California had been appearing in the papers.* The papers mention that a few days ago a ship arrived at Liverpool from the Pacific Ocean, bringing as part of her freight fourteen thousand dollars worth of Californian gold. This is, I believe, the first gold from California that has been brought to England. It is said that the most absurd prices are asked and obtained in California for articles of clothing and other common necessities of life – as £4 for a shirt. (*Diary*).

Sidmouth sketches. 49/2/?/1-4 *February. Confined indoors because of his painful*

49/2/?-3. *View from No.4 Coburg Terrace, looking nor'-nor'-west.* (Date cut off) (DRO, Z19/2/8D/169)

49/2/?-4. *View from No.4 Coburg Terrace, looking west north-west.* (Not dated). (DRO, Z19/2/8D/171)

knee, Hutchinson continued the series of Sidmouth sketches viewed from his house in Coburg
Terrace started in July the previous year, working methodically round the compass.

Painful knee. *Friday February 9.* Hemmed three kitchen cloths for my mother
and marked them, after which piece of needlework I walked for a quarter of an
hour in the Blackmore fields. I can't make out what my knee means; it seems to
get no better and yet I cannot say that it gets worse. I begin to think that a
change of air to a more bracing and invigorating atmosphere would be my best
physician. The damp and mild climate of Sidmouth always pulls me down so
much that I cannot combat my ailments here. (*Diary*).

Evening in. *Tuesday February 13.* This evening a sedate party celebrated their
orgies under our roof, to wit Miss Rose of the discrete age of eighty-five, Miss
Lock of a certain age, Miss Jouenne of an uncertain age *and* Mrs. Theophilus
Jenkins, a buxom widow. (*Diary*).

Valentine's Day. *Wednesday February 14.* Valentine's Day! Sent no valentine
whatever. Goodness knows how many years it is since I omitted such a duty to
the ladies. (*Diary*).

Second fytte. *Friday February 16.* Sent the second fytte of '*Ye Merrie Geste of
Exancester*' to the editor of Woolmer's Gazette. (*Diary*).

Visit to the editor. *Monday February 19.* Started to pay a visit to the Joneses at
Uffculme. Left at half past eight AM and got to Exeter soon after eleven. Called
at Woolner's Gazette office and had a chat with the editor. He told me he
intended to print the second fytte of '*Ye Merrie Geste of Exancester*' next Saturday
and a notice of my article on Moridunum in the current number of the
Gentleman's Magazine. He also said in reference to my '*Essay on the Present State
of the Literature of the Day*', printed two or three months ago, that the editors of the

49/3/12-1. Bridge over the Culme
at Uffculme, Devon. Coloured on
the spot March 12, 1849.
(DRO, Z19/2/8D/199)

Western Miscellany, a new periodical, wish to reprint it in that periodical and would I have any objection? I said no, but on the contrary felt complimented at the intention.

I missed the quarter to three train so I took the half past five one *and* got safe to Uffculme, having suffered little by my knee for this exertion. (*Diary*).

Literary criticism. *Friday February 23.* Finished skimming through Dr. Oliver's *History of Exeter,* 1821, and his *Historic Collections relating to the Monasteries of Devon*, 1821. Oliver abuses his predecessors. He speaks of the time-honoured old Izacke as 'the careless Izacke', *and* at page 32 he says 'Izacke disgraced the name of an historian'. *Also,* 'Godwin, who is rather an elegant writer than a faithful historian', page 37, *and* 'Jenkins, in what he is pleased to call his *History of the City of Exeter*'. I question whether the *History* of Oliver is so supremely perfect as to warrant him in using such language of his predecessors. (*Diary*). *For unsurpassable disdain, Hutchinson's quotations hardly do justice to Oliver's lofty disparagement of earlier Exeter historians. Izacke 'betrays a lamentable deficiency of good taste and judgement, and that to excessive credulity and puerility he unites no inconsiderable share of dogmatical assurance', Hooker whose 'mind indeed appears to have been soured with religious bigotry', and Jenkins who 'should not suppose that what may satisfy his mind will content a discerning public'.*

River Culme at Uffculme. *Monday March 12.* The morning fine and the air quite balmy. Made my first out-of-door sketch this year. Walked down to the mill, where I seated myself on a grass slope by the river under some poplar trees and made a coloured drawing looking down the Culme to the bridge. Came back with a sore throat. So much for sitting upon damp grass after having been shut up invalided all the winter. (*Diary*).

49/3/12-2. *Uffculme, Devon, from the bridge. Coloured on the spot April 2, 1849.* (DRO, Z19/2/8D/ 201)

49/3/12-3. *Hackpen Hill, from Uffculme. Coloured on the spot April 3, 1849.* (DRO, Z19/2/8D/203)

49/3/21. *Uffculme market. October 13, 1847.* (DRO, Z19/2/8D/69)

Besley's Road Book. *Thursday March 15.* Received from Mr. Harvey, the bookseller of Sidmouth, a letter in which was enclosed a proof sheet beginning about page 64 of part of the new edition of the *Road Book of Devon*, being published by Besley of South Street, Exeter. He wished me to insert a few words relative to High Peak Hill and Moridunum. This I did and sent the proof sheet to Mr. Besley. (*Diary*).

Wombwell's zoo. *Friday March 16.* Wombwell's itinerant collection of animals came to Uffculme, a kind of sight that had never before greeted this retired place. The Uffculmites were stricken with extreme wonderment when the elephant walked into the market place with a lady riding on his back seated in a houda. In the afternoon I went to see the collection with the Joneses and their children. (*Diary*).

Criticism of Uffculme. *Wednesday March 21.* Received Woolmer's paper from home.   There is a paragraph on *Uffculme* by me, which has awoken the

Uffculmites.   It reflects on their dirty roads *and* neglect of their local duties and public spirit.   There is nothing like a paragraph in a newspaper to make people look about. *(Diary).   His unsigned article, which must indeed have upset the townsfolk, opens:* This place must be situated either at the north or the south pole, since every other place moves forward but Uffculme seems to stand still.   There is a great lack of public spirit there, and even of morality amongst the lower orders.   *After more in the same vein, Hutchinson ends with a query he had presumably received from a Sidmouth doctor:* A physician practising in one of the watering places on the south coast of the county recently applied to know whether there was a respectable lodging in Uffculme with a view to recommending some of his patients a change of air there, but the reply to his question was No!   *(Exeter and Plymouth Gazette March 17, 1849, extract).   The accompanying sketch of a market stall in Uffculme was done on a previous visit eighteen months earlier.*

Uffculme to Chudleigh.   *Thursday April 5.*   Left Uffculme and travelled to Exeter from the Tiverton junction by rail, the Rev. Francis Jones with me.   My cousin Mary Roberton met me in Exeter and took me in the carriage to Heightley Cottage, near Chudleigh.   Besides my aunt Mrs. Cocks, I found my aunt Mrs. Stairs at Heightley and her daughter Ann. *(Diary).*

Black Rock.   *Monday April 9.*   Walked to the Black Rock, where I sat down and for half an hour and enjoyed the beautiful view.   Then went on to the cliff over-looking the quarry.   I had a hammer with me and remained an hour knocking out geological specimens containing organic remains, being madrapores and mollusca of different species.   These are nearly the earliest traces of animal life in a geolog-ical sense, occurring in the oldest rock and nearest to the series of igneous origin, this limestone being designated the Transition Primitive. *(Diary).*

Bone from Chudleigh Rock.   *Thursday April 12.*   Went to Chudleigh Rock and took shelter in the mouth of the cavern from a shower of rain.   Whilst there, I found a mass of stalagmite out of which I knocked a bone resembling a rib.   Some twenty years ago Dr. Buckland searched this cavern and found many antediluvian and pre-Adamite osseous remains. *(Diary).   Hutchinson sketched the cavern entrance about a year earlier.*

Chudleigh Rock from a distance.   *Friday April 13.*   Went to the field in which Mr. Hill's house stands near the old Hennock road and made a drawing of Chudleigh Rock, Heightley Cottage, etc. *(Diary).*

49/4/12.   *Entrance to the cavern in Chudleigh Rock. Coloured on the spot May 16, 1848.*
(DRO, Z19/2/8D/115)

49/4/13.   *Chudleigh Rock, from the old Hennock road. Coloured on the spot April 13, 1849.*
(DRO, Z19/2/8D/205)

49/4/30-1. Part of the vallum and foss of the ancient camp in Ugbrook Park. Coloured on the spot April 30, 1849.
(DRO, Z19/2/8D/207)

Walk to Black Rock. *Sunday April 16.* In the afternoon took a walk through the trees below the Black Rock to the quarry, then climbed up and returned over the top of the Rock. (*Diary*).

Pixie's cave. *Wednesday April 25.* Took candles and went into the cavern in Chudleigh Rock. By pacing, I found that the length of the passage to the anterior chamber to be about 150 feet. The ramifications tending towards the left hand extend about the same distance. When I went into this cavern as a boy the passage inwards was scarcely eighteen inches high, so that I crawled on my hands and knees. A few years ago however, the floor of this passage, which was a bed of stalagmite, the accumulation of centuries probably, was dug through and cleared away, so that one can now enter nearly upright. In this stalagmite or crust a quantity of fossilised bones have been found, *and* I remember years ago having procured some there, especially the crown of a bear's double tooth. Today I found part of a large bone of a stony texture, nearly half an inch thick from the surface to the cavity of the marrow. At the ends there are the marks of teeth as if it had been gnawed by some wild beast, a former inhabitant of the cavern. Today I was alone, and after a solitary half hour my candles were getting low, so I returned once more to daylight. (*Diary*).

Return to the cave. *Thursday April 26.* Went into the cavern this afternoon with my cousin Ann Stairs. We made no particular discoveries. The spaniel dog that accompanied us got so frightened when we plunged into the obscurity, that no caresses which we paid him could stop his whining and trepidation. Neither could we persuade him to remain there. He made his escape and waited for us outside until we returned. (*Diary*).

49/4/30-2. Part of the earthwork and dry ditch of the ancient encampment in Ugbrook Park, near Chudleigh. Coloured on the spot 1848. (DRO, Z19/2/8D/119)

Survey of Ugbrook Camp. *Monday April 30.* Went to measure the dimensions of the ancient hill fortress in Ugbrook Park. Found the gates shut but I scaled the Park palings. Some evil disposed persons have recently fired on and killed several of the deer and the public in consequence have been excluded. The camp is an ellipse approaching to a circle. I made the north and south diameter 650 feet and the east and west diameter 770 feet. Then sat down on the fosse for an hour and coloured a sketch. (*Diary*). *Another sketch of the earthwork is dated the year before. Hutchinson returned to make a more exact survey and plan of the Camp some years later (see September 22, 1853).*

Stalactite from Chudleigh cave. *Wednesday May 2.* Went to the caverns at the west end of Chudleigh Rocks with hammer and chisel and was engaged for nearly two hours in getting off a mass of stalactite, out of which I mean to turn a box. (*Diary*).

View from Chudleigh Rock. *Monday May 7.* Went with my cousin Ann Stairs to the top of Chudleigh Rock to enjoy the view. (*Diary*). *The annexed view from the summit was done the previous year.*

49/5/7. Chudleigh, Devon, from the top of the Rock. Coloured on the spot June 31, 1848. (DRO, Z19/2/8D/129)

Sidmouth again. *Thursday May 10.* Left Heightley Cottage for home. My cousin Mary Roberton took me into Exeter in the carriage, where I got on the Sidmouth coach at four and arrived home at seven, having been away since February 19th. (*Diary*).

New vegetable. *Tuesday May 15.* Planted some haricot beans in the garden by way of experiment. It was in America that I learned to like these. Since the failure of the potato they have been recommended and imported for use into this Country. Such however, is the foolish prejudice here against anything new or not well known that many persons won't even do themselves and the beans the justice to try them. 'Our fathers did without them and why shouldn't we?' Small minds these, methinks. (*Diary*).

Drawing of High Peak. *Saturday June 9.* Made a pen and ink drawing of the summit of High Peak Hill. (*Diary*).

Bronze centaur from the River Sid. *Wednesday June 13.* Engaged all the morning in making a pen-and-ink copy of the centaur belonging to Mr. Heineken, which I borrowed from him yesterday. This bronze centaur was found by a man called Barnes at the mouth of the River Sid in 1840 and is described in the Gentleman's Magazine and other places. (*Diary*). The annexed representation was etched by me for my *History of Sidmouth*. (*Soc. of Antiq. Ms. 250*). *Mr.*

49/6/13-1. *Bronze centaur.*
(Hist. of Sid. I,90a)

49/6/13-2. *Bronze centaur.*
(Hist. of Sid. I,90a)

Heineken presented the centaur (Cheiron with Achilles riding on his back) to the Exeter Museum in 1871.   It has been identified as a Roman tripod ornament, probably dating from the second century AD.   (Allan and Timms 1996).

Blackbury Castle.   *Thursday June 14.*   Started at half past eleven this morning on an expedition with Mr. Heineken to take a plan of Blackbury Castle.   We ascended Trow hill by the eastern continuation of High Street, the old Roman road, and at the distance of about three miles and a half from Sidmouth turned northwards towards Broad Down.   Attaining the Down, we veered to the east and after journeying about six miles from Sidmouth we reached the object of our search.   The road runs immediately on the north side of it, a line of road which is likely to be ancient, but we first went on a quarter of a mile and took a sketch of an octagonal tower covered with ivy.

Blackbury Castle is made on a ridge and is approached on the east and west on the level, but the ground descends towards the north and south.   It is an oval, the conjugate or east to west diameter measuring 634 feet whilst the transverse dimension measured 324.   The works are not of remarkable strength and resemble those of Silbury Castle.   The earth of the fosse outside is thrown up to form the agger, *which* measured 36 feet on the slope on the south by east side.   But the most interesting part is the grand and apparently only entrance on the south side.   A road flanked by embankments runs south for 180 feet and two angular embankments with ditches are constructed outside it, so that the last mentioned works form a large triangle whose apex points south and whose base is attached to the great oval.   This great entrance points towards 'Long Chimney', the principal British and Roman thoroughfare from the old maritime stations to the east.   We were unable to trace the line of connection from Blackbury Castle across the valley to the south or up the opposite hill towards Long Chimney, and yet there was a light green line across a corn field near Long Chimney, and below this there were the traces of a ruined causeway.   But still, these few indications were too indistinct to warrant any certain conclusion.   It is past conjecture that none of the camps towards the west, Sidbury, High Peak, etc., could be seen from Blackbury Castle, for Broad Down rises too high to admit of it.   On the east, none of the camps are now visible in that direction owing to the plantations of trees which obstruct the view, but doubtless when the hill was bare the stations at Hawksdown, Musbury, Membury and others were visible with ease.   Blackbury Castle itself is a mass of thick plantation.

On returning home, we diverged northwards over Broad Down to look for the barrows and see 'Roncombe's Gurt'.   On the highest ground the road passes between two *barrows*, further north *there are* one or two more on the east, and lastly we saw three opposite Roncombe's Gurt in a cornfield recently enclosed.   Roncombe's Gurt is the reputed head and source of the River Sid, though not the most distant source from the sea.   There are two or three deep and wild chasms here, in the northernmost of which is a little stone-built well filled by the spring.   We had a drink and the water was clear and cold.   The tradition runs that an exciseman by the name of Roncombe was some years ago murdered and thrown in here by some smugglers, *and* the whole valley is now called Roncombe from this spot to Sidbury.   By this route we returned, and a rough route too, stopping a few minutes to look at the old house at Sand.   When near Sidford our attention was arrested by the appearance of a parhelion round the sun, though only a portion on the south side was then visible.   It was nearly as bright as a piece of a rainbow, the red colour being next to the sun.

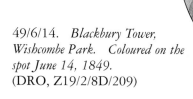

49/6/14. *Blackbury Tower, Wishcombe Park.   Coloured on the spot June 14, 1849.*
(DRO, Z19/2/8D/209)

When we got to Sidmouth and the sun was lower, the entire semi-circle, like a halo, was discernible though not so bright in tint. By an observation with the sextant, the distance of the halo, or the angle subtended, by was 22 degrees 8 minutes *and* the width of the halo was about that of the diameter of the sun. It was the first appearance of the kind I had witnessed. (*Diary*).

High Peak from Sidmouth. *Saturday June 16.* Went down to the beach and made a coloured sketch of High Peak Hill from Sidmouth. (*Diary*).

Sketch of Lime Park. *Tuesday June 26.* Went and made a coloured sketch of Lime Park from the river *and* lunched there on pigeon pie. No bad thing either. (*Diary*). *This drawing is not in the sketch books.*

49/6/16. *High Peak Hill, from Sidmouth. Coloured from nature June 16, 1849.*
(DRO, Z19/2/8D/211)

First swim. *Monday July 2.* Had a swim in the sea. This is the first time I have bathed for several years. (*Diary*). *Hutchinson now bathed most days whatever the weather in yet another attempt to cure his painful leg,, but the exercise was eventually to bring on an even more severe illness (see October 9, 1849).*

Otterton Church and Budleigh Salterton. *Friday July 13.* Started at 3 PM in a fly with Mr. and Miss Heineken and Mr. Smith for Budleigh Salterton. They put me down in Otterton and drove on to see Bicton. I went into the church and took rubbings of the two brasses recording the deaths of Robert Duke, anno 1641, and of Sarah, wife of Richard Duke who died the same year. We then proceeded to our destination where Mr. Heineken transacted some business with his house agent. Took outlines of his houses *and* made a coloured sketch of Otterton Head, which Miss Heineken also sketched. We got home at nine. The hedges near Otterton were studied with glow-worms *and* we brought home one. (*Diary*). *Though not precisely dated the accompanying sketch of the pebble bar at Budleigh Salterton is very likely the one referred to.*

49/7/13-2.   *The Duke brasses.*
(Hist. of Sid. I,187b).

Camera lucida.   *Monday July 16.*   Spent the evening with Mr. Heineken.
Reduced with the camera lucida one of my rubbings of the Otterton brasses.
(*Diary*).

Telescope.   *Tuesday July 17.*   Finished the brass work of my two-lens Galilean
telescope.   Bathed *the* seventh time.   (*Diary*).

George Hudson.   *Wednesday July 18.*   George Hudson, the 'Railway King', a
quondam haberdasher of York who is supposed to have made upwards of a million
sterling by railways, is now discovered to have done so by the most fraudulent
transactions.   This man has been lauded to the skies, courted by Dukes, made
Member of Parliament, and I saw him elbow Lords in the crowd with much
pomposity at the Marquis of Northampton's.   As if he did not make money fast
enough, his admirers subscribed and gave him £10 000.   It comes out that by one
dishonest transaction alone he pocketed £140 000!   He is likely to forfeit all his
ill-gotten gains and deservedly sink back to his former obscurity.   (*Diary*).

Oil painting of Sidmouth.   *Tuesday July 24.*   Bathed, *the* eleventh time this year.
Sea roughish.   A heavy shower came on as I was returning, but I got shelter in
the cavern under the limekilns.   These cliffs are much fallen away since my recollection and are still continuing to do so.   The rain is most welcome to the country
though inconvenient to oneself.
        Began oil painting after an interval of several years.   Put in the sky of a view
of Sidmouth taken from near the Preventive House and looking towards High
Peak Hill.   (*Diary*).

Wednesday July 25.   Oil painted five hours *and* then took a walk up Salcombe Hill.
(*Diary*).

Monday July 30.   Painted five hours.   Oil painting is certainly much more
satisfactory than water.   Went to Sidbury in Smith's 'della' and called on
William Henry Fellowes, just come over from Canada, and on the Hunts.
(*Diary*).

Poor old Tommy.   *Tuesday July 31.*   Painted four hours at my view of Sidmouth,
looking west, and finished it.   These four added to the seventeen before make
thirty-one in all.
        Poor Mr. Tommy, the white drake, makes a very disconsolate widower.   He
and his wife, Mrs. Tommy, were sitting as usual under the current bushes, after

being tired of walking about looking for slugs, when Mrs. T., who had not been very well for several days, very quietly leant her head forward and died. The drake was found sitting beside her perfectly contented but was very loath to go to roost without her in the evening. All the next day (Saturday) she was left in the same position and it was amusing to see with what complacency he sat beside her. In the evening however, it was decided that she must be buried, and in order to convince Mr. Tommy that his wife had not been stolen from him by the hand of man but that she was really dead, he was present at the solemnity. He was even put into the grave on his wife before she was covered that he might know what had become of her. This seems to have had a salutary effect, for although he appears disconsolate, he does not wander about the premises to search for her. She was not above eight years old, but about a month ago we were obliged to kill an old duck, Mrs. Mooty, which must have been upwards of twenty. Mrs. Mooty was roughly used by the Muscovy drake (not Mr. Tommy), otherwise she might have lived on. My sister had her eight years, the Rev. Prebendary Dornford of Plymtree had her eleven, and before that she had been brought from Italy a full-grown duck. I should think that twenty years is an advanced period for a duck. (*Diary*).

Another oil of Sidmouth. *Monday August 6.* Began painting in oil a view of Sidmouth looking east and was at it six hours. This is a companion to the view done a week ago. (*Diary*). *He continued with the painting over the next few day, carefully noting how much time he spent on it.*

Friday August 10. Painted four hours and finished my view of Sidmouth looking east. This four added to the twenty before makes twenty-four. (*Diary*).

Cholera. *Saturday August 11.* By the returns given, the cholera has been steadily increasing for several weeks. The weekly mortality in London for the week ending August 4th was 1967 for all diseases, *though* the average for the season is but 1008. In the three previous weeks it was 1369, 1741, 1931 and the last just

49/8/13. Schooner blown upon Sidmouth beach. Coloured on the spot August 13, 1849.
(DRO, Z19/2/8D/175)

mentioned 1967.   The cholera for several weeks has numbered deaths as follows: 49, 124, 152, 339, 678, 783 and 926.   (*Diary*).

Wreck of a schooner.   *Monday August 13.*   Made a sketch of the unfortunate schooner that was wrecked on the beach near the river. (*Diary*).

Family farewell.   *Tuesday August 14.*   I went into Exeter with the Rumleys and saw them and their servant, John Lawrence, off on the train for Plymouth to join the ship 'Constance', which is to take them to Australia.   I wonder if we shall ever meet again, and if so, whether the meeting will take place out there or in England or indeed in a further off country than the Antipodes? (*Diary*).

Sunday August 19.   The schooner that was driven ashore here a week ago was sold by auction yesterday.   Mr. Lousada and Captain Mathews bought her hull and lower rigging for £44.   This evening at high water she was floated off by means of casks. (*Diary*).

Monday August 20.   The schooner was floated to Topsham. (*Diary*).

Early reference to Moridunum.   *Saturday September 1.*   On turning over the leaves of Polwhele's history of the county, I saw in a note (Ch.2, Sect. IV, p.183) a quotation from a work by Gen. Simcoe, where the remains of a fortress are cursorily mentioned as existing on High Peak hill, and that this spot is at the same distance from Exeter as Moridunum is described to have been.   It is eight years since I discovered the remains of this fortress and I was not aware till now that any writer had spoken of its existence.   But my view respecting Moridunum thus receives confirmation.   (*Diary*).

Sketch of High Peak Hill.   *Friday September 7.*   *There is no Diary entry recording this colourful sketch of High Peak Hill viewed from the north-east.*

49/9/7.   High Peak Hill from Peak Hill.   Coloured on the spot September 7, 1849. (DRO, Z19/2/8D/215)

Otterton churchyard and East Budleigh.   *Tuesday September 11.*   Went to Otterton and East Budleigh.   Examined the parish register and made two extracts under date 1656 attested by Ro. Duke.   I paid two half crowns.   At Otterton I copied John Green's effigy and ship on his tomb in the churchyard (*see June 17, 1873*) and made a coloured sketch of the stocks as an interesting feature amongst the romantic scenery.   Coming home I made a coloured sketch of High Peak as seen from Pinn, or more properly Pen Farm.   From the top of Peak Hill, Portland looked more distinct than I ever remember to have seen it.   (*Diary*). *The stocks have gone as has the decorated end slab depicting the ship on John Green's tomb* *(d.1687) in the churchyard, though the shipbuilder himself is still just recognisable from the thighs upwards.* The punishment of the stocks has been falling into desuetude within my memory. I once saw a man in them, I believe for drunkenness. This was the only time, and it was somewhere between 1830 and 1840. This took place at the lower or south-east gate of [*Sidmouth*] churchyard between the steps (which were then narrower) and the road. The stocks, for three pairs of legs, now (1872) are kept at the top of the stone stairs of the Town Hall, rusting for want of use. I give a sketch of them. (*History of Sidmouth II, 35a*). *Hutchinson's copy of a Sidmouth lithograph dated 1819* shows the stocks beside the narrow steps leading up through the churchyard. *They are now on display in Sidmouth Museum.*

49/9/11-3. *From a tomb in Otterton churchyard to commemorate Rd. Green, a ship builder. 1849.* (DRO, Z19/2/8D/ 223)

49/9/11-1. *View in Otterton churchyard. Coloured on the spot September 11, 1849.* (DRO, Z19/2/8D/213)

49/9/11-2. *Sidmouth stocks.* (Hist. of Sid. II,35a)

49/9/11-5. *High Peak Hill from Pinn. Coloured on the spot September 11, 1849.* (DRO, Z19/2/8D/219)

49/9/11-4. *Copy of a lithograph showing the stocks beside Sidmouth churchyard steps.* (Hist. of Sid. IV,58)

Wood engraving. *Tuesday September 25.* Prepared for some wood engraving. Began one of the inscriptions taken from the East Budleigh register, namely the second one which is the shortest. (*Diary*).

Wednesday September 26. Engraved four hours on wood at the inscription beginning 'Item' etc. I am obliged to do it on beech, not being able to obtain boxwood in Sidmouth of sufficient size. During the evening I made use of one of my lenses

49/9/26-1. *Sidbury Castle Hill from Sidford. Coloured on the spot September 26, 1849.* (DRO, Z19/2/8D/221)

or bullseyes to throw the concentrated light from a candle onto the wood. I found it answered very well. I have seen the wood engravers in London use a globular bottle of water for this purpose. (*Diary*). *According to the date, Hutchinson also went out to Sidford and sketched Sidbury Castle Hill from the bridge. Sidmouth Bridge was the subject of his first etching, done in 1830.*

49/9/26-2. *Sidford bridge. My first etching on copper, circa 1830.* (Hist. of Sid. I,48a).

Saturday September 29. Michaelmas Day! Mild rainy weather. Engraved two hours today, say sixteen *altogether*, and finished the inscription. Took several impressions. Gardened two hours, pruned the raspberries and trimmed the ivy on the wall. (*Diary*).

Author's advice. *Tuesday October 2.* Bathed, *the* forty-ninth time this year. Rather cold. Gardened, made a fire and burnt the weeds. Immolated nearly a hundred copies of my first puerility '*Branscombe Cliffs*', *and* thus I advise all authors to devote their first works. Roasted some potatoes in the ashes *and* eat them too. There is a very nice flavour in potatoes dressed in this way. (*Diary*).

Cold swim. *Saturday October 6.* Bathed *the* 51st time this year, *but it was so cold and cheerless that I don't think I shall bathe again.* (*Diary*). *Hutchinson goes on to discuss the current theory of the cause of cholera known as the 'Fungoid Theory', minute germs in the air and water in infected places.*

Severe illness. *Tuesday October 9.* My bathe on Saturday did me no good. I got chilled before I could dry myself and dress. I feel flushed in the face and chilly in the body and the rheumatism has come on terribly in my left leg. Heaped on blankets and perspired all night. (*Diary*).

Wednesday October 10. No better. The warm bed increased the rheumatism. (*Diary*).

Thursday October 11. Little better. Went to a small party at Lime Park because I would not confess I was unwell, but I was unable to conceal my aches and pains. (*Diary*).

Friday October 12. A trifle better. Hobbled to Mr. Heineken's and showed him my recent labours on wood. The exercise seemed to do my rheumatism good. (*Diary*).

Saturday October 13. Worse again, and flew to galvanism. (*Diary*).

Friday October 19. Had a shocking week, the worst rheumatic attack I ever had. Took a warm bath *and* called in Dr. Cullen. Amid all this I have had little inclination for reading. From London the cholera accounts are most satisfactory. Last week the deaths from the epidemic were 110, so here is a cheery return. Our new form of prayer has not been offered in vain. (*Diary*).

Thursday November 1. Oh, such a time as I have had! Such miserable days! Such sleepless nights! (*Diary*).

Leaving Sidmouth. *Tuesday November 6.* Today Mother and Bingham went to the Rev. Charles and Mrs. Webber of Staunton on Wye, and the agreement to let the house was signed by the two principals and witnessed by Bingham. We are to leave on Friday. (*Diary*).

Friday November 9. Left Sidmouth for a few months and took a lodging at 5 Bouverie Place, Mount Radford (*Exeter*). (*Diary*). *In fact, Hutchinson did not return to Sidmouth for nearly a year, moving to London after a stay in Exeter.*

Monday November 12. Had a painful day but hope crisis has passed. (*Diary*).

Gratitude. *Thursday November 15.* Today was set apart as a day of solemn humiliation before Almighty God in acknowledgement of his having so immediately removed the pestilence of the cholera, after our prayers for that purpose were put up only a few weeks ago. (*Diary*).

Essay in the 'Western Miscellany'. *Monday November 19.* Bought 'The Western Miscellany' for the current month. It contains the first half of my *'Essay on the Literature of the day'* (see February 19, 1849). Though this is a country publication printed in Exeter, it is creditable. Woolmer's Gazette of this week pays me a compliment on the same article. If they did not think more of the essay than I do, they would hold their tongues. (*Diary*).

Literary labours. *Friday November 23.* Tried today for the first time to resume my literary labours, though I am obliged to write with great difficulty on the sofa. Had out the rough draft of my proposed article on 'The Dukes of Otterton' with the extracts, notes, etc., made some weeks ago at Sidmouth, looked them over and prepared to arrange them. (*Diary*).

Tuesday November 27. Beautiful day! Took a turn out of doors for a quarter of an hour, the first time I have been out since I left Sidmouth. (*Diary*).

Saturday December 8. A letter of mine, reflecting on the fact that there is no museum in Exeter for the preservation of local antiquities, appears in Woolmer today. (*Diary*). *It was a provocative letter initiating, as no doubt Hutchinson intended, a long but not altogether favourable debate in the correspondence column of the Gazette. Eventually, four hundred of the 'largest' ratepayers requested a public meeting to consider the proposal, and on January 20, 1851, it was agreed almost unanimously to establish a Free Library and Museum in Exeter. Nevertheless, it was not until 1865 that the corner stone was laid and a further three before Hayward's magnificent front block was finally completed.*

Amusing forgery. *Tuesday December 25.* Christmas Day! Passed it very quietly. This week a literary forgery of mine appears in Woolmer. It is entitled '*Helas ffor Bennet*', and purports to be an old poem recording the death of Bennet who was burnt at Liverydole in 1531, and that the said poem written on vellum was recently found in an old oak chest discovered in the remains of the alleged Sidmouth Priory. (There was no Priory at Sidmouth. It was at Otterton, and Sidmouth was attached to it). (*Diary*). *The account of its finding and decipherment* what with mildew, rotten vellum as brown as the oak itself and the fading of the writing, the task was one of some perplexity (*Exeter and Plymouth Gazette, Dec. 22, 1849*), *was rather too convincing. Despite such clues as the suspicious coincidence of the date (see March 13, 1850) and the signature of that rather prolific balladeer Petrus de Sidemue, Hutchinson's poem was accepted as authentic by some, appearing almost in full for instance in Notes and Gleanings 1892, V, 144.*

Chit Rocks, Sidmouth.

1850

Another counterfeit. *Saturday January 19.* At last an agreeable change in the weather. For the last fortnight we have had a cutting easterly wind and the country has been bound up in ice. Fine weather for skaters and Esquimaux perhaps, but I prefer something more genial. I have been keeping the fire warm and reading. I have gone through the *'Perambulation of Dartmoor'* by the Rev. Mr. Rowe of Crediton which has made me long to be touring in that wild region. A letter of mine respecting the 'Farming Interest' and signed Jan Chawbacon, written in the Devonshire dialect, is printed in Woolmer's Gazette today. (*Diary*). *Hutchinson's long and amusing letter to the editor of* 'Oolmer's Gazette' *opposed Free Trade and the hardship it was causing in the countryside:*

Honoured Zur.

This comes hoping youme well. 'Tis ever zo long zince I rote to you. We varmers be down in the mouth. I've been zo dashed about the loss of Purtection that I've had no heart to hould my pen – no more than to hould my plou. I've been as wished as a dishclout and ave a got no sproil in me. *After describing the fall in price of wheat and its effect on rent and employment 'Jan' continues:* When I zeed mysel going downhill we no drag to stop me, I vound I was obligated to turn off my man Urchit – I mane Urchit Pook. It went agin the grain cruel bad, vor he had worked vor me man and boy vor nigh vive-and-twenty year. I goes into the yard one day and Urchit was a sot down pun the zool. He had a got a sliver of bird and a rasher of bacon in one hand and his stick-knife in the t'other, a eating his ten-o-clock.

'Urchit', sez I, 'Urchit'.

'Ees Maister', cries Urchit, a jumping up pon his veet, vor he never knowed I was zo near.

'Urchit', sez I, rather solemn, 'do you know what Vree Trade is?'

'Well', he sez, a shoving his hat off and scratching the right side of his hade, 'I baint quite certified as I do; is it a rabid dog Maister?'

'No, no'.

'May be 'tis a plant. Is it henbane or ratsbane?'

'Tis a wus bane than that comes to. 'Tis the varmer's bane, and everybody else's bane'.

'Then 'tis the wire-worm!' cried he in triumph, 'vor that is the varmer's bane'.

'You hant hit it yet'.

'The turnip-fly may be?'

'No, no Urchit, 'tis wus I tell 'ee'.

'Then I don't know what it is, vor the very life of me'.

'I see you don't, and I spose I must just give you a notion. Vree Trade is a murrain wus than all your banes and worms. It makes a man wear his coat two years instead of one, it makes him drink small beer when he used to drink strong ale, and it makes a varmer like Jan Chawbacon obligated to turn off Urchit Pook who have a sarved um faithfully vor vive-and-twenty year. Urchit, we must part. I be cruel zorry vor it. Indeed, I must give you your walking ticket. You be dashed and I be dished, zo there a regular hash of both of us. And now you know what Vree Trade is'.

According to the letter, some time later Jan Chawbacon met Urchit working on the waterfront in Exeter. Urchit however had found employment unloading 'Vree Trade carn imported from Prussia'. (*Exeter and Plymouth Gazette, Jan. 19, 1850, extract*).

50/1/24.
*Younge of
Puslinch*
(Hist. of Sid.
I,189)

50/1/26.
*Upton of
Upton.*
(Hist. of Sid.
I,190)

50/2/1-1. *Sarah Duke's brass,
Otterton church.* (Hist. of Sid.
I,187b)

50/2/1-2. *Richard Duke's brass,
Otterton church.* (Hist. of Sid.
I,187b)

50/2/1-3. *Arms sculptured on
Mr. Duke's house, Otterton.*
(Hist. of Sid. I,187b)

Genealogical studies. *Tuesday January 22.* Made out the pedigree of 'Duke of Otterton' compressed into the size of the pages of the 'Gentleman's Magazine'. (*Diary*).

Thursday January 24. Made out the pedigree of 'Younge of Puslinch'. (*Diary*).

Saturday January 26. And the pedigree of 'Upton of Upton'. (*Diary*).

Etching. *Friday February 1.* Got up to breakfast, the first time for the last three months. Laid an etching ground to engrave the brasses in Otterton Church to the memory of the Dukes. (*Diary*).

Saturday February 2. Traced the subject of one of the brasses (to Sarah) on the etching ground in white chalk. (*Diary*).

Monday February 4. Used the etching needle on the plate representing the brass in Otterton to the memory of 'Sarah, praecharissima uxor Roberti Duke'. After my illness however, I find my hand very shaky and unsteady. Worked at it for two hours. (*Diary*).

Tuesday February 5. Etched two hours, and the two yesterday totals four. (*Diary*).

Wednesday February 6. Etched two and a half hours, and the four before making six and a half, and finished the plate. (*Diary*).

Friday February 8. Put nitric acid on the plate, proportion one part acid to two of water. It was only on half an hour but bit very vigorously. Stopped out what was corroded enough, to wit the crests, mantling, outer border and figures. (*Diary*).

Saturday February 9. Put acid on again. On twenty minutes and the former thirty totals fifty. Cleaned off the plate and thickened the letters, etc. with the graver. Took two impressions. (*Diary*). *Hutchinson made a second plate of Richard Duke's brass over the next few days.*

Monday February 18. Went over to the workshop of Mr. Parrot, carpenter, opposite Bouverie Place, and worked three hours filing the two plates down to the margin of the work, soldering tacks by the heads to their backs and mounting them on wooden blocks the height of the type. (*Diary*).

Thursday February 21. At last, after many days owing to my illness, my article on the 'Dukes of Otterton' which has been some six months in hand is finally completed. Made it into a parcel with the blocks and engravings and sent it to Mr. J.G.Nichols, 25 Parliament Street, London. Perhaps he won't print it. (*Diary*).

Record voyage. *Friday February 22.* Heard of the Rumley's safe arrival in South Australia. They sailed from Plymouth on the 18th of last August and arrived at Port Adelaide on the 4th of November, having made the voyage in 78 days. This is the shortest passage on record, the average run being 100 to 120 days. (*Later note:* It is now done in 34 days – 1892). (*Diary*).

Verse on love. *Saturday February 23.* My quatrain on '*Love*' is in Woolmer. (*Diary*).

> Love is a forge, a furnace, or a fire,
> A fret, a fever, or some sore disease,
> A hunger, thirst, a want, a fond desire –
> In short, this Love is anything you please.
>   *Signed* Peter. (*Exeter and Plymouth Gazette, Feb. 23, 1850*).

Valentine post. *Wednesday February 27.* The papers mention that on last

Valentine's Day in London, 22 000 letters above the daily average were delivered. (*Diary*).

Verse on hate. *Monday March 4.* In Woolmer of last Saturday is my notice of the arrival of the Rumleys in Australia and the quatrain on 'Hate'. (*Diary*).

> Hard is that heart where Hate doth lie enshrined –
> Hard as the rocks and blocks of old Stonehenge:
> And Hate is venom for your foe designed,
> Commingled with a longing for revenge.
> *Signed* Peter. (*Exeter and Plymouth Gazette March 2, 1850*).

Bennet's stake. *Wednesday March 13.* Went out to Liverydole to see the new almshouses. They form a fine row of buildings. The old chapel of red Heavitree stone still remains, but will probably come down soon. I enquired the spot where the stake was found to which Bennet was supposed to have been chained when he was burnt here three hundred and eighteen years ago. The place pointed out is immediately within the doorstep of the small wing attached to the east end of the range of buildings. The man described the stake as being about the size of one's leg, that an iron ring was driven into the top to prevent its splitting, and that into this top end, so fortified, an iron spike with an eye at one extremity was driven home and this was secured by a pin going through it and the stake too. When the old almshouses were cleared away last year and this relic turned up, there was much talk in the neighbourhood concerning the finding of 'Bennet's stake', *and* in order to preserve it from destruction, Lady Rolle had it carried to Bicton. (*Diary*).

Heavitree churchyard. *Thursday March 14.* Went to Heavitree churchyard where I have not been for three years. The new church is certainly handsome and it is to be hoped they will soon raise the required funds to build the new tower. Had a look at the Hutchinson monuments in the north-east corner *and found them* much out of order. Uncle Tom's is leaning on one side and almost out of the ground, and Uncle William's tombstone is cracked in half. (*Diary*).

Gorham versus the Bishop. *Saturday March 16.* The long-pending case of 'Gorham v. The Bishop of Exeter' has been terminated by the decision of the Judicial Committee of the Privy Council, which pronounced judgement last Friday. This reverses the decision of Sir H.J.Fust in the Arches Court, which was in favour of the Bishop – the present being against him. The Bishop refused to institute the Rev. Mr. Gorham to the living of Brampford Speke near Exeter because he held opinions contrary to what the Bishop held to be orthodox. It was on the subject of Baptismal Regeneration. 'The doctrine held by Mr. Gorham', said Lord Longdale, the Master of the Rolls, when reading the judgement, 'appears to us to be this – that baptism is a sacrament generally necessary to salvation, but that the grace of regeneration does not so necessarily accompany the act of baptism that regeneration invariably takes place in baptism; that the grace may be granted before, in or after baptism; that baptism is an effectual sign of grace by which God works invisibly in us, but only in such as worthily receive it – in them alone it has a wholesome effect; and that without reference to the qualification of the recipient it is not in itself an effectual sign of grace. That infants baptised and dying before actual sin are certainly saved, but that in no case is regeneration in baptism unconditional'. Mr. Gorham therefore restricts the spiritual efficacy of baptism to those only who 'worthily receive it', and *thinks* that baptismal regeneration is not unconditional. This the Bishop thought to be contrary to the doctrine of the church. But the Judicial Committee of the Privy Council, which is not composed of ecclesiastics, and I believe may be composed of heretics and infidels, has thought otherwise. Let's see the end (*see August 12*). (*Diary*).

Sidmouth tenant. *Thursday March 21.* Our tenant at Sidmouth, the Rev. C. Webber, having died, his widow has determined to go, though they engaged the house to the seventh of next May. Today she sent the halves of three five pound notes, the rent till the seventh now being fifteen pounds, and intends to leave tomorrow. (*Diary*).

To London. *Thursday March 28. With the early departure of their tenants, Mrs. Hutchinson and brother Bingham resolved on a return to Sidmouth, whilst Peter decided that a further period of recuperation in London would be beneficial. He moved into lodgings in Hampstead, reading, sketching, etc., and whilst there determined to finish his three volume historical novel . . .* called anything you please. The first two volumes I wrote four or five years ago in London and then threw the work aside. Being alone during the past summer at Hampstead I thought I might as well finish it, even if it is never published. *Apparently it never was. In the autumn he moved to a Paddington address, which had its disadvantages.* Oh the bugs! I have encountered bugs in London before and I have encountered them still more in America, but I never encountered so many as I have here. *Hutchinson finally returned to Sidmouth on October 1, 1850.*

Gorham victorious. *Monday August 12.* So the 'Gorham Controversy' has terminated and the Rev. G.C.Gorham preached for the first time at Brampford Speke, near Exeter, yesterday. He was inducted at the Court of Arches, I think last Tuesday, after the fiat of the Archbishop of Canterbury, so that he has fought his way into the diocese of Exeter in spite of the Bishop and with nothing from him but opposition up to the last moment. The Bishop has even written a letter to the churchwardens of Brampford Speke, warning them of their new pastor and telling them to note down any heretical sentiments he may utter in his pulpit. *(Diary).*

Photographic portrait. *Friday October 11.* Mr. H. Johnson took my portrait with his apparatus at Mr. Heineken's, the one that Mr. H. took with his yesterday not being satisfactory. *(Diary).*

Height of Sidmouth church tower. *Monday October 21.* Went up on Sidmouth church tower *and* measured the height on the west side. From the doorstep to the top of the parapet it was seventy-four feet six inches, or there about. Also took the inscriptions on the six bells. *(Diary).*

Hazards of coach travel. *Tuesday October 22.* Went into Exeter by the Mail. When we were within a mile and a half of Ottery, the horses ran away and we were turned over. John Hook, marker at the Billiard Room, jumped off and broke one of his legs very badly just above the ankle. We then ran on nearly a quarter of a mile and were all pitched into a garden on the left side. If we had been thrown against a house or a wall our brains must have been dashed out on the spot. I lighted on the hedge upon my back, and unhurt. A woman made a grasp at the luggage to save herself but by mistake caught hold of the guards bugle, and then flew over me. Dr Marshs' groom had his green livery coat torn from the skirts up to the collar and presented the most ludicrous appearance. Everybody was more or less hurt but myself. When we were all righted and ready to proceed, one of the passengers, a lady, was so tearful that no entreaties or arguments from the coachman or passengers could make her take her place. It is said that a joke will prevail where a sober argument will sometimes be urged in vain. I tried it. 'Madam', said I, 'you never heard of a coach being turned over twice in one day'. The remark was convincing. Everybody burst out laughing and the lady got in. *(Diary). Hutchinson published a lengthy and amusing account of the accident in the Exeter and Plymouth Gazette (October 26) describing each passenger's fate. Of himself:* Mr. Peter Hutchinson of Sidmouth was ejected headlong and when the bewilderment went off he found himself comfortably lodged on his back upon some dry blackthorn bushes which had been used to mend the fence. *It seems it was not an entirely unexpected event on the Sidmouth run (see June 23, 1852).*

Design for new vicarage. *Friday October 25.* Spent the evening with the Rev. Henry Fellowes, vicar of Sidbury, and his family, now at Fort Cottage since his vicarage burnt a few weeks ago. *We* talked over plans for a new house and *I* took with me a plan which he had asked me to draw for him. *(Diary).*

Inscription on bell. *Tuesday October 29.* Went up to the tower again especially to take a plaster cast of the Latin inscription on the fourth bell, which appears very

ancient and is difficult to decipher.   Passed the evening with Mr. Heineken to have some music *and* took the casts of the inscription to him.   (*Diary*).   *With the assistance of Dr. Oliver of Exeter (see November 5) Hutchinson interpreted the inscription as 'Jesus, that beloved name, is given to me'.   He later wrote an article on the 'Jesus' bell in Harvey's Sidmouth Directory March 1851, and again in Notes and Queries 1854.*

50/10/22.   Coach from Sidmouth turned over half way to Ottery by the horses running away, October 22, 1850.
(DRO, Z19/2/8D/233)

Authors revenge.   *Thursday October 31.*   Assisted in planting the privet hedge in the garden.   Read Mrs. Mary Molesworth's two-volume novel of *Claude, or the Double Sacrifice, and* wrote a review of it for the Exeter Gazette.   This work, though only a novel, is causing a great stir in Sidmouth.   About two years ago the authoress was down here on a visit to Gen. Slessor's family, and she has now amused herself in her book by many severe personalities played off upon the inhabitants amongst whom she visited.   Their wrath is much excited.   (*Diary*).   *No doubt they were even less amused when Hutchinson's only mildly critical revue was reprinted in the December issue of Harvey's Sidmouth Directory.*

Visit to Heightley Cottage.   *Tuesday November 5.*   Went from Sidmouth to Heightley Cottage, Chudleigh.   Took the same conveyance from which I was pitched a fortnight ago.   Left my plaster casts of the inscription on the bell at Dr. Oliver's, for him to try and decipher.   Great preparations for an anti-popery demonstration are being made in Exeter for tonight.   The recent aggressions of Rome in the appointment of an archbishop of Westminster and other popish dignitaries seems to have aroused all England.   Went by South Devon rail to Newton where my aunt's carriage was waiting for me *and* got to Heightley by five.   (*Diary*).

Creation theory.   *Saturday November 16.*   Finished reading *Vestiges of the Natural history of Creation*, sixth edition.   This work has been much talked of but with very little approval by those who pay greater deference to the Mosiac account of the Creation than to the new theories of philosophers, however learned in philosophical and geological studies they may be.   The work cannot be otherwise than hurtful when it tends to materialism and runs into speculations not only independent of, but in some cases opposed to, the inspired account of the formation of all things. The theory is that of 'development' or progression, a theory however which is not new in as much as Lord Monboddo and Monsieur Lamarck have already propounded it to the world, though with less particularisation. That man originated from monkeys, and monkeys by development from the inferior animals, is not in accordance with what we read in the Bible, yet we here have another stickler for such a notion. The work is anonymous, but Sir Richard Vivian, Bart., MP for Helston in Cornwall, has been suspected of being the author. *Hutchinson was not entirely sceptical about evolutionary theories however, as a few days later he adds*: But though its opponents have put before me one or two difficulties, it is not without hesitation that I reject it. (*Diary*).

50/11/30. *Ugbrook Park, near Chudleigh, Devon. May 1836.* (DRO, Z19/2/8A/132)

Noble neglect. *Saturday November 30.* Took a drive in Ugbrook Park – a beautiful park for which nature has done a great deal, but which is falling into great neglect owing to the absence and poverty of Lord Clifford. What a pity so many of our nobility live too fast. The day of retribution is sure to come. (*Diary*).

50/12/3. *The lighthouse on the Den, Teignmouth. Coloured on the spot without sketching in pencil June 1848.* (DRO, Z19/2/8D/125)

Day in Teignmouth. *Tuesday December 3.* Went to Teignmouth in the carriage *and* called on the Rev. Mr. Cresswell, heretofore of Sidmouth, and on the Misses Cousins whose house we formerly occupied. Took a turn around the Den and then went to the harbour to see what was going on among the shipping. Returned to Heightly by five for dinner. (*Diary*). *The sketch of the lighthouse on the Den was done over two years previously.*

Visit to Dr. Oliver. *Monday December 9.* Accompanied Mary Roberton in the carriage to Exeter. Left her to return to Chudleigh whilst I took the Sidmouth coach, after having had half an hour's chat with Dr. Oliver, and got home for dinner. I have made Dr. Oliver's acquaintance at a remarkable time. I first called on him on the fifth of November when Exeter was making extraordinary preparations for burning the 'Old Pope', as also the Cardinal Archbishop and the twelve new Romish bishops. The country is everywhere in an uproar, roused by this act of 'Popish aggression'. Considering that Dr. Oliver is a Roman Catholic, the circumstance was a little amusing but our topics of conversation were antiquarian. (*Diary*).

Papal aggression. *Wednesday December 11.* Put my name to the petition shortly to be presented to the Queen on the subject of the 'Papal aggression'. The fact of the Queen's father having died at Sidmouth and she having stayed here some time ought to have been more dwelt on. Her residence here is only alluded to in parenthesis. (*Diary*). *To Hutchinson, a staunch Low Churchman, renascent Roman Catholicism and the inroads 'ritualism' was making within the Church of England were a constant concern throughout his life. Some years later when the parish church was being rebuilt, he was to find himself embroiled at the centre of a particularly acrimonious dispute with the 'ritualists' of the parish, an affair which assumed a more than local prominence.*

Type setting. *Friday December 13.* Tried my hand at setting up type. Some fourteen years ago or more I set up and printed a small book, but I thought I had nearly forgotten where to find my letters in the case. At first I was puzzled but after half an hour I began to feel more at home. My subject was the antiquarian *Notes on Sidmouth, No. III*, in Harvey's Directory. (*Diary*).

Hail to the New Year. *Tuesday December 31.* Last day of the year *and* wonderfully mild weather. Gardened for an hour or two, coat and hat thrown aside and quite in a perspiration. My *Ave, Anno Nove!* appears this week in Woolmer and my *Notes on Sidmouth, No. IV* in Harvey's Directory. (*Diary*). *Ave, Anno Nove! was yet another discovery of an old poem by Petrus de Sidemew*, drawn from the same sources as the others (*see December 16, 1848 and December 25, 1849*). Dust, corrosion, mildew and damp as usual all combined to render the original somewhat difficult to decipher. (*Exeter and Plymouth Gazette December 28, 1850*).

Mount Pleasant, late the residence of Mrs Tyrrell, Salcombe parish.
Coloured on the spot April 14, 1848.
(DRO, Z19/2/8D/101)

1851

51/1/9. Roman coin. (Hist. of Sid. I,97)

Roman coin from Mill Lane, Sidmouth. *Thursday January 9.* Engraved in wood the obverse side of the Roman coin recently found near Mill Cross, Sidmouth, and which now belongs to Mr. Heineken. The discovery of this coin is important when coupled with that of the centaur found in 1840, as going to establish the idea that the Romans at one time made use of the harbour formerly existing at the mouth of the Sid. As it is also likely they occupied the camps on High Peak and Sidbury Castle Hills, and had a station at Sidmouth, the discovery of this coin adds much to the notion of their permanent occupancy of the shores round the harbour. The coin was found by William Sweet junior, rope maker, whilst digging to repair a pump about two feet below the surface, *and* I went yesterday to enquire the exact spot where it was turned up. The man was not in, but I was shown the place in the yard where the pavement had been taken up. The place where Mill Lane, that runs on the south side of All Saints Church, abuts onto the top of High Street is called Mill Cross. There was probably an ancient cross here, perhaps on the east side of High Street opposite the Lane. Forty or fifty yards below this, also on the east side, stood the old mill that belonged six hundred years ago to Adam de Radway. This mill is in the recollection of persons now living but it was falling into disuse, as the present mill down by the river was erected about fifty-five years ago. I can remember the hollow in the ground where the water-wheel worked, and some paltry cottages there which were burnt down one evening when I was dining with the Mortimers at Salcombe Lodge. We went out on the lawn to look at the blaze and when I went home at eleven o'clock, six or eight houses were all in flames. I forget the date but I think I entered it in my diary at the time, some three years ago. At the east end of Mill Lane, by Sidlands and between High Street and the turning into Blackmore Fields on the south side of the Lane, are the entrance doors into two houses, *and* I was led into the most westerly one. I passed through a passage about five or six yards long, and emerging into a small courtyard the pump stands against the wall of the house immediately on the right hand and close to the back door. I believe they were digging on the south-east side of the pump when Sweet found the coin. It is the size of the old Roman semi-libella, or about the bigness of a farthing. It appears to be a Claudius, and on the reverse there is a female figure with what looks like the word 'Felicitas' around it. (*Diary*).

Another schooner wrecked. *Wednesday January 15.* Today an unfortunate schooner was wrecked upon Chit Rocks, but the crew consisting of six men and a boy were saved. She was from Poole to the Severn with pipe clay. It blew tremendously from the south. Her bowsprit and foretopmast were carried away so that she became unmanageable, and running for the shore she came stem on upon the rocks. The vessel was soon swamped but the crew took refuge in the rigging where they were kept many hours wet, cold and without food. After several unsuccessful attempts, a shot with a rope attached to it was fired over her. Towards night the wind moderated and two boats put off and brought the crew ashore half dead. Warm baths and hot broth revived them. (*Diary*).

Thursday January 16. The wind has got up and the gale blows stronger than before. Waves are flying over the vessel and it is surprising that she holds together. (*Diary*). *The vessel was the 'Jane and Eliza' of Caernarvon and within the week had become a complete loss. (Exeter and Plymouth Gazette Jan. 25, 1851).*

Visit to the Joneses. *Saturday January 18.* Went to Exeter by the Mail via Ottery, without being turned over. Called at Dr. Oliver's and left him some casts of the Roman coin and some impressions of the inscription on the fourth bell in Sidmouth Church. Went over from Northernhay to take a look at 'Dane's Castle' *which* is about forty paces in diameter, *and* then went on to Uffculme, taking the rail as far as Tiverton junction. Arrived at the school house about four and found the Joneses well. (*Diary*). 'Dane's Castle, behind Exeter jail, was a small earthwork, perhaps an outpost. It was destroyed when the reservoir for the Exeter waterworks was made (*in 1852*), all but a portion of its eastern slope. I have paced it several times and made it 38 paces in diameter. It is mentioned in my paper in the number for March 1862 of the Journal of the Archaeological Association. (*Soc. of Antiq. Ms. 250*). *The twelfth century Castle reappeared in 1993 with the emptying of the reservoir, and is now preserved in landscaped surroundings.*

Friday January 24. The Joneses started this morning for Leamington, Warwickshire, leaving me to look after five children and four maidservants for the next ten days. After the children had had their tea, had a good romp making noise enough to tear the house down and gone to bed, I enjoyed a little peace, first having an hour at the piano and then reading Layard's *Ninevah*. (*Diary*).

Uffculme Church. *Sunday February 2.* At church twice with the children. Uffculme church is unusually handsome for a small country town. (*Diary*). *Hutchinson sketched details of the church on a number of occasions, unrecorded in his Diary.*

51/2/2-1. *Cross on the south porch of Uffculme church. November 2, 1847.* (DRO, Z19/2/8D/45)

51/2/2-2. *Monuments of the Walrond family, Uffculme church, Devon. Coloured on the spot November 4, 1847.* (DRO, Z19/2/8D/85)

51/2/2-3. *The organ in Uffculme church, Devon. Coloured on the spot November 4, 1847.* (DRO,19/2/8D/47)

51/2/28. *Columns in Uffculme church. Sketched on the spot February 28, 1851.* (DRO, Z19/2/8D/239)

Monday February 3. Mr. and Mrs. Jones returned from their visit to Leamington and Worcester. Gladly returned the keys into their hands before the children had succeeded in dethroning me and setting up a republic. (*Diary*).

Around Uffculme. *Tuesday February 11.* Took a walk on Uffculme Down. (*Diary*).

Wednesday February 12. Walked down to the factory and returned through the meadows on the south-east side of the River Culm. (*Diary*).

Smithincot. *Thursday February 27.* Walked to Smithincot (if it is so spelt) then up to Gadden Down and returned to Uffculme down the hill by the three elms. (*Diary*). *The annexed sketch of Smithincot bridge was apparently done a week earlier.*

Walk to the 'Five Fords'. *Friday February 28.* Took a walk up the river to the 'Five Fords' and returned through the meadows on the Craddock side of the river. (*Diary*). *According to the date, Hutchinson also went to Uffculme Church and sketched the columns in the nave.*

51/2/27. *Smithincott bridge over the Culm, Uffculme. Coloured on the spot February 21, 1851.* (DRO, Z19/2/8D/237)

Stroll on Uffculme Down. *Saturday March 1.* Rubbed over the second round ash table that I finished last Thursday staining and polishing. Took a ramble over Uffculme Down. In some of the county histories I have seen it observed that the continuation of a Roman road from Exmouth passed over this Down. Also that there existed an old British work known as 'Pixie Garden' somewhere on it (*see September 8, 1854*). I have failed to discover any traces or intelligence of either of these remains, whether by examination or by enquiry. Many parts of the Down however, have been enclosed and brought into cultivation during the last half century. (*Diary*).

Sidmouth bells. *Thursday March 6.* Received Harvey's Sidmouth Directory. The March number contains my article on the Sidmouth bells *and* there is a complimentary letter signed JDS addressed to me. Who is JDS? (*Later note:* James Davidson of Secktor). (*Diary*).

Kite flying. *Monday March 10.* Went to Uffculme Down with the boys and the children to fly Thomas Hodge's kite. (*Diary*).

Uffculme to Sidmouth. *Tuesday March 11.* Left Uffculme for Sidmouth. Called on Mr. J.Norris and C.J.Williams in Exeter. (*Diary*).

Sidmouth parish map. *Wednesday March 12.* Had the first look at my new *Map of the Parish of Sidmouth*. I reduced the large map measuring some seven or eight feet high, and this has been lithographed from mine by Spreat of Exeter for Harvey, the bookseller of Sidmouth. It is very neatly executed. I spent the evening with the Fellowes, now at Fort Cottage. (*Diary*).

Thursday March 20. Coloured some of my maps of Sidmouth and mounted them in cases. (*Diary*).

51/4/2. *Edward VI shilling.* (Hist. of Sid. I,98)

Shilling of Edward VI. *Wednesday April 2.* Finished engraving in boxwood Mr. Mortimer's shilling of Edward VI, to be published in Harvey's Directory for May. The reverse side, which I did first, I was eight hours about, and I was five hours at the obverse. A practised hand would have done them in half the time. Printed off twenty copies *and* called on Mr. Heineken and showed him the result of my work. (*Diary*). It was found at Sid in Salcombe parish in 1850. (*History of Sidmouth I, 98*).

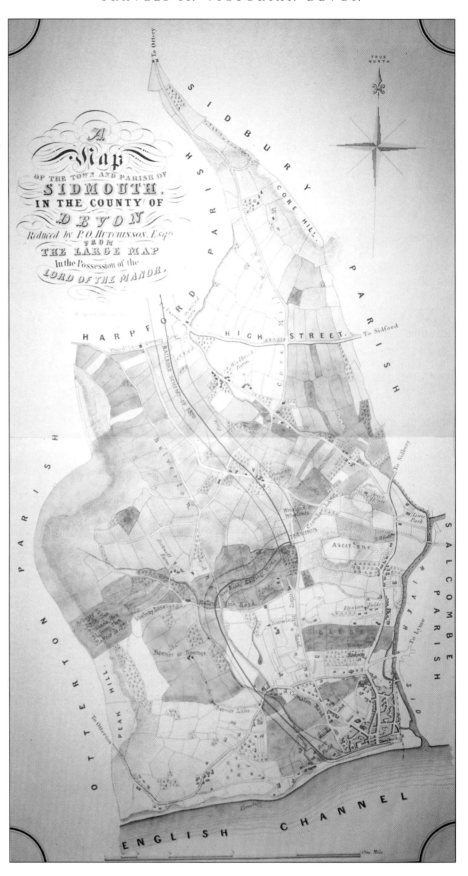

51/4/13. *Map of the parish of Sidmouth.* (Hist. of Sid. III,170b)

Enclosure of Salcombe Hill. *Thursday April 3.* From Coburg Terrace I watched some workmen burning the furze bushes on the top of Salcombe Hill. By virtue of an Act of Parliament they are proceeding to enclose the top and steepest parts of the sides of the hill, so they are burning the furze and dividing it by hedges. I am almost sorry to see this wild and romantic place enclosed, over which I have rambled so many scores of times, but as mouths increase I suppose more land must be cultivated. (*Diary*).

Otterton Cartulary and John Coke of Thorne.
Tuesday April 8. Went over from Sidmouth to Ottery to
see Mr. F.G.Coleridge about the *Otterton Cartulary* from
which I wish to make some extracts. Saw him and
received the book, on which he justly sets great value.
Went into the church and made a coloured drawing of
the monument of John Coke of Thorne in the north
aisle. The story goes that this man was murdered by his
brother who coveted the estate. (*Later note:* The story
seems to be only a fiction).

The *Cartulary* is a volume about an inch thick
containing forty-nine leaves and a mutilated half leaf of
vellum, several more having been cut away. It measures
seven inches by nine and is literally 'bound in boards', to
wit beech boards, covered with skin, but the one at the
end has been split longitudinally through the middle
and one half lost. The whole is now kept in a modern
crimson embossed morocco case to protect it from
injury. First we have three plain leaves much scribbled
over subsequently to the death of the last male heir of
the Duke family, when the book seems to have fallen
into the hands of the servants and to have been taken
little account of. Then we have six leaves devoted to a
calendar or almanac, each month occupying a page. The
days are not numbered as days of the month according to
the modern plan, but by ides, nones, dominical signs,
saint's days and by certain notable events . . . And it may
be remarked that there are some uncancelled entries
highly offensive to Henry VIII. (*Diary*). *Hutchinson*

John Coke, of Thorne.
North aisle, Ottery church.

Coloured in the church
April 8. 1851.

51/4/8. *John Coke of Thorne,
north aisle, Ottery Church.
Coloured in the church April 8,
1851.* (DRO, Z19/2/8D/241)

worked on the Cartulary all day and every day *for several weeks and eventually transcribed it into the second volume of his History of Sidmouth. His published account, still
in medieval Latin complete with the pot-hooks and hangers of the original, appears in a
series of articles in Notes and Gleanings for 1888.*

Progress of enclosure. *Tuesday May 13.* Took a ramble along the cliff through
the fields to the top of Salcombe Hill to see the progress of enclosing. *I have* not
been this way for a year and a half. Some men were grubbing up the roots of the
furze bushes recently burnt *and* on the flat summit of the hill I see the plough has
been at work for the first time. (*Diary*).

51/5/25. *The summit of High
Peak Hill with he signal staff,
seen over Peak Hill, from the top
of Bulverton Hill. May 25,
1851.* (DRO, Z19/2/8D/243)

New lenses. *Wednesday May 21.* Received my lenses for a Galilean telescope
from Chadburn, Sheffield, but they have not followed
my instructions in grinding them. This won't do.
After breakfast, took a walk to Mutter's Moor, Bulverton
Hill, and from the ridge enjoyed the view northwards
and westwards over and beyond Ottery towards the
Blackdown Hills in one direction and towards Dartmoor
in the other. (*Diary*).

Walk to Bulverton Hill. *Sunday May 25.* Took a walk
to Mutter's Moor and then to the summit of Bulverton
Hill. This last must be higher than many in the neigh-
bourhood. The cone of High Peak is seen rising over
Peak Hill and the horizon line of the sea is much above
the flagstaff on High Peak. This will make Bulverton
Hill perhaps about 600 feet high, for High Peak is 511.
(*Diary*).

Charles II at Sidford. *Tuesday May 27.* Went with
mother in a carriage to pay some visits. Returned
through Sidford, over the river into Salcombe parish.

51/5/27. House dates, Sidford.
(Hist. of Sid. V,142)

There is a tradition that Charles II, when he was a fugitive passing through this part of the country, stopped and slept one night in Sidford. I observed the dates on the three oldest houses in the place. In the street running north and south leading from Sidmouth to Sidbury there are two houses close together on the west side, one bearing the date 1640 cut in stone on the chimney, and the other 1633. Some have pointed to one of these as likely to be the house, but on the south side of the street leading to the bridge over the Sid and about half way down, there is a house bearing the date 1574 occupied by a baker, and this is the one most confidently believed to have been the one in question. (*Diary*).

The student however, who looks into the Boscobel Tracts will see that the king, in his flight after the Battle of Worcester, never came near Sidford at all. Romantic traditions are very pretty no doubt, and it is rather cruel to attack them. In our mind's eye, that wonderful eye that never goes blind, the picture like a sham fight only wants to be real in order to be perfect. (*History of Sidmouth III, 90*).

Reclamation of Salcombe Hill. *Wednesday May 28.* Took a turn on Salcombe Hill to look at the alterations. The hedges are finished and a number of men were engaged in burning the furze bushes, grubbing up roots and in 'subduing the land'. The race course on the top of the hill is cut up into various enclosures, and hedges bound the road all the way to Salcombe. On making my way to the edge of the cliff, I passed the conical block of stone which I remember more than twenty years, in line from the edge of Maynard's Hill towards Portland and standing about four feet high. I have sometimes observed this stone looking quite polished and shiny with oil rubbed out of the sheep's wool, for the sheep are given to collecting round it and rubbing against it. (*Diary*). It is unhewn, but its sides east and west are parallel, and it rises wedge-shaped north and south. From being so upright in the ground, this stone looks like one leg of a cromlech, though it may not have been so. There are many other blocks of stone on the hill, but none of them are so upright. (*History of Sidmouth I, 119a*). *The monolith was still standing in place in 1946 but has since been dragged to the corner of the field (Pollard 1978). Another 'Great Stone' once stood in the field on the other side of the road, half a kilometre almost due north (see June 1, 1871).*

Close to the edge of the cliff there is an acre of ground recently belonging to the crown, on which during Napoleonic times a signal staff and telegraph were erected. The electric telegraph and the use of steam have rendered these things useless and the spot of land has been sold. I was told that Charles Farrant, upholsterer of Sidmouth, gave £22 for it. It is now in potatoes. On the Sidmouth slope of the hill near the cliff some men were skimming off the turf and burning it, so I amused myself for some time feeding their fires. (*Diary*).

Oak Apple Day. *Thursday May 29.* Restoration of King Charles. Had up the flag again. (*Diary*).

Lime Park. *Friday May 30.* After breakfast I went up to Lime Park. Made a coloured drawing of the house from the hedge near the road. Taking the front at right angles, point blank, the only place I could get a sight of it the trees are grown so much. Lunched there and gave my morning's work to Mrs. Walker. (*Diary*).

Pen Beacon. *Saturday May 31.* After breakfast I walked over to Pin, or Pen, Beacon Hill, being the south-western spur of Peak Hill. I think it must be nearly twenty years since I was over on this hill. At the extreme point where the beacon fire was lighted, there is a mound like a tumulus. Whether the faggots of wood were heaped up and lighted or whether the alarm was given by any other process of illumination, there is no evidence to show. I dug down a few inches with the point of my stick on this mound to see if I could discover any traces of charcoal, but I failed to distinguish anything of the sort. I regretted I had no spade with me. There are no marks of any stone building here, as on the Beacon Hill rising over Harpford Wood. I doubt whether the trees on Pin Beacon can have been planted within fifty years - the trunks of many of them are more than a foot or fifteen inches in diameter, which bespeaks considerable age.   This hill may be about 550 feet high.   I merely judge so by remarking that the horizon line of the sea appeared thirty or forty feet above the top of High Peak, which is 513 feet. Nearly a hundred yards or so north from the beacon is another mound having the appearance of a tumulus.   Also, two or three hundred yards east of this, on the small promontory, I observed a slight rising like a tumulus.   I have laid these down on my copy of the Ordnance Map.   (*Diary*).

Sketch of Sidmouth limekilns. *Tuesday June 3.*   Went down to the beach and made a coloured sketch of the limekilns.   I have long been intending to do this, as I expect that before very long these limekilns will tumble into the sea.   There has recently been another large fall of the cliff between them and Sidmouth. (*Diary*).

51/6/3.   *The lime kilns, Sidmouth.   Coloured on the spot June 3, 1851.*
(DRO, Z19/2/8D/245)

Stay in Exeter. *Saturday June 7.* Up between seven and eight. Got on the coach and went to Exeter, to turn over some books at the Institution. Mr. T. Norris introduced me there. (*Diary*). *Hutchinson stayed in Exeter for about four weeks, mostly at work in the Institution copying out manuscripts, and incidentally noting Oliver's mistakes in his histories (see February 23, 1849).*

Donkey parade. *Wednesday June 25.* Today is the first day of the 'Synod' in Exeter. It was a question of whether the Bishop was not acting in opposition to the law by proposing the course he has adopted. The learned in the law have alleged that though he has the right thus to call his clergy about him, he would have no right to pass canons. Being in Exeter at this time I would have got into the Chapter House and have heard the deliberations, but none but the delegated clergy of the diocese have been admitted. Many persons have been very much opposed to the whole proceedings. An attempt has been made to get up a procession of several dozen donkeys on whose backs were to be seated persons dressed in clerical habits, one of them with a mitre on his head. The intention was to parade them through the streets and Cathedral Yard but it has failed, either because they could not collect donkeys enough, though agents had been sent for the purpose to some neighbouring towns, or, as someone told me, because people were afraid to ride them for fear of getting taken into custody by the police. (*Diary*).

Flower show. *Friday June 27.* Went to see the Horticultural Show at Northernhay and remained there for a couple of hours. There was a tolerable exhibition of flowers, many of them very fine and pretty. However, I am not sure whether the prettiest flowers were not walking about. (Diary).

Donation to the library. *Saturday June 28.* As they accept any donation for the library of the Institution at Exeter, I gave them today my *Geology of Sidmouth*, the *Guide to the Landslip*, third edition, and one of my maps of Sidmouth parish, coloured and mounted. (*Diary*).

Rougemont Castle. *Monday June 30.* Went and had a look at Mr. Gard's lawn and grounds at Rougemont Castle, as I think his residence is called. As I had no friend at leisure to take me, I went and presented myself for admission, for I had heard that any 'respectable person' on giving their name at the door would be admitted. On ringing the bell and giving the footman my card, he politely told me I might enter and walk about wherever I liked. The lawn comprises the only remaining part of the ancient ditch or fosse, sweeping round under the south-west wall of the castle. I was surprised at the depth and width of the fosse. It is now dry of course, dotted with venerable trees and covered with fine grass, beautifully kept and closely mown. The place is certainly very picturesque. After walking about in different directions to admire the undulations, I ascended the tower on the Northernhay side and commanded a fine view towards St. Davids and the Exwick Hills.

51/6/30. North-east gateway of Rougemont Castle, Exeter, Devon. April 26, 1833. (DRO, Z19/2/8A/2)

Mr. Gard has been one of the fortunate ones in his passage through life. I have been told that his father was a clothier of Exeter, but by some mishap lost his earnings before he died. This son was first a clerk in the bank of old Sparks the Quaker, *and* from thence he went to London where he soon made a moderate fortune. He then paid a visit to Devonshire and some chance took him to Cornwall. Here he was persuaded to invest some money in a mining speculation. Unlike most mining speculations, it succeeded beyond expectations, so that the original one pound shares rose to be worth between £300 and £500 apiece. This soon made his riches flow in at a great pace and now he is the owner of the best residence in Exeter. I believe he has two brothers now in trade in the City. (*Diary*). *Rougemont Castle seated the Devon Sessions, whilst the entrance to Mr. Gard's pleasure grounds of Rougemont Lodge 'tastefully laid out as a terrace walk' adjoined the Castle gate (Murray's Handbook 1859). Hutchinson,s annexed sketch of the gateway is dated some eighteen years earlier.*

Local historian. *Thursday July 3. Hutchinson visited Dr. Oliver again and mentions for the first time that he was contemplating writing a History of Sidmouth. He must already have had a reputation as a local historian for he was engaged in providing a long series of articles on various aspects of the history of the town for Harvey's Sidmouth Directory.*

51/7/9-2. Piece of charcoal taken out of the buried stratum of charcoal by reaching over the cliff, High Peak Hill. July 9, 1851. (DRO, Z19/2/8D/251)

View from High Peak. *Wednesday July 9. The page containing this entry has been cut out of the Diary, but Hutchinson seems to have spent the day sketching on High Peak. The first sketch is entitled:* a piece of charcoal taken out of the buried stratum of charcoal by reaching over the cliff, High Peak Hill. There was an ancient camp on this hill and the charcoal seems to have been the remains of a signal fire made by the Britons or Romans, or other occupiers of the camp to communicate intelligence to other stations. *The second is a view of the earthworks bounding the camp on the summit, with a small figure breaking into an 'apparent tumulus' (later note:* more likely where the

51/7/9-3. The earthwork on High Peak Hill, looking towards Sidmouth. Sketched on the spot July 9, 1851. (DRO, Z19/2/8D/249)

51/7/9-1 *View from the summit of High Peak Hill, looking south-west towards Otterton Point and Bury Head.*
(DRO, Z19/2/8D/247)

oxen were roasted.   See September 29, 1871 *and November 13, 1851). The third sketch shows* the view from the summit of High Peak looking south-west towards Otterton Point and Bury Head.   The signal staff, erected in 1850, was soon shattered by lightening (*later note: it was* removed November 15, 1851). The conical mound of turf was made by the Ordnance surveyors in May 1851, visible from their other stations at Littleham, Beer Head, etc., after they had completed their angles with the theodolite on that spot.   (*Sketchbook D*).

Enclosing Mutter's Moor. *July 10.   The missing page may have contained a Diary entry for this date, when Hutchinson did a sketch of a new enclosure on Mutter's Moor looking down towards Sidmouth.*   The nearest field, having been recently enclosed, yielding its first crop of corn. (*Sketchbook D*).

Church reminiscences. *Friday July 11.*   Went to Sidmouth church, where I found Wheaton the sexton.   He told me that the Rev. W. Jenkins, father of the

TRAVELS IN VICTORIAN DEVON

present vicar, built the north gallery but not the north aisle. That, at that period, there was an old stone pulpit standing against the south columns of the archway going into the chancel; that this was removed and a wooden pulpit on legs or supports was put up in the middle of the archway, so that people passed under it in going to the communion table, and that when this was taken down, the present pulpit on the north side of the arch was made. He said that he recollects a carved wooden screen across this part of the church, with the royal coat of arms over it, an angel or cherub with a trumpet on each side, and scrolls, one on each side, bearing respectively the words 'Fear God' and 'Honour the King'; that this screen was taken down about 1803 or 1804, etc. (*Diary*). *The rest of this entry continues the sexton's reminiscences of the alterations that had been made to Sidmouth church during the early nineteenth century.*

Hemyock Castle. *Thursday July 17.* Went with Mr. Heineken over to Hemyock from Sidmouth to try and find Hemyock Castle, not having been aware till lately that the remains of a Norman Castle existed in this neighbourhood. After passing through Honiton and Combe Rawley and ascending the hill beyond, we had a fine view of Dumpden Camp on a high conical hill. On arriving at Hemyock, two round towers overgrown with ivy soon attracted attention. Mr. Heineken took photographic views of these, having brought his camera and some prepared paper with him, whilst I set to work with my sketch book. The plan of the castle is a square of about 60 yards on each side, with a round tower at each corner and a round tower in the middle of each side between the corners. The whole was surrounded by a moat, still mostly remaining. The walls are from 3 to 4 feet thick, where they are in existence, and the round towers about 20 in diameter from outside to outside. The principal gateway, which is in the middle of the east

51/7/10. View of Sidmouth from Mutter's Moor. Sketched on the spot July 10, 1851. (DRO, Z19/2/8D/253)

51/7/17-2. Inner gateway, Hemyock Castle. Sketched on the spot July 17, 1851. (DRO, Z19/2/8D/257)

57

51/7/17-1. *East gateway, Hemyock Castle, Devon. Sketched on the spot July 17, 1851.* (DRO, Z19/2/8D/255)

51/7/31-2. *East end of the granary at Sand, in the garden. Sketched on the spot July 31, 1851.* (DRO, Z19/2/8D/259)

wall, is immediately opposite the west door of the parish church and not above 40 or 50 yards from it, a small stream of water flowing between. The gateway has a pointed arch flanked by two round towers, and the place remains where the portcullis descended. A modern farmhouse has been built just within this gateway, and an old doorway evidently taken from part of the ruins of the castle has been built into the house. It is of rude design and execution and it is remarkable that the sides and arched top are of granite. There is no granite nearer to be had than Dartmoor. (*Later note*: I learn that this close moulding was brought from a distance). The area within the outer walls and the towers is now an orchard. The citadel, or principal part of the building, once probably occupied the centre. There are stony mounds overgrown with grass about the orchard, and there are seemingly the remains of former erections now ruined. It is strange that none of the County Histories make any particular mention of this Castle and I heard of it only by chance. (*See August 4, 1851*). On returning, we visited Dunkeswell Abbey, of which little remains but ruined walls and pointed gables overgrown with ivy. (*Diary*).

Photography. *Thursday July 24.* Made a 12 x 8 frame for taking positives by the photographic process. (*Diary*).

Tuesday July 29. Made my first photographic positives, being duplicates of a view of Sidmouth from the west end of the beach. (*Diary*).

House at Sand. *Thursday July 31.* Took two rubbings from the small brass of Henry Parsonius in Sidbury Church. Went on to Sand and made three sketches of some of the old sculptures there. (*Diary*). On the east end of the granary is the inscription EYOYMIAS FONS BENE CONVENIRE CUM DEO. By some clever

51/7/31-1. *The granary at Sand, in the parish of Sidbury, Devon. Sketched on the spot July 31, 1851.*
(DRO, Z19/2/8D/261)

fellows, hot from college and touring into the West Country, this sentence has been rendered thus: 'To be well with God is the fountain of joy'. (*Soc. of Antiq. Ms. 250, p. 26*).   The inscription below the armorial bearings on the gate reads HORTUS JOHANNIS CAPELLI, 'Lord Capel lived here'. (*Sketchbook D*).

Salcombe Church altar.   *Friday, August 1.*   Walked over to Salcombe Church and made a coloured sketch of the interior.   The stone altar piece, put there, as I have heard, by or through the influence of some ladies since turned Roman Catholics (the Misses Morris, late of Sidcliff) has just been removed and a massive wooden table put there instead. (*Diary*).

Hemyock Castle again.   *Monday August 4.*   Started for Hemyock again with Mr. Heineken, driven by Wellington Smith.   We first made for Dunkeswell Abbey after passing through Honiton, where we took two photographic views.   Then we proceeded to Hemyock Castle where we took two or three more.   Mr. Heineken returned to Sidmouth but I stayed where I was *and* slept at Hemyock.   Took a rough plan of the Castle and adjoining land *and* went into the church, where

51/7/31-3. *Gate and armorial bearings at the north-east end of the garden at Sand. Sketched on the spot July 31, 1851.*
(DRO, Z19/2/8D/267)

there is nothing worthy of record except the old font of Purbeck stone, about the recent exhumation of which, nearly under one of the columns on the north side of he nave, the village schoolmaster had much to say.   The stained glass in the head of the window at the east end of the south aisle *was* executed, as I was told, by the Misses Simcoe of Woolford Lodge, *but* there is no monument more than a hundred

*51/8/1. Interior of Salcombe
church, Devon, looking towards
the east. Coloured in the church
August 1, 1851.*
(DRO, Z19/2/8D/269)

*51/8/4. North side of the moat
and ruins of Hemyock Castle, in
the County of Devon. Coloured
on the spot August 5, 1851.*
(DRO, Z19/2/8D/271)

years old within the walls. Admired the great yew tree in the churchyard and was told a story about the curate who planted the small one to the south of it some thirty years ago.

If I had Hemyock Castle, I would soon make a pretty place of it. I would clear away the ugly and dirty farm buildings and the mass of apple trees by which it is choked up, and repair and restore the towers and battlements of the castle itself. I am surprised that the owner should neglect it so much. Hired a vehicle and went to Uffculme, preferring the route over Hackpen Hill for the sake of the view. Went to the schoolhouse and found the Joneses well. (*Diary*). *Hutchinson would have been pleased with the present state of this picturesque castle, which has since been consolidated and partly restored and is occasionally open to the public.*

Culmstock Beacon and the Wellington Monument. *Thursday August 7.* Mr. Caines took me a drive in his gig. First we went through Culmstock and up the high hill to the Beacon. The Beacon is a stone building about twelve feet diameter, with walls nearly two feet thick. There is a doorway on the south side and slits or loopholes on the east and west. Inside there are several blocks of masonry like seats, built up from the ground. The perpendicular wall rises about eight foot high, then there is a slightly projecting string course, and then the building is arched over with a hole in the top about two feet in diameter. The arch is of rubble work, with the edges turned to the centre, and these are cased in mortar and stones laid on flat. From this small edifice in a northerly direction over the wild and heath-covered summit of the hill, there runs a straight ridge pointing to a tower on a hill some miles off, having much the appearance of a British or Roman road. A similar also runs from the Beacon in an easterly direction, but they are soon lost where they dip down into the cultivated grounds. What the age of this building may be I am unable to learn. *The beacon hut, said to be the only one surviving from the days of the Armada in its original form, remains much as Hutchinson depicts it.*

From hence we went along the top of the hills till we came to the Wellington Monument, a triangular obelisk on a base erected in honour of the 'Iron Duke'. At a distance it looks round and very ugly, but its appearance improves on a nearer approach. It is built of chert rubble cased with well-dressed and squared blocks of sandstone *and* there is a staircase within that leads to the top. The eastern angle

51/8/7. Culmstock Beacon on the Blackdown Hills. Sketched August 7, 1851. (DRO, Z19/2/8D/273)

at the summit has been struck by lightening and many of the stones knocked away.   From this monument, the views all round, but especially towards Wellington and Taunton, are fine and extensive.   Leaving this spot, we descended into the valley and passing through Culm Davey and Culmstock, retired to Uffculme. (*Diary*).

Return to Exeter. *Friday August 8*.   Left Uffculme for Exeter.   The five little Joneses, from Marion to Agnes, accompanied me to the station and saw me start. (*Diary*).

Coffin at St. James Priory. *Sunday August 10*.   At St. Lawrence's Church in the High Street, Exeter.   In the afternoon I went down to Countess Weir village and dined with the O'Briens, who have removed there from Whipton.   Returned through the fields by the river, remembering that when I was with Mr. Pitman Jones last month, he told me that in the cottage garden on the site of St. James' Priory there used to be an old stone coffin lying on the ground.   After some enquiry, I came to it.   But it is broken in two and the two halves are turned bottom upwards and now used as two steps going up to a new iron pump.   'To what base uses . . . etc.' (*Diary*).

View of Exmouth. *Friday August 15*.   Walked over Marypole Head and found Stoke Hill Camp, which is nearly obliterated.   Enjoyed the view and made a coloured sketch of Exmouth and the river from this point.   (*Diary*).

51/8/15.   *Mouth of the River Exe from Stoke Hill Camp, near Exeter.   Coloured on the spot August 15, 1851.* (DRO, Z19/2/8D/277)

Sketch of Heavitree Church.   *Tuesday August 19*.   Walked to the quay, to St. James Priory, to Heavitree where I made a sketch of the church, to Mount LeGrand and back to Exeter through St. Sidwells. (*Diary*).   *The sketch shows the rebuilt church before the new tower was added in 1889.*

Exeter to Sidmouth.   *Friday August 22*.   Left Exeter for Sidmouth.   (*Diary*). *For the next few days Hutchinson amused himself at home with photography before leaving for London to carry out further researches into the history of Sidmouth.*

51/8/19. Heavitree new church with the old tower. Coloured on the spot August 19, 1851. (DRO, Z19/2/8D/279)

Return to Exeter by coach. *Friday August 29.* Went to Exeter from Sidmouth by the mail, the fee-mail as I jocularly called it some time ago in Woolmer's paper, owing to the fees which the coachman and guard looked for from the passengers. *(Diary).*

Uncomfortable journey to London. *Saturday August 30.* Went from Exeter to London by one of the 'excursion trains'. The cheapness of the fare, being one third of the ordinary fare to London, whereas this comprised the return also, induced great numbers to go. We started at 8.30 instead of 8.00, for the crowd and confusion were immense, and laboured on very slowly, stopping at almost every station to take up more people. It was not until we had passed Bristol that we ceased taking up and proceeded at a better pace. We were ten minutes going through the Box tunnel as I proved by my watch, the usual time being about five. At Swindon we were let out for refreshment and a strange turn out it was. I tried to count the number of carriages but found it very difficult, the train was so long. I made out above thirty. We did not get to Paddington till eight, though we were led to believe that four would have been the hour. It was now getting dark and the confusion was indescribable. The railway officials omitted the care and attention usually paid to passengers on other occasions. The luggage was thrown out anywhere and people had to find it as best they could. After a deal of searching with lanterns I found my carpet bags lying in the mud and, as I discovered afterwards, my clothes were wet through. There were lots of women there who were strangers in London and had lost their friends and, unable to find their boxes, *were* in extreme tribulation. Some of these I assisted out of their difficulties, but I had much ado to get out of my own. Loud and vehement were the complaints which the passengers raised against the railway officials at being treated in such a way. *(Diary).*

Red duster. *Thursday October 23. In London Hutchinson spent several days reading and copying manuscripts at the Record Office in the Tower, searching out any ancient documents relating to Sidmouth. He also went to the British Museum, Kensington Gardens, Westminster Abbey and was so impressed with the Great Exhibition at Crystal Palace that he visited it five times. He found the time to take the train to Croydon to try to find some memorial to his great-grandfather, the ex-Governor of Massachusetts, in the church, and on one occasion visited a chandlers:* Went down to the marine store dealers today to see if I could get a good-sized second hand flag to hoist in the tree before the house in Coburg Terrace, Sidmouth. By a little enquiry I found a whopper. It is about fifteen feet by twenty, and a red ensign. The man told me that such a flag would cost me three guineas and a half, *but* after some little fighting I got it for fifteen shillings. *(Diary). Hutchinson then undertook a short walking tour through the Home Counties sketching castles, churches, etc., before returning to London with badly blistered feet. He caught the evening train from Paddington to Exeter.*

London to Sidmouth. *Friday October 31.* Travelled all night. Most of my fellow travellers slept but this I never do. At half past four this morning we arrived safe in Exeter (so the expense of insuring my life for the journey was useless as it happened) and here I got out. Had a good warm at a fire in the New London Inn, took a brisk walk in the dark up and down High Street, and a little before six, just as the dawn was beginning to appear, I got on the mail for Sidmouth. (*Diary*).

Unfurling the flag. *Wednesday November 5.* Old Pope Day! Had up my flag for the first time. Amongst the admirers of my new display is Wheaton, the sexton, who gazed at it from the churchyard. He wants to beg it of me to hoist on the top of the tower! I reminded him that I had given a considerable sum of money for it, that perhaps the vicar would not mind two or three guineas for a flag for his own tower, or that if the parishioners would subscribe for such a purpose I would contribute. (*Diary*).

Excavation at High Peak. *Thursday November 13.* Went with Mr. Heineken to the top of High Peak Hill to examine the earthworks. We went in a vehicle over Peak Hill, past Pinn Farm, and then on perhaps half a mile before we found a lane towards the south; and after that we had to turn back again, having got too far. In this circuitous way we reached the upper cone of High Peak Hill. We examined the beds of charcoal, which I regret to say are fast wearing out. The flagstaff, which the lightning shattered, we measured with a quadrant and made it 49 feet 9 inches. The 'apparent tumulus', as I have termed it in my plan in the Gentleman's Magazine, next took our attention. (*B.R.No.1. See sketch July 9, 1851*). We had brought a spade wrapped up in brown paper to escape notice, for we had no permission to dig, and I had fortified myself with the kitchen poker! With these tools I set to work. He took an opportunity, when he thought I was not looking, of dropping a Roman coin into the ground. We had a good deal of laughing when the coin was turned up, but I charged him with the fraud. My tools, I found, were not efficient enough to make much progress amongst the closely packed stones and earth, *but* I still think it may have been a barrow. We were only able to make a slight examination of the spot. *Much later, Hutchinson had second thoughts about this mound.* The stones near the south end of the agger,

51/11/23. Sidbury Castle Hill as seen from the summit of Core Hill. From a sketch taken on the spot November 23, 1851. (DRO, Z19/2/8D/297)

which I have spoken of as an apparent tumulus, I now think are not so.   About the commencement of the present century some oxen and sheep given by the late Lord Rolle were roasted on the hill and the spit was supported by stones.   Perhaps this is the spot. (*History of Sidmouth I, 30*).

On returning, we sent the carriage round.   We walked to Peak Hill where we joined it and got in to descend to Sidmouth.   The weather was beautiful. (*Diary*).

Walk around Sidbury Castle. *Sunday November 16.*   Walked to Sidbury this morning.   Before I came back, I took a turn on Sidbury Castle Hill.   Walked all round, remarked the ancient flanked entrance at the western end and the various points of interest I had before dwelt upon.   Descending through the wood on its south side, I walked back to Sidmouth. (*Diary*).

Birds-eye view of Sidmouth. *Wednesday November 19.* Laid an etching ground on a copper plate and traced thereon a birds-eye view of Sidmouth, being the modern view in contradistinction to the 'Sidemew Brito-Romana Restaurata' which I mean to engrave. (*Diary*). *Hutchinson continued working on the etching for the next two weeks.*

Sidbury Castle viewed from Core Hill. *Sunday November 23.*   Walked to Sidbury *and on* returning took a turn over Core Hill.   Went up the field on the north side of the hedge dividing the parishes.   It is as steep as the roof of a house.   This field was enclosed and cleared last year *and* it now bears a crop of turnips.   They are obliged to hold on tolerably tight with their roots, otherwise they would roll down the hill. (*Diary*).

Bird's-eye view engraving. *Friday December 5.*   Engraved two hours and finished the work – the 'Bird's Eye View of Sidmouth, Devon'. (*Diary*).

Ladram Bay expedition. *Wednesday December 24.*   Beautiful day!   Clear sky- bright sun.   Made a geological expedition along the beach to Ladram Bay and back and made drawings of the faults, dislocations and principal features of the cliff all the way.   From observation, I find that the strata of Peak Hill rise two and a half degrees towards the west.   From the face of the cliff in Sandy Cove, just beyond Picket Rock, I knocked out some large specimens of the alcyanite. (*Diary*).   *The accompanying view from the west side of Ladram Bay looking towards Sidmouth is one of Hutchinson's earliest sketches.*

51/12/24-1. *Sidmouth from the further side of Ladram Bay, Devon. 1836.* (DRO, Z19/2/8A/121)

51/12/24-2. *Geological view of the cliff from Sidmouth to Ladram Bay.* (Hist.of Sid. I,7a)

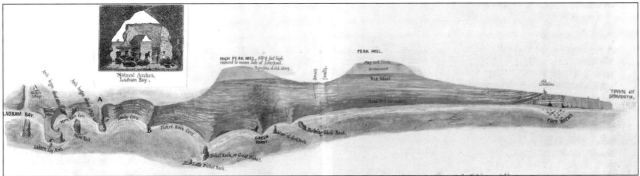

51/12/24-3. Geological view of the cliff from Sidmouth to the old limekilns. (Hist. of Sid. I,7a)

1852

New Years Day 1852. *Thursday January 1.* Beautiful, bright, fine day. Gardened all the morning and dined with the Walkers at Lime Park. (*Diary*).

Optical work. *Friday January 9.* Finished turning the brass setting of my achromatic object lens on Mr. Heineken's lathe. (*Diary*).

Semiramide. *Monday January 12.* Music at Mr. Heineken's. Played the overture to Semiramide as a quartet, Miss Heineken on the piano, her father double bass, Mr. Jackson of Barnstaple the flute and I the horn. (*Diary*).

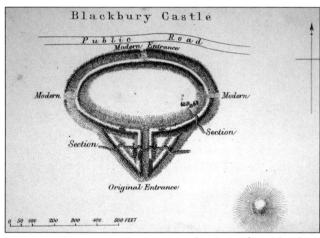

52/1/13. *Engraving of Blackbury Castle.* (Hist. of Sid. I,54)

Blackbury Castle engraved. *Tuesday January 13.* Finished my engraving of the plan of Blackbury Castle. (*Diary*).

Semiramide preparations. *Wednesday January 21.* Finished writing out the overture to Semiramide, arranged for French horn, clarinet or violin, and piano forte. (*Diary*).

Drumsticks. *Saturday January 24.* Put a half dozen of port and ditto of sherry into the cellar and made a pair of drumsticks for playing Semiramide. (*Diary*).

Semiramide performance. *Monday January 25.* Music at Mr. Heineken's. We had the overture to Semiramide with piano, horn, violin and drum. (*Diary*).

Another engraving. *Friday February 13.* Finished engraving the 'Bird's-eye View of Sidmouth, Devon, from the Sea', the second attempt. By referring back to December 5, I see I was fifty-five hours about the last. This one I did in thirty-seven hours, but there is not so much work in it. (*Diary*).

Valentine Day, 1852. *Saturday February 14.* Received four valentines but have no idea who any of them are from. (*Diary*).

Musical evening at home. *Monday March 8.* A party of about twenty-five at home. Mostly music. I played the French horn to an audience in accompanying Mr. Heineken's voice in the song 'Angel of Life'. The general notion was that so large a brass instrument would be deafening if played in a room, but when they heard it they were surprised how soft it was. (*Diary*).

Musical evening. *Tuesday March 9.* At a party at Mr. Walker's, Lime Park, mostly music. I played the horn again, as well as the flute. When I brought it into the room, much doubt was manifested by those who had not heard it as to whether so military and so large an instrument would not either stun them or blow them all out of the window. I assured them that the French horn was the most mellow of all the brass instruments. I accompanied Mr. Heineken in two songs and they were surprised to find that his voice was even stronger than that fierce-looking instrument. (*Diary*).

Gardening. *Monday March 15.*　Gardened as usual for an hour or two and have nearly got all the seeds in. (*Diary*).

Amelia Elphinstone. *Tuesday March 23.*　Spent the evening at Mr. Walker's, Lime Park, where I met the three Miss Elphinstones.　Came home and dreamt of Miss Amelia. (*Diary*).

Coin engraving. *Monday April 5.*　Engraved the small copper Carolus coin, recently found in the Fort Field, Sidmouth, on box wood, (*Diary*).　It was found on a gravel path at the higher side of the field by John Snell the letter carrier or postman in 1851 (*History of Sidmouth I, 101*).

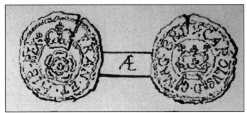

52/4/5.　*Carolus coin.*　(Hist. of Sid. I,101)

Sidbury Castle and the 'Money Heap'. *Tuesday April 6.*　Started in a phaeton with Mr. Heineken to make some examination of the top of Sidbury Castle Hill. The western extremity of the camp has lately been cleared of the coppice, so for the first time I had an opportunity of examining the plan of the ancient enclosure and of laying it down.　Here I dug a trench with a spade in the vain hope of turning up some coin, spear head or bronze weapon, but I dug to no purpose.　I found two greensand nodules as large as apples, and these I pocketed.　In the centre of the camp on the highest ground, near the ash tree, we placed our compass and found that the mouth of the Sid lay due south of us.　With a water level we took observations of all the surrounding hills.

Before we started in the morning, we sent a man onto the top of High Peak with a long fishing rod and a flag on it.　This he was told to hold up at an appointed hour and wave for twenty minutes.　We were anxious to find out whether signals could be made from the hill fortresses on High Peak to Sidbury Hill.　There seems little doubt that intelligence could at one period have been conveyed between the two stations, but as the plantations on Peak Hill now intervene and have grown so high, we were unable to discover the little flag.　Having discussed our sandwiches and beer (into which we dived with considerable avidity) we proceeded to the plantation at the east end of the hill.　We measured the slope of the agger and found it forty-five feet.　We then examined 'The Treasury' or 'Money Heap', a tumulus of dry bleached flints.　Some persons had been sinking a hole into the top of it, into which I descended, but no kistvaen has been come to.　On descending the hill we found a large globular stone wonderfully like a human skull, but it is a mass of chalcedony.　I brought it home.

A boy near Castle House told us a legend about the 'Money Heap'.　He said there was one Joe Lugg, a day labourer living at Sidbury, who once conceived a strong desire to penetrate into that supposed depository of hidden treasure.　He used to steal up into the plantation to dig, but strange to say, the hole that he made during the day was all filled up again during the night following, so that he never progressed in his work.　That some supernatural hand did this he had no doubt, especially as he was much troubled when on the hill by certain airy figures flitting round him.　The unaccountable filling in of the flints as fast as he turned them out and the dread forms by which he was haunted, were quite enough to scare him from the work.　So much had he been frightened that nothing could afterwards make him willingly go near the spot.　However, the boy described old Joe Lugg as being 'a terrible fellow for cider'.　A pic-nic or Gypsy party was to take place on the hill, and Joe could not resist the hogshead of cider which was carried there.　He joined the party but 'he valled away' as the boy expressed it, by which I understand Joe fainted or fell away, probably at the sight of the airy figures which appeared to him, though they remained unseen by his friends.　The story ends that they were obliged to carry him home. (*Diary*).

Camera lens. *Thursday April 8.*　Ground the glass for my camera. (*Diary*).

Sidbury Castle beacons. *Friday April 16.*　Walked again to Sidbury Castle, having heard that there were two outworks of which I was before ignorant.　There is certainly a small platform against the outer and lower agger in the middle of the flank of the camp, both on the south and north sides, the latter however being scarcely perceptible.   I know not what these could have been for, unless for burning wood on to act as beacons.   Possibly they avoided making their fires on the crown of the hill within the entrenchments as it might interfere with their habitations.   The idea that such situations were used as beacons receives confirmation when we bear in mind that it was on the agger, similarly placed, that I discovered the charcoal at High Peak. (*Diary*).

Harpford Beacon. *Sunday April 18.*   At All Saints Church in the morning.   In the afternoon, the weather still continuing dry and beautiful, I walked to Beacon Hill overlooking Harpford Wood.   The view is splendid.   The former beacon seems to have been a building like Culmstock Beacon on the Blackdown hills (see August 7, 1851).   It was about twelve feet diameter outside but all that remains is part of the circular stone wall which is two feet thick, standing about five feet out of the ground.   But it is very ruinous. (*Diary*).

Photography. *Wednesday May 12.*   Tried some photographs on glass with collodion, but did not succeed to my satisfaction. (*Diary*).

Salcombe parish map. *Wednesday May 26.*   Called on Miss Cornish of Salcombe Hill by appointment and copied some parts of the map of Salcombe parish, especially the Sidmouth poor lands and the boundary line between that parish and Sidmouth which in my published map is wrong. (*Diary*).

52/5/28. *Engraving of High Peak from Peak Hill.* (Hist. of Sid. I,36c)

Supper at Sid Abbey. *Friday May 28.*   At a small party at Sid Abbey.   Music, prayers and supper.   Finished engraving 'High Peak Hill from Peak Hill, near Sidmouth. (*Diary*). *This engraving* 'sketched and engraved by P. O. Hutchinson' *is a close copy of the coloured drawing done on September 7, 1849.*

Normandy excursion.   *Wednesday June 2.*   Started from Sidmouth by the mail for an excursion to Avranches and St. Michael's Mount in Normandy, to search the cartulary and other old manuscripts belonging to that Abbey, in which I hope to find some memorandums relating to Sidmouth. (*Diary*).   As the Manor of Sidmouth had pertained to the Abbey of St. Michael's Mount during the long term of 350 years, it occurred to me that there might be documents over there still in existence that referred to its English possessions. (*Soc. of Antiq. Ms. 309*).

Embarkation. *Thursday June 3.*   Walked about Plymouth, called on my aunt Lady Parker, heard the band play on the Hoe, went over the Citadel and procured a passport at Luscombe and Driscoll's, Vauxhall Street, for five shillings. Embarked on the steamer at half past five in the afternoon and steamed away for Jersey.   The Queen, three-decker and two frigates were lying inside the breakwater.   I was sea-sick of course but I had companions in my distress – even four French nuns who were as sick as any heretic could well be.   Slept on the sofa all night. (*Diary*). *Hutchinson was away in Jersey and France for two weeks, copying a charter of Edward the Confessor at Avranche, sketching and visiting Mont St. Michel and St Malo.*

Brother's marriage. *Wednesday June 16.*   At half past four this morning, after a rainy and boisterous night, we got to Torquay.   We landed in the rain and our things were looked at in the Custom House.   I then went to an Inn and got some coffee, and at eight took the rail for Exeter.   On arriving at my lodgings, I found a note from Bingham saying he had got married the day before to Miss Augusta Kingdon at Heavitree, so I was just twenty-four hours too late to be present. (*Diary*). *Despite having missed his brother's wedding, Hutchinson stayed on in Exeter for a week.*

Exeter manuscripts. *Thursday June 17.* Called on the Dean of Exeter and got permission to see the Exeter Domesday and other manuscripts belonging to the Dean and Chapter Library. Called also on Dr. Oliver and gave him an account of my researches in France, in which he took much interest. Left him my sketchbook and the copies of the manuscripts at Avranches for him to turn over for a few days. (*Diary*).

Well met. *Saturday June 19.* Went to Mr. Ralph Barnes' office by appointment about the Exeter Domesday Book. On coming away I fell in with the Rev. F. Jones, who is a candidate for the Exeter Grammar School. (*Diary*).

Overloaded coach. *Wednesday June 23.* Travelled on the mail from Exeter to Sidmouth without being turned over. The coach however, was so disgracefully overloaded and we were consequently in such danger of accident so many times, that I mean to reprove the proprietors through the medium of Woolmer's paper. I have been away just three weeks. (*Diary*). *After his previous experience (see October 22, 1850) Hutchinson had good reason to censure the coach company in a letter to the Exeter and Plymouth Gazette.* Much praise is due to Mr. Arundell who drove on this occasion for conveying one of the most memorable loads in modern times so great a distance without losing a single life. On the back of his coach are painted the words 'Constructed to carry four inside and ten out', to which words his attention was drawn at the time. If then he had sixteen outside and four in from Exeter to Ottery, and seventeen or eighteen outside and four in from Ottery to Sidmuoth, he may estimate the amount of mercy which we in this instance show to him if we refrain from bringing an action against him in a court of law. It may be stated that the luggage was heaped up several feet above the roof and instead of being confined within the iron railing round the roof, the trunks were built out over more than a foot on each side. On top of this load three personages were allowed to travel. To say that twenty times the coach was nearly over last Wednesday is to speak within bounds. The general exclamation was 'If we get to Sidmouth alive we will never travel this road again'. Regret is frequently expressed because Sidmouth does not enjoy the advantages of a railroad. What substitute is enjoyed instead? Why, one coach which travels as much on its head as it does on its heels. *Signed:* One of the passengers. (*Exeter and Plymouth Gazette July 3, 1852, extract*).

Consultation. *Wednesday July 21.* There now! A long interval and no record. The interval has been filled up with a few evening parties, as at Mrs. Clarke's, No. 2, Coburg Terrace, at Mrs. Walker's, Lime Park, etc. The horn and flute have been plied, gardening attended to, the fruit and vegetables now being abundant, and certain photographic experiments made. The weather has been beautiful and remarkably fine. Today after breakfast, I went down to the beach with Captain Lang to survey and consult as to a new plan for drawing coals up an incline from the sea to a depot in the Marsh field. (*Diary*).

Back to Heightley Cottage. *Monday July 26.* A cold day, especially striking after the hot weather we have had. Went to Exeter in a four-wheel with mother, taking in Mrs. Jenkins and her daughter Clare. They did some shopping and returned, whilst I went down to Heightley Cottage with Mary Roberton. (*Diary*).

Voyage to Jersey. *Thursday July 29.* Left Heightley Cottage for Jersey. Embarked this evening at six from Plymouth on board the Sir Francis Drake steamer. (*Diary*). *As the following page of the Diary has been torn out, the details of this excursion are lost, but presumably Hutchinson was following up the researches started in June. By August 17 he was back at Heightley Cottage, returning to Sidmouth the following day.*

Photographic experiments. *Wednesday August 25.* All the morning making collodion photographs. Made a portrait of myself in which I have my face reflected in a looking-glass. I was anxious to know whether the reflected light would have sufficient power to produce a picture. It seems it has. Took a profile of Mr. Heineken who happened to call, and also took a group of musical instruments. (*Diary*).

Photographic failures. *Wednesday September 1.* Have had many failures in my photographic amusements and some satisfactory results. My apparatus however, is rather rude and I doubt whether it is worth while to be at the expense of procuring a better camera and a good compound achromatic lens, without which few really creditable things can be produced. (*Diary*).

Hedge laying. *Thursday October 14.* The Terrace within the boundary of our own railings is now having shrubs planted along it, by way of enclosing it and making it more private. I cannot go outside to garden or look after the flowers or take a turn up and down without having the eyes of Amyat Place opposite and the rest of the neighbourhood on me. I am rather fearful however, lest the salt winds which sometimes blow somewhat strong from the sea may cut off the tops and prevent them growing. This has before now been an evil with us, but we have now selected such shrubs as are reputed best to stand the sea air, so blow soft ye breezes and grow away ye shrubs. (*Dairy*).

52/10/19. *Farway Castle.*
(Hist. of Sid. I,61)

Farway Castle and Widworthy. *Tuesday October 19. This entry describes an excursion with Mr. Heineken first to Ring-in-the-Mire, omitted here as it is again described on July 25, 1854. The entry continues:* At about a mile from Hunter's Lodge eastward and on the north or left side of the road, there is a circular plantation of firs. This place has a regular agger with a ditch outside it. The man at Hunter's Lodge said it is known as 'Farway Castle'. Doubtless it is an ancient entrenchment. On measurement it proved to be 210 feet in diameter and 204 feet by taking it in the other direction. The agger is 16 feet wide, but the width, height and the width of the ditch are so irregular that no precise measurements can be assigned. The site is on the crown of the hill and most of the old camps in the neighbourhood can be discerned from it. The top of High Peak Hill with its earthworks can be seen rising over Peak Hill. A small portion of Sidbury Castle could be detected and numberless hill fortresses all round could be descried, as those at Musbury and Membury and away into Dorchester, on the north at Dumpden and Hembury Fort and westward over to Cadbury. Though hazy, Woodbury Castle seemed to be apparent in the dip between Core Hill and Ottery East Hill. (*Diary*). No remains have been found there; indeed this camp never seems to have been noticed by any writer except myself. (*Soc. of Antiq. Ms. 250*).

On leaving this locality, we proceeded to Bishop Coplestone's Tower at Offwell, of which Mr. Heineken took a photograph. At Widworthy he took two or three. Mr. Mathews, the recently appointed Rector, took me into the church where I was surprised at the number and beauty of the monuments. There is one by the elder Bacon and another of a rich farmer of the parish. The bust, by Rouw, he had made during his lifetime and kept it in his house and it now surmounts his monument. An ancient recumbent figure is a gem of antiquity. I then accompanied the Rector to the hill called Widworthy Castle. There is a sort of platform on the summit but no trace of stonework. The parish almost entirely belongs to Sir Edward Elton of Widworthy Court. We dined at the Rectory and got back to Sidmouth before nine. (*Diary*).

Bingham leaving for Australia. *Wednesday October 20.* Bingham and his wife left us this morning and in a few days they sail for Adelaide, South Australia. (*Diary*).

Crowded performance. *Tuesday October 26.* At a musical party at Mrs. Walker's, Lime Park, where I played the flute and the horn. There were sixty people there. How ill-judged it is, in those who form the audience, that they should so often crowd round the performers! People would hear the music much better if they would keep a few yards off. Instead of this however, they thrust themselves up to the piano forte and other instruments, looking over the music and watching every note that is produced. All this is an annoyance to those who play. It distracts their attention from what they are about and thereby does much to make them commit errors when they might otherwise go creditably through their parts. There is a want of delicacy and a want of reflection in those who do this and it was particularly the case tonight. Mr. Heineken, who played the violoncello on one side of the piano, could scarcely work his bow, and I on the other had much difficulty in finding a place to stand, and even more in holding, in some pieces the flute, and in others the horn. All this was most disagreeable. (*Diary*).

Greenwich time. *Wednesday November 3.* This morning the church clock was altered to Greenwich time. Here we have an innovation superinduced by the new requirements of railway travelling. The subject of altering all the clocks in the country to the time agreeing to the meridian of Greenwich Observatory has been much canvassed of late. The Mayors and Corporations of some of the cites and greater towns have adopted the plan, some still hesitate and some have discountenanced it. Yesterday it was adopted in Exeter and the example of the capital will probably influence most of the places in the county. If we were on a large continent like Europe, perhaps it would be impossible to attempt it, as the discrepancy would become so egregiously glaring at the extreme east and west limits. As Great Britain is so small, the evil may be bearable, but they now talk of laying down an electric telegraph to America as they already have to France. If the system is to be extended it will become absurd. Indeed, although I have listened with some attention to the arguments adduced in favour of the plan, I confess I do not think them thoroughly satisfactory. The difference between Greenwich and Sidmouth meridians is about twelve minutes and ten seconds. (*Diary*).

Letter from Bingham. *Thursday November 4.* Another letter from Bingham on board the Walrisch in Plymouth Sound, unable to put to sea owing to the violent winds from the south and south-west. As the wind moderated last night and veered somewhat to the north of west, it is probable he has sailed. He and his wife ought to be at Adelaide early in February. I hope my six hundred sovereigns will get out safe! (*Diary*).

History of Sidmouth. *Friday November 5.* Began today to write out a clear and fair copy of my History of the Town , Parish and Manor of Sidmouth from the notes and memorandums which I have been collecting for the last two or three years. (*Later note:* This was not the same as the five green volumes. That came later). (*Diary*).

Tree house. *Friday November 12.* Finished laying the beams, joists and planking of the floor of my summer house up in the elm tree opposite No. 4, Coburg Terrace. This will make a pleasant eyrie in the summer. (*Diary*).

Doubtful prospects. *Thursday November 25.* Finished etching and biting in the '*Plan of Sidmouth and Neighbourhood*' for my history of Sidmouth. I wonder if this history will ever get printed? I have no certain idea what it would cost to publish, but considering it would make a thick Royal Octavo volume with a dozen plates, I dare say not much under two hundred pounds. It would be absurd to throw away a large sum of money even on a rational and useful whim, and it scarcely likely I should secure two or three hundred subscribers at fifteen shillings or a pound each. However, I will issue prospectuses when I am ready. (*Diary*). *This is the only occasion Hutchinson records even considering publication of his 'History of Sidmouth', doubting that even a single volume*

52/12/8. *Sidemew yn the olden tyme.* (Hist. of Sid. I,88a)

would pay for itself. This version, the 'Second Transcription', without illustrations apart from a few small maps, was eventually deposited in the Devon and Exeter Institution.

Emily Fitz-Gerald.   *Thursday December 2.*   This morning Miss Emily Fitz-Gerald, daughter of Major Fitz-Gerald of Mount Edgar, was married to Lieut. I. Darnell.   I was at her sister's wedding in September 1849.   I was told I behaved very badly today.   I borrowed a horn and blew it out of the carriage window all the way to Sidbury (three miles) and all the way back again.   The ceremony went off very well in Sidbury church, though the ring was a little too small.   I asked Miss Emily whether she was not in an immense fright, to which she answered 'only a little shaky'.   We had a capital breakfast at Mount Edgar and sat down about twenty.   I was between Mrs. J. Jenkins of Lime Park and Miss Amelia Elphinstone.   I have since made a coloured drawing of the scene in the church and given it to the Major. (*Diary*).

Sidmouth engraving. *Wednesday December 8.*   I finished engraving 'Sidemew yn ye olden tyme', in imitation of an old print. (*Diary*).

December storm. *Monday December 27.*   Last night we had a gale of wind from he west and a violent storm of rain.   I was kept awake nearly all night with the noise and shaking of the house.   The cook got up at four fearing the roof was coming in.   The sea was over the walk into the town.   Much damage has been done, many large trees blown down, some walls laid flat and chimney tops carried away. (*Diary*).   *The scene showing the flooded banks of the Sid presumably depicts the aftermath of this storm, the only one recorded this December.*

52/12/27. *Sketch of the River Sid and the Salcombe fields, Salcombe, after the flood of December 1852. Coloured on the spot.* (DRO, Z19/2/8D/329)

1853

Foundations on Sidmouth beach. Saturday January 1. *Winter gales frequently exposed substantial foundations of an unknown building outside the sea wall on Sidmouth beach, almost opposite Portland House. Towards the end of 1852 Hutchinson and some friends decided to investigate. There is no relevant Diary entry corresponding with Hutchinson's sketch but the circumstances are recorded in his article in the Sidmouth Directory.* The frequent on-shore winds having removed the shingle to an unusual degree, suggested the idea that a favourable opportunity presented itself for making some examination of the spot. With this view several men were employed on the last day of December 1852 to excavate. It was found however, that in order to prosecute the work in a satisfactory manner between tide and tide, it would be necessary to put on more hands. The day following therefore, that is on the first of January this year, twelve men were directed to commence operations as soon as the tide should have sufficiently receded to admit of it. By eleven o'clock in the forenoon they were able to get to work and before low water their excavations exposed to view some masonry of very massive construction. A wall eighty feet long and three feet thick runs parallel with the beach wall and about thirty feet outside it, mostly constructed of blocks of stone the entire thickness of the wall, the interstices being filled up with stones of less size and the whole cemented together with mortar and grouting. They are all unhewn and in their rough state *and* no trace of a tool is discoverable on any of them. If these foundations formed part of a habitable building, it should appear that the sea must have encroached since the time it was inhabitable, in as much as the tide now flows over them. (*Harvey's Sidmouth Directory and General Advertiser, February 4, 1853*).

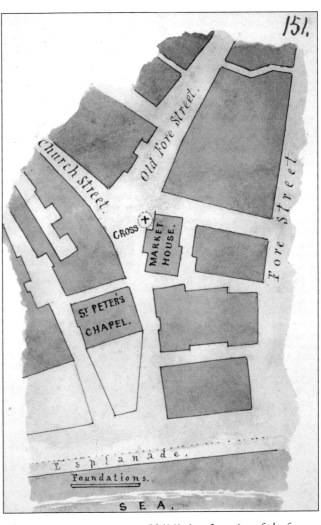

53/1/1-1. *Location of the foundations.* (Hist. of Sid. IV,151)

Several of the older inhabitants contributed opinions from their own local knowledge, unfortunately mostly contradictory. One such was John Radford, another native worthy, who said that the tradition was that these foundations were the remains of an old store house for ships and their cargoes at the time when the Newfoundland fishery was flourishing. My own idea, from its position, is that this massive wall was probably originally built as a protection or breakwater to St. Peter's Chapel. (*History of Sidmouth V, 28*).

Pump repair. *Thursday January 23.* For a long series of years the plumber has been accustomed to send in a Xmas bill for repairs to the pump. Suspecting that the pump got out of order oftener than it ought to, I took out the sucker about two years ago and put a new leather to it. It cost about four pence to do and from that day to the present it has done admirably with no plumber being near it. As the leather was now beginning to wear and the water to go, I resolved to try my hand again at this new line of occupation, so have again renewed the leather for about four pence, and expect it to go on right and

53/1/1-2. Foundations in the beach, Sidmouth. (Not dated). (DRO, Z19/2/8D/331)

tight for another couple of years.   So much for the honesty and good faith of tradesmen.   (*Diary*).

Wreck of the Laurel.   Wednesday *February 2.*   The ship Laurel was wrecked under High Peak Hill.   (*History of Sidmouth V, 160*).

Valentine Day 1853.   *Monday February 14.*   Valentine's Day.   Received five valentines and sent thirteen!!   Bless the girls!   Why don't they put their names to them?   (*Diary*).

Saturday February 26.   Three more valentines!   The lady in one of them asks me to kiss her!   Why did she omit to put her name in some sly corner?   In times past it has not been the custom for gentlemen to receive valentines but only to send them.   The times however are changed, as of last year - a leap year - and now the gentlemen (in Sidmouth at all events) get as many as the ladies. (*Diary*).

Tree House.   *Monday February 28.*   Myself and three men proceeded to hoist the roof of my summer house up into the tree.   I borrowed a ship's block and plenty of good rope.   I fixed the block to a branch sufficiently high and whilst myself and one of the men hoisted the roof, the other two guided it into place on the top of the upright posts, let down upon them and fixed it securely with iron bolts. (*Diary*).

April Fool.   *Friday April 1.*   Received a sham cheque for £19 19s 113/4d drawn on Messrs. Hookey Walker by the post.   Who made me the April Fool I guess not.   (*Diary*).

Rail petition.   *Friday April 15.*   Signed my name to a petition to the House of Commons, praying that the Sidmouth branch of the proposed Exeter and Dorset railway may not be thrown out.   Doubtless a rail to Sidmouth would much benefit the place and as this conviction is general of course the petition is numerously signed.   (*Diary*).

Uffculme again. *Tuesday June 3.* Went over to Uffculme to see the Joneses at the School, whom I had not seen for two years. Went for ten days and tarried near ten weeks! My time was fully occupied in mending toys, drawing pictures and romping with six children. Made three attempts at taking the right hand of my little god-daughter Agnes in plaster of Paris. She did not like the operation at first, and being only four and three quarter years old I had much difficulty in putting her hand in an easy position and getting her to keep it still. However, mamma sat by and due attention was purchased at the price of one half-penny. (*Diary*). *Whilst at Uffculme, Hutchinson did a coloured sketch of the road between the town and Park Station, now the A3391. He returned to Sidmouth on August 13.*

53/6/3. Sketch on the road between Uffculme and the Park station, looking towards Uffculme. Coloured on the spot July 1853. (DRO, Z19/2/8D/333)

Death in the family. *Wednesday September 1.* Went from Sidmouth over to Piermont House, Dawlish, on account of my aunt's death at Heightley Cottage, Chudleigh. She will be buried in the family vault in the churchyard, some fifty yards south-east of the church. The Joneses and Uncle Roberton were at Dawlish. (*Diary*). *The aunt was Jane Cocks, Hutchinson's mother's oldest sister and mother of Mary Roberton. He did the accompanying sketch of the family tomb in Dawlish churchyard some five years earlier.*

53/9/1. Tomb of the Cockses and the Robertons in Dawlish churchyard. Coloured on the spot September 29, 1847. (DRO, Z19/2/8D/61)

Ramble on the Ness. *Tuesday September 7.* Uncle, Marianne and the children went over to Heightley to see Mary Roberton who is still too unwell to leave her bed, whilst Frank Jones and myself went to Teignmouth. We took a ramble on the Ness and enjoyed the beautiful view, the glass making every object discernible. All the hills round Sidmouth were plain even to the naked eye, though the town itself was hidden by Exmouth Hill. (*Diary*). *The two accompanying coloured sketches were done some years earlier. One, undated but probably 1847, depicts the Ness and the mouth of the Teign. The other shows the coast eastwards towards Sidmouth.*

53/9/7-1. *The Ness Rock, Teignmouth, Devon, and entrance to the harbour.* (Not dated) (DRO, 19/2/8D/29)

53/9/7-2. *The 'Parson and Clerk' rocks, as seen from Teignmouth, with Exmouth Head and the coast beyond Sidmouth. Coloured on the spot without sketching in pencil June 1848.* (DRO, Z19/2/8D/123)

53/9/7-3. *The Ness Rock, Teignmouth, Devon. May 1836.* (DRO, Z19/2/8A/125)

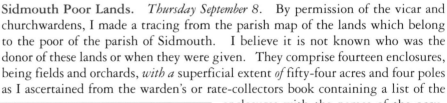

Sidmouth Poor Lands. *Thursday September 8.* By permission of the vicar and churchwardens, I made a tracing from the parish map of the lands which belong to the poor of the parish of Sidmouth. I believe it is not known who was the donor of these lands or when they were given. They comprise fourteen enclosures, being fields and orchards, *with a* superficial extent *of* fifty-four acres and four poles as I ascertained from the warden's or rate-collectors book containing a list of the enclosures with the names of the occupiers. The rent charge to the vicar is £5 14s 7d, and that to the appropriators £2 14s 2d. (*Diary*). What with sundry landed estates lying scattered in three different parishes, let at liberal and improving rents, and a good round sum of money in the funds, some think the poor of Sidmouth rather rich. (*History of Sidmouth II, 111*). *Hutchinson later traced the history of the Poor Lands as far as he was able and wrote an account of them in the History of Sidmouth, Volume II.*

Took a walk to look at the Sidmouth lands, *which* lie two miles south-west at Higher Southwood. I went up the road above Holcombe Down, though the Down, as given on the Ordnance Map, is now enclosed and cultivated. From the top of this hill there is a fine view. The Sidmouth lands run from the valley at Southwood up to the road on the ridge. Looking over towards Dawlish and Exmouth, all the Sidmouth hills and even every field on their sides, are clearly seen with the naked eye. From the neighbourhood of Sidmouth, therefore, these lands ought to be discernible. I made a coloured sketch of the view looking towards Sidmouth. (*Diary*).

Little Haldon Camp and the Sidmouth Lands. *Friday September 9.* This morning after breakfast, with some sandwiches in my pocket, I started for Little Haldon to look at the camp. I had a warm walk till I got to the summit of the hill. The camp is not remarkable for size, position or strength. It is circular, measuring 124 yards in diameter and the agger is only fifteen to twenty feet from ditch to its summit. There is a hole about eight feet across near the centre which may be a modern pit to collect water for cattle, but if ancient it may have been of the nature of a well. Openings, apparently modern, are found at the four cardinal points. The highest part of Haldon prevents Berry Head and any camps in that direction from being seen, but the Ugbrook Park Camp was seemingly visible and all those towards the north, Hembury, Dumpden, Woodbury, High Peak, etc., which latter were very clear.

On leaving the Camp I came down over the heath and fields to Smallacombe and ran against a wasp's nest in a hedge. I retreated from that *and* proceeded till I got opposite Higher Southwood and the Sidmouth lands. Here I pulled up, eat my sandwiches and made a coloured sketch of the said Sidmouth lands as they lay spread out before me. I then returned home and got back at five, having been out seven hours. (*Diary*).

53/9/8. Sketch taken from the Poor Lands belonging to the poor of Sidmouth, situated near Higher Southwood in the parish of Dawlish. Looking over Dawlish and Exmouth towards Sidmouth. Coloured on the spot September 8, 1853. (DRO, Z19/2/8D/337)

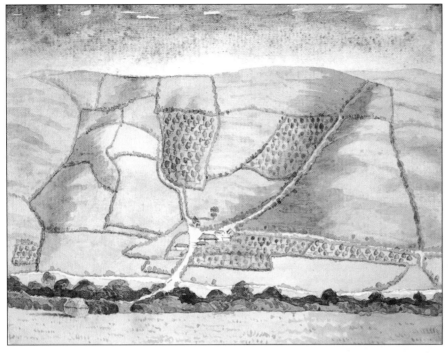

53/9/9. The Higher Southwood estate, Dawlish. (Hist. of Sid. II,109)

Parson and Clerk. Saturday September 17. Being spring tides and low water at noon, I took the opportunity to walk along the beach from Dawlish towards the Parson and Clerk Rocks. Got nearly as far as the foot of the Parson, but on no occasion is the tide ever low enough to permit of quite reaching it, and of course not of passing it. Made a sketch of his features and walked back. (Diary).

Little Haldon Camp. *Monday September 19.* My article on the subject of Little Haldon Camp, just completed, is to be printed next Thursday in the Dawlish Directory. (*Diary*).

Mary Roberton's illness. *Tuesday September 20.* Started for Heightley. Left the Joneses at Piermont House, Dawlish, in the forenoon and went by rail to Newton Abbott. From thence I walked to Heightley Cottage near Chudleigh, five miles and a half, where I found my cousin Mary Roberton still very unwell. The house, since the death of her mother Mrs. Cocks, is in a dismantled state and preparations are being made for removal and a sale. (*Diary*).

Camp in Ugbrook Park. *Thursday September 22.* Measured the camp in Ugbrook Park. Made it 270 yards east to west and 218 north and south. (*See April 30, 1849*). The agger is from 45 to 50 feet on the slope, from the middle of the ditch to the centre of the top of the agger at its most perfect part. (*Diary*).

Saturday September 24. Went to the Park again to examine the outworks. These outworks on the south side form a large curve nearly concentric with the agger of the Camp and about 300 yards in advance of it. At the south point of this work, which is a ditch and agger, there is a zig-zag bank running a hundred yards towards the Camp, by an opening in the work. The south-west part of this work is as bold in features as those of the Camp itself. The advanced work runs irreg-

53/9/17. Near view of the 'Parson and Clerk Rocks', between Dawlish and Teignmouth. Or rather of the 'Parson' only, for the 'Clerk' is round the corner and invisible from this point. Coloured on the spot September 18, 1853. (DRO, Z19/2/8D/347)

ularly eastward down the hill to the pond at the head of the lake. It then turns back at a sharp angle towards the Camp for nearly 200 yards, at which point it alters course northwards flanking all the east side of the Camp. There are also slight traces of the same kind of work commencing from the north-east side of the Camp, running straight towards the north-east boundary of the Park. It seems obvious that these works were intended as additional security on the south and east sides of the Camp, but it is hard to say

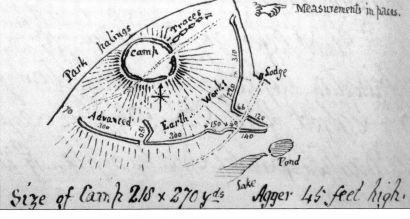

53/9/24-1. *Plan of camp in Ugbrook Park.* (In letter to Mr. Heineken)

at what period they were constructed. They are not of a nature to be of equal age with the camp itself, but perhaps were made by troops that may have occupied the camp during one of the civil wars of the middle ages. *(Diary). The only plan Hutchinson did of the camp is contained in a letter to Heineken dated September 29, 1853 (and copied into Soc. of Antiq. Ms. 250). The accompanying coloured sketch of the lakeside drive was done some five years previously.*

53/9/24-2. *Sketch in Ugbrook Park – lower end of the upper lake. Coloured on the spot June 20, 1848.* (DRO, Z19/2/8D/127)

Thursday October 20. My article on Ugbrook Park Camp is in the Dawlish and Teignmouth Directory today. *(Diary).*

Milber Down Camp. *Saturday October 22.* Took the rail from Dawlish to Newton in order to examine Milber Down Camp. The interior area is squarish in form, measuring 134 by 154 yards, with the road from Newton running through it. There are three aggers and ditches *and* outside these there are some extensive circumvallations too irregular to describe, but I have a plan of them in my sketchbook. After being five hours on the hill in a sharp wind examining and measuring the interior works, and the exterior ones which are probably modern, returned to Newton and then by rail to Dawlish. The outworks of this Camp (locally called the Castle) were probably thrown up by the Prince of Orange (William the Third), *or* at least Lysons says so. The land is Sir William Carew's. One of the game keepers told me that about seven years ago, at a spot a half mile north, or north by east, of the Camp where the outworks extend, some 'pence' were dug up; also a coin like a sixpence and some knives and forks decayed with rust. *(Diary). Excavations by Cottrill in 1937-8 revealed that the fort was occupied some time after 300 BC and peaceably abandoned in the first century AD, when the small* *rectangular enclosure just to the south-east, shown on Hutchinson's plan, was constructed as a homestead. There was no evidence to show that the outer embankment was of a more recent origin than the rest of the entrenchments (Fox et al. 1949).*

53/10/22-1. *Plan of the camp on Milber Down, near Newton Abbot, Devon. Surveyed October 1853.* (DRO, Z19/2/8D/335)

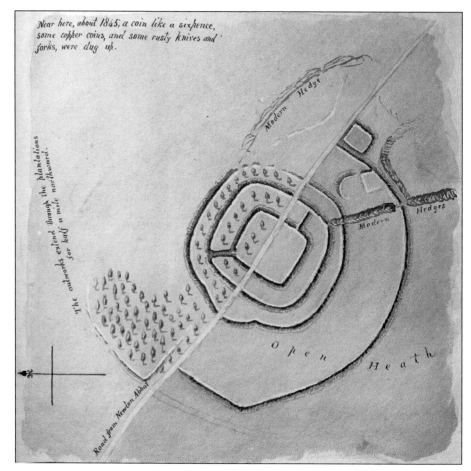

53/10/22-2. *Old camp on Milber Down, near Newton Abbot, Devon. Sketched on the spot October 22, 1853. Half the camp is hid in the plantations.* (DRO, Z19/2/8D/349)

Denbury Down Camp. *Saturday October 29.* Went over to Denbury Down Camp. Took the rail to Newton and from that place walked to the neat village of Denbury (where Archdeacon Froude has a house), distant three or three and a half miles from the station. This Camp occupies the crown of a conical hill, which rises by itself out of the plain like a molehill in a field. A horizontal section of the hill shows, not a circle, but an ellipse, and the form of the Camp naturally enough assumes the elliptical shape according to the shape of the hill. The sides of the hill are cultivated, but the summit, first planted about forty years ago, is not only covered with large trees overhead, but is so matted and entangled below with ferns, weeds, brambles and coppice wood that there is no getting through it, and no means of examining the earthwork satisfactorily.

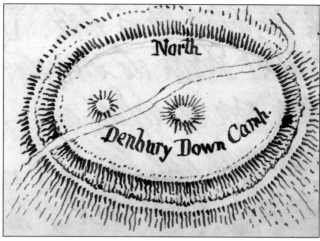

53/10/29. *Plan of Denbury Down camp.* (In letter to Mr. Heineken)

There is a kind of trackway from the north-east to the south-west across it, and from an imperfect measurement through this I am disposed to think the long diameter may be about 250 yards. Near the middle of the area there is a great mound like a tumulus, and towards the west end apparently another, visible among the brambles and bushes. There is a ditch with a small agger outside, and the high acclivity of a steep agger inside. The most perfect parts are at the west end and south side. The short diameter I could not measure for underwood. From the ditch to the top of the agger on the south (the only place I could get at it) the measurement was 18 yards, or 54 feet, but it may be still bolder in other places. The views all round are very fine . . . There is a tradition in Denbury that this Camp was either attacked by the Danes or occupied by that people. (*Diary*). *The accompanying plan is taken from a letter to Heineken dated November 2, 1853.*

'Old Popes' Day, 1853. *Saturday November 5.* Sundry 'Old Popes' or 'Guys' were brought about this morning by the boys, something after the Sidmouth fashion only they were mounted on donkey back and the verses the boys repeated were not exactly *the same.* In the evening, tar barrels predominated over fireworks. (*Diary*).

Dawlish Water barrow. *Friday November 11.* On taking a walk on the high hill on the east side of Dawlish water, I espied some sheep feeding on a mound in a grass field. Having an eye to antiquities, I conjured up a tumulus in imagination, and at once scrambled over the hedge to make a closer examination. Sure enough it was, a mound like a molehill about 14 yards in diameter. Some persons have been endeavouring to sink a hole in the centre, trying, doubtless, to find the treasure – the 'crock of gold'- which universal tradition affirms to be usually buried under such mounds. (*Diary*). *Hutchinson was to record many visits to this tumulus over the years and at one time applied for permission to excavate, which was declined. The monument is no longer accessible, the site having been enclosed within a semi-fortified enclosure surrounding a water treatment works.*

53/11/11. *Tumulus or barrow on Dawlish Water Hill, half a mile north of Dawlish, Devon. Diameter fourteen yards. Coloured on the spot November 17, 1853.* (DRO, Z19/2/8D/343)

Sunday worship. *Sunday November 20.* Went to the parish church in the morning and to the chapel on the west side of the Lawn in the evening. (*Diary*). *Hutchinson's pen and ink sketch shows the Lawn twenty-one years previously.*

Dawlish, Bishop's Parlour. *Tuesday November 22.* Made a coloured drawing of the Bishop's Parlour. (*Diary*).

53/11/20. *The Lawn, Dawlish, Devon. 1832.* (DRO, Z19/2/8A/134)

Return from Dawlish. *Saturday November 26.* Returned home. Took the express train at Dawlish for Exeter where I did a little shopping and a little gazing into shop windows to see if there was anything new. Got on the mail at half past three, passed through Ottery and arrived in Sidmouth by six. (*Diary*).

53/11/22. *The Bishop's Parlour, Dawlish. Coloured on the spot November 22, 1853.* (DRO, Z19/2/8D/339)

Pew rents. *Thursday December 1.* People in Sidmouth are beginning to resist the payment of pew rents to the vicar. For twenty years my late father paid four guineas a year for a pew in the parish church, a sum amounting to eighty guineas, knowing that the law did not require him to do so. Many persons have been quietly growling for some time past, but now several families have declared that as residents in the parish, they have a right to seats in the church without such a demand and they consequently decline paying any more. Such is the state of rebellion in which I find Sidmouth on my return. After being five days in the parish, I have openly joined the rebels by the letter I have just written to the churchwardens. Pretending to understand that a general distribution of seats is about to be made to the parishioners, I have requested on the part of my mother that they will assign four sittings for her use and the use of her household. The vicar need not charge me with wronging him. If he has asked and taken eighty guineas from my father illegally, on which side does the commission of wrong lie?

I believe the living of Sidmouth is worth £350 or more per annum to which may be added the vicarage house and some thirty acres of glebe, and besides this there are surplice fees which are very high in this parish. It is not therefore on the score of poverty that the vicar, Rev. William Jenkins, has let out the pews in the church at a guinea a sitting. I await an answer to my letter. (*Diary*).

Alcyonites. *Friday December 2.* Took a walk on the beach to Picket Rock and made some sketches of the alcyonites, and got some specimens. (*Diary*). *Hutchinson later had some doubt about the nature of these specimens and decided to get a second opinion.* Some years ago (*November 10, 1858*) I carried two or three specimens to the Geological Museum in Jermyn Street, London, and they told me that these snake-like forms were now believed to be only infiltrations. I do not know whether this explanation will satisfy everybody, but we must be content with it till we get a better. (*History of Sidmouth I, 8*).

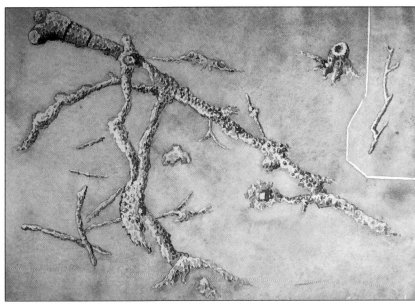

53/12/2-1. *Specimens of the Alcyonite {crossed through} on a flat slab near Picket Rock, Sidmouth.* (Later note: *only infiltrations*). (DRO, Z19/2/8E/3)

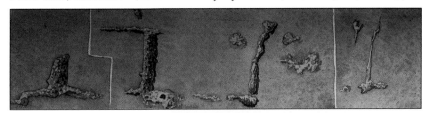

Robbery at Knowle Cottage. *Thursday December 15.* This morning after breakfast, as I was walking over the Chit Rocks towards High Peak Hill at low water to look for some fossils in the red rock, something shining attracted my attention that I at first thought was an oyster shell. I passed it several paces, but thinking that the glitter was more like that of a silvery metal than mother-of-pearl, I turned back to look again. Nothing was visible but a piece about the size of a dollar, but on pulling it out of the sand it proved to be a silver-plated square dish. After having washed it in a pool of water, I discovered a crest, a leopard's head or something of that nature, with the initials T.L.F. underneath. Remembering that about six months ago a robbery of plate had been committed at Mr. Fish's, at Knowle Cottage, and knowing these initials to be the same as his, it occurred to me that I had found part of the lost plate, the thief having secured to himself all that was pure silver and throwing away what was only plated. A short time ago, Harding the watchmaker found a tray in the river, and Sweet the rope maker another at a different place but also in the river. On these the marks of the chisel are plain where the solid silver edgings were ripped off. My portion of the treasure trove I took to the Reading Room and Billiard Room in order to make the circumstances known. The magistrates were afterwards told of it and the piece of plate given into the custody of a policeman. (*Diary*).

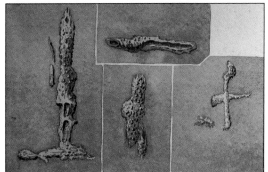

53/12/2-2. *Specimens of the alcyonite {crossed through} as seen in the perpendicular face of High Peak Hill near Sidmouth, Devon. They occur near Picket Rock. The above sketches comprise detached examples but all within a few yards of each other.* (Later note: *these are only infiltrations*). (DRO, Z19/2/8E/1)

Saturday December 24. Finished my watercolour drawing of the destroyed weir in the Salcombe fields for my leather work frame of ivy, but now it is done I don't like it. (*Diary*).

Roman coin from the churchyard. *Wednesday December 28.* Finished engraving on wood a coin of Faustina Augusta as an illustration to an article in the Sidmouth Directory in January. This evening went to a small party at Lime Park. (*Diary*). It was found in Sidmouth churchyard about ninety yards north-east of the church tower in 1850. (*History of Sidmouth I, 96*).

53/12/28. *Coin of Faustina Augusta.* (Hist. of Sid. I,96)

1854

Possible runic letters on Iona. *Wednesday January 4.* Sent a communication to the Archaeological Institute, London, on the subject of a sculptured slab in Iona having some characters cut on it resembling Runic letters. (*Diary*).

Blackmore field. *Monday March 13.* For the second time accompanied Mr. Paul Hayman in surveying the premises and part of the Blackmore field I propose buying of Sir John Kennaway. (*Diary*).

Late night. *Wednesday March 22.* Mozart's 12 Mass came off tonight in the great room in Exeter by the Exeter Society. Mr. Heineken and myself went in and took part in it. We did not get back until near three tomorrow morning. (*Diary*).

Sketching in Teignmouth and Dawlish. *Thursday March 30.* Went over to Dawlish today to see my cousin Mary Roberton. (*Diary*). *Whilst staying there for nearly a month, Hutchinson sketched some local beach and harbour scenes.*

54/3/30-1. *Sketch in Teignmouth harbour. Coloured on the spot April 3, 1854.* (DRO, Z19/2/8E/7)

Crimean war. *Saturday April 1.* So war with Russia is declared at last. Much forbearance have we shown certainly, and tried every argument to turn the Emperor from his determination of unscrupulous aggression against Turkey. France and England now unite as friendly allies (unusual alliance) in defending

54/3/30-2. *Mount Pleasant and the coast near Dawlish, from the warren. Coloured on the spot April 15, 1854.*
(DRO, Z19/2/8E/9)

Turkey against the attempt of Russia. The London Gazette of 28th ultimo contains a declaration that active hostilities must begin. The allies have a powerful foe to contend with and everyone looks out anxiously for every morsel of intelligence that may come from the seat of war. (*Diary*).

Sketch on Dawlish beach. *Friday April 21.* Made a coloured sketch on Dawlish beach. (*Diary*).

54/4/21. *Sketch on Dawlish beach. Coloured on the spot April 21, 1854.*
(DRO, Z19/2/8E/11)

Sid Abbey. *Monday May 15.* At Sid Abbey (a few nights ago) where there was mostly music, and where Mr John Wolcott of Knowle sang several Italian songs, whom I accompanied on the flute. (*Diary*). *The accompanying sketch of Sid abbey from across the Sid was done some years earlier.*

54/5/15. *Sid Abbey, near Sidmouth, Devon. Coloured on the spot, July 29, 1847.* (DRO, Z19/2/8D/35)

Gardening pains. *Saturday May 20.* Yesterday and today I poured nine large watering pots onto the rhubarb in the garden. Since the shower on the 1st we have had scarcely any rain, and only a sprinkle or two during the three preceding months. Gardening of late has made my back ache terribly. Weeding is stooping and tedious work, much digging is tiring and mowing tries the back, shoulders and limbs immensely. (*Diary*).

Illuminated tree house. *Monday May 22.* Made some bluelights, the composition being one part of sulphuret of antimony, two of sulphur and six of nitre, all powdered well mixed and driven into a case. Lit two of them successively up in my summerhouse in the tree by way of experiment. They answered satisfactorily and illuminated the tree and objects nearby very brilliantly, much to the surprise of the neighbours. (*Diary*).

54/5/30. *Review of the Yeomanry Cavalry on Salcombe Hill, near Sidmouth. May 30, 1854. Sketched on the spot.* (DRO, Z19/2/8E/15)

Yeomanry cavalry on Salcombe Hill. *Tuesday May 30.* Went to Salcombe Hill to see the review of the Royal First Devon Yeomanry Cavalry. It would have been a pretty sight had not the day been showery. Made a hasty sketch of the scene by way of a momento. (*Diary*).

Letter to Lord Palmerston. *Monday June 5.* Wrote to Lord Palmerston. A man may serve his country sometimes without fighting. (*Diary*). *The letter has not been traced but probably contained details of a new type of artillery shell Hutchinson had designed (see September 29, 1854).*

Walk on Bulverton Hill. *Wednesday June 14.* Walked to Mutter's Moor, Bulverton Hill, *where* by appointment I was soon followed by Mr. and Miss Heineken and the two Miss Horsfalls in a carriage. On the ridge of the hill they got out and admired the view looking over the valley of the Otter, etc. We then walked through 'Lord Rolles Plantation' on Bulverton Hill to examine the cairn of dry flints which is fast vanishing to mend roads with. Having returned to the carriage, we went, some riding and some walking, along Peak Hill out to the cliff, where we enjoyed the view and then returned down Peak Hill to Sidmouth. The distance by the Ordnance Survey map taking all the turnings into account was five miles and a fraction. (*Diary*).

Parting friends. *Friday June 23.* The Miss Horsfalls returned to Yorkshire. What a pity! (*Diary*).

Purchase of No. 4, Coburg Terrace. *Thursday July 6.* Signed the deeds concerning the purchase of the house, No. 4, Coburg Terrace, Sidmouth, from Sir John Kennaway of Escot, together with the premises, garden and strip of the adjoining lower Blackmore field. Which strip of field, now being attached to the house, may now be designated Coburg Meadow. (*Diary*).

Caterwauling. *Thursday July 13.* Walked out to Sidbury and played chess with the vicar. Went via Snogbrook and the lanes. Coming home at eleven I picked up some glow-worms in the hedges and carried them back to Sidmouth. Wanting to speak to Mr. Hutchinson, I called on him at this unseasonable hour but did it in a novel way. As he has been much troubled with the caterwauling of the tomcats of late, I resolved to play him a trick by stealing under his window and imitating their notes. Soon, he stealthily opened the front door and crept out and then shied a couple of coals (the first missiles he could lay hold of in his hurry) in the direction of the sound. When I could contain my laughter no longer he discovered who the tomcat was. We then went in and chatted till nearly two in the morning. (*Diary*).

54/7/25-1. *Plan of trenches in barrow.* (Diary)

54/7/25-2. *The barrows etc., on Honiton Hill.* (Diary)

Barrows near Ring-in-the-Mire. *Tuesday July 25.* Went with Mr. Heineken to the top of Honiton Hill, to open a barrow lying close to the fifteen milestone from Exeter. My, how hot it was! The thermometer at home stood at 75, but out here in the sun it was scorching. Nothing to drink but beer and spirits but the attempt to satisfy one's thirst with such drinks only endangers one's head. I would have given a great deal for water or tea. The barrow had been nearly all

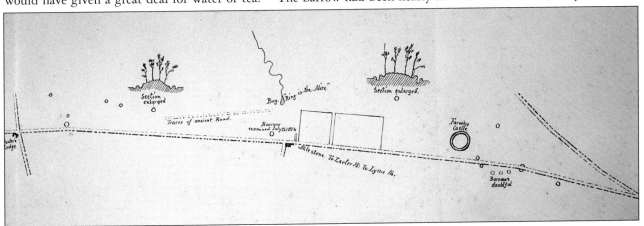

54/7/25-3. *Section of barrow on Honiton Hill.* (Diary)

54/7/25-4. *Section of barrow on Honiton hill.* (Diary)

54/7/25-5. *'Ring in the Mire' on Honiton Hill, Devon. The four parishes of Sidbury, Gittesham, Honiton & Farway all meet at a spot in the middle of this pond, or rather bog.* (Not dated). (DRO, Z19/2/8E/17)

removed level with the ground. We had two men with us with spades and pick-axes and commenced at the centre of the area, and dug trenches in various directions as per plan annexed. We dug down till we came upon tough yellow clay which appeared never to have been disturbed. We came upon this clay at depths varying from one to two feet. All our attempts, carried on for several hours, failed to discover any pit in this stratum of yellow clay such as could lead us to conclude that a cist-vaen had been made. We either missed the right spot or the men who some two or three years ago levelled the mound unconsciously removed the urn or other depository of bones, ashes, or similar exuvia.

About a hundred or hundred and fifty yards north-west of the milestone, close by, is a bog of oval form some 60 yards or so long known as 'Ring-in-the-Mire'. The circumstance that led to imposing such a name on such a spot are related in most of the county histories. Isabella de Fortibus, Countess of Devon at an early period, owned all the land in this neighbourhood. A dispute having arisen respecting the boundaries of several of the parishes adjacent, this lady settled matters both promptly and permanently. She rode up to this place on horseback, and throwing a gold ring into the mire, told the persons who attended her that the spot where the ring fell should henceforth indicate the place where the parishes met. True enough, for many centuries this locality has been known as 'Ring-in-the-Mire', and moreover the parishes of Farway, Honiton, Gittesham and Sidbury all meet here. A man whom we found on the hill told us that about ten years ago the boundaries were being fixed, on which occasion a pole was erected in the middle of this bog, so that the spot is indeed still recognised by authority.

Some of the large barrows on the hill vary in construction. The large one close to the road 170 paces from Hunter's Lodge has a ditch round it, and the one about 700 paces east of Hunter's Lodge and 150 on the left or north has a hedge or vallum around it. Can this hedge, though now somewhat eroded and looking like an ancient vallum, have only been thrown up to protect the young fir trees when first planted? The barrow on the highest part of the hill and about 400 paces north-west of Farway Castle has perpendicular sides with a ditch and vallum outside it. It occurs to me that these outer works may be modern, unless similar features of known antiquity can be identified elsewhere,

Having finished our observations we returned to Sidmouth by nine, having been away just twelve hours. (*Diary*).

Treasure trove. *Friday August 4.* Walked to Mr. Charles Cornish's farm at Salcombe, occupied by Trump. One apartment in this old house has a flat ceiling divided into squares by carved cross-beams, with bosses in the middle of the panels and escutcheons in the corners. Some of them bear a sort of rude fleur-de-lis in a position that would be upside down if the shield were upright, *but* perhaps it is rather a fanciful than an heraldic device.

54/8/4. *Ceiling escutcheon, Charles Cornish's farm.* (Diary)

Went with Mr. Trump westward to a field on the hill overlooking Sid Abbey, to see a curious pit about four feet across and the depth uncertain. Stones thrown down rattled a long time *and* it may be thirty or forty feet deep. After many strange conjectures, Trump's idea that springs may have excavated a hollow below ground and the top sunk in seems the more likely cause, rather than that it should have been a smuggler's cave.

This man Trump is the nephew of the man whom the tradition of the neighbourhood declares found a 'crock of gold' when ploughing a field near Trow. Trump pointed out the field at a distance, but to examine it must be the subject for another walk. He said in answer to my questions that his uncle's name was Sanders, and that he was still living. The circumstance occurred about forty years ago but he thought there was no truth in the story. His uncle, he said, speculated in one or two ways and was fortunate. The story goes that Sanders was ploughing the field when his horses suddenly sank down, the ground giving way under them, *and* wishing to examine this strange occurrence alone, he sent away the boy who was with him on some errand. In the pit he found a large crock full of gold coins, *and becoming* rather 'well to do' not long after, the tale was set agoing. His own taciturnity and denial only served to spread and confirm the suspicion. (*Diary*).

Half a segar. *Monday August 7.* The box of clothes for Fanny goes to London today. I called at the Elphinstones and found the Captain all alone. We cut a segar in two and each smoked half, neither of us being suckers, and even this made my nerves all of a shake. I then had a cup of coffee, which took away the effect, and then a glass of liqueur with a German name made of white brandy, syrup and caraway seed. We gossiped for three hours. Later I had a practise with Mr. and Miss Heineken, trying over Handel's 'Mount of Olives', I taking the horn. (*Diary*).

Death of Col. Roberton. *Tuesday August 15.* Heard of the death of my uncle Col. Roberton, St. Andrew's St., Tiverton, and am requested to go over on Thursday. He was eighty-six on Sunday 13th and died on Monday at 2AM. (*Diary*).

Thursday August 17. Went to Tiverton – on the mail to Exeter and on the rail to Tiverton. (*Diary*).

Cranmore Castle, Tiverton. *Friday August 18.* The funeral took place this morning at half past ten, his daughter and her husband the Rev. Francis Jones being in Tiverton but the former not attending. The latter, myself, Dr. Paterson and the Rev. Spurway being the only persons except the servants who went. My uncle was buried across the path south of St. George's Chapel near his eldest daughter Jane, buried some sixteen or seventeen years ago, and his wife Mary, my mother's sister, whose funeral I attended (see May 10, 1848). In the afternoon the Rev. Jones and myself went to look at Cranmore Castle on the hill over

54/8/18. *Plan of Cranmore Castle, Tiverton.* (In letter to Mr. Heineken)

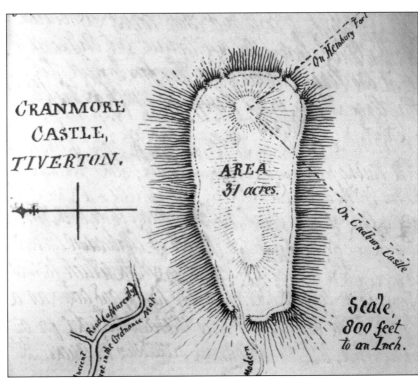

54/8/22. Marine subjects sculptured on Greenway's Chapel, St Peter's Church, Tiverton. Sketched on the spot September 6, 1854. (DRO, Z19/2/8E/23)

Collipriest. (*Diary*). *Hutchinson described this excursion in a letter to Heineken:*

My Dear Mr. Heineken. I have just stormed Cranmore Castle, and taken it. This afternoon, feeling inclined for a quiet walk, I went down to Collipriest towards the encampment that lies on the high hill over Collipriest Cottage. I stopped the farmer's men and women in the lanes to enquire of them the name of the camp on the hill but none had ever heard of it, though they had heard of a great battle once fought thereabouts. On referring to Col. Harding's *History of Tiverton*, this camp turns out to be the veritable 'Cranmore Castle', though the name is quite lost on the spot. Col. Harding's account is brief but he gives a plan. The highest part of the camp is the east end though it is a good tug to get up from the Collipriest side. I had intended to survey it but its immense size put that out of the question, and as it is divided into several fields of corn and other crops separated by high thick hedges, the eye cannot see one half of it at a time. I was glad therefore to find Col. Harding's *History* in the house. (*Letter to Heineken dated August 18, 1864, extract*). *The accompanying plan is taken from the letter to Heineken.*

Tiverton Church and Castle. *Tuesday August 22.* Went into St. Peter's Church to see what progress had been made since last year in the rebuilding. With the exception of the tower, Greenway's Chapel and the south wall, it will be a new church. The ancient circular-headed zig-zag doorway in the north wall I see they have preserved and built in again.

I then went to look at the castle. Sir Walter Carew has recently been having the battlements over the east gateway and the adjacent turret known as the Duke of Devonshire's Chair repaired, added to or altered. Some persons were alarmed lest injudicious alterations were made to the venerable building, and I cannot say that the repairs are satisfactory inasmuch as they are not strictly restorations. One day when I was a boy, I climbed up in the Duke of Devonshire's Chair with Timothy Featherstonehaugh, whose mother was a Carew. (*Diary*). *Some days later Hutchinson returned to St. Peter's Church to sketch some of the sculptured slabs inset into the south wall and porch, depicting a unique series of early sixteenth century armed merchant vessels representing Greenways fleet. The four sketches are particularly valuable as recutting and erosion have since destroyed many original features then visible.*

Brass gun. *Thursday August 24.* The curious brass gun given me by my cousin Marianne Jones I conveyed this morning to the station to go by the luggage train to Exeter, and from thence by carrier to Sidmouth. This gun was captured by my cousin, the late John Roberton, on the 29th of January 1845, from a pirate prahu on the east coast of Borneo. The circumstance is mentioned in Captain Sir Edward Belcher's *Narrative of the Voyage of HMS Samarang during the Years 1843-46* in the eastern archipelago. John Roberton was lieutenant on board the Samarang and the Captain was so pleased at the gallant way in which he attacked and took the pirate that he made him a present of the gun when he brought it on board. My cousin's health failed so much on the voyage home that he was put on shore at the Cape where he died. The gun was sent to Tiverton where it remained till it was given to me. It is four feet long, small bore of about an inch and a quarter, and ornamented with arabesques and scrolls. I must have a carriage made for it. (*Later note*: Now in Exeter Museum). (*Diary*).

Seven Crosses, near Tiverton. *Wednesday August 30.* Walked out to 'Seven Crosses' near Tiverton. At this spot there is nothing now but the divergence of three or four roads, though formerly I believe there existed some monument commemorative of a curious circumstance which the historians of the neighbourhood relate; how a certain Countess of Devon , passing that way one day, met a man carrying a basket, the contents of which he seemed anxious to conceal; how she asked him what he had got there, to which he hesitantly answered 'seven puppies which he was going to drown in the River Exe; *and* how she forced him to uncover and show his 'puppies' ,which turned out to be seven male children. When she drove him to an explanation he confessed that he had deserted his wife for seven years in dread of a large family, but having returned a twelvemonth ago his wife had recently presented him with seven boys at a birth! The Countess, having severely reprimanded him for the course he was pursuing, directed him to

54/8/30. *'Seven Crosses' near*
Tiverton. Coloured on the spot
August 30, 1854.
(DRO, Z19/2/8E/21)

take the contents of the basket to her residence, Tiverton Castle, saying that she
would in future take them under her care. The story goes that she brought them
all up and put them into the church, where through her influence they all rose to
be high dignitaries. (*Diary*).

Artillery hints. *Wednesday September 6.* Returned Major Hole's book on
Artillery, which I borrowed to get some hints for the benefit of my gun. (*Diary*).

Tiverton to Uffculme. *Thursday September 7.* Left Tiverton with the Rev. and
Mrs. Jones for Uffculme. (*Diary*).

Pixie Garden. *Friday September 8.* Went out with a determination to find 'Pixie
Garden' on Uffculme Down if possible, a thing I had many times resolved to do
before. The description given of this place by Lysons and others is that it is a
quadrangular enclosure about 20 paces square with an opening at the corners, the
enclosing hedge being about two feet high, that it is divided into four compartments by a hedge each way, and that there was a mound in each compartment. I
proceeded from Uffculme to Hillhead, all the summit of which fifty years ago was
open Down. After rambling over hedge and ditch for an hour or two in various
directions without discovering the sign of an earthwork, and after failing to obtain
any information from persons I met on the hill or at Hillhead Farm, I espied an
old fellow on a corn stack thatching. Him I hailed, and demanded whether he
had ever heard of such a place as Pixie Garden? 'Yes, to be sure', was his reply,

54/9/8-2. *Plan of Pixie*
Garden. (Diary)

54/9/8-1. *Sketch on Uffculme*
Down, looking towards Hill
Head. Coloured on the spot
September 8, 1854. Pixie
Garden stood in the corner of the
field where the figures are.
(DRO, Z19/2/8E/25)

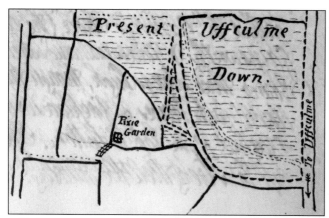

54/9/8-3.　*Location of Pixie Garden.*　(Diary)

'and when I was a boy I ran over it scores of times'. This was encouraging. After some parleying I bribed him to come down and lead me to the place. I refer to the Ordnance Survey Map. He led me to a spot about a tenth of an inch below the letter N in the word Down of Uffculme Down. This region is now enclosed and under cultivation. I made a haphazard plan of the enclosure as far as I now recollect; Pixie Garden stood in the corner of the field where I have placed it. The man, whose name was Baker, so asserted. He took my walking stick and drew a plan of what he could remember of the earth-works, and they were like the annexed. He said there was a 'mump' in the middle, which may have been a tumulus, but Lysons speaks of a mound in each compartment. He agreed with Lysons on describing the ridges as about two feet high, over which he had run and jumped many times with his school fellows. It was destroyed some forty or fifty years ago when this part of the Down was enclosed. What this small but curious work could have been is hard to conjecture, but that it is of considerable antiquity seems generally supposed. It was from twenty to thirty yards square. (*Diary*).

Blackborough and the Whetstone Hills.　*Wednesday September 13.*　Walked from Uffculme via Ashill and Allhallows to Blackborough Hill and Punchey Down and a tolerably fagging walk I had. Put the sketchbook and colour box in one pocket and my lunch in the other, and was out all day. I witnessed the process of making whetstones (the range is called the Whetstone Hills), went part of the way into one of the burrows in the side of the hill where they are dug (I was told it entered three hundred yards), walked to Garnsey's Tower (the correct name I have heard is Gainsworthy), measured and sketched it. It is a circular tower three stories high, though the floors are ruined and fallen, with traces of fireplaces. The wall is two feet thick but cracked from top to bottom. The windows have been blocked up to strengthen the building, but nevertheless it is so tottery that it threatens to fall. The tower is twelve feet in diameter. The conical hill near the church with the fir trees on it is called Beacon Hill and from it the view is splendid. I could see Aylesbeare Hill and the sea beyond, the hills near Sidmouth such as Pinn Beacon and some others. In other directions the view is equally extensive. (*Diary*). *Bracken-covered waste dumps now mark the site of the whetstone quarries above the village. The church has been demolished, finally defeated by the elements after*

54/9/13-1.　*Mode of trimming whetstones for scythes on the Whetstone Hills, Punchey Down, and one of the entrances into the side of the hill. This passage entered 300 yards horizontally. Sketched September 12, 1854.* (DRO, Z19/2/8E/31)

54/9/13-2. *View from Punchey Down looking down on Blackborough Church, Beacon Hill (with the firs on it) and Lord Egremont's house (on the extreme right). Coloured on the spot September 12, 1854.* (DRO, Z19/2/8E/27)

54/9/13-3. *Garnsey's Tower, Blackborough Hill. Coloured there September 12, 1854.* (DRO, Z19/2/8E/29)

little more than a hundred and fifty years and, as Hutchinson feared, Garnsey's Tower is now reduced to a three metre stump concealed in the woodland on the summit.

Lidwell Chapel. *Friday September 22.* After many enquiries, I discovered where Lidwell Chapel was situated and went there. Took a sketch of it and made measurements. (*Diary*).

Wednesday September 27. Went to Lidwell Chapel again. Mrs. Willis, the wife of the farmer who rents the estate, lent me a paper today drawn up by the Rev. owner, in order that I might copy it. It contains some memoranda relating to the Chapel, and the following is the copy:

54/9/22-1. Remains of Lidwell Chapell, near Dawlish. Coloured there September 22 and 27, 1854.
(DRO, Z19/2/8E/37)

'The ruined Chapel which stands on this estate was dedicated to the V. Mary. At the west end there is a spring of water with the remains of some artificial stonework, which I suppose once constituted the well; so that the Chapel was dedicated to Our-Lady-of–the Well, from which the name of the estate, anciently written Lythewell or Lyddewell, was borrowed. The length is 35 (or 37?) feet within the walls and the breadth 17 feet within, and the west wall is 2 foot 6 inches thick. The ruins consist only of the western gable containing an arched doorway composed of four large stones, 4 feet broad and 6 foot 4 inches high, over which is a square or oblong window. The line of the walls may be traced round the other side by the stones which still remain'.

The following are the only notices which I found of it:

'At Ludwell, an estate of Mr. Richard Widborne near Haldon, in a field called Chapel-park, is the ruinated Chapel of St. Mary; of which the proprietor can give no other account, than that he has heard his father say, 'it is prayed for in Roman Catholic countries by the name of the Holy Chapel of Ludwell'. He added that his father, when he gave him the estate, exacted a promise from him that he would never remove any of the stones or any part of the building. There are no

54/9/22-2. Sketch shewing Lidwell Farm and the site of Lidwell Chapel (over it). September 22 and 27, 1854.
(DRO, Z19/2/8E/41)

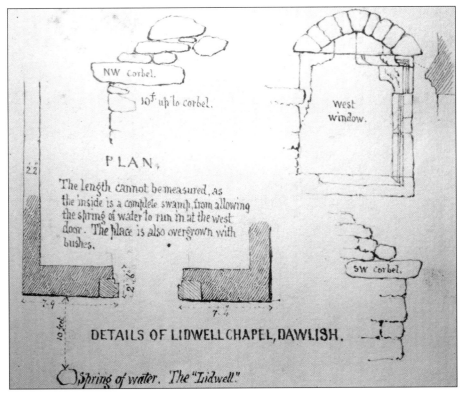

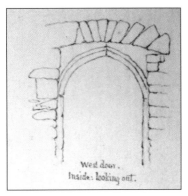

54/9/22-3. *Details of Lidwell Chapel, Dawlish.* (Not dated) (DRO, Z19/2/8E/39)

monuments remaining of any person buried there. This chapel is called in the Liber-regis, Lithewyll'. (Polwhele, *History of Devonshire*).

'Bishop Stafford further licensed him (Thomas Fayrforde) on 11 August 1411 to celebrate mass in St. Mary's Chapel at Lidwell on the 15 August, the feast of the Assumption of the Blessed Virgin Mary'. (*Stafford's Register Vol. 1*).

'On 25 May 1426, Bishop Lacy licensed this vicar (Walter Chiterwell) to officiate 'in capella beate Marie ate Coketon et Lydewell infra parochiam de Dawlysh'. (Oliver, *Ecclesiastical.Antiquities in Devon,Vol 2, p 144).".*

So much for the memorials of the owner of the place. In White's *History, Gazetteer and Directory of Devonshire* for 1850, one of the legendary notices of the Chapel is alluded to:

'About three and a half miles north-west of the town [Teignmouth] are the venerable ruins of Lithwell or Lidwell Chapel, where a villainous priest, popularly called St. Simon, is said in a legendary tale of the 16th century, to have committed many murders on the surrounding heath, for the sake of hoarding up gold in a secret chest under the altar, at the foot of which was a deep well in which he is said to have buried his victims. This Chapel was in Dawlish parish, and the well may still be seen in the middle of the ruined walls, covered with a large granite slab'. (White's *Directory*, 1850).

Nothing, however, seems to be known of such a well in the present day. Examination might decide. A more amplified version of the above tale I have read somewhere, but where I cannot think unless it were Woolmer's *Gazette* about the year 1850. I was told at Lidwell Farm that the monk above alluded to died at last in prosecuting his nefarious practices. The legend says he one night attacked a traveller on Haldon to rob him, but the traveller drew some weapon and so wounded the monk that he drew off. He was just able to get back to the Chapel, where he died. The ghost is said still to haunt the spot. I have another legend of two children , Jon and Janthe, who died and were buried there. It is entitled *The Little Chapel, or the Children of Consolation.* The writing, on a sheet of notepaper, is lithographed and a lithographed view of the building is given at the head. No author, publisher or date is given. (*Diary*). *The article Hutchinson remembered seeing was probably the anonymous one entitled 'Legend of Lidwell Chapel' published in the Exeter and Plymouth Gazette for May 5, 1849. It adds little but embellishments to the tale told above.*

54/9/26. *Sketch in Teignmouth Harbour. Coloured on the spot September 26, 1854.* (DRO, Z19/2/8E/43)

Teignmouth harbour. *Tuesday September 26.* Went to Teignmouth and Shaldon and called on several friends. (*Diary*). *According to the date, he also sketched this harbour scene.*

Report of a new shell. *Friday September 29.* In the Illustrated London News of the 23rd instant, I see the following paragraph at page 274. 'The Committee of Ordnance have had their attention drawn to a new projectile; it is a shell charged with a liquid which, when released by the concussion of the ball, becomes a sheet of liquid fire consuming all within its influence, the smoke emitted also destroying human life'. Now, I have reason to suspect that this is my shell as it is so exactly like what I communicated to the government in my letter to Lord Palmerston of last (?). (*Diary*). *The letter was presumably the one sent on June 5. The Committee must have considered the possibilities of this fearful missile for the notice to appear in the I.L.N., but there is no indication of whether it was actually tested. Hutchinson resumed his investigations into shell design some years later (see September 13, 1859).*

Premature rejoicing. *Tuesday October 3.* The news of the alleged fall of Sebastopol has set Sidmouth rejoicing, I fear prematurely. This evening the Sidmouth band paraded the parish. When the players came near our house into Coburg Terrace, by way of a lark I took my French horn and went out and mingled with them. I had a good blow with them for half an hour. (*Diary*).

Friday October 6. So Sebastopol has not fallen! No, it was too good to be true so soon. There has been a great battle however on the River Alma between Kalamuta Bay in the Crimea and the city, where the allies attacked a Russian camp. The loss to the English in killed and wounded was 1895 rank and file, 96 officers, 114 sergeants and 23 drummers, and to the French 1400 men an 60 officers. The Russians were driven from their camp and the victory has been celebrated in London. (*Diary*).

Musical interludes. *Friday October 13.* Had a capital musical meeting this morning at the Heineken's, *where we* played Reissiger's Trio in F. Took the violin part on the flute, Sir George Pocock the violincello, Miss Heineken the pianoforte *and* Mr. Heineken put in a few deep notes with his double bass. After that we went through Hummel's 6th Trio. Our audience consisted of Lady and Miss Pocock, Lady Knowles and Sir John and Lady Claridge. Lady Claridge and Miss Heineken then played some things from Mozart's 12th Mass. Before we broke up appointments were made for tomorrow. (*Diary*).

Saturday October 14. As by appointment, had an hours practise with Lady Claridge at Don Juan and subsequently with Sir George Pocock and the Heinekens. (*Diary*).

Monday October 16. Had a 'grand crash' at the Heineken's, in concert with Lady Claridge, Sir G. Pocock, Miss and Mr. Heineken. (*Diary*).

Three barrows. *Saturday October 21.* Went with Mr. Heineken and Mr. Waterhouse to Ottery East Hill, to enjoy the view and to show the latter a piece of Devonshire. We took the route in our vehicle by way of Sidford, and then to the left up the old Roman road ycleped High Street. From that we turned into the lane which took us all the way along the north side of Core Hill, and so on till we reached the top of Ottery East Hill. Here we halted, and taking out our spyglasses searched the countryside for half an hour on all sides, naming the Dartmoor tors, the camps on the principle eminencies and examining the houses of Exeter, Ottery and other places just discernible. Thence we started northwards until we came to the three barrows, the situations of which we noted in order to lay them down on the Ordnance map, where they are not (*B.R.Nos. 18-20*). These barrows are cut into peculiar forms by the ditches made round them. The most southerly one is in the shape of a star with six points, like a fort or battery; the second is like a square but bounded by curved lines bowing inwards, and the most northerly towards Chineway Head is merely circular. These ditches are not likely to be ancient and perhaps were made at the time the barrows were planted with fir trees, some of which remain growing on them. (*Diary*). One fir on the four-pointed barrow is fifty-two feet high as measured with Mr. Heineken's apomecometer, a little instrument subtending an angle of 22.5 degrees, being half 45, which is described in the 'Student' for April 1869. (*History of Sidmouth I, 69*).

From here we went along Chineway Head to Honiton Hill, the scene of our operations on the 25th of last July. Having taken our station on the great barrow some 170 paces east of Hunter's Lodge Inn, we pointed out the most remarkable sites within view to our Yorkshire friend, especially Ring-in-the-Mire. After entering the carriage, we descended Honiton Hill homewards but turned out of our way to give him a look at Sand, he being connected with the Huyshes, the owners. We entered the house and garden, and having satisfied our curiosity, we drove back through Sidbury to Sidmouth. (*Diary*).

No news from the Crimea. *Saturday October 28.* Great anxiety exists at the present moment for news from Sebastopol. The allied forces are said to amount to 120 000 men, though all are not in the Crimea. The siege operations commenced on the 9th and it was thought that by the 17th two hundred guns of large calibre would be ready to open fire upon the devoted city. It seems scarcely possible that the Russians can withstand this, and yet the nation naturally feels anxious. By this time we ought to have had ample intelligence of the proposed attack and some persons are loudly complaining that news should be so long coming. A Sidmouth woman named Hill stopped me the other day to enquire if I knew the result of the battle as one of her dear boys, who enlisted last June in Sidmouth unknown to her, was out there. I did not know her before but am frequently asked questions about the war, for some people fancy that the gentry by reading the papers have superior advantages in picking up information. I have not seen the name of Edward Hill of the 95th among the killed or wounded, so I hope he is safe. She had heard that another Sidmouth man had got through the battle quite safe. Howard Elphinstone, son of Captain Elphinstone of Livonia, is

54/10/21-1. *Two barrows, Ottery East Hill.* (Diary)

54/10/21-2. *Mr. Heineken's apomecometer.* (Diary)

54/11/4-1. Gunboat design
(Diary)

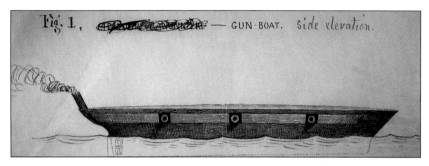

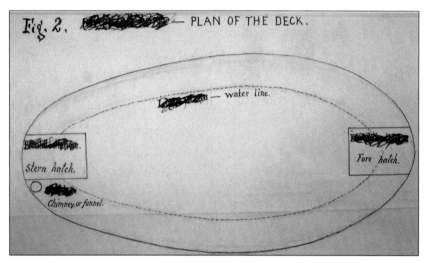

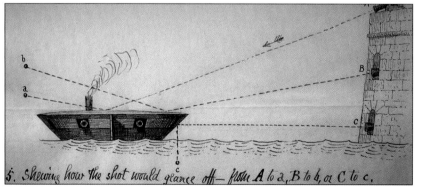

now before Sebastopol in the Engineers. These are the only Sidmouth people out there that I know of. There are however about twenty Sidmouth men in the Baltic and Black Sea fleets. (*Diary*).

Gunboat. *Saturday November 4.* Had lunch with the Elphinstones and then had a private confab with the Captain on the subject of my gunboat, some further particulars about which I am soon to send to the Government. (*Diary*). *Hutchinson took a great interest in ships but this entry is the only indication that he actively worked on an innovative design for an iron-clad warship, some eight years before the first was commissioned. It seems he was prepared to test his design by steering it through the fleet under bombardment. Many years later the plans for the gunboat turned up in an old portfolio and are included here (see January 19, 1886 for a brief description).*

Guy Fawkes Day 1854. *Sunday November 5.* Gunpowder Plot. Hoisted my flag, though *being Sunday* the noisy demonstrations are reserved for tomorrow. (*Diary*).

Monday November 6. And a noise I made, as well as other folks. (*Diary*).

Patriotic Fund. *Friday November 10.* Today a meeting was held in the Market House on the subject of the 'Patriotic Fund' for the benefit of the widows and orphans of those who fall in the Russian war. Sent down my flag which was fastened up against the wall at the end of the room, where it made a very good background. The speeches made were very appropriate and the room was filled with company. It is expected on sufficient grounds that about or nearly £300 will be collected in this parish and neighbourhood. I was asked whether I would assist in collecting from the inhabitants, but I said I would rather be excused if they could do without me, though I would not shirk a disagreeable duty if requisite. They did excuse me. Some people are fond of running from house to house gossiping but I am not. To thrust myself into half the houses in the parish and ask for money, even for a good purpose, is most repugnant to my feelings. But I was let off. (*Diary*).

More from the Crimea. *Saturday November 11. Hutchinson regularly recorded news from the Crimea into his Diary. The vicissitudes and suffering of the Army there was causing considerable concern to the population at home.* The accounts from the seat of war are most trying. The siege of Sebastopol is going on slowly, we hope surely, but the task is a most arduous one and the frequent encounters with the enemy are harassing and diminishing the troops of the Allies. News is sought after with the greatest anxiety. Two curious circumstances are related to have occurred in the siege batteries before Sebastopol. One was that a cannon ball fired by the Russians entered the mouth of an empty gun in the English lines and stuck fast about one third down the bore. This strange event caused much amusement amongst the soldiers. The other was somewhat similar but even more remarkable if possible. The besiegers were on the point of firing a shell when another shell fired by the Russians entered the mouth of the piece. Thus charged, and on the point of going off, the two shells exploded together inside the howitzer (or whatever it was), killing and wounding most of those who were standing near. Strange chances were these. (*Diary*).

Gun carriage. *Thursday December 7.* The carriage for my gun (see August 24, 1854) is at last so far completed as to have it home. Richards made the wheels and woodwork, Coles the elevating screw, Burgoyne the rest of the ironwork and Hayman bouched the touchhole (*added the copper lining to the vent*). The browning of the elevating screw box and giving the carriage its last coat of paint I mean to do myself. A brief history of it is contained in the following inscription I recently engraved on a brass plate and which I mean to screw on the tail-piece. 'This gun was captured from a pirate on the east coast of Borneo, Jan. 29, 1845, by Lieut. J. Roberton, H.M.S. Samarang (Capt. Sir Ed. Belcher, Bart.), on whose death it went to his father, Col. Roberton; on the death of the latter it passed to his nephew P. O. Hutchinson, 1854'. (*Diary*). *An interesting account of the capture of the gun written by Lieut. Roberton to the Captain is copied into the Diary.*

Concert performance. *Monday December 10.* This afternoon I went into Exeter with Mr. Heineken and Mr. H. Johnson *and* played the horn at the Oratorio, the Mount of Olives and part of the Creation. Mr. Heineken played double bass *and* Mr. Johnson was among the audience. Did not get in till nearly dusk, for we stopped on the top of Aylesbeare Hill to examine the two barrows planted with

54/11/4-2. *Two ships. Sketch, not from reality.* (DRO, Z19/2/8A/130)

firs that lie about a hundred yards on the north of the road. However, before the concert I also found time to go and see the works at Bodley's Iron Foundry. We had a moonlit night returning but did not get home till three hours after midnight. (*Diary*).

Laurel for the victors. *Thursday December 21.* All England, especially the ladies of England, now having nearly finished making the flannel shirts, 'mitts' and sundry other articles of warm clothing for our brave soldiers shivering there in the Crimea outside the walls of Sebastopol, it struck me that as they were prepared to send out so many things of which the Army was in need, I myself would send something which it so well deserved. The victors of Alma, Balaclava and Inkermann, thought I, merited a wreath of laurel, so a crown of laurel I made. I enclosed it in a light box together with some verses and sent the whole by post to London, to the agents there. (*Diary*). *The panegyric addressed 'To the Army of the Crimea', perhaps not one of Hutchinson's best compositions, is copied into the Diary.*

Gun re-bored. *Saturday December 30.* My brass gun, which I sent to Bodley's Iron Factory in Exeter a few days ago to be more perfectly bored, was sent back today. Where this gun was originally made is hard to say, though many of my friends have offered their opinions on this point. Some think it Malacca, some China and others Manilla. The pirates who last had it are not likely to have been able to cast such a thing as a piece of ordnance. The gun had been cast with a block or core which had afterwards been removed, leaving the bore very irregular. The drill however, will remove the irregularities and make it true. (*Diary*).

New Years Day, 1855. *Monday January 1.* New Years Day. I wonder what this year will bring, a thought suggested by the events of the year past, which to me has been the most eventful year within memory. For England to be at war is a thing quite new to me. No doubt we have made the most egregious blunders. Never have troops suffered as ours have before Sebastopol for want of sufficient food, clothing and shelter. All the papers are full of this subject. As we have been at peace ever since the Battle of Waterloo, we are novices in the art of fighting but great efforts are now being made to retrieve past mistakes. (*Diary*).

First outing with the gun. *Wednesday January 3.* Went out with the brass gun for the first time to try its new carriage and capabilities. Pushed it up to Cotmaton and showed it to Captain Carslake, who was much amused at my new toy. (*Diary*).

East Budleigh Church. . *Saturday January 13.* Went with Mr. Heineken to East Budleigh *where Heineken had some business to attend to.* We then went into the church where a new organ was in course of erection. Whilst Mr. Heineken went up and tried the organ, I made a copy of the tablet erected to the memory of Mrs. Frances Elizabeth Yeates, and then made a rubbing of the slab in the middle of the nave over the vault of Johanna Ralegh, I believe the mother of Sir Walter Ralegh, or Rawleigh. The inscription on it is curious, in as much as some of the letters are upside down, the rest being the right way. Copied the date 1537 on the woodwork of the pew close by on the north, and lastly went round and admired the old carving on the ends of the open seats, and copied Roger Vowles' slab in the south aisle. Mr. Heineken and myself then walked to Hayes Barton where Sir Walter Rawleigh was born, taking the way through Hayes Wood where we lost ourselves, and returning by the road. We got back to Sidmouth by seven and I passed the evening at his house. (*Diary*).

scale—one inch to a foot.

55/1/13. *Inscriptions in East Budleigh church.* Copied January 13, 1855. (DRO, Z19/2/8E/45)

Gun practise on the promenade. *Tuesday January 16.* Had a trial with my gun on the promenade *and* fired iron shot out to sea. Made 'ducks and drakes' along the water, which was calm, much to the amusement of a number of people who were looking on. (*Diary*).

Thursday January 18. Gun and self went to call on the Rev. Kestell Cornish of Salcombe Hill. He fired two shots in front of the house. (*Diary*).

Friday January 26. Being a fine calm day I went out with the gun, taking Edward Slessor and Brine (cadets in the Artillery who are off again for Woolwich next Wednesday) and we made 'a jolly row' in the Fort Field and on the beach. (*Diary*).

Wreck under High Peak. *Friday February 2.* Walked along the beach to Picket Rock under High Peak Hill to see the wreck. Last Wednesday morning in the snowstorm and before daylight, a bark of 800 tons ran upon the rocks about 100 yards on the Sidmouth side of Picket Rock. The crew, about twenty-four men, reached the shore in safety, but they must have suffered much from the cold. It

55/2/2. Wreck of a vessel on the rocks at the foot of High Peak Hill, near Sidmouth. February 2, 1855. (DRO, Z19/2/8E/47)

is not clear how she met with this fate.   Even allowing that she could not see where she was going on account of thick weather and snow, still, one might have supposed that the lead or the sound of breakers would have warned her of her danger if a good lookout had been kept.   However, in merchant ships great carelessness and neglect of duty too often exist, as I myself have seen.   The rocks presented a strange scene, strewed as they were with spars, broken pieces of cabin furniture, cushions, ropes, sails, iron bolts, planks and timbers and splinters of all sizes and shapes.   The crew were doing what they could to carry away their clothes and other property and several score sailors and other persons from Sidmouth were there assisting in collecting and removing what they could, it then being low water.   One person told me that the crew of the vessel mistook High Peak Hill with the snow on it for a cloud and thus ran upon destruction.   The general impression however, is that blame attaches elsewhere.   She was insured.   I heard she was laden with guano from Callao to London.   Cold as it was, I managed to get a sketch, which I coloured when I reached home. (*Diary*).

Government falls. *Monday February 12.*   Made a respirator of a new design, of tin and zinc wire.   The plan is to carry it in the mouth instead of outside *it*, by which contrivance the unsightly appearance is got rid of.   The breath is drawn in through a wire grating, several times reduplicated, as a segar flusher draws in the air.

A pretty to-do there has been in Parliament during the last fortnight.   The old ministry with the Earl of Aberdeen at its head has gone out and Lord Palmerston has succeeded.   The country has been disgusted and highly indignant at the gross want of management in the conduct of the war, and deeply sympathises with the unheard-of sufferings which our brave soldiers have endured in the Crimea in consequence.   Neither will the country be satisfied until the Commander-in-Chief, Lord Raglan, be recalled from the Crimea. (*Diary*).

Thursday February 15. Today there was a sale on the beach of the remains of the unfortunate vessel that was wrecked last week under High Peak. (*Diary*).

Icy weather. *Friday February 16.*   Our winter has been the coldest that ever I remember.   For weeks it has frozen in my bedroom, but last night it was more intense than ever. The frozen water in my jug split it and my water bottle cracked into a dozen pieces. Since the cold set in so severely, I have been accustomed to gnaw my toothbrushes before using them in order to crush the ice and soften the hair, and having hitherto used cold water to wash and shave, it is time to take to warm. Last night even the chamber utensil was frozen, a most unusual thing. (*Diary*).

Mamma unwell. *Thursday March 1.* The sudden change in the weather has caused a great deal of sickness. Mamma, who has had one or two bilious attacks in past years, has been losing her appetite for the last day or two and remained in bed today. (*Diary*). *At first nothing serious was apprehended, but over the next few days Mrs. Hutchinson's condition gradually deteriorated. She died peacefully in bed the following Monday and was buried in Sidmouth churchyard close to her husband.*

RUBBING.

THE WOOD CUT.

55/3/27. *Bactrian coin.* (Hist. of Sid. I,96)

Bactrian coin. *Tuesday March 27.* Engraved on wood Mr. Heineken's Bactrian coin, for an article in the *Sidmouth Directory.* (*Diary*). It was found on Sidmouth sea beach opposite Marine House near the chapel of the Independents, in or about January 1851. Obverse: the king's head, sceptre in hand. Reverse: The king on horseback. Ancient Bactria was on the eastern side of the Caspian Sea and is now called Chorasan, Samarcand being the chief town. My account of this coin and a woodcut of it appeared in Harvey's Sidmouth Directory, April 5, 1855. It may be surmised that either Phoenician or Greek traders may have brought it to England. (*History of Sidmouth I, 96*).

Sidmouth Miscellany. *Monday April 2.* The *Sidmouth Miscellany,* a local publication to come out monthly, has made its appearance. The first number is well enough, but it is impossible that the town can long sustain such a publication. (*Diary*). *As Hutchinson correctly guessed, the newspaper died of neglect in June after the third issue.*

Gardening invention. *Friday April 13. We are informed that Mr. Peter Orlando Hutchinson has received a letter of thanks from the Horticultural Society of London for a lately invented instrument to be employed in the culture of strawberries, which he presented to the Society a short time ago. (Contemporary newspaper cutting).* The instrument resembled a large punch such as is used for making gun cards. By pressing the cross handles on top, all the runners are cut off at the same length with great rapidity. Where strawberries are much cultivated such a simple instrument ought to be of use. Whether it is known beyond the garden of the Horticultural Society, I don't know. (*Diary*).

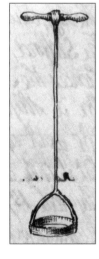

55/4/13. *Strawberry cutter.* (Diary)

Lampreys and Porch House, Sidford. *Thursday April 19.* Took a walk to Sidford with my cousin Anne Stares, going by way of the Salcombe fields and so on up the river and all through the fields near the 'Byes'. We saw some boys in the river catching lampreys, or lamprey eels as they called them. I had never seen these fish before. There is a popular notion that they have got nine eyes, the vulgar probably mistaking the breathing holes in the place of gills on either side of the head and neck. They were about five or six inches long and have suckers instead of mouths, that is mouths like those of the sturgeon. The boys, who were fishermen's sons, said they used them for bait at sea.

In Sidford we went to look at 'Porch House', the house where King Charles II is said to have slept one night whilst looking for a ship at Lyme and elsewhere along the coast to effect his escape (*see May 27, 1851*). We went upstairs into the room (where I have been before) but it is in a sad state. A number of cocks and hens are kept there now. The date 1574 is on the outside of the building. The whole place seems to be getting very rickety.. (*Diary*). *The accompanying sketch of Porch House is dated nearly three months later.*

London again. *Monday April 23.* Left Sidmouth for London to prove Mamma's will and do other matters of business. (*Diary*). *In London Hutchinson worked at the Record Office in the Tower again, copying ancient documents referring to Sidmouth, but there were more than he expected and he decides he will have to come again.*

55/4/19. *House in the village of Sidford, near Sidmouth, in which Charles the Second is said to have slept one night. The room he occupied is at the nearest corner, where the figure at the window is. The date 1574 is cut on the chimney. Coloured on the spot July 9, 1855.* (DRO, Z19/2/8E/53)

Return journey. *Tuesday May 8.* Returned from London to Sidmouth *but* met with an adventure at the outset. Having called a cab and got my baggage into it to go to Paddington Station, scarcely had the man driven a dozen paces when the horse sprawled on the flagged pavement. He either *slipped* on the smooth stone or he had been so overworked, like most London horses, *that he* fell from exhaustion. Several people came to render assistance to try to get him up again and very soon a crowd collected. After much ineffectual labour, he was unharnessed on the ground and the shafts of the cab withdrawn. I was grieved to find that the horse was to be pitied, since his refusal to rise was due to want of strength. The driver, seeing it was a desperate case, told me I might as well have another cab, *and on* this I alighted and sent for one, leaving the unfortunate animal on the ground apparently on the point of death. London horses are too often driven till they drop. (*Diary*).

Tidwell. *Thursday June 7.* Went to Budleigh Salterton with Mr. Heineken, he having business there connected with his houses. On our way we went a little out of our way to find the veritable spring of Tidwell or Tide-well, a spring that is spoken of by most of the historians of this county. It is opposite Tidwell Farmhouse and nearly opposite Tidewell House. The spring, a copious rill, issues from the ground, and a rough stone arch has been built over it. The water, from neglect, now stands as a marshy swamp, though once it formed fishponds. In the orchard on the east side of the swamp, there are traces of raised terraces running along the margin of the water. I made a coloured sketch of the scene. Risdon mentions it, Sir W. Pole gives a genealogy of the owners of the estate, and Westlake records that the spring is sufficiently warm never to freeze in the coldest weather and that it ebbs and flows. I may add that a belief in these alleged facts still exists in the neighbourhood, as I was told it in East Budleigh and at Tidwell.

In the farmhouse there are some pieces of curious old oak carving, a coat of arms having a shield of pretence on it (Arscot and St. Clair?), the coloured figure of a man some eighteen inches high used as a corbel in the apartment on the left side of the entrance, etc. Also, there is a curious jug having the date 1793 (I think) on it, by which the unwary drinker pours the liquor onto his bosom through some small holes round the rim but which the wary drinker stops with his fingers. I tried to buy this from the farmer's wife but she would not sell it. (*Diary*).

55/6/7. *The spring of Tidwell in the parish of Budleigh, Devon. In the Cartulary of Otterton Priory, under date about 1260, the word is Todville. It is two or three miles from the sea. Sketched on the spot June 7, 1855.* (DRO, Z19/2/8E/49)

Salcombe Church, Branscombe Church and a stone coffin. *Friday June 22.* Started with Mr. Heineken on an exploring expedition over Salcombe Hill. For the first time made use of my new leather bag with the brass clasp, just made in Sidmouth according to my own design. Never remember seeing the atmosphere clearer to the westward. The Babbicombe quarries and the whole coast towards Torbay were easily seen with the naked eye, and the glass showed the houses and every tree quite plainly. In the village of Salcombe we examined the church, particularly remarking the band of carving outside and under the east window, also the cross over *it*, both evidently very old, and the tablet outside the south wall of the chancel on which one of the Garter King-at-Arms is referred to. Inside, since the restoration and repair of the church some five years ago, what most strikes the eye is the pointed arch between the nave and the chancel, the Norman columns in the nave now divested of their whitewash, the tower arch and the Norman font. The transition from the Norman period into the Pointed is here discernible. There are several monuments to the Mitchells of Thorn close by. The east window, given by Miss Elizabeth Walcott of Knowle now Mrs. Goddard (her initials are on it), and the window at the east end of the south aisle, erected as a memorial to the Cornishs, are *both* handsome.

We then took a look at Thorn farm, the ceiling of the entrance hall of which is divided into square compartments by carved oak joists. In the panels are bosses and shields each bearing a fleur-de-lis, but these do not appear to be armorial bearings. Some parts of the building bear marks of age and a chapel was once attached to it, traces of which still exist. Some of the Mitchells of Thorn were buried in front of the west entrance to the tower, an altar tomb remaining, the dates beginning in 1611. On the north side of this altar tomb and close to it, is *another* of the Cornishs of Salcombe House, and inserted into the south side of it is a piece of stone with part of an old inscription (older than most others in the churchyard) said to have belonged to a Mitchell tomb. The person referred to on this fragment seems to have attained the age of 104 years.

Leaving Salcombe, we pushed on to Dunscombe where tradition says there was once a priory, but persons who profess to be better informed declare that this tradition has no foundation in truth. The oldest part of the farmhouse, some years since burnt down, shows the remains of windows with stout stone mullions somewhat in the ecclesiastical style, but these are said to have been only parts of a substantial private residence. After making a circuit to pass Slade, we proceeded through Weston and then made an attempt to find a stone coffin lying buried in one of the fields by the roadside, to which we had been directed. Having taken an iron rod, about two and a half feet long, we thrust it into the ground in many places to feel for the coffin, but not knowing the exact spot, or even the field, we gave up the search in despair. We therefore resolved to go on to Branscombe to see John Parrott, the sexton, who knew all about it, or so we had been informed. Before entering Branscombe, we stopped to look at Berry (Bury) Farm, reputed to be haunted by the lady who lies in the said coffin.

55/6/22-1. Branscombe church, slab with cross and inscription. (Diary)

55/6/22-2. Branscombe church, Wadham tomb. (Diary)

55/6/22-3. Branscombe church, Holcombe (?) tomb. (Diary)

55/6/22-4. Shield of Smith of Exeter and Illminster. (Diary)

The first cluster of houses on entering Branscombe from the west, is locally called 'The Dean', some supposing that the Deans of Exeter had a residence here, but Lysons calls it the 'village of Dean'. Branscombe church and tower are of great antiquity (at Salcombe the church is older than the tower). The tower bears the distinguishing Norman features – square, without buttresses or battlements and a surrounding corbel table. A similar corbel table is seen under the eaves of the south side of the church. The staircase turret on the north side of the tower is circular, its octagonal summit evidently a subsequent addition. The oldest inscription in the church is on a slab about four feet long in the floor of the south transept. Under a cross on its pedestal are the words ORATE PRO ANIMA JOH - - -. Near this, and under the window, was formerly an upright sculptured slab, but as it kept out the light it was removed to the north transept opposite the left hand part of the wall. This bears two male kneeling figures, said to be father and son but the coats of arms over their heads are not the same. The first here annexed is over the left hand or oldest figure, the reputed father, behind whose back are portrayed ? children. The wife's arms are not here copied. The second escutcheon which I here give is over the head of the right hand or younger male figure, and he seems to have been a Wadham, the Wadham arms according to Lysons having been a chevron between three roses. On the other side of the end of the north transept, there is another tablet sculptured with armorial bearings but suffering much with damp, as the whole church is. The husband's bearing is a chevron between three blackamoor heads for Holcombe of Hole, *and* the wife's is three lambs. In the churchyard near the south-west end is an ancient stone coffin lying on its face *and* I put my hand under it to feel that it was hollowed. This is said to have been brought, some three or four generations ago, by a person named Payton from Budleigh Salterton (more probably East Budleigh) who alleged that it had belonged to his ancestors. Descendants of this person live in this neighbourhood and some of them are lace makers in Sidmouth. The coffin measures seven feet long, two feet two inches wide in the middle and about a foot high. A few yards south of it almost buried in the grass lies a block of stone about six feet long and fifteen inches square, brought as the sexton phrased it 'from our ebb', meaning from Branscombe beach between ebb and flow of the tide or high and low water. He could not say why it was brought *here*. Some five yards north-west from this block and near the west end hedge of the churchyard, is a massive altar tomb almost buried in the ground except the top slab. Around the edge is cut, on the east end, north side and west end, the following inscription: 1586 IOHN TAYLER BURIED THE X APRILL. There is a slab now leaning against the outside south wall of the church but which once belonging to a tomb, the verses on which have often attracted attention. The lines annexed which I copied from it are somewhat like the utterance of a professed wrestler. The stone is inscribed to one Joseph Braddich who died June 27, 1673.

> Strong and in labour
> Suddenly he reels,
> Death came from behind him
> And struck up his heels
> Such sudden strokes
> Surviving mortals Bid ye
> Stand on your watch
> And to be also ready

Leaving the churchyard we went to look at an old house called 'The Clergy'. It lies about fifty yards north-east of the church across the road. There is a tradition, or a superstition, that some of the priests or other clergy connected with the church before the period of the Reformation occupied this building *and* Mrs. Somers, the chatty landlady, showed us all over it. Immediately inside the entrance a large trap door can be pushed up. The space above has no communication at present with the rest of the house *but* is lighted by a loophole through the wall over the door. In one of the bedrooms are two bas-reliefs (there was once a third, larger, on the ceiling) of the coat of arms annexed. The walls in some places, especially in the lower apartments, are three feet thick. A belief exists that there is another house under this one, and in support of this opinion Mrs. Somers stamped on the stone floor in several places to let us hear how hollow the sound

was.   She also added that her husband had dreamt 'a hundred times' that the
entrance to this underground house is by a flight of steps still existing beneath the
soil immediately outside the dairy window.   Perhaps there may be some cellars
still undiscovered.   (*Diary*).   *In his manuscript account of 'The Clergy', Hutchinson
elaborates slightly and adds a sketch:* There is a sort of fortified doorway.
Immediately over the entrance is a slit or loophole through which arrows or other
missiles could have been shot.   Over the door and under the loophole inside there
is a trapdoor which lifts up, so that if an enemy forced his way in he might be
speared from above.   There is a belief that some chamber exists under the dairy
floor, as it sounds hollow.   In one of the upper chambers towards the west part of
the building there is a small hole in the wall down which, if a pebble is dropped,
it is heard to descend a great way.   Tradition says this house was occupied by some
of the clergy of the neighbouring parish church.   (*Soc. of Antiq. Ms. 250, p.26*).
*These features are no longer visible, though perhaps still exist, in the ancient building now
known as Church Living just across the road from Branscombe Church.   A short distance
further on is the Blacksmith's Shop, said to be the only working thatched forge left in the
country, looking very much as it did in Hutchinson's sketch, undated but probably done in
the 1840s.*

55/6/22-5.   *Doorway and loophole at The Clergy, Branscombe.*
(Soc. of Antiq. Ms. 250)

55/6/22-6.   *Blacksmith's shop,
Branscombe, Devon.*   (Not
dated)   (DRO, Z19/2/8D/23)

We now left Branscombe, returning back to the field, taking the sexton John
Parrot with us.   It is necessary to enter from the road by the gate A, and then pass
through the hedge at B to reach the coffin at the east end of the field called
Littlecombe Three Acres.   The site of the coffin as indi-
cated by Parrott is at 43 feet from the east hedge of the
field and immediately within the hedge bounding the
road.   At about 200 yards from the entrance at A, along
the road towards Sidmouth, there is a pond of water
under the hedge, and this will serve as a guide to the
locality.   We probed the ground at the place pointed out
and were much deceived if we did not come down upon
the object sought.   If so, the upper edges of the sides were not more than three
or four inches from the surface.   I longed to cut up the turf at once, but John
Parrott warned me to desist, as it was a grass field and the man who rented it was
a 'queer customer'.   His story was this.   About sixty-five or six years ago, when

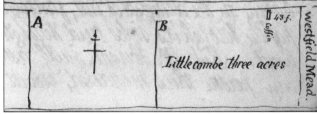

55/6/22-7.   *Site of stone coffin.*
(Diary)

there was a way through by which the farmers used to convey their produce, a man was taking a cart; that on passing over this spot one of the cart wheels sunk in and made an opening; that the man who drove the cart, being attracted by this circumstance *and* having examined the hole, thought he had discovered the hiding place of a 'crock of gold'; that he thrust his arm therein to secure the treasure but was much surprised when he pulled out a skull; that this skull was taken to the vicarage at Branscombe; that some years afterwards, when John Parrott himself was a boy (he told us he was now 65 on the 17th), he took out of this coffin some finger bones, a collar bone and two or three ribs; that he put them back again; that a Mrs. Chick (ancestors of the Chicks of Sidmouth) who then rented the field, wanted to have the coffin destroyed and offered to give it to him, but he would have nothing to do with the matter; and that the coffin and its contents have not been disturbed since.   He further told us that the common belief in the neighbourhood is that some woman was murdered at Berry Farm, was buried here and that her ghost still haunts a certain apartment in the farmhouse, appearing in the form of a woman having on an antiquated hat fastened by a long pin passing through the hair over the crown of her head.   But Mr. Heineken justly asked whether it is likely that any person thus murdered would have been so carefully interred in a stone coffin?   And secondly, that if a body was buried here in the regular way, whether it is not likely that other coffins might not be found if searched for?   It is a matter for surprise that any evidence of interment should be discovered in so remote a locality *and* so far from any habitation.   Three fields off towards the south-west there is a barn, but we have no evidence to prove that this was ever an inhabited building or that any burial ground existed there.   Berry Farm is the nearest house, and that may be half a mile. (*Diary*).

Death of Rumley.   *Wednesday July 4.*   Received an 'Adelaide Observer' newspaper from my brother, in which the death of Rumley my brother-in-law is announced.   Poor Fellow!   He suffered much for more than three years from rheumatic gout caught from getting a chill, having got out of bed and gone only in light clothing to render assistance, his dray and bullocks and driver having been overturned. (*Diary*).

Search for Belbury Castle.   *Friday July 6.*   Went out on an exploring expedition with Mr. Heineken, chiefly to try and find Belbury Castle.   Devonshire writers mention this as 'commanding the vale of the Otter' and some I think say on Ottery East Hill.   This last we took.   We drove out to Sidford up High Street, and mounted the hill above Buscombe.   Then we went north along the ridge enjoying a most splendid view till we got to the point of Gittesham Hill opposite Hembury Fort.   This we thought the most likely place, but first we selected a beautiful spot on the slope of the hill where we could look down upon half the county and here we took our lunch.   This ended, we plunged into the plantations leaving the man with the carriage.   In these plantations there are many deep trenches and high banks, and several times we fancied we had come to the object of our search, but a few paces more showed us that they were apparently only gravel pits.   All round the point of Gittesham Hill on both sides of the road we prosecuted our hot, thirsty, wearisome and entangled search, finding plenty of irregularities certainly but no symmetrical earthwork.   We met a lad in the wood who told us that there was a heap not far from where we had been in which persons had once dug for treasure, and I suppose this was a barrow believed to contain, as usual, 'a crock of gold'.   Whortleberries and wild raspberries abounded in some places.   Going up this hill in despair, we drove to Putt's Corner, or Hunter's Lodge, and then turned back northwards along the Honiton road and made an equally laborious search around the point of the hill over Combe House.   Here however, and much to our surprise as well as disappointment, we were equally unsuccessful, for we felt certain that Belbury Castle must be somewhere in this neighbourhood.   None of the writers who mention it seemed to know where it is, or was.   They describe it as having one enclosing trench of an oval figure, measuring, I think, 400 feet by 200.   The first syllable Bel, or Belus, may indicate great antiquity.   *Strangely, Hutchinson seems to have forgotten about an article he had read some years before (see November 22, 1848).   In 'Nooks and Corners of Devon' (Exeter Flying*

55/7/6-1.   *Great Stone, Putt's Corner.*   (Hist. of Sid. I,119)

Post for November 16 and 23, 1848), W.P.Shortt described in some detail both the camp and its location. Eventually the two friends found the site for which we have been enquiring for a dozen years *on May 31, 1861.*

We returned to Putt's Corner and halted whilst I sketched the large stone that lies at the crossroad. There are some traditions connected with this stone which I cannot now recall. One person told us today that formerly someone used to bury his money under it 'by a hundred pounds at a time', at which an old woman added 'and I once seed a half-crown and a shilling pulled out from under thick stone'. How these coins got to the base of the stone is hard to say unless perhaps some traveller sitting upon it dropped them, but this fact is quite enough to raise the belief that treasure lies concealed here. *The 'Witche's Stone', probably an old boundary stone, has been moved slightly out of its original position in recent years and reset in front of the Hare and Hounds Inn.* From this spot we went eastwards towards Roncombe Gate, passing the scene of our operations on the 25th of last July. Passing over Broad Down we examined all the barrows we could see and laid down the positions of two or three not on the Ordnance map. We reached Sidmouth before nine and I supped at Mr. Heineken's. *(Diary).*

Leasing Coburg Terrace. *Tuesday July 10.* Signed the agreement letting the house, No. 4 Coburg Terrace, with the garden but excluding the field, to Captain and Mrs. Hamilton for three, six, nine or twelve months. Rent £70 per annum. *(Diary).*

Leaving Sidmouth. *Thursday July 19.* Having let the house in Coburg Terrace for a year, I left today. Passed several hours in Exeter. It so happened that the judges came in today and I had an opportunity of seeing their arrival, and of being much disappointed. From what I had heard of coaches, javelin men and cavalcades, I expected something striking. So it was, only striking for its meanness. First there were two men on horseback looking like grooms and carrying trumpets, then a double file of awkward men carrying sticks tipped with a bit of metal – these were the imposing javelin men. Then a private carriage, then a coach and four with two big-wigs, and lastly a string of farmers on horseback in two rows wearing different costumes and riding horses of different colours and sizes taken rough from their

55/7/6-2. Block of stone on Honiton Hill at Putt's Corner of Hunters Lodge, concerning which several traditions are current in the neighbourhood – as how the witches used to sacrifice their victims on it. Sketched July 6, 1855. (DRO, Z19/2/8E/51)

ploughs. This was all. I went on to Dawlish and found my cousin Miss Roberton in Belmont Villa, one of the new villas on the east cliff. (*Diary*).

55/7/20. Practising guns, a six pounder and a thirty-two pounder, at the 'Battery' on the Warren, opposite Exmouth. Sketched there July 20, 1855.
(DRO, Z19/2/8E/55)

Target practise on the Warren. *Friday July 20.* Walked out to the Warren, near Exmouth, to see the gun practice. The men are exercised for six weeks and the period is now nearly over. They are taken from the preventive stations and I recognised three Sidmouth men there. First there was practising with a six-pound brass field piece at targets pitched on the sandbanks at 300 yards. These targets were knocked to pieces and most of the shot buried in the sand. These they generally dig out and use again. After the firing was over, I walked to the spot and picked up one of the balls, asking leave to take it away as a momento. This was granted so I shall send it to Sidmouth. The men then exercised a 32-pound ship gun in the 'battery', as they call the wooden house, the back and sides of which are removed when exercising. They fired at a target pitched on the bar at the mouth of the river, about half a mile off. First, I stood behind the breech of the gun but the smoke so concealed the target that I could not see the effect of the shot. So I then went out on the sandbank nearest the sea about 70 yards in advance of the battery, and at an angle of 40 or 50 degrees to the right of it. The concussion here was rather strong, and the sound which the ball made in rushing by struck me as peculiarly viscous in its tone . . . After this I had the curiosity to try what the effect would be if I let the ball pass over my head. I therefore, whilst they were loading and unknown to them, got down beyond the sandbank and placed myself in a line between the gun and the target, crouching down low enough to be safe from accidents. As soon as I heard the report there was a violent noise, between a hiss and a scream, close above my head as the mass of iron passed – it was some three or four yards but it seemed quite close – and on looking towards the target I distinctly saw the ball for half a second or so. It went through the target and was the only shot that hit it all the afternoon. Lastly, I stood at about three or four yards abreast of the muzzle of the gun, and here the concussion was the strongest and the noise made my head ring all day. (*Diary*).

Leaving for France. *Thursday July 26.* Left Dawlish for France. I wish to go over to Avranches again to search among the manuscripts formerly belonging to St. Michael's Mount, Normandy. I took the rail at 11.20 and got to Plymouth, where I obtained a passport and paid five shillings for it. Took the steamer at 6.00 for Jersey, after having walked about Plymouth visiting the Citadel and other places. (*Diary*). *Dissatisfied with the result of his previous investigations in France (see June 2, 1852) Hutchinson was returning to make a more extensive search in the libraries of Avranches and St. Lo for any documents referring to Sidmouth. After some success, he took a leisurely tour through the cities of northern France before returning to England eight months later.*

1856

Return to England. *Thursday March 13.* After nearly eight months residence in France, I left today for England. I would willingly have taken over many pretty things, either for my own use or as presents for my friends, but I selected only a few - a half dozen of the thick and heavy coffee cups and saucers such as are used in restaurants so different from our own, a tray of glass gilt with two decanters and a dozen glasses, two dozen iron four-pronged forks for the kitchen, etc., etc. (*Diary*). *The journey was not a pleasant one, as the passage across to Folkstone was very disagreeable and by some mistake my luggage was left behind in Paris. But Hutchinson was in no hurry to return home and stayed on in London to sort out various financial matters and to continue his Sidmouth researches at the Record Office. In spare moments he visited the National Gallery, Crystal Palace, British Museum, etc. Whilst in London, he records that a treaty was finally signed with Russia formerly ending the Crimean War.*

Elizabethan map of Devon coast. *Tuesday July 1.* Traced off and copied part of a map of the coast of Devon made in 1588, including Sidmouth and Torbay. The map exhibits a plan for fortifying the coast of Devonshire and Cornwall at the time Queen Elizabeth apprehended attack from foreign enemies. (Diary). *The colours are as in the original map, and the accompanying sketch, an imaginative enlargement showing the coastal defences around Sidmouth, form the frontpiece to Volume III of the History of Sidmouth.*

Jury summons. *Wednesday July 16.* Hearing that my tenant in Sidmouth intends to leave the house on the 20th (the year's end), I go home. But I have also received a summons to appear at the Castle of Exeter at ten o'clock on Wednesday the 23rd on a special jury case at the assizes, the first time I have been summoned. Here are two reasons for going down. (*Diary*).

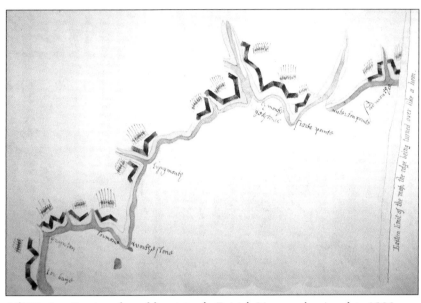

56/7/1-1. *Portion of an old map in the British Museum, bearing date 1588.* (Hist. of Sid. III,67b)

56/7/1-2. *View representing the town of Sidmouth as proposed to have been fortified in 1588, against an attack from the ships of the Spanish Armada.* (Hist. of Sid. III, frontpiece)

Home for tea. *Wednesday July 23. Going via Dorchester and stopping off in Exeter to do his duty as a juryman, Hutchinson finally reached home.* Left for Sidmouth and got home to Coburg Terrace for tea. My cat Louis knew me after a year's absence. We had tea together and he held out his right paw to have it buttered, an accomplishment I taught him before I left and which he had not forgotten. (*Diary*).

Sidmouth Choral Society. *Sunday August 31.* During the month I have been settling down, seeing my friends, been out to Sidbury and perceived that old Court Hall has been half pulled down and rebuilt during my absence. On going in and seeing the Hunts, I was told that it had become so rickety that it was necessary to rebuild the southern part. I spent the evening at the vicarage with Mr. Heineken's family.

I have just been elected one of the committee of the Choral Society, a society embodied a few months ago by some musical people here, the intention being to cultivate music generally, and for singing glees, madrigals and the performance of more difficult pieces. Many of the town's people who have joined sing very well but are in a great degree ignorant of the theory and practise of music, so I have volunteered to teach any who choose to come their notes, rests, keeping time, the common chord, the seventh, flats, sharps, the different keys, and so on. Just enough in fact to enable them to sing from the sheet and have a general idea what music is. (*Diary*).

Wednesday September 10. Gave ten or twelve members of the Choral Society an hour at their notes and time this evening, before the singing began. Then we had our practise. (*Diary*).

Walk to Ladram Bay. *Monday September 15.* Walked to Ladram Bay along the beach to make a new geological examination of the cliff *and* remarked that they are somewhat changed by falling away since I was there last. Being now full moon and spring tides and so calculating the time to get to Ladram Bay by noon, I had no difficulty in getting through the natural arch. Two other new arches nearer Sidmouth have been excavated in the cliffs since my recollection. I returned over Peak Hill and examined the earthworks again. In the hedges I feasted on blackberries and found so many sloes that I filled my pockets, and brought them home to see what sort of pie they would make. (*Diary*).

Funeral custom. *Sunday September 28.* Had to conform to that disagreeable Devonshire custom which requires that on the first Sunday after a funeral, one should appear in church in one's hatband and scarf. I sat in the same pew with Frederick Tyache and the medical man Dr. Miller who were similarly attired. (*Diary*).

Rail project. *Monday September 29.* Michaelmas Day. Fine warm sun but showery weather. Attended a meeting today at the Market House to listen to statements brought forward by a Captain Moorsom, with a view to consider whether or not a rail could be made from the trunk line from Exeter, Honiton, Yeovil, etc., now in course of preparation, by means of a branch from Fairmile or Fenny Bridges to Sidmouth. Captain Moorsom's arguments were not quite satisfactory to me and therefore not altogether encouraging. A committee however was appointed, of which I am one, to examine the case and report accordingly. (*Diary*).

Saturday October 4,. Attended at two this afternoon the first meeting of the committee for the proposed railway at the Market House. It sat for two hours and a working committee was appointed to go round and canvas for shares. I excused myself from this, not liking the office to beg at people's homes. However, as a preliminary, several members of the committee present put their names down as shareholders, the shares being £10 each. Mr. Lousada of Peak named 200 for himself which amounts to £2 000 in value, Sir Henry Floyd I think 100, Sir John Claridge 50, Major Brine, myself and the bulk of the gentry 20, representing £200. (*Diary*).

Saturday October 11. Attended another railway meeting at the Town Hall. The shares are taken up very slowly. Up to this time only 890, which at £10 a share represents £8 900 whereas £24 000 are wanted. (*Diary*). *Hutchinson seems to have become more enthusiastic about the project and opposed the immediate winding up of the committee due to lack of support, but he was outvoted and the committee was disbanded. The project was however soon revived (see November 3).*

New Vicar. *Thursday October 16.* The Rev. Arthur Pardoe who married the eldest of the late Vicar's two daughters, was today inducted into the living of Sidmouth, and went through the usual ceremony of shutting himself into the church and tolling the bell. (*Diary*).

Railway project resumed. *Monday November 3.* Attended a railway meeting at the Town Hall. New arrangements were entered into but excused myself from being on the new committee. (*Diary*). *This project also came to nothing and it was not until July 6, 1874 that the branch line to Sidmouth finally opened.*

Guy Fawkes Day, 1856. *Wednesday November 5.* Had up my flag and got all the other people who have flagstaffs and flags to hoist them on all the great days as I do. I wrote out several copies of the list of the days on which they should be hoisted. The fireworks this evening were very meagre. (*Diary*).

Lecture on Normandy. *Monday December 1.* Latterly I have been busy making some large coloured drawings to illustrate my lecture on 'Normandy and the Normans', to be delivered about the middle of January in the great room of the London Inn. Also latterly making several Norman caps, hats or head-dresses, which I must get some girls to wear at my lecture to illustrate the costumes of Normandy. (*Diary*).

Thursday January 8, 1857. This evening came off my lecture on 'Normandy and the Normans'. The room was well filled, for I believe that the rumour of four girls wearing Norman caps excited the curiosity of the community and served as an invisible attraction. Though the lecture was written, I spoke the greater part of it as the subject was well in my head. It lasted about an hour and twenty minutes. I took my hearers across the Channel and amused them for some twenty minutes with descriptions, and then came to the costumes. The appearance of the girls caused great fun, and such was the curiosity that the back rows stood up on the benches to get a glimpse of them. Considering it was my first lecture, I acquitted myself as well as I had expected. A map and four large drawings were hung up further to illustrate the subject. (*Diary*).

56/12/1. Lecture on 'Normandy and the Normans', delivered in the ballroom at the London Inn, Sidmouth, January 6, 1857; illustrated by drawings and by four girls wearing Norman costumes.
(Not dated).
(DRO, Z19/2/8E/71)

1857

New Years Day 1857. *Thursday January 1.* December went out quietly enough, a few parties and Christmas games, but not many. January of the new year has come in without much ado. (*Diary*).

Visit to Mary Roberton. *Monday January 12.* Went from Sidmouth over to Dawlish to pay a visit to my cousin Mary Roberton of Belmont Villa. (*Diary*).

Another lecture. *Monday February 2. Hutchinson repeated his Normandy lecture at Dawlish about a month later but it was rather less successful.* The weather was bad, several friends disappointed me and my Norman princesses were shy and awkward. (*Diary*).

Smuggled brandy. *Sunday February 22.* There were thirty-five tubs and six flagons of French brandy seized at Woodash, near Branscombe, hidden under some straw on the premises of Farmer Bray. The magistrates fined him £630, which was reduced to £100. (*History of Sidmouth V, 161*). *Smuggling was still rife along the south-east Devon coast and the Bray family were notorious practitioners in Jack Rattenbury's league, having had more than one brush with the Preventive Officers. Bray's rather weak defence was that 'he did not know about its coming, but he declined to answer when asked whether he knew it was there'. (Exeter and Plymouth Gazette February 22, 1857). Refusing to pay even the £100 fine, he was sent to prison for six months.*

Ankern Firs. *Thursday March 5.* Went to Budleigh Salterton with Mr. Heineken. On our way we stopped at Otterton to ascend the hill on the northern side of the village, on which grows the clump of firs. These trees are called 'Ankern Firs', but I am unable to guess what the word comes from. They are planted apparently on an old tumulus and hedged round. In the face of the low cliff east of Salterton, towards the river, I observed organic remains much resembling those at Picket Rock and Sandy Cove in High Peak Hill two miles west of Sidmouth. We got back to Sidmouth before nine. (*Diary*).

Sidmouth Guide. *Thursday April 9.* Mr. Perry, one of the booksellers here, having asked me to write him a new guide book for Sidmouth and its neighbourhood, which he is anxious to bring out, I have set to work on the undertaking. As I have been nearly ten years collecting materials for a large history of this place (and which is partly written) and as I have lived here for so many years and ferreted so much about its neighbourhood, the task to me is an easy one. I can write it out at a great pace with little or no further research. The first guide book to Sidmouth I believe was the Rev. Edmund Butcher's published in 1810, which subsequently reached its fourth edition. Then came Marsh's, followed by Dr. Mogridges '*Descriptive Sketch* etc.' in 1836 and then '*The Tourists and Visitors Handbook*' 1845, no name but by the Rev. Richard Cresswell. (*Diary*).

Thursday May 21. Finished my new Sidmouth guide. It will fill about 120 or 130 pages. Indeed, the bookseller did not wish it to much exceed 100, for a large book cannot be sold for a small price, which is his desire. And I myself do not wish to say too much in this guide for fear of damaging my large History of Sidmouth, for which I have been so long collecting materials but so slow in writing it out fair. There are always so many things in hand and so many interruptions that there is no getting on. I have also finished engraving on wood some slight outline diagrams of the old camps in the neighbourhood so as to give my readers an idea of their shape. I have corrected the first proof sheet but I do not think the book will be printed for two or three months. (*Diary*). *Two days later Hutchinson left home for a general sightseeing tour of Sussex and London, returning to Sidmouth on June 20.*

Hangman's Stone. *May.* Nearly six miles E.N.E. from Sidmouth, on the Lyme road, there is a large block of stone by the roadside called Hangman's Stone. It is on the south side, where one of the lanes turns down to Bovey House. The name is down on the Ordnance Map, on the spot just above the final letter E. It is a mass of the chert conglomerate found so plentifully on these hills, planted in the earth with scarcely more than two feet of its length above the ground exposed to view. According to popular belief it obtained its name from a man having been strangled or hanged against it. The story runs to the effect that a man one night stole a sheep in one of the fields near Branscombe. In order to carry it he tied the forelegs together, and then leaning forward he placed its body on his back, with the legs round in front of his forehead. When he got to the top of the lane, feeling tired or wishing to re-adjust his burden, he sat down with his back against this stone with the sheep resting upon it. The animal now made an effort to get loose, and in its struggles shifted its legs down over the man's face and under his chin. With his back against the stone and unable to extricate himself, the weight of the sheep pressing against his throat soon served to strangle him.

It may however be remarked, that in other parts of the country there are great stones on the hills to which a similar legend attaches. It has been conjectured that instead of Hangman's Stone, the expression should be Hanging Stone, in allusion to some cromlech. If this be the case, the stone about which we are speaking may have been one of the legs which supported the top stone of a cromlech. On the south side of the stone there is the Ordnance mark. (*History of Sidmouth I, 95*). *There is no mention of making this sketch in the Diary, one of Hutchinson's best known scenes. As he says, similar tales and the name Hangman's Stone are common elsewhere, attached to many an isolated menhir or boulder (Notes and Queries 1856). A legend is told about one of the Combe Martin boundary stones in almost identical terms by Westcote (View of Devonshire, 252). This inconspicuous stone, now set in a concrete plinth, still stands beside the busy A3052.*

57/5/?-1. *Hangman's Stone, north side.* (Hist. of Sid. I,95)

57/5/?-2. *Quod fecit.* (Hist. of Sid. I,95)

57/5/?-3. *Quod subiit.* (Hist. of Sid. I,95)

57/5/?-4. *'Hangman's Stone', near Bovey House, about five miles east of Sidmouth. Sketched May 1857.* (DRO, Z19/2/8E/73)

Archers only. *Thursday June 25.* Got the mule and went out with the gun. Drove down to the beach, unlimbered, and fired several shots out to sea. Limbered up and drove to the Archery Ground at Cotmaton, where I found a dozen ladies and gentlemen. I fired one shot with powder only, just to make 'a jolly row' and amuse the girls, but they would not let me have a try at their target with ball. No wonder perhaps. (*Diary*).

Indian Mutiny. *Wednesday July 1.* News has arrived of an extensive and serious insurrection of the native population in the East Indies against the Europeans. They have massacred the whites, men, women and children at Meerut, Delhi and other places, and great anxiety exists for the next news. (*Diary*).

Smuggling again. *Saturday July 4.* Ch. Blackmore and another were fined £700 for smuggling forty-one tubs and three flagons of spirits, together with some other prohibited articles. (*History of Sidmouth V, 161*).

Musbury sale and house at Ash. *Tuesday July 14.* Mr. Heineken and myself went over to Musbury to a sale at the Rev. Mr. Tucker's, the vicar. I there bought a piece of Roman tessellated pavement about the size of an octavo volume containing thirty-four square tesserae of apparently white lias stone, some fragments of black Roman pottery and about a peck of loose tesserae of the same kind. They come, I believe, from Uplyme where the remains of a Roman villa were discovered in 1851. The whole cost me two shillings and sixpence. (*Later note:* I have given them to the Exeter Museum, except some of the tesserae - 1880).

We then went to the church where the monuments of the Drake family, heretofor of Ash, attract most attention.   There are three couple of figures, male and female, in a kneeling posture in the south-east part of the building.   In the organ loft we saw a double-base made by Mr. Tucker.   Then we climbed the hill to Musbury Castle, *and* a pretty fag it was considering the heat. We lunched on the summit and then, with Davidson's 'Axminster' in hand, we examined the camp and verified his description of it.   But during the last twenty-five years since he wrote several parts have been altered or obliterated. After descending the hill and taking another look at the sale, where two little reputed Rembrandts were knocked down for twenty pounds, we went on to Ash, now belonging to John Wolcott of Knowle, Esquire. I made one sketch of the house from the garden and another of the chapel.   The buildings must at one time have been very extensive. We also went a quarter of a mile on towards Axminster where a brook crosses the road *at a* place called Warlake or War Lake.   Tradition says that a great battle between the Danes and Saxons took place here, that the brook ran blood and that the battle continued till the combatants reached Colyton (see August 9, 1872). We then started for home, where we arrived about nine.

In the Archaeological Journal for March 1854, p. 49, there is some account of the above mentioned tessellated pavement.   Mr. Tucker, whose house we had been to, made the discovery of some pavement in a field called 'Church Ground', part of Holcombe Farm in the parish of Uplyme.   There was a heap of ruins and a popular notion prevailed that an ancient church had stood there.   But on making a search a tessellated pavement was found.   The apartment was about eighteen feet square and more than half the pavement was perfect.   A broad border of two bands ran along the side of the room *and* within was inscribed a circle about ten

57/7/14-1. South side of Ash from the garden, near Musbury, Devon. Formerly the residence of the family of Drake. Sketched on the spot July 14, 1857. (DRO, Z19/2/8E/75)

57/7/14-2. *Remains of the Chapel belonging to Ash, now used as a cellar. Sketched on the spot July 14, 1857.* (DRO, Z19/2/8E/77)

feet in diameter with foliated ornaments in the spandrels and enclosing a figure of four intersecting circles with a hexagon in the centre.   The circles were ornamented with the guilloche pattern, the colours being red, blue and white.   At first the colours were bright.   Fragments of pottery, bones which soon crumbled, charred substances, and a piece of metal (which I also have) which had been subjected to very strong heat were found on the floor.   Also some roofing tiles, in form somewhat pentangular.   An adjoining room was floored with lime and sand, and a third with square red tiles.   Also, the remains of a bath were met with, in shape octagonal, in depth three and a half feet, *and in* width from side to side eleven and a half feet except where there were benches.   The discovery was made in August 1850 – 52. (*Diary*).

New vicar. *Sunday July 19.*   The new vicar, Rev. H.J.Hamilton, 'read himself in'. (*Diary*).

Excavation of coffin at Littlecombe Three Acres. *Monday July 27.*   At last I had a dig at the stone coffin (*see June 22, 1855*).   Mr. Heineken, myself and a man went over to 'Littlecombe Three Acres'.   Provided with spades, pickaxes, rakes and probing iron, we at once went to work.   On taking up the turf we found the coffin at the spot before pointed out to us.   It lay nearly north and south, or to be exact, the north end (apparently the head) lay 14 degrees west of north.   That end was five feet from the hedge and forty-three feet from the eastern hedge of the field.   There was a slight depression in the ground at the spot.   The top edge of the coffin was only six inches under the surface.   It was made of chalk stone from the Beer quarries and soft in texture.   It was rudely hollowed out from one great block, the marks of the tool being visible.   It was in great fragments except for a portion of the end near the hedge.   The bottom

57/7/27-2.   *Coffin.*   (Hist. of Sid. I,83)

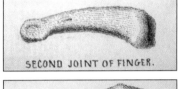

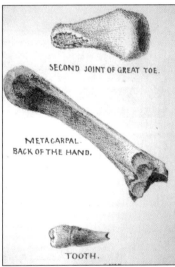

57/7/27-3.   *Bones from coffin.* (Hist. of Sid. I,83)

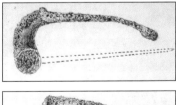

57/7/27-5.   *Bronze fibula from coffin.*   (Hist. of Sid. I,84)

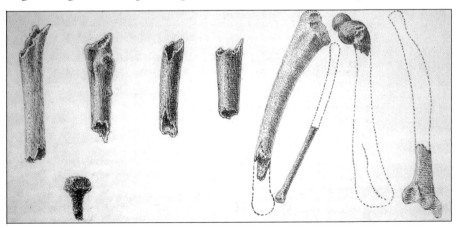

57/7/27-4.   *Bones and iron nail from coffin.*   (Hist. of Sid. I,84)

57/7/27-1. *Excavation of stone coffin, July 27, 1857, in a field near Branscombe. All the remains seem to have been removed by the farmer before 1871.* (DRO, Z19/2/8E/79)

of this piece was, or is, entire, with the head and east side, but the west side of it is broken away. The thickness of the stone is from three to four inches. The coffin was eleven and a half inches deep, length about seven feet but the width could not be ascertained. We carefully examined all the earth as we took it out. In filling in again, we first laid down all the fragments of stone, then put in the earth, again raking and carefully examining it, and lastly laid down the turf. We found about thirty pieces of bone, all in small fragments except for three or four. These were two finger bones (apparently), a metacarpal, a toe bone and a tooth. Also we found an iron object like a nail or rivet, and part of a bronze fibula. These we brought away, as well as two or three pieces of the coffin which had tool marks on them. From all these we hope to ascertain to what nation or people the corpse had belonged and at what period the interment may have taken place. It is worthy of remark that many of the bones belonged to some small animal and not a human being. (*Diary*).

Choral Society dissension. *Friday July 31.* Attended a meeting of the Sidmouth Choral Society. I was made chairman, but after introducing the general business of the evening, the proceedings became perplexing and almost stormy. How is it that in associations and societies got together for the purpose of amusing people and giving them pleasure, little and despicable jealousies so frequently arise which cause discord? It is almost always the case. Our society, after a year's existence, is threatened with dissolution. It is impossible apparently to please everybody. Where everybody wants to play first fiddle what is to be done? (*Diary*). (*See January 11, 1858*).
On August 11 Hutchinson went over to Dawlish to stay for a few days before going on to Northamptonshire.

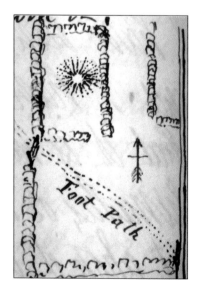

57/8/?. *Site of Water Hill barrow.* (Diary)

Water Hill barrow again. *August.* My dear Mr. Heineken. One whole hour and more I have been perched upon the barrow and I have come to the conclusion that it is not a toot-hill but a tumulus, or barrow supulchral. I sat upon it and stood upon it for an hour, turning in different directions, scrutinising all the glens and valley ridges and hills spyglass in hand, but failed to detect any object visible from it that I could not see when off it, or any advantage derivable from an elevation of eight or ten feet. The hill on which it stands is considerably lower than Little Haldon a mile west, and even before the plantations of the Luscombe grounds existed, Little Haldon camp could never have been seen from it.   It lies about a hundred yards west of the road that runs towards Mamhead.   The hill is a ridge, the barow is on the crown of the ridge and the road runs along the east side of the ridge a little below the crown.   (*Extract of letter to Heineken, with plan, dated August 1857*).

Leaving for Northamptonshire. *Thursday August 20.*   Left Dawlish to visit the Joneses at Moreton Pinkney in Northamptonshire.   (*Diary*).
Apart from spending a considerable time in Lichfield Cathedral and calling on other relations in the Midlands, Hutchinson was able to examine the manuscript diary of Governor Hutchinson of Massachusetts for the first time.   He also travelled to Lincolnshire in search of those of his ancestors living there at the time of Charles I.   He returned to Sidmouth via London on November 18.

Book review. *Friday November 20.*   This evening I sat down and wrote a review of my own book, the *New Guide to Sidmouth*, for Woolmer's Exeter and Plymouth Gazette.   Perry the publisher thought it was the best plan to adopt and I thought he was right.   (*Diary*).

Tumulus on Bulverton Hill. *Friday December 4.*   Beautiful day!   Clear sky, mild air and not a breath of wind.   I walked via Bickwell to the cairn on Bulverton Hill *(B.R.No. 8)*.   It does not seem to have been disturbed since I was last time there, though a good quantity of the flints have from time to time been taken away to mend the roads.   There are eight or ten large masses of stone lying about which are apparently parts of some outer works.   I am however, inclined to think that the kist-vaen itself has not yet been disturbed. (*Diary*).

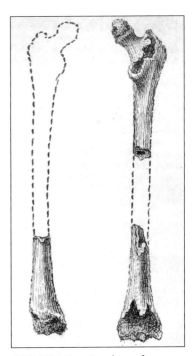

57/12/11-1. *Leg bones from Duncombe quarry.* (Hist. of Sid. I,81)

Quarried bones. *Friday December 11.*   After breakfast I walked over Salcombe Hill to Dunscombe, to see the place where a skeleton was found about six years ago, some of the bones of which I have (*B.R.No. 87*).   Turned in at Dunscombe House, some of the ruins of which remain, went through the farmyard and down the road a hundred or so yards to the kiln.   Poked about the quarry and returned. The men who found the bones were called Gosling and Bond and I found the former in Salcombe.   He told me that they were digging out the place for making the kiln when they came upon the bones, close up against a sort of cliff and covered over with earth and stones.   The body was not lying flat but rather in an inclined position.   Whether the person had really been buried there or whether a quantity of undermined cliff had fallen down and buried a man who had been working there, is impossible to say.   The latter supposition is within reason, as the hills here seem to have been quarried for stone at some remote period. Gosling further said that no trace of clothing or ornaments were found, and indeed many of the bones were so decayed as to fall to pieces.   I then asked him whether they ever turned up any old coins or other relics of antiquity about that neighbourhood, but he said no.   I said that if he ever did, or if he ever heard of any such things coming to light, to be sure to secure them for me.   (*Diary*).   *Hutchinson's Barrow Committee Report adds a few further details:* Gosling told me some years afterwards that most of the bones were taken to Miss Leigh, who owned the Dunscombe property, at Hill's Cottage near Sidmouth *where* the skull was buried in the garden.   Mr. Heineken has three of the detached teeth, the crowns of which are much worn by mastication.   I got portions of leg and other bones with part of the left side lower jaw with four teeth in place, which I sent to Exeter.   This was an interment without cremation, but under what circumstances it is impossible to say.   The bones adhered strongly to the tongue and there was every appearance of great age about them. (*Second Report of the Barrow Committee, 148*)

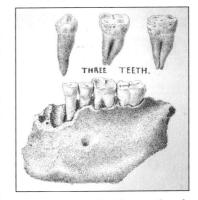

57/12/11-2. *Jaw bone and teeth from Dunscombe quarry.* (Hist. of Sid. I,81)

Ringing out the old year. *Thursday December 31.*   Last day of the year, a mild and beautiful day.   Spent the evening at Lime Park and saw the new year in of course.   The bells were ringing.   The custom is to ring occasional peals during the latter part of the day up to midnight, and again beginning early in the morning of New Years Day and through the greater part of the day.   This is 'ringing the old year out and the new year in'.   (*Diary*).

1858

New Years Day 1858. *Friday January 1.* Was awoken by the church bells at some unknown hour this morning, but fell asleep again. Today I hoisted the large flag but there was not a breath of wind to display it. This evening our old Christmas friends the Mummers came round. (*Diary*). *The accompanying sketch, done a few months previously, shows the flag and staff in the garden outside Coburg Terrace.*

58/1/1. *Sidmouth churchyard and Coburg Terace, 1857.* (DRO, Z19/2/8E/107)

Choral society troubles. *Monday January 11.* This evening at eight o'clock there was a meeting of the musical committee of the Choral Society of Sidmouth at my house, to see what could be done to go on. There are two or three rebellious and mischievous members who have long given a great deal of trouble and have created much discord where (amongst musical people) everything ought to be in harmony. It is a curious thing that most musical societies are troubled in the same way. There is a stock of music in hand and £11 0s 0d in money. The opposition want to divide and scramble for all this. That won't do. (*Diary*).
The following day Hutchinson received twenty-five copies of his 'Tour of Lincolnshire' from the printers, for distribution amongst his friends and relations. Over the next few days he records the preparations in Sidmouth for the Princess Royal's wedding.

Lecture on local history. *Tuesday February 16.* Gave my lecture on 'The Antiquities of Sidmouth and the Neighbourhood' in the ballroom of the London Inn. The room was well filled. I had four illustrations: 'two women grinding at the mill', a large drawing of the Roman brooch found in the stone coffin, the Roman standards and the skeleton found at Dunscombe. The coins and different antiques I produced were all found at Sidmouth or in the neighbourhood. The time occupied in delivering it was an hour and a half. (*Diary*).

Dartmoor petition. *Saturday February 27.* The memorial to Prince Albert which I drew up some weeks ago has got into the 'Western Times', an Exeter paper. Dr. Croker of Bovey Tracey, to whom I sent it for signature in his neighbourhood, informs me that he made several copies and sent them round Dartmoor to collect signatures elsewhere. One copy was sent to Exeter and I suppose Latimer the editor got hold of it. (*Diary*).

The memorial was a petition protesting at the destruction of antiquities on Dartmoor. We have viewed with concern or heard with regret of the many acts of destruction that have from time to time taken place among the relics of a bygone age on Dartmoor. Rock idols, cairns, ancient British dwellings, Druidic circles and other remains, mostly formed of granite, have been broken up or are occasionally being broken up either for making fences or for mending the roads. To corroborate these remarks, allusion need only to be made to the mutilation of the old Stannary Court at Crockern Tor, the removal of the Druid circles at Manaton, Bottor and other places, the destruction of the sacred avenues on Shuffle Down, etc. (*Extract from Hutchinson's 'Memorial', printed in the 'Western Times'*). *The petition snowballed, 'traversing Devon and Cornwall', and copies were soon available for the public to sign at Exeter, Plymouth, Torquay and other places. The response from the Duchy was distinctly negative however, and several years later Hutchinson raised the matter again with the influential Society of Antiquaries in London (see letter March 7, 1867).*

Russian guns at Exeter. *Thursday March 25.* Went from Sidmouth to Dawlish on a visit to my cousin, Mary Robertson. Had several hours in Exeter, so went and examined the two Russian guns on Northernhay, placed behind the Courts of Law. They are of iron, nine feet long, bore about six or seven inches and mounted on wrought iron English carriages. They are like those I saw last autumn at Boston and Newark. One has a piece near the muzzle knocked out by a shot – an English shot I presume (*see sketch June 8, 1893*). (*Diary*).

Geological specimen. *Tuesday March 30.* Walked at low water (spring tide yesterday) to the 'Parson and Clerk'. In the cliff line there are large hollow nodules filled with spar. I procured one and carried it back, but being a rough walk over gravel and rocks and being pressed by the rising tide, the mass of stone made my arms and legs ache considerably. I thought it was heavy and guessed it might weigh about ten pounds. The servants weighed it and to my surprise it amounted to nineteen. (*Diary*).

Agreeable guests. *Tuesday April 6.* Spent the evening next door at Mr. and Mrs. Ermen's. Aside, and don't tell anybody, *but* Miss Matilda and Miss Emma Ermen, two nice girls, *were there.* (*Diary*).

New villas. *Friday April 9.* Walked to the hill over the 'Parson and Clerk' and looked at the new villas being built there in the fields. Two are nearly finished. On the top of the cliff a little on the Teignmouth side of the Parson and Clark, they have erected a stage and windlass and they are quarrying stone on a shelf half way down the face of the cliff over the sea, and are hauling it up to build the new houses with. I walked back to Belmont Villa in the rain. (*Dairy*).

Circus. *Monday April 12.* Wombwell's wild beast show arrived. I went at feeding time with Elizabeth Hands. I was surprised at the small quantity of animal food they give the beasts and was told they only feed them once in twenty-four hours. The performance of one of the elephants was the most striking part of the exhibition – that of standing upon half a tub with all four feet together, then stretching out two feet and standing on only two, and lastly standing on its head on the ground. These animals are not only sagacious but are tractable. (*Diary*).

Dislocated strata. *Thursday April 15.* Made a coloured sketch of part of the cliff (a fault) near the Preventive House. (*Diary*).
Hutchinson left Dawlish for Sidmouth on April 21.

58/4/12. *Performing elephants.* (*Diary*)

58/4/15. *Fault or dislocation in the cliff near the Preventive station, Dawlish, Devonshire. Coloured out of doors April 15, 1858.* (DRO, Z19/2/8E/99)

Sidmouth photographic exhibition. *Wednesday April 29.* Wrote a short article for Perry's Journal on the photographic exhibition. (*Diary*). *Photography seems to have been a popular pastime at Sidmouth, with some five hundred specimens on show at the exhibition,* some of great beauty.

Bury Camp survey. *Friday May 7.* Mr. Heineken and myself made an expedition to examine Bury Camp. On the maps the word Bury is usually spelt Berry, but according to analogy Bury ought to be right. Bury Farm stands at the western end of Branscombe. We mounted Salcombe Hill, passed through the village of Salcombe by old Dunscombe House, then Slade, Weston, the field where we examined the stone coffin (see July 27, 1857), and stopped at Bury Farm. Here we turned off along a lane towards the cliff. The annexed is a rough plan, but there is a more correct one in the private quarto copy of my *Sidmouth Guide.* There is no known name to this camp, but it was anciently and par excellence called Byrig, Burgh or Bury in all probability, and the farm close by called Bury Farm after it. The side along the edge of the cliff measures 952 feet and the width in the middle 350. It has a vallum inside the ditch, 19 feet high at the north end from the bottom of the ditch, and a small vallum outside. The ground is level all round. Whether any of it is lost by the falling away of the cliff is impossible to say, and therefore it is impossible to say whether there was ever an outer vallum or hedge on the side of the cliff. At present there is none. There are traces of a hedge near the opposite or inland side. We are told that a man had a garden there some years ago. From this camp are visible High Peak Hill, the town of Sidmouth, Blackbury Castle and apparently Membury and Musbury Castles beyond the Axe. The Camp is a sort of irregular parallelogram but not sufficiently regular to warrant its being considered Roman. It is sufficiently rude to make us assign it to the Britons. We had never heard of its existence until recently.

Walking out at the end in the Sidmouth direction we came to three large masses of stone almost buried in the grass. The first is of sandstone of the Greensand Formation and the two others of chert. Tradition as usual declares that there is treasure buried under them. Pursuing our route for nearly half a mile, measuring with the pedometer, we examined and took down a number of barrows or tumuli. I believe they have never been opened, but Mr. Ford of Branscombe has given leave. Some of these do not bear the semblance of genuine barrows but only heaps of dry flints thrown up after clearing the land for cultivation. All along here is a beautiful undercliff, a sort of stage or platform half way down to the sea, well cultivated with corn, potatoes, etc. The mule that drew us we had turned adrift in the camp for several hours to graze, and the lad who drove us, whom we have reared up in these sort of expeditions during the last ten years and bears the immortal name of Smith, lay down and went to sleep after half emptying the quart bottle of beer we gave him. We lunched on the hill and returned home somewhat tired after so much measuring and walking about. (*Diary*).

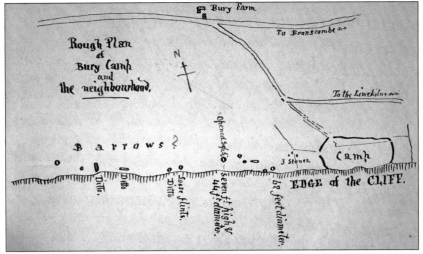

58/5/7. *Rough plan of Bury Camp and neighbourhood.* (Diary)

Site of possible barrows on Salcombe Hill. *Tuesday May 10.* After breakfast, I went up Salcombe Hill with a hoe to grub about where an apparent barrow has been recently levelled. The spot is on the crown of the hill twenty-five yards into the field on the right, or south, side going to Salcombe. We walked up this hill last Friday with Mr. Charles Cornish of Salcombe House, whose land it is, and he said that a good many stones large and small had been removed but no antiquities were found. I scraped about for an hour on the spot and then went to another place some hundred yards south-west in the same field where a similar apparent tumulus had been, but all my hoeing was in vain. (*Diary*).

Budleigh Salterton encroachments. *Friday May 21.* *Hutchinson was in Budleigh Salterton for the day, assisting Heineken with his business affairs.* Took a walk half a mile eastward to the mouth of the River *Otter*. There was a small cutter yacht and some boats lying in smooth water inside. The inhabitants of Budleigh Salterton have recently been loudly complaining of the injury done to the harbour by the Rolle family for twenty or thirty years past, by enclosing some of the flats and thereby curtailing the size of the basin. A public meeting was held a week or two ago about it. I was told that about thirty acres of land had been enclosed. Before this large shallow basin was thus curtailed, the inhabitants assert that the rising tide poured in so large a body of water as effectively to keep the mouth well open and secure a deep channel when it rushed out at the falling of the tide, but that since these encroachments have been made the channel and the mouth have been filling up. When the tide was only two hours up from low water, boats I was told could enter, whereas now they can only enter when the water is nearly high. It was decided at the meeting to memorialise the government with a view to having the encroachments thrown down, but an amendment was subsequently adopted by which it was decided first to make an amicable application to the Rolle family. (*Diary*).

Diamond cut. *Monday May 24.* This evening, Mr. Drew came to me and with a mysterious and significant air drew from his pocket what he declared to be a petrified orange filled with diamonds! He found a round pebble on the beach some time ago and recently cut a slice off one side and polished the exposed surface. On examining the thing, it proved to be nothing more than an echinus, or sea-egg, infiltrated with chalcedony with a cavity in the centre sparkling with crystals. I showed him an echinus I had got out of a flint on Peak Hill, but as some of the prominent features had been rubbed off his specimen on the beach and mine was rough and fresh, he could not distinguish the resemblance. Nothing I could say in delicate language shook his confidence in being the happy possessor of an orange full of diamonds. (*Diary*).

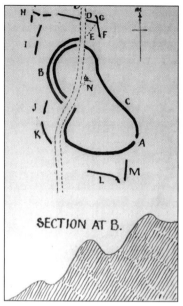

58/5/27. Plan and section of Woodbury Castle. (Hist. of Sid. I,41)

Woodbury Castle survey. *Thursday May 27.* Started with Mr. Heineken to examine Woodbury Castle. We drove over Peak Hill, through dirty Otterton, past Bicton Cross and the great lodge. A little beyond this we turned out of our way by passing Hayes Mill to go to Hayes Farm, of which we took two photographs. There was a great meeting of farmers there, it being rent day. We then pushed on westwards, out upon the open heath towards Black Hill, but before we reached it we turned north along a mere track so rough we were nearly over more than once - the better the fun. Nearly two miles across this wild and romantic country brought us to the camp. The views are splendid and most extensive on all sides, but high as this hill is, the cone of High Peak rose considerably above the horizon line of the sea. The camps visible were High Peak, Sidbury Castle, Dumpden, Hembury Fort, Mary Pole Head, and various others towards Cadbury, Tiverton, Haldon and Milber Down. Woodbury Castle is thickly planted with trees, a practice I should discourage if I owned these places, for it prevents any satisfactory examination of their interiors and conceals their features from a distance. We examined and measured it as well as we could.

The camp is irregular as mentioned in my *Guide*, having been originally an oval but subsequently (apparently) added to on the south. There are two ramparts on the north-west portion. The fosse was 45 feet deep and very steep, and from the top of the inner agger across the fosse to the top of the outer one, 62 feet. There is a little ditch and agger outside all, at A in the section attached. The interior is like a basin as the agger rises all round. All the rest of the camp has but one agger. The outworks, supposed to have been added in 1549, are not quite accurate in Shortt's *Collectanea Curiosa* but I have corrected them in the little plan annexed. B - double agger, C - single agger, D - straight outworks to defend north entrance, being a bold hedge and ditch, E - traces of a low hedge, F - partly obliterated but running down the hill to where there is a spring, G - doubtful or obliterated, H - ditto, I - earthwork to defend the south entrance, J - a similar work, K - another running back to the camp, and L - woodman's cottage inside, the woodman called Gordon. We walked round the agger and made it 920 yards, or more than half a mile. Of the outworks, the piece b measured 68 yards, short piece a 23 yards, from that to the road 34, and across the road and down the slope of the hill 84, where the traces become broken and confused. The piece I is about 30 yards long, J 66 yards and K 30 yards. There are one or two cultivated fields just outside the south-east side of the camp, but the crops are usually destroyed by the rabbits that abound on the heath.

I told the Gordons that I had heard some shot or cannon balls had been dug up in the camp, but they had never heard of this. The only antiquities they had heard of as having been found there were 'three old ha'pence' as Mrs. G. called them. She gave them to a Miss Swan of Woodbury Salterton in about 1847, but Miss Swan left the neighbourhood about 1849. I should like to know what they were. They told me a story still well known all about here in reference to the battle fought on this hill in August 1549 between Lord Russel's forces just come down from London and a detachment of the Cornish rebels who were besieging Exeter. There is a brook, almost dry except after rain, nearly half a mile down towards Woodbury Salterton. The place is called Red Slew. The battle at one period is said to have raged here, and the combatants fought 'up to their knees in blood'. Mrs. Gordon added, very seriously, that when she passed that way after a shower of rain she had seen the brook quite red still. I could have told the good Mrs. Gordon that there is an abundance of oxide of iron down there and that the redness is more likely to be from this than human blood. Outside the outworks, marked a and b, and against them, some hollows are seen, as if the bank had been cut down. Could the soldiers of Col. Simcoe's time have built huts here?

As a mem. of this neighbourhood, I may mention that when some old cottages near Woodbury were some short time ago pulled down, it was found that they had been originally thatched with rye straw, for the lowest stratum of thatch was of rye though the higher and more recent ones were of wheat. Rye has not been cultivated in the neighbourhood within the memory of man.

We left the camp not till half past six in the evening and descended to Yettington, a neat and clean village - the ancient Yettemetone of the Otterton Cartulary, 1260. Here we enquired about manganese, for it used to be dug on the hill north-west of this place and all about it. The diggings are now given up as they did not pay. We got home soon after eight, somewhat tired. (*Diary*).

Fossil hunting under Peak Hill. *Thursday June 3.* After breakfast I walked to High Peak Hill. Went out on the undercliff to grub about for greensand fossils and antiquities and got a few imperfect specimens. As for antiquities it is possible, though not likely, that something from the camp might be met with here. A thunderstorm with lightening and rain made me hurry away for shelter. The storm was very solemn and grand approaching from the sea. When it held up, I managed on returning to go into the gravel pits on Peak Hill and found a couple of petrified sea eggs. (*Diary*).

Sidmouth parish chest. *Monday June 21.* The last three vicars have given me leave to turn over the contents of the parish chest, to assist me in my historical researches. Today I availed myself of the permission for the first time. I got one key of the chest from Webber, the churchwarden, and went to the vicarage for the other. Mr. Hamilton was up in a field haymaking and Mrs. H. took me up to him. He showed me a spot on the high ground of the glebe where a new vicarage would stand with advantage, an idea that probably will never be carried out. I went to the church and examined some of the old deeds. By means of a ladder, I mounted and copied the piece of painted glass in the east window, and copied also the arms on Harlewin's monument, recently cleaned and the colours brought out. Came home and made a coloured drawing of the painted glass. (*Diary*). *Hutchinson continued work on the contents of the parish chest for several weeks (see August 28).*

58/6/21. *Harlewin's monument.* (Hist. of Sid. II,68)

Furzehill and Ebdon. *Wednesday July 14.* Walked to Sidbury. Called in at Furzehill on my way to look again at the old cast iron fireback. I sounded Mr. and Mrs. Hook as to whether they would part with it but it belongs to the house. A man there who lives at Ebdon close by, told me that an iron ball as large as his fist was recently dug up on the side of Sidbury Castle Hill and that it is at his house. I promised to come out and look at it soon. (*Diary*).

Friday July 16. After breakfast, walked out to Ebden, or Ebdon, the farm lying on the east flank of Sidbury Castle Hill (see last Wednesday). I saw and handled the iron ball but which however is not above two inches in diameter and much rusted. It was dug up in the road or side of the road in front of the old farm-house. The farmer promised to bring it to me the next time he came to Sidmouth. (*Later note*: But he never did). (*Diary*).

Summons. *Saturday July 24.* My summons into Exeter is for the assizes on Monday, but as I am summoned for ten in the morning and the Sidmouth coach does not get in till twelve, I go today to my cousin's at Dawlish from where I can get in conveniently at the required hour. Went to Exeter by the Mail, stayed a few hours in Exeter and then went on to Dawlish. (*Diary*).

Salute to the losers. *Tuesday August 3.* The Exeter cricket club came down and a match (which they lost) was played in the Fort Field. Took the brass gun down and fired them a few shots. (*Diary*).

Parish documents. *Wednesday August 4.* Finished my researches and memoranda taken from the documents in the parish chest kept in the vestry. From these notes I now proceed to make my catalogue and shall number the deeds and books and arrange them chronologically. (*Diary*).

Archery prize. *Tuesday August 10.* Gave a brooch, a 'moss-agate' Sidmouth pebble set in silver, to be shot for by the Sidmouth Archery club. The match came off today on their ground at Cotmaton, and Miss Radford, eldest daughter of George Radford, solicitor, got it. (*Diary*).

Vaccination. *Thursday August 19.* This morning I was vaccinated. What a whim! The smallpox has been flying around the place of late and several old maids, old bachelors and old fidgets have had themselves re-vaccinated. I was vaccinated in my infancy and though I go everywhere and come in contact with all sorts of people, I never trouble my head about the danger or think about infection. I have among my acquaintances several of these fidgets and they have been bullying me about vaccination, so to please them Dr. Miller did it this morning and laughed at the whim too. (*Diary*).

Cataloguing parish documents. *Saturday August 28.* Finished writing out my chronological catalogues of the contents of the parish chest from my rough notes. I must prefix a preface and number the documents in the chest and then my work will be done. (*Diary*).

Prout the artist. *Tuesday August 31.* The Everetts left this morning for Greenhill. I called on young Prout, son of Prout the artist. The widow and three daughters of the artist have lived here, in the Bridge Cottage, for several years. Prout looks about thirty. I suppose he will not equal his father and I am told that he builds too much upon his father's fame, forgetting the saying that 'every man must be the architect of his own fortune'. I saw in the house some good interiors of Norman and French churches by the father, the colouring rich, mellow and true. (*Diary*).

Perils of barrow digging. *Monday September 6.* Went to Branscombe and opened a barrow near Bury Camp (*B.R.No. 84*). Nothing in it. (See May 7, 1858). (*Diary*). *This rather brief account in the Diary is amplified in Hutchinson's Barrow Report:* Between three and four miles east of Sidmouth, on a farm called Bury, there is a quadrangular camp... and on the plain covered with fine grass that stretches away westwards of it there lies, scattered about within fifty yards of the cliff, twelve or fourteen heaps of stone. In our visits to the camp, Mr. Heineken and myself had often contemplated these mounds but considered them only as 'clearance heaps', commonly so called... . Mr. Heineken remarked however, that some of these were covered with a foot thick of good mould, and as it seems unlikely that any farmer would cover a mere refuse heap with earth, it might be inferred that possibly these may be designedly made burial mounds after all. The opening of 84... did not produce any results. The fine turf and the earth were removed from the top, and the labourers descended down to the ground line. The work was most difficult. All the interior was composed of loose dry flints, and as fast as any were removed the sides slipped down and threatened to bury the men. Only standing room for one man was laid bare at the floor, although the top was completely open. Nothing but the removal of the whole heap would have proved whether it was a sepulchral mound or not. (*Second Report of the Barrow Committee*).

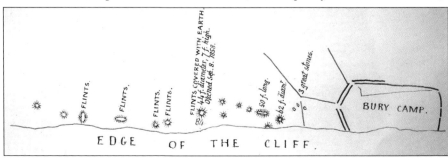

58/9/6-1. Location of stone heap. (Hist. of Sid. I,85)

This cairn has since been levelled almost to the ground, and like most of the others in the group is now a mere undulation of the surface. Their identification as burial mounds remains uncertain.

58/9/6-2 Opening stone heap on Littlecombe Hill, Bury Camp, September 8, 1858.
(DRO, Z19/2/8E/101)

Quarry near Salcombe Church. *Saturday September 18.* Walked over Salcombe Hill to examine the quarry near the church. Several churches in the neighbourhood have been built from this quarry and tradition asserts that part of Exeter Cathedral came from here. The quarry consists of beds of sandstone covered by the usual stratum of flints and clay. It was a geological walk. I found specimens of oysters and other bivalves, but I looked long before I found a perfect one as they are mostly broken. (*Diary*). *At this period Hutchinson spent many a day collecting fossils and geological specimens from the quarries and cliffs around Sidmouth.*

Sidmouth Fair. *Tuesday September 21.* Sidmouth Fair, second day. The remainder of the Regatta sports took place today. There were two rowing matches, the signals for which I gave with my gun. After the races were over, I amused myself with throwing balls out to sea. They pitched about a mile out, considerably further than the two colliery schooners that were lying off, much to the amusement of the bystanders. Indeed, the gun seems to be taken much interest in by all Sidmouth, for I am generally cheered whenever I appear with it. 'Three cheers for Mr. Hutchinson' were given when I arrived on the beach. Today I dispensed with the mule to draw the gun and used the drag-ropes, having two boys on each rope and one to hold up the shafts of the limber, myself mounted as usual. They enjoyed the exploit amazingly. They ran with all their might, rather incautiously round corners, nearly capsizing sundry people. (*Diary*). *A week later Hutchinson left Sidmouth for Warminster and a tour of the Midlands, returning to Sidmouth on November 4.*

Church restoration fund. *Friday November 19.* Called at the vicarage. Gave Mr. Hamilton £5 towards the restoration of the parish church, soon to be begun, with an intimation that more would be forthcoming before the work is completed. (*Diary*).

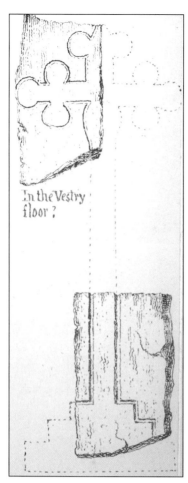

In the Vestry floor?

58/12/16-1. *Sidmouth Church, two fragments of an incised cross.* (Hist. of Sid. IV,63)

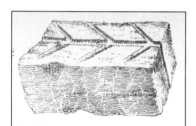

58/12/16-2. *Fragment in the west wall of the Old Chancel, Coburg Terrace.* (Hist. of Sid. IV,63)

58/12/16-3. *Lost fragment.* (Hist. of Sid. IV,63)

58/12/16-6. *Column capital, fixed outside the south wall of the Old Chancel.* (Hist. of Sid. IV,63)

58/12/16-4. *Toothed moulding, now lost.* (Hist of Sid.IV,63)

58/12/16-5. *Norman zig-zag, in the north transept gable outside.* (Hist of Sid.IV,63)

58/12/16-7. *Stone now over south door of chancel.* (Hist of Sid.IV,63)

Romanesque carving in Sidmouth church. *Friday December 16.* Discovered a piece of stone built into the south wall of the chancel, outside, having a Norman zig-zag moulding on it. This is a remnant of an older church at Sidmouth. (*Diary*). This stone . . . was put in the gable of the north transept outside when the church was rebuilt in 1859 and 1860. (*Sketchbook E*). *Many more Romanesque and later fragments were shortly to turn up when the old fabric of the church was dismantled, and some years afterwards Hutchinson was to record their fate at a vestry meeting, later published as an article in the Exeter and Plymouth Gazette (written in the third person).* He wished to say that when the rubbish in the mason's yard was being cleared away, some children were found hacking with a hatchet the capital of a Saxon or Norman column of unusual type which had been discovered whilst taking down the walls of the old church. Several other highly interesting fragments were met with, as incised crosses, toothed mouldings, zig-zags, etc., all of which he was particularly anxious to have preserved in the new church. He collected them together with his own hands and got a friend to photograph them. These carved stones, by the patterns which appeared upon them, indicated the age of the building to which they had belonged almost with the same precision as if the date had been cut upon them, and they were therefore valuable. He regretted that the Restoration Committee never appreciated these things and most of them have been lost sight of. The said capital was a spherical block of stone with incised devices and a band of quatrefoils round the middle. To rescue it from destruction he had it carried over to his own premises. It was fixed in the small blank window outside the south wall of the Old chancel where anyone was welcome to examine it. As soon as the churchwardens could find a place for it, he should be happy to restore it to the church. (*Exeter and Plymouth Gazette April 18, 1862*)

58/12/16-8. *Part of the stonework of the former chancel of Sidmouth parish church, showing the Norman zig-zag imbedded in the wall.* (Not dated). (DRO, Z19/2/8E/109)

Church restoration committee formed. *Friday December 17.* At a vestry meeting called to consider the plans for rebuilding the chancel and other works connected with the church, it was found necessary to adjourn to the Town Hall. Mr. Hamilton, the vicar. presided. There was some contention respecting the re-seating in the body of the church and a committee was formed of which I was one (see my book headed *Restoration of Sidmouth Parish Church in which I enter all particulars*). (*Diary*). *This 'contention' was an ominous prelude to one of the most disagreeable periods in Hutchinson's life. An increasingly bitter feud developed between Hutchinson and the rest of the Committee, with Hutchinson strongly opposing the 'Romanising tendencies' of the other members. On his side, Hutchinson had some influential supporters such as the Earl of Buckingham as well as the majority of parishioners. Over the next two years the dispute escalated to involve the Bishop of Exeter and eventually Queen Victoria herself, finally leading to the resignation of the vicar, Mr. Hamilton. Recording the events in later years,*

Hutchinson wrote in unusually vehement terms: After an interval of many years, I look
back upon the talents, knowledge and capabilities of this Committee with feelings
of the utmost contempt. Their ignorance and mismanagement soon threw everything into confusion and led to very serious quarrels. As the High Church party
was at that time rather strong, they took the opportunity of trying to introduce
novelties to which the great mass of the inhabitants were strangers and manifested
a very great dislike, living as they did in a secluded country town. The whole
parish became divided into two parties with consequences to society and the place
at large most lamentable at the time and injurious to the community for many
years afterwards. (*History of Sidmouth IV, 53*).

Monday December 20. First meeting of the new committee at the vicarage.
(*Diary*).

Delphinus tursio. Friday December 24. This morning at daylight Henry
Conant, a fisherman, having gone out with his companions in a boat to catch
herrings, entangled a large fish in their net which at last they brought to the
shore. It measured eleven feet four inches long, and if I may judge from the
description given in books, it is Delphinus tursio. The sailors knew nothing
about it. It is surprising how ignorant the fishermen here are about the differ-
ences between even the common large fish on this coast, such as the shark or
dogfish and the porpoise tribe. (*Diary*). *Hutchinson's account of its capture appeared
in Harvey's Sidmouth Directory for January 1858. Despite the discrepancy in the date,
the extended caption of the coloured sketch identifies it as the fish described in the Diary.*

Thursday December 30. Finished a drawing of the great fish. (*Diary*).

Friday December 31. This morning the fish was taken beyond the mouth of the
Sid on the beach, to have the oil boiled out. It was entirely covered with a coat
of blubber or hard fat, about an inch thick on the sides but three or four inches
thick on the back. The dorsal fin was merely a prolongation of this fat, without
any bone or muscle in it. Strange to say, four bullets and a stone marble such as
boys play with were found embedded in the fat and the skin was entirely healed
over. They were of different sizes and had apparently been fired into the fish at
different times. I saw them cut out and I have preserved them. (*Diary*).

*58/12/24. Fish caught at
Sidmouth, February 1859. It
was the Delphinus turseo, a species
of grampus.*
(DRO, Z19/2/8E/121)

Last of the 'fish'. *Saturday January 1.* Went down to the fish again. Several gallons of oil were procured. The carcass was opened. The anatomy was like that of a land animal and the flesh looked like coarse red beef. Assisted in cutting off the head, the skull of which I had set my heart on getting, but Heneage Gibbes, son of the incumbent of All Saints, also wanted it, and as he took the trouble to dissect off the greater part of the flesh, a disagreeable job, I let him have it without dispute. The blow-hole was double, that is, like two nostrils close together. For sanitary reasons the carcass was towed out to sea and set adrift. (*Diary*).

Evening with the Lousadas. *Friday January 7.* I dined at the Lousada's at Peak House. We sat down fifteen to dinner at a round table. The days of King Arthur are come back, or at all events one of the fashions thereof. Many ladies came in the evening. We had chatting and music, and I was scolded for not having put my flute in my pocket. (My flute doesn't dine out). (*Diary*).

Stone for re-building church. *Sunday January 9.* Beautiful day. After some two months of rain, the weather seems to have again settled. After church, I walked over Salcombe Hill to see the new quarry they have opened at a spot on the slope of the hill on the Sidmouth side of Salcombe Brook and at about half way between Salcombe church and the sea, perhaps nearer the sea and nearly over the farmhouse. The stone for re-building some parts of the parish church, now in contemplation, is to be brought from here, and indeed some has been brought. Some of the blocks I had seen appeared to me to be so soft and friable that I was not satisfied with it. On examining the quarry I see that the upper stratum is the best. I found one or two fossil shells. (*Diary*).

Old chestnut. *Monday January 10.* Committee meeting at the vicarage about the church. I sold my horse chestnut tree at the further end of the field and today it was loosened all round the root and felled. I condemned it for two reasons. First, nothing would grow under it and second, I never could keep the place neat after the blossoms and nuts came, for the boys were perpetually throwing stones and breaking my hedge down to get at them. I mean to plant a young sycamore or lime tree in the place of it. (*Diary*).

Ill-timed. *Tuesday January 18.* My lecture was announced for tonight. Inadvertently, the Committee of the Institution forgot that there was to be a tradesman's ball this evening at the London Inn, so that after the bills were printed and out, they had to be called in and others printed for next Thursday the 20th. But after that was done Lord and Lady Buckinghamshire issued cards for a ball for Thursday, and I realised that I should lose many of my gentry. In this predicament a sudden thought struck me, that I would pretend my cousin Miss Roberton in Dawlish was taken dangerously ill and that I must go over. Notices were printed and sent to all the principle inhabitants regretting my 'unavoidable absence', and appointing my lecture for Tuesday next. The crier was also sent round the town. But instead of going over, I shut myself up in my house for four days and drew the blinds down. Not a soul in the place knew the trick except Mrs. Webber my housekeeper. (*Diary*).

Saturday January 22. Today I was supposed to return from Dawlish. (*Diary*).

Ill-founded. *Monday January 24.* At a party at Mr. and Mrs. Clements, one of the curates, Mr. Hamilton the vicar told me there was a report about that my cousin was dead and that she had left me a fortune. I laughed and said that she was neither dead nor had left me a fortune, and as she had poorer cousins than myself, I did not expect she would leave me one halfpenny. (*Diary*).

Lecture. *Tuesday January 25.* And my lecture did come off and I had a very good audience. In spite of the apparent gravity of my subject, 'On the restoration of churches in general and that of Sidmouth church in particular', I managed to make my listeners laugh a good deal. (*Diary*).

Sidbury walk. *Friday February 4.* Lunched at Lime Park and started for Sidbury. It began to rain but I went on. Went into Sidbury Church and looked round. The south wall of the chancel leans out and is dangerous, but they talk of restoring it. I gave them a sovereign for their chancel and walked home. Very dark, still raining and the roads very muddy. (*Diary*). *The accompanying sketch of the organ and west end of the church was done a dozen years previously.*

Fossil hunting at Hook Ebb. *Saturday February 26.* Went again to Hook Ebb for fossils. The tunnel made from the mouth of the Sid some three-quarters of a mile through the cliff in 1837, to fetch stone from Hook Ebb to construct the proposed harbour still remains as a monument to foolishness. Beyond it, over to Hook Ebb, in places are seen the piles on which the rail was laid. I procured two or three new fossils and found others for which I must come again. (*Diary*).

Party host. *Tuesday March 1.* A small party at home, ten ladies and four gentlemen beside myself. I generally elect the oldest married lady as the lady of the house for the evening. I was disappointed at two or three of my singers so we danced all evening instead of having music. We had supper at eleven and broke up at twelve. (*Diary*).

59/2/4. Nave of Sidbury church, Devon – looking west. Coloured on the spot November 20, 1847. (DRO, Z19/2/8D/87)

Church numbers. *Wednesday March 2.* Church committee meeting held in the vestry. We went into the church and made a number of measurements and calculations about pews and seats. (*Diary*).

Joanna Southcott. *Thursday March 3.* Walked out to Sidford immediately after breakfast to see John Pound, one of the last remaining followers of Joanna Southcott, who has several sons in Australia living near my sister, concerning whom I had news for the parents. Found old Mrs. Pound at home, told her my news and received some messages from her to send out. Something led her to speak of her husband and his religious views, for she is a church woman. She told me her husband was turned this way of thinking by a man called Bailey who died at Sidford or thereabouts some years ago. There was another follower called Johnson, whom I remember, who was found dead in his room a few months back. Pound is now the last in Sidford. She told me that his conversion, or perversion, had been a source of much misery to her. He believes he shall never die but be translated direct to heaven, and those who die were not 'true Israelites'. They never shave, perform their religious duties in secret and practise circumcision. She told me the queer bit of news that her husband was circumcised about a dozen years ago. (*Diary*). *Joanna Southcott (1750-1814) was born nearby at Taleford Farm, Ottery St. Mary, and grew up at Gittisham and Sidmouth where her brother had a farm. Though her career as a prophetess only started after she moved to Exeter, her influence in her native district seems to have become widespread.* Long within my memory Joanna's followers were numerous in the neighbourhood of Sidmouth, and especially at Sidbury and Sidford. They were generally called the 'bearded men' and the children were afraid of them. They were mostly common labourers in the fields, untaught and ignorant to a degree. It was said that one point in their belief was that they would never die, and they held to this in spite of seeing their numbers dwindle away one by one, to be put in coffins and carried to the burial ground. Finally they all dropped off leaving John Pound as the last survivor. It was supposed that he was in possession of the books, papers and canons pertaining to this moribund sect, and in the event of his death, as a matter of curiosity, I had thought of trying to get possession of them. I failed to secure these valuable documents, and neither have I succeeded in meeting with the Silver Cradle, but if I should do so I will present it to the Exeter Museum. (*Joanna Southcott, extracts*). *The more important papers were given to the British Museum Library, though the whereabouts of Joanna Southcott's Box seems to be uncertain. The cradle is at present kept by the Panacea Society in Bedford, but other important items of the sect's paraphernalia did indeed eventually find their way to the Royal Albert Museum in Exeter. (Lewis 1997)*

Return to Hook Ebb. *Friday March 4.* Walked out to Hook Ebb, dug out some fossils and made a plaster cast of a large one I marked the other day. (*Diary*).

Thirsty work. *Thursday March 10.* Again at Hook Ebb. Every time I go I find two or three new specimens. I should be glad to bring out a new edition of my *Geology*, for the first was a childish production and is wrong in two or three places. I started this morning at 9.30 and got back at 6.30, nine hours altogether, and I only sat down whilst I discussed my sandwiches and sucked an orange. I would have given a trifle for something to drink. Towards the latter part of the day I drew from a spring that issued from the cliff, and used the water also to make a plaster cast of a shell from the matrix in a great stone, having come provided. With iron hammer and chisels and every pocket full of fossils, it was a weary walk home over the loose shingle of the beach. Had tea, I forget how many cups, as there is nothing like tea after a fagging walk. (*Diary*).

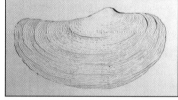

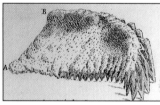
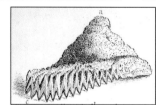

59/2/26. Sketches of a few of the fossils from Hook Ebb and Dunscombe Cliffs. (Hist. of Sid. I, 27)

Church restoration discussed. *Thursday April 7.* Meeting in the Town Hall about the church restorations, the vicar in the chair. All members of the committee were of course present. The meeting was better attended than I expected, but the only actual fact brought forwards was that the faculty for re-building the chancel and doing the other proposed works will be granted only when the money is subscribed. We want £1500 before we pull down a single stone and we have about £1100. I spoke for about a quarter of an hour. (*Diary*). *The accompanying view of the church was sketched shortly before restoration work started.*

Peak Hill undercliff. *Thursday April 21.* Went where I never went before, out over the sea face of Peak Hill on the undercliff, to see if I could find any traces of the old road to Otterton said to have passed that way till about eighty or ninety years ago. They seem to be nearly all obliterated. (*Diary*).

High Peak and an iron gun. *Saturday May 7.* After breakfast I went again to High Peak Hill and explored the sea face of the cone. I searched it carefully both for geological specimens and for any stray antiques from the camp above. Pulled out a tooth like that of a young horse from the eastern end where the charcoal is.

59/4/7. *East end of Sidmouth parish church, taken in 1859, shortly before the church was taken down and rebuilt.* (DRO, Z19/2/8E/111)

Near the western end I found a piece of pottery and some bones, but as yet I will not venture to give an opinion on them. All the greensand fossils in this hill are broken to pieces.

Today arrived from the Smethwick foundry near Birmingham my new three pound iron gun. If any of our enemies try to invade us at Sidmouth, I shall be able to give them a warm reception. It is 4 foot 8 inches in diameter at the breech, weighs 3cwt 2qtrs 20lbs and cost £3. 3s. 0d. Carriage from Birmingham, 13s. (*Diary*). *Over the next few days Hutchinson worked on the gun and adapted the old carriage to take it.*

the may not have

59/5/7. *Tooth of horse from High Peak camp.* (Hist. of Sid. I,10b)

Reinforcement for the Yeomanry. *Thursday May 19.* This morning the town was all alive. Flags were flying and triumphal arches of laurel spanned the streets. The soldiers were to meet on Peek Hill at 2 P.M and the gun and limber being all ready, I determined to go up and meet them. The gun is of iron, but nevertheless by rubbing it over yesterday with some drying oil and then dusting over it a little bronze powder and here and there a little green paint which looked like verdigris, it was taken for a brass gun. I ascended the hill by way of Cotmaton, Jenny Pine's Corner and Mutter's Moor because the ascent is more gradual. On reaching the summit, rather a hard pull, I found a full array of cavalry, I believe nearly five hundred. My appearance soon attracted their attention. I made a circuit of the hill and fired four times. I was surprised to find that I was heard down in Sidmouth, though I only put in half charges. I descended along with the regiment by way of the cliff, Peak House, Cotmaton, Mill Lane and down the town to the beach. (*Diary*). *Much later, this event was recalled by Rev. H. Clements: . . . one of the earliest things I can remember about him was his going about the place in a sort of uniform of his own devising, driving a donkey attached to a light cannon! And, on one memorable occasion, on a sort of field day of the Yeomanry on Peak Hill, I recall the indignation of the Colonel and officers at finding themselves on the return to Sidmouth solemnly preceded all the way home by Mr. Hutchinson in this somewhat ludicrous semi-military equipage.* (*Clements, 1903*).

59/5/19. (Diary)

Saturday May 21. Hutchinson seems to have provided further unsolicited military assistance throughout the week: Drove the gun to the esplanade. Fired one charge there this evening at parade on the beach and another in the Fort Field. (*Diary*).

Monday May 23. This evening at parade I drove the gun round the Fort Field and then took up a station near Fort Cottage and fired six half-pound charges, the last ten ounces. (*Diary*). *This unexpected artillery reinforcement seems to have been accepted eventually however, for on the last day of manoeuvres Hutchinson was invited to dine in the mess.*

Loss of the brig William. *May 26.* The brig William, 125 tons, foundered at sea but the crew landed safely at Sidmouth. (*History of Sidmouth V, 162*).

59/5/30. *Mr. Smith's solo.*
(DRO, Z19/2/8F/1)

Rifle Corps proposed. *Monday May 30.* At six PM there was a public meeting at the Town Hall to consider a circular from the Lord Lieutenant of the County (Earl Fortescue) on the subject of forming a Rifle Corps. Considering the uncertain position of political affairs on the Continent the Government has expressed a wish that Volunteer Rifle Corps should be embodied all over the country. Gustavus Smith Esq. J. P. was in the chair. As people are required to find their own rifle and equipment, everybody pleaded poverty and little was done. Mr. Lousada read a letter from the Earl of Buckinghamshire in which the Earl expressed his willingness to subscribe £20 if money was wanted. (*Diary*).

Bushy Knap, Buckerell Knap and Hembury Fort. *Monday June 6.* Mr. Heineken and myself resolved to visit Hembury Fort, distant nearly twelve miles. We started at nine, passing through Sidbury. We pulled up at Hunter's Lodge and took some observations with the sympiesometer to ascertain the height of the hill, which however has been levelled from Sidmouth and found to be 800 feet. We then made a steep descent and crossing the Honiton road passed Weston to Awliscombe. Here we got out to see the church. The village was full of flags and holiday people and as they were now all in church we altered our plans. We explored Bushy Knap and Buckerell Knap. The former is an immense mound or tumulus at the southern part of the hill, which we climbed in spite of the heat, from where a fine extent of country is seen. The latter is the northern and higher end of the hill, rising like a mound about 200 feet in diameter, surrounded by an earthwork and having other earthworks south of it across the hill to dispute the approach. These places look strongly as if they had been outposts connected with Hembury. We came down and entered Awliscombe church. It is curious that the stone floor rises by a slope from the west door towards the chancel. It is a handsome building in the Perpendicular style. There appears to be no monument in this church to Mrs. Amelia Elphinstone as mentioned by Lysons and which I copied into my guide-book. The tower is square, without buttresses.

We then made for Hembury Fort, discussing our sandwiches and beer by the way to save time. It is a wonderful camp. It is a long square with the corners rounded off, the southern end more pointed, having a circular place as if a beacon had been there. Length from north to south is 1035 feet, width across the middle 285 feet and nearer the north end 330 feet, from the tops of the aggers. We measured from the top of the inner agger at the north end to the bottom of the

fosse and made it 57 feet.   On the west side from the top of the
inner agger to the top of the second, 85 feet.   Sidmouth tower is
only 75 feet.   The camp is surrounded by three aggers with their
ditches.   Across the middle of the interior run two hedges or earthworks, the purpose of which is disputed.   There is a mound in the
middle of the south one.   The entrance was on the west and perhaps
another at the north-east.   An iron figure of Mercury is said to have
been found here and I should like to know what has become of it.

We varied the route home by taking the lane to the south-west,
which is straight and perhaps occupies the line of the Roman road
and got back by nine, having been out twelve hours (see also August
24). (*Diary*).

Trip to Dawlish.   *Thursday July 14.*   Went to Dawlish by way of
Exeter.   Besides my cousin Mary Roberton at Belmont Villa, I found
my cousin Mrs. Jones and her two children Fanny and Agnes, Miss
Gordon from Dumfries and her niece and nephew Mary and
Alexander Roberton. (*Diary*).

Teignmouth harbour.   *Monday July 18.*   I took little Alexander
over to Teignmouth to look at the harbour and shipping, he having
a strong desire to be a sailor.   We then crossed to Shaldon by the
ferry boat and took a walk around the Ness before returning to
Dawlish. (*Diary*).   *On another occasion perhaps Hutchinson took young Alexander to
watch the crew unloading ballast and drying the sails on Dawlish beach, as pictured in the
accompanying sketch.*

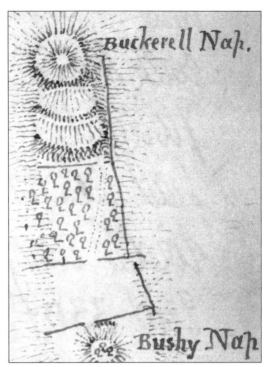

59/6/6.   *Plan of Buckerell Nap
and Bushy Nap.*   (Diary)

59/7/18.   *Sketch on Dawlish
beach, July 1859.*
(DRO, Z19/2/8E/113)

Bed bugs. *Sunday July 31.* Obliged to go into Exeter this evening to sleep in order to be in court sufficiently early tomorrow morning. Annoyed by the bugs! This hot weather they abound everywhere, even in the best hotels, and one is enough to keep me from sleeping. Their attack is just like that of a stinging nettle on my skin. Some say that to touch the edges of the nightcap, waistbands and collar with essential oil of lavender or other strong scent will keep them off. Others recommend sponging the face, neck, hands and other exposed parts with vinegar, letting it dry before going to bed. They say they will not touch the skin where vinegar has been. *(Diary).*

Bible mystery. *Wednesday August 10.* When running a trench round the south-east corner of the south transept of the church on August 9, 1853, the men struck into a vault in which they could see a skeleton extended to full length with the remains of a book under the skull. After some excitement at such an unusual discovery, it was ascertained that Mr. Ximenes, late of Rose Mount, a gentleman of Jewish extraction, had been buried there about twenty years before, and that he had expressed a wish to have his Bible, or Old Testament, placed under his head. The remains of the book were taken out, shown to the vicar and several other people, and the next day a brown paper parcel was put back and the vault closed up. A strong suspicion arose as to what was in that parcel. I wanted to get the vault re-opened for the sake of examination but could not get it done *(see April 23, 1860).* The cover was of tortoise shell, well preserved, ornamented with hand-some silver mountings. *(History of Sidmouth IV, 61).*

Voluntary service. *Thursday August 11.* Was present at a meeting of the Artillery Corps Committee at the house of Gustavus Smith Esq. It was decided that the best way to annoy or harass an enemy that might attempt to land (ideas of a French invasion being again rife) would be nine pound field pieces in prefer-ence to guns in battery or riflemen. Fifty volunteers are required, but as yet only thirty-three have offered. In spite of my lameness my offer is accepted. If I can go out with my field piece and fire for my amusement at a target why may I not go out in earnest and fire at an enemy.

I examined the works in the churchyard. *(Diary).*

Bury Camp, Blackbury Castle and a barrow. *Wednesday August 17.* Went with Mr. Chick and Mr. Heineken to Bury Camp on the cliff and examined it and the flint heap which we opened last September. Drove inland to Blackbury Castle. This we examined and surveyed years ago. Mr. Heineken killed a viper and took the head home for preservation. Some persons have spoken of traces of earthworks as existing on the west of this camp but we were unable to discover any. About half a mile west of the camp there are the remains of a barrow in a field on the south side of the road, in one part of which was found a coin fifty years ago. Mr. Higgins, miller of Colyton, has the coin, and we must enquire what it is.

Approaching Broad Down, we stopped at a cottage and saw an old man aged 89. In answer to our questions, he said that when the road over the Down was made, now about a hundred years ago, his grandfather was one of the men employed. They cut right through a barrow near Roncombe's Girt and found one or two urns of pottery with bones in them *(B.R.No.42).* Parts of weapons (he appeared to mean arrow or spear heads) were also met with. This testimony shows the mode of burial here. Some men further on near Ring-in-the-Mire corroborated the story, and said the vessel or vessels they believed were taken to Netherton Hall. We returned home via Hunter's Lodge, Sidbury and so on. *(Diary).*

59/8/7. *Roncombe's Girt barrow.*
(Hist. of Sid. I,72)

Gun practise on the beach. *Friday August 19.* Drove the gun down to the beach at low water to have some practise, across the sand and shingle to High Peak Hill. Erected a target and fired six shots and think I will send the particulars to one of the journals. On returning, I found the mule quite unable to draw the gun up the steep bank of shingle and I was obliged to send for a horse. The place is so inconvenient that I doubt whether I shall go there again, though I know of no other. *(Diary).*

Artillery Corps meeting. *Saturday August 20.* Attended a meeting of the Volunteer Artillery Corps at the Town Hall. I was proposed as second lieutenant but excused myself as I wished first to know what were the duties and responsibilities of taking command. I also said that I had some misgivings as to whether my lameness might prove to be an impediment, and I wanted to know what the expenses of an officer's uniform were likely to be. Some discussion about swords etc. We broke up with three cheers. (*Diary*).

Hembury Fort and Payhembury Church. *Wednesday August 24.* Mr. Heineken and myself went again to Hembury Fort. When we had mounted Honiton Hill we turned half a mile out of our way to examine the remains of the barrow near the fifteenth milestone from Exeter (see July 26, 1854). We scraped about it but found nothing. I went a hundred yards to the bog called Ring-in-the-Mire and found it dried up, that is, sufficiently to walk over. We then turned back to our previous route and pursued our way through Awliscombe to Hembury. As soon as we attained the summit of the hill we sat down to enjoy the view and discuss our sandwiches. That done we dug about in various places, but dug in vain. We then went down to Payhembury to see Mr. Venn, the owner of the Camp, and examined Payhembury Church. It was put in a state of repair some four years ago. The tower is square and Norman in appearance and the present windows are Perpendicular. Embedded in the walls are many fragments of the Devonshire igneous rock. Inside, down the nave the original low oak seats are handsomely carved and there is a good old wooden screen with fan tracery painted white and blue. There are a few ancient square tiles in the floor on the north-east side. In the churchyard at the north-east part there is a remarkable yew tree of great size. I thought it was four yew trees growing close together with just space enough to walk between the trunks, but the sexton's wife who accompanied us said that it was one tree which many years ago had been struck by lightening and split into four portions down to the ground. We did not get back to Sidmouth till near ten. (*Diary*).

59/8/26. *Foundation stone.*
(Hist. of Sid. IV,66)

'Foundation stone' of Sidmouth Church. *Friday August 26.* The so-called 'foundation stone' was laid at the Church today. The particulars are in the book I devote to the subject. (*Diary*).

Saving the old chancel. *Tuesday September 6.* Mr. Noah Miller, builder, and myself have entered into a contract which we signed today. For £45. 0s. 0d. he is to erect for me on my grounds at Coburg Terrace the old chancel of Sidmouth Church in miniature. I thought it a pity that the old windows, especially the great east window, the buttresses and other parts should be lost or broken up, so I mean to rescue them and re-erect them on my premises. (*Diary*).

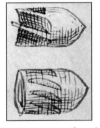

59/9/13. *Shot design.* (Diary)

Shot designs. *Tuesday September 13.* Attended a meeting of the Artillery Corps at Mr. Gustavus Smith's (Belgrave House) and took with me several new shot of my own pattern which I have just had cast in Exeter. The intention is that they should revolve and go point first, though fired out of a smooth bore. (*Diary*). *Two designs accompany the entry. The relative advantages of rifled ordnance had been tested by a Parliamentary Committee the previous year and the Armstrong gun had been put into production. One dilemma was the vast number of smooth bores actually in service and Hutchinson was attempting to achieve similar results by redesigning the casing of the shot. He published his conclusions in 'Rifled Shot in Smooth-bore Guns' the following year.*

Target practice. *Wednesday September 14.* Went along the beach to the base of High Peak and fired five shots at a target against the cliff. Firing very unsatisfactory. (*Diary*). *Displeased at these results, Hutchinson began work on a new casing design, with rather more success (see February 15, 1860).*

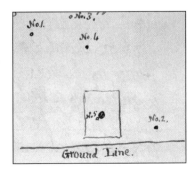

59/9/14. *Firing results.*
(Diary)

Lovehayne Farm tumulus and Blackbury Castle. *Monday September 19.* Went with some friends to examine a tumulus near Lovehayne Farm (*B.R.No. 78*). The farmer, Mr. Power of Elverway, was already there with his two labourers. Half the tumulus was dug down a few years ago. Its construction is thus: first the earth

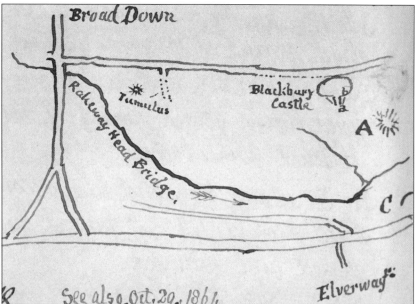

59/9/19-1. Sketch map of Blackbury Castle area. (Dairy)

59/9/19-2. Tumulus in 'Stone Barrow Plot' near Lovehayne Farm, examined and remains found, September 19, 1859. (DRO, Z19/2/8E/117)

was lowered two feet below the natural surface, a mound of dry flints was made four feet six inches high and this was covered with earth to a depth of five feet. On digging, the men in time came to some pieces of bone, which we picked out. For an hour we continued to pick out pieces of bone, then some pieces of rude, black, unbaked pottery, and I found what appeared to be two or three arrow or spear heads of flint. From appearances in the section of this barrow, it is plain that it had been opened before by sinking a hole from the top. It had been clumsily done, for the vase had been broken and parts left, well mixed with the soil along with the bones and flints. The bones had been calcined. We found what appeared to be slight traces of charcoal but these were doubtful. The barrow had been seventy feet in diameter. It is in a field called 'Stone Barrow Plot' belonging to the feoffees of the Poor Lands of Colyton. Report says that fifty or sixty years ago some bronze spearheads or similar weapons, were found in the south side of this heap. The discoveries we made seem to point to an earlier age. Report further says that the said feoffees have one of these weapons at Colyton and we must enquire. (*Later note:* They have not). I am disposed to think that there are the bones of a child as well as an adult among these remains. There is the left side of the lower jaw, very minute, but perhaps the bones shrank in burning.

We then went on to Blackbury Castle with one of the men. At a (*on the map*) on the east side of the entrance the man (James Mutter) told us that about 1825, he had taken away some seventy cartloads of what was believed to have been burnt or calcined flints. Amongst these were many pieces of charcoal, as much as would have filled a cart. There has always been a tradition about calcined flint at Blackbury Castle. Some have ascribed it to the burning of the wood, but this is

vague and the burnt flints would be equally scattered everywhere. Others ascribe them to the action of a fire beacon, but no beacon would ever be made on such a low situation. Query – did they burn their dead here? The man told us a fact hitherto unknown. He said that after his fellow workmen of that day had left the spot, he (James Mutter) saw a round hole where these flints had been dug. It was about fifteen inches in diameter and eighteen deep. Query – whether there had not been an urn burial here and whether the men had not removed the vase? The flints were sifted and used in the mortar for building the house at Wiscombe Park. But there is also a bed of burnt flints at b on the agger of the camp. This is higher and a more likely place for beacon signals. At C there are traces of a half moon entrenchment. At A there is a large, low mound. Tradition says the slain were after a battle buried here. (*Diary*).

59/9/19-3. *Flint from Lovehayne tumulus.* (Hist. of Sid. I,78)

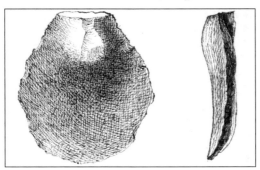

59/9/19-5. *Flint from Lovehayne tumulus.* (Hist. of Sid. I,80)

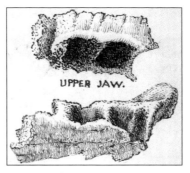

59/9/19-6. *Adult jaw bones.* (Hist. of Sid. I,79)

59/9/19-7. *Pottery fragment.* (Hist. of Sid. I,80)

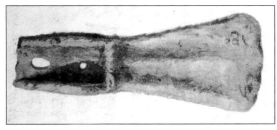

59/9/19-4. *Bronze celt from Lovehayne tumulus.* (Hist. of Sid. I,78)

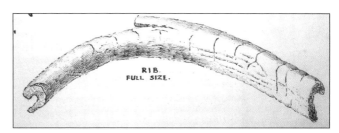

59/9/19-8. *Rib bone.* (Hist. of Sid. I,79)

Three Horseshoes earthwork and Beer quarry. *Monday September 26.* Another antiquarian expedition. Mr. Heineken and myself went to examine point C opposite Blackbury Castle (see map September 19, 1859). We drove up Salcombe Hill and came out at Trow. We stopped at the Three Horseshoes, rented by William Webber, one of my housekeeper's sons. The earthwork is in his field and he took us out to see it. The vallum begins almost imperceptibly not far from the turnpike road behind the Inn and runs in a northerly direction in a straight line for, I should think, two or three hundred yards, and then turns towards the east nearly at right angles. The angle is rounded off. It runs into the hedge but I am inclined to think that it originally ran on and occupied the line of the present hedge at the top of the copse B. This makes two sides of a square like a Roman camp. Report says that the ditch of this entrenchment was on the inside, along the sides a and b, though I scarcely know whether to believe it or not. With respect to the east and south sides of the square (if square it were) we could not trace them, nor learn whether they ever existed. Supposing this to have been a Roman camp, one may imagine that it had been made there to watch Blackbury Castle, occupied by the Britons. The idea is supported by the tradition that a battle was fought between the two and that the slain were buried in the mound at A (but see July 3, 1861).

It set in a rainy day, but nevertheless we went on. We passed Bovey House, approached Beer and drew up the vehicle in the road to eat our sandwiches, for it rained so hard that we scarcely knew what to do. We had heard of the finding of a vase with bones in it near Watercombe (the spot was at D) but as it occurred six or seven years ago we fear we shall not recover any of the remains. (The annexed representation is a rubbing of a piece of pot found in Crossway Close near

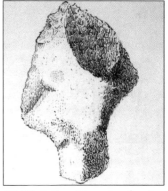

59/9/19-9. *Flint spearhead (?) from Lovehayne tumulus.* (Hist. of Sid. I,79)

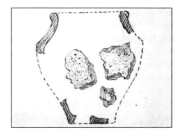

59/9/19-10. *Attempted restoration of urn.* (Hist. of Sid. I,79)

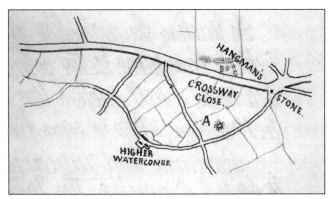

59/9/26-1. *Location map of mound in Crossway Close.* (Hist. of Sid. I,86)

59/9/26-2. *Pottey fragment from Crossway Close.* (Hist. of Sid. I,86)

59/9/26-3. *Column of chalk, Beer Quarry.* (Hist. of Sid. I,19)

59/9/26-4. *Entrance to the stone quarries near Beer. September 26, 1859.* (DRO, Z19/2/8E/119)

Watercombe. The vase was about eighteen inches in diameter by three quarters of an inch thick, and the pattern was impressed with twisted cord).

We visited the Beer stone quarries. The largest is the most curious, the passages extend*ing* under eight acres of ground. At some places the roof is not more than 20 feet thick, at others 120. A man called Cawley who rents the quarry, or works in it, was our guide. Each person carries a candle. The beginning of the excavations is very ancient *and* there are no traces of the use of gunpowder in blasting. The roof is supported by immense square columns of chalk *and* in the ancient workings these columns have a sort of rude capital. We saw two stone troughs, one triangular and full of water, the other square *and* leaky. We went through many turnings round about, beside which there is a horse track for part of the way by which the stone is drawn out. The largest chamber where stone is now procured is at the end, some sixty feet long *and* twelve or fifteen feet high. Several blocks of stone from two to three tons in weight had been detached, *which* are sold at one shilling the cubic foot. Cracks or fissures are met with in the excavations *and* as a test to find out whether these are dangerous or disposed to go further, clay is rubbed into them and watched. If it does not crack, the fissure is not increasing. The fine stone for architectural purposes lies about six to eight feet thick and separates into beds of two to three feet. Above this the stone is coarser and is used for lime, *and* lime kilns in an open quarry are nearby. On emerging the light has a peculiar effect on the eye. (*Diary*).

Re-building the Old Chancel and wall painting discovered in the church. *Thursday September 29.* Michaelmas Day. The masons began the stonework of 'The Old Chancel' in my grounds. At noon there was an artillery meeting where some twenty-nine or thirty of us were enrolled as volunteers by taking the oath of allegiance etc. (*Diary*). In taking down the masonry *in the church*, several blocks of stone painted with various devices in distemper were discovered. The prevailing colours were yellow, red, black, blue and puce-colour brown. In many places also abundant traces of gilding were apparent. Over the chancel arch in the nave, under sundry coats of whitewash, were found patches of wall covered with inscriptions. Some portions of the Commandments were legible. The initial letters were coloured; the rest of the writing, in old English type, was black on a white ground. From these and other traces we may conclude that at one period the greater part of the interior was covered with inscriptions and mural paintings. (*A History of the Restoration of Sidmouth Parish Church, 12*). *The illustrations show* specimens of colouring dug out of the wall.

Dismantling the chancel arch. *Thursday October 13.* Laid the foundation stone of my Old Chancel. (*Diary*). The great chancel arch in the church was taken down after two or three days labour. The soffit had been shored up to prevent its falling in when the keystone was removed. (*History of the Restoration of Sidmouth Parish Church, 12*).

Mr. Miller's accident. *Saturday October 15.* One of the scaffold poles in *the chancel* arch fell upon Mr. Miller the contractor, giving him a violent blow on the crown of the head. He did not recover from its effects for a considerable time afterwards. (*A History of the Restoration of Sidmouth Parish Church, 13*).

Artillery business. *Tuesday October 18.* Another meeting at Mr. (or Captain) Smith's on the subject of artillery. I was again offered a commission (for the third time) but refused as before, and for two reasons. That is, the fear that my lameness may be an impediment, or at least a disadvantage, and also a dislike to incur the expense. Subscriptions have been paid in to the amount of £160. 18s. 0d. (*Diary*).

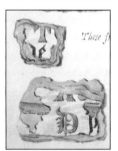

59/9/29. *Specimens of painted stone found during restoration.* (Hist. of Sid. IV,63 and 69)

59/10/19. *Barrett's arm.* (Diary)

Deformed hands. *Wednesday October 19.* A man called Barrett, a fisherman from Budleigh Salterton, called on me with oysters. Both his hands are deformed in a very peculiar manner. He has only a misshapen thumb and forefinger, not unlike the claw of a crab. The tarsus is carried back, not flat like the back of a hand, but irregularly round to the wrist bone which projects a good deal. His neighbours, in order to account for the circumstance, say that his mother was frightened by a crab before he was born. It did not occur to me to ask him what he knew about this part of the affair. (*Diary*).

Commission accepted. *Monday October 24.* Decidedly there is no trust in man. I have just done what I have all along refused not to do. I have accepted a commission after refusing three, or I think four, times. Captain Smith sent Lieutenant Ede to me, who found me busy with the masons at work on the Old Chancel, and requested I would go to Belgrave House. Capt. Compton, R. N., First Lieutenant of our Volunteer Artillery Corps, has retired and a vacancy occurs. Mr. Ede wished to put me over his head as First Lieutenant in Capt. Compton's place, he remaining as Second Lieutenant, but this I of course would not hear of. After a long discussion I was persuaded and my name is to be sent to the Lord Lieutenant. (*Diary*). *In fact Hutchinson was to serve enthusiastically for the next three years, eventually resigning partly to avoid promotion to Captain (see August 16, 1862).*

Wet weather. *Tuesday October 25.* After several days frost, we have today a most boisterous, windy and rainy day. I scarcely remember the like. Went down to the beach to see a small vessel that had been driven on shore. The hail and rain were incessant, and the wind hard to stand against. The driving hail was quite painful against the face. After remaining there half an hour I got drenched, and feeling the rain running down my legs inside my clothes, I came back and changed. (*Diary*).

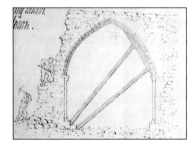

59/10/13-1. *Last arch of the nave supported from falling.* (Hist. of Sid. IV,70)

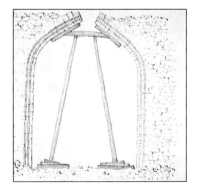

59/10/13-2. *Chancel arch being taken down.* (Hist. of Sid. IV,70)

Aftermath. *Wednesday October 26.* 'After a storm comes a calm' saith the proverb, and today it was calm and quiet. But what a scene of desolation on the beach. At six yesterday evening the sea broke over the esplanade and ran into the town carrying shingle and gravel along with it. The market place and all the lower part of

the town was flooded and the lower rooms of the houses were filled with water, mud and gravel. The esplanade and all the roads and walks near it are now covered with sea beach. The little vessel lies high and dry. A man on board told me he had sent word about his disaster to Jersey (where she belongs) and that endeavours to launch her will be made as soon as an answer is received. Such a storm as this has not occurred here since the memorable one of November 1824. (*Diary*). *The pen and ink sketch from the History of Sidmouth III, 148, illustrates the pebble-strewn street and battered appearance of a house after the earlier storm of 1824.*

59/10/26. *The calm after the storm.* (Hist. of Sid. III,148)

Drill practice. *Wednesday November 16.* We of the Artillery Corps met this evening in the ballroom of the London Inn. Wanting the guns, Captain Smith thought it a good plan to have the men twice a week in the evening after their work, to be taught the facings, how to turn and march and so on. Only half of them are as yet in uniform. (*Diary*).

Arrival of guns and Sidmouth Fort. *Friday November 25.* The guns are to be sent in wagons today. At noon the Corps mustered at the London Hotel. We first had an hours drill by our drill sergeant, Mr. George Gosling, and by one o'clock, when we heard that the guns were in the Market Place, we all went down, formed in two divisions, one marching before the wagons and the other in rear. In this way we went along the beach, up by Denby Place and in front of the houses of Fort Field Terrace into the field. The guns were to be placed on the grass fifty feet from each other pointing out to sea on either side of the flagstaff. The flag (Union Jack) was hoisted. The two guns were on a timber wagon and the two carriages on a common wagon. We were disappointed at the form of the carriages. Each gun with its carriage weighed 50 cwt. Removing them from the wagons and placing them onto their carriages took till half past four. In order to give the Sidmouth men some idea of how the guns were to be worked, the sergeant and six gunners who had come with them from Plymouth, went through the actions of loading and firing several times, our men being drawn up round the guns forming three sides of a square. (*Diary*).

59/11/25-1. (Diary)

Fort Cottage, Fort Field *and* Fort Terrace all take their names from the existence of a fort standing in the corner of the said field, on the rising ground close to the west side of Fort Cottage. When that defence of the town was first erected does not seem to be known, but I can at all events show from the parish books that its *history* can be carried back nearly two hundred years. Besides the fort proper, there was a small house or magazine in which ammunition or side arms were kept, which stood in rear or right rear of the former. The fort was dismantled after the Battle of Waterloo and the general peace. All I can recall of it, is a rough place and the foundations of some stone walls, soon after my father came to Sidmouth in January 1925. At the spot where Fort Cottage now stands there used to be two small cottages and a potato plot *and* I have been told that one of the tenants left because the firing of the guns broke the windows.

Old people who could recollect all the arrangements have often described them to me. There were four iron twelve-pound guns, two of which pointed rather to the eastward and the other two inclined to the westward. The 'Sea Fencibles', who had the handling of these guns, used to direct their shot, sometimes against the Chit Rock as a mark. There was also a brass six-pound field piece. Two of the guns were removed to the east end of the beach and stood on end as posts, and the other two were stood on end in the tower of the parish church to support the floor of the belfry and the organ gallery, but these were cleared out in 1860 when the church was rebuilt.

59/11/25-2. (Hist. of Sid. IV,156a)

One dark cloudy evening one of my playmates and myself, having considered the upturned mouths of these guns, went and bought a quantity of gunpowder

and some crackers. Thus prepared, we got on the trunnions of one of these guns and emptying our packet in the muzzle, let the powder run down to the breech. We then lit a cracker and let it drop down upon the powder. In an instant, oh my, what a row! We jumped or tumbled off the trunnions somehow and ran – my, how we ran! The explosion roused the town and there were many anxious enquiries about the earthquake. We were never found out but the guns were afterwards filled up with beach gravel, and after that they put plugs in the muzzles and have fixed gates to them.

The annexed sketch of the Fort I drew at the dictation and description of the late Mr. Hugh Wheaton, the sexton of Sidmouth, standing at his elbow and jotting down all the arrangements of the interior, until he was satisfied that my drawing was a correct representation of what he could recollect of its appearance before it was dismantled. (*History of Sidmouth IV*).

59/11/25-3. *The Fort, Sidmouth.* (Hist. of Sid. IV,158)

Sword exercises. *Saturday November 26.* Today I received my sword. It has a steel scabbard and the blade bears the words 'Sidmouth Artillery'. Unfortunately steel scabbards blunt the edge of a sharp sword. Tonight we had a drill that made our arms ache but is good exercise for the muscles of the shoulders, back, chest and arms. And others for the legs. (*Diary*).

Commission received. *Friday December 2.* Received my commission as Second Lieutenant dated November 15, for which I paid five shillings. (*Diary*).

Squints. *Wednesday December 7.* This day 600 years ago (not allowing for the change of style) Sidmouth Church was consecrated. A squint or hagioscope, that opening pierced through the wall from the nave into the chancel behind the chancel arch, was found on the north and on the south sides of the building. The largest was that on the north side. (*A History of the Restoration of Sidmouth Parish Church, 13*). *The two squints are shown in the accompanying illustrations.*

59/11/26. *Exercises.* (Diary)

59/12/7-1. *Hagioscope on the north side of the chancel.* (Hist. of Sid. IV,67)

59/12/7-2. *Hagioscope on the south side of the chancel.* (Hist. of Sid. IV,66)

Re-erecting the Old Chancel. *Saturday December 13.* The gables and gable crosses of my Old Chancel were up a few days ago and today the masons completed the chimney and crowned it with a spare gable cross. I then gave the men half a gallon of hot cider with sugar, ginger and nutmeg in it, which they relished amazingly, for the day though fine was cold. It froze in the shade all day. (*Diary*).

59/12/8-1. *The old chancel of Sidmouth parish church re-erected at Coburg Terrace, 1859.* (DRO, Z19/2/8E/115)

Chancel complete. *Thursday December 8.* Today the masons completed the exterior of my Old Chancel. The walls are all up, the steps placed at the door, the garden wall brought up against the buttresses where it had been pulled down to put in the north wall of the building and the rubbish cleared away. Another payment of £15 is now due. *The chancel of the parish church, shown in the annexed sketch painted about this time, was thus saved from destruction and re-erected, though in rather shorter and narrower form than the original, on Hutchinson's ground in Coburg Terrace. At this stage he intended it merely as a private museum and workshop, but as more old materials became available, another window from Awliscombe church, ship timbers from a wreck, etc., the idea grew of enlarging the building into a dwelling for himself. Piecemeal additions in the gothic style were made over the next decades as finances allowed, he was still adding embellishments in his 80's, but in the end Hutchinson was far from happy with the result (see February 4, 1881). Nevertheless, he bequeathed to Sidmouth, a town that has retained more than its share of notable buildings, one of its most picturesque residences.*

59/12/8-2. *Strange clouds.* (Diary)

A few nights ago, as I was going to drill, I saw a very curiously defined cloud. The annexed is a representation. It was like five gigantic figures springing upwards, with the young moon between two of them. (*Diary*).

Icy weather. *Tuesday December 20.* Since last Thursday the weather has been intensely cold. Pump frozen, water in my bedroom frozen, everything frozen. On Sunday night the thermometer in my room went down to 23 degrees Fahrenheit. All outdoor work has been stopped. This morning the wind changed to the south and it blew and rained and thawed. (*Diary*).

1860

New Years Day 1860. *Sunday January 1*. Very mild. Several window flies have shown themselves. The Corps again went to church in uniform, being New Years Day. It rained miserably when we came out *so* the Captain dismissed us at once, the wisest thing he could do. (*Diary*).

Promotion. *Monday January 16*. For good conduct George Robbins, one of our men, was called out of the ranks at drill tonight by Captain Smith and told he should be made a corporal. (*Diary*).

Tuesday January 17. Alas, there is no selecting one man for promotion without offending all the rest *and* this morning fourteen men sent in their resignations. George Robbins happens to be young and in an inferior position in life, and the older and better-to-do did not like the idea of his advancement. (*Diary*).

Sword practice. *Thursday January 19*. There is a jolly row in the town about the 'mutiny', as it is called. Robbins, much annoyed by the taunts of his companions and wishing to compose the present agitated spirit seeing that the safety of the Corps was at stake, wrote a very proper letter to the Captain thanking him for his kindness but begging to remain in the ranks where he was before. At our drill tonight, there was a very full attendance and an immense number of spectators drawn to see what would come next, *but* the resignation of Robbins of the honour offered him has served to compose matters. Captain Smith read some comments on recent affairs from a paper and things passed off peaceably.

By way of keeping my hand in at sword play, I went down to the butchers and decapitated a sheep with a single blow of my sword. I did not succeed every time I tried, but I am inclined to think that, as there is as much a knack in it as actual force, a little practice would make one tolerably sure of doing it without much risk of failure. (*Diary*).

Target practice on Sidmouth beach. *Wednesday February 15*. Took my 3-pound gun down to the beach for some practice. The drill sergeant and half a dozen men of our Artillery Corps took it down with the drag ropes. We halted on the shingle near the Preventive House and fired against the cliff near the mouth of the river. Our target was a piece of board a foot square painted white, range two hundred yards. The first was a round shot with half a pound of powder. It struck to the right *so* I therefore readjusted the sight by shifting it a little to the left. The second shot struck the board right in the centre and shivered it to pieces. Nothing could be more accurate. The practise with my conical shot was satisfactory in one case but not in the other. The shot, feathered behind like this sketch, were found embedded in the cliff point first, but the shells did not answer so well. One of the round shot we fired away, having been bruised. We elevated the gun a good deal and pointed it eastwards towards Salcombe mouth, *but* when fired the shot made a sweep round to the left and pitched on the beach about a mile off instead of in the water. This made us throw away another shot. We now took a perfect one that had not been bruised, *which* went as straight as an arrow and either struck or dashed the water over a small rock in the sea off Salcombe Hill, a mile from Sidmouth. (*Diary*).

60/2/15. *Another shell.*
(Dairy)

145

60/3/8-1. *Mural painting discovered in Sidmouth Church.* (Hist. of Sid. IV,72)

Painted plaster in the church. *Thursday March 8.* Under the whitewash at the west end of the north aisle a very rudely executed mural painting in distemper was discovered. It was so rudely done that it was not worth preserving as a work of art, and its destruction was unavoidable as a window was opened at that spot. But I secured a sketch of it before it was destroyed. Little could be made out except the hind leg and tail of some strange animal, coloured dark red, and part of a scroll in front of it bearing an inscription with nothing legible but **...an...olbre...** or something like it. Or perhaps **...art...olbre...** (*History of Sidmouth IV, 72*). *Various other fitments were taken out of the church during the rebuilding and either replaced or lost:* In one of the old puttock holes in the eastern spandrel of the northern arcade, the headless bust of an angel bearing a plain shield was found, as here portrayed. Like the niche, it had been coloured red. It was about nine or ten inches high and being of no sculptural value, as the hands plainly showed, it was put back again. (*History of Sidmouth IV, 73*).

60/3/8-2. *Carved figure, front view.* (Hist. of Sid. IV,73)

60/3/8-3. *Carved figure, side view.* (Hist. of Sid. IV,73)

60/3/8-4. *Bottom slab of the old piscina.* (Hist. of Sid. IV,69)

60/3/8-5. *Front view of the piscina.* (Hist. of Sid. IV,69)

60/3/8-6. *Niche, now over east window outside.* (Hist. of Sid. IV,70)

60/3/8-7. *Arm of stone seat, now lost.* (Hist. of Sid. IV,70)

Stormy meeting. *Friday March 23.* Attended a vestry meeting of a very stormy kind. From the church (or rather the tower, for the church is not finished), we adjourned to the Town Hall. An address was recently issued by the Rev. the Earl of Buckinghamshire discouraging the putting up of certain Tractarian symbols in the church and advising the parishioners to attend and vote against them. This brought a large attendance. Although one of the Building Committee, I have felt lately that I could not pull with the other members *and* sided more with the Earl's views than with those of the Committee. It was a most unpleasant thing for me today, to make a speech condemnatory of the course now proposed to be taken by those gentlemen with whom I have worked for fifteen months. When the votes were counted the parish (including the Earl's views and mine) had a majority of four to one over the Tractarians. (*Diary*). *The Tractarian symbols complained of included such things as a high altar with reredos, moving the organ to the east end of the church, choir in surplices, etc.*

Saturday March 24. This morning I got a very friendly letter from the Earl, approving of the part which I had taken. (*Diary*). *Having won the vote the Earl, perhaps unwisely, now spectacularly enlarged the quarrel in a letter to the Exeter and Plymouth Gazette complaining of the 'small party of Tractarians in the parish'. Over the next few weeks the simmering fury of several members of the Building Committee at having been outvoted exploded in a deluge of acrimonious and mostly pseudonymous attacks on the Earl and 'Mr. H.', whom they regarded as at least partly behind the troubles.*

Tessellated pavement. *Thursday April 5.* Finished my piece of tessellated pavement, begun on the 7th of January and carried on at sundry intervals. The tesserae came from the remains of a Roman villa discovered some years ago in a field near Uplyme. I bought a peck of them in a sale at the vicarage, Musbury, in August 1858. The colours are blue (blue lias), fawn (white lias), white (chalk) and red (brick). My pattern is a sort of Greek fret surrounded by a border of guilloche pattern, *and* the whole is set with Portland cement in a basin an inch deep cut in a slab of Portland stone. I design this piece of work for the centre of the floor of the Old Chancel at Coburg Terrace. (*Diary*).

Quarrel continues. *Saturday April 21.* In Woolmer's Exeter and Plymouth Gazette of today, there is a long letter of mine on the subject of the late parish quarrels and a defence of the Rev. the Earl of Buckinghamshire in the steps which he has taken. This evening I received a kind letter from his lordship, thanking me for what I had done. (*Diary*). *The next issue of the paper (April 28) published the vicar's insulting response to Hutchinson's letter, amongst other accusations alleging rather inaptly that 'the muse of history never smiled upon his birth'. The correspondence spluttered on for another month, ending with the Earl's triumphant claim that he would 'now be no longer apprehensive of such objectionable matters as were clearly in contemplation but which are now to be withdrawn'. The 'ritualists' had retired but were not yet defeated (see September 12).*

60/4/23. *Bible found in the vault.* (Hist. of Sid. IV,61)

Buried Bible. *Monday April 23.* At five this afternoon there was a Committee meeting of the members of the Church Improvement Committee at Mr. Churchwarden Webber's. Present were the Rev. H. J. Hamilton the vicar, J. B. Lousada Esq., Rev. G. Deacon, Mr. Webber and Mr. Prettyjohn, besides myself. The chairman, the vicar, read a reply to my letter in Woolmer of Saturday, to certain parts of which I objected. It was then sent to the post. The vicar was then called away to a funeral and Mr. Lousada took the chair. Mr. Plaice, the Clerk-of-the-Works, came upstairs and said he had some complaints to make about me *and* I understood his ill-humour. A month or two ago I offended him by conveying to him a censure from the Committee, especially *from* Mr. Deacon and Mr. Lousada, respecting the shameful and unworkmanlike way in which large and jagged holes had been cut in the tower to insert some ends of timbers. Though he was saucy to me at the time, he subsequently apologised for what he had said, *but* he appears to have thought that the present would be a favourable moment for a little revenge. He said that last Autumn I had gone down into the churchyard early one morning and tried to bribe or induce some men to open a vault and show me the remains of a Bible which had been examined and reburied. My counter statement was that the Bible had been found on the 9th of August, that towards the afternoon of that day I had talked to him about it, that I expressed my regret that I had not seen it and asked whether he could show it to me. He replied that it was only under a few stones, but as there were a good many people about he had rather not remove them then, but if I would came down the following morning early he would give me a sight of the book. I went down but he failed to keep his promise *and* when I saw him a little later he made excuses and I did not see it.   My sketch of the book in ms. memoranda on the restoration of Sidmouth Church was taken from a drawing of his. (*Diary*).

Calumnies unanswered. *Wednesday April 25.* Wrote to the vicar to request he would call an early meeting to give me an opportunity of refuting the calumnies spoken against me last Monday, before the same gentlemen who had heard them. He excused himself. *Diary:*

Company drill. *Wednesday May 9.* We had a pleasant drill. First worked the guns in the field, *then* marched four deep to the Town Hall where more men joined us *and then* marched back to the field via Church Street.   Had half an hour's company drill there *and* then marched via the beach (whistling a tune) up through the town *before being* dismissed in Upper High Street. (*Diary*).

Friend in need. *Saturday May 19.* A friend of mine, a gentleman of property here, bought some chains and other jewellery off a travelling Jew, giving him besides money a quantity of furniture, under the idea that they were good gold. He, being in Exeter today, pawned one of the chains.   The man took the chain and gave four sovereigns for it.   He allowed the other to go and then found out that it was not gold, *though* he ought to have tested the article whilst the other was in the shop.   He then sent a policeman after him and had him taken into custody, and as there was no one in Exeter who could speak for him, he was locked up.   His wife, on her return to Sidmouth, sent and told me, *and* at half past nine I started for Exeter in a gig, hoping to get there in time to bail him out.   I did not arrive till near twelve, the distance being little short of sixteen miles, *but* I saw his lawyer by calling him out of bed.   I also went to the Guildhall but it was too late to do anything.   I determined to get back to Sidmouth as soon as I could *and* went to bed at one in the morning of: (*Diary*).

Sunday May 20.   Woke at three AM, got up at four or a little after not much refreshed, at five got into the mail and arrived in Sidmouth at half past seven. Had breakfast at eight, for I had eaten nothing since my tea at home the evening before. (*Diary*).

Monday May 21. Started *for Exeter* again. His wife took a carriage and Mr. Harris and myself went with her to the Guildhall. The case was adjourned till Saturday for want of further evidence *but* we bailed him out, £50 each, and returned. (*Diary*).

Dawlish visit. *Wednesday May 30.* Went to Dawlish via Exeter to stay a week or two with my cousin Mary Roberton at Belmont Villa on the north-east cliff. Found my cousin Marion Jones there. (*Diary*). *Among other things, Hutchinson had some Artillery business to attend to before returning to Sidmouth on June 12.*

Churchyard enquiry. *Thursday June 14.* Today the churchyard enquiry took place. The reporters of two of the Exeter papers dined with me. (*Diary*). *The enquiry was in response to complaints that human bones from the churchyard had been found scattered all over the parish and resulted in a further embarrassment for the vicar. The circumstances are described in the History of Sidmouth:*   In November 1859, that portion of the burying-ground lying to the north of the church was lowered by a depth of about two feet, beginning at the church and thinning northwards to nothing. The Vicar had given orders that if any bones were met with they should be put aside and re-interred, and that the earth should be screened or sifted. There had been a great deal of rain late in the autumn so that the earth was too wet to pass through a sieve and was so clammy and muddy that it held together in clods. Consequently all but the larger bones, many of which I saw picked out and put into a basket for reburial, remained unobserved. The earth was offered for sale to dress or manure the land with and a great quantity was put in the road outside the south-west wall of the churchyard. Churchyard earth that has been buried in for centuries must necessarily be full of fragments of osseous remains, but at first these were not very obvious in the muddy clods that were distributed

over the fields.   A few good showers of rain however soon served to alter the case.
The earth was washed into the ground and disappeared and then the fields were
discovered to be strewn all over with bits of bone.   As I was walking to the church
one day, I picked up as many bits of ribs, skulls, finger bones, teeth and toe bones
a I could hold in my two hands, and before I threw them down in the yard I
showed them to a man who was working there.   He gave an uneasy hurried glance
around but made no comment, for such was the terrorism created in the parish
owing to the violent clash of sentiments, that trades people were afraid to commit
themselves to remark on what they saw.   I have heard it said that Mr. Harris the
grocer, who had openly spoken against the measures of the Committee, lost eleven
of his best customers, and Mrs. Farrant the upholsterer, alluding to passing events,
said to me 'I can't afford to have an opinion, Sir'.   Mr. Ede of Lansdowne
forwarded to the Chancellor of the Diocese a fragment of a child's skull thrown
down on the public turnpike for the purpose of repair, whilst Mr. Vane of Camden
picked up some pieces of bone near Jenny Pine's Corner, and thinking it high time
that these irregularities should be looked into enclosed them to the Bishop.
Upon this the Bishop sent a gentleman down to make enquiry on the spot and
after an interval of some months issued a commission for a court of enquiry.   The
verdict was that the removal of the earth without a faculty was illegal and that
there were sufficient prima facia grounds for instituting further proceedings – if
anyone chose to follow them up.   (*History of Sidmouth IV, 80-82, extracts*).   *The
Bishop declined to do so and it seems that nobody else was prepared to either.*

Harlewyn's monument.   *Wednesday June 27.*   Gilt and painted the armorial
bearings on Harlewyn's monument (*see sketch of June 21, 1858*).   The shield bears
Harlewyn impaling Parker (Earl of Morley's family).   (*Diary*).

Page's trial.   *Monday July 2.*   Page's case came on today (see May 21).   Started
at half past seven AM and drove into Exeter.   He was acquitted.   Got back by
nine PM.   (*Diary*).

Official re-opening of Sidmouth Parish Church.   *Thursday July 12.*   Today
the parish church was formally opened to the public, although much remains to
be done in the way of finishing.   Fourteen clergymen in surplices made their
appearance!   At the end of the morning service a collection was made *and* I could
not resist a practical joke having reference to the quarrels, contentions and party
animosities that have been so much mixed up with the rebuilding of the church.
In all these quarrels, I regret to say, I have seen as much spite, ill will, and
ungentlemanly conduct in the clergy as ever I have seen in any other persons what-

60/8/1-1. *West window of the
bell chamber, Sidmouth church
tower. January 22, 1848.*
(DRO, Z19/2/8D/103)

ever.   Before I went to church this morning, I
selected a piece of paper as near in size and appearance to that of a £5 or £10 note as I could find and
wrote the following sentences on it:
'Except the Lord build the house, they labour in
vain that build it'.   *Ps. 127.1*
'It is an honour for a man to cease from strife'.   *Prov.
20.3.*
'And a house divided against itself shall not stand'.
Math. 12.25.
When I put the paper in the plate, it certainly looked
very like a bank note.   I would have given a trifle to
have seen the countenances of those fourteen clergymen when they opened it. (*Diary*). *As it turned out,
Biblical injunctions were insufficient to compose the feud
and the 'ritualists' now contrived a rather underhand ploy
to attain at least part of their goal (see September 12).*

Illustrations for book on Sidmouth Church.
Wednesday August 1.   Having recently done the six
subjects for illustrating my little book on the
Restoration of Sidmouth Church on stone (or rather on

60/8/1-2. *North side of the parish church before the alter-*
ations were begun. (Hist. of Sid. IV,59).

60/8/1-3. *North-east view of the parish church as rebuilt.*
(Hist. of Sid. IV,59)

60/8/1-4. *West doorway, Sidmouth Church. January 14,*
1848. (DRO, Z19/2/8D/93)

60/8/1-5. *West doorway, Sidmouth church.* (Hist. of Sid.
IV,122)

transfer paper) I am now busy about the interior views of
the new parish church on copper. (*Diary*). *Two illustra-*
tions from the book show the north side of the church before and
after restoration. The window of the bell chamber and the first
picture of the west doorway were sketched in 1848.

Enlisting the band. *Friday August 10.* The Captain
and myself attended at the Town Hall this evening at
seven, to receive candidates as bandsmen *and* also to
examine the drums, fifes, etc. Brass fifes have been
recommended by Mr. Pinney of Exeter, now organist at
Sidmouth, whom we have got for £20 per annum as our
bandmaster. The candidates handled the drums and fifes
and a pretty noise they made. (*Diary*).

Wreck of the 'Enterprise'. *Thursday August 16.* A
sudden gale of wind came on last night. Yesterday, two
schooners and a brig were anchored off Sidmouth discharg-
ing coals. Two vessels rode out the storm, but the chain cable
of the 'Enterprise' schooner of Brixham parted between four
and five this morning and she was driven on shore opposite
Fore Street. There she lies high and dry. (*Diary*).

Friday August 17. As the schooner was leaning outwards
towards the sea, ropes were fastened to her mainmast and
when the tide rose they tried to drag her over. The strain
however, broke the mast clean off. (*Diary*).

Saturday August 18. The schooner is abandoned to her
fate. The weather is so boisterous and she has become so
leaky that little hope now remains of doing anything to
save her. (*Diary*).

Engravings for book. *Monday August 20.* Finished
engraving on copper the plate representing the east and
west interior views of the parish church, destined for my
little book on the restorations. (*Diary*).

Saturday September 1. Finished engraving, all but a few
touches, the plate representing the west end of the church
with the organ. (*Diary*).

Unchivalrous charge. *Wednesday September 5.* Attended
at the Captain's, to investigate a case of assault in which
our Drill Sergeant's name was implicated - he being near

the woman who was struck and did not interfere to protect her. Afterwards, we drove to Sidmouth to see the woman and then to Cotford and saw Mr. Bailey the magistrate. (*Diary*).

Last of the 'Enterprise'. *Friday September 7.* Fine warm weather at last. The wrecked schooner was sold today *and* I went down to the beach to see. Her hull fetched £60 *and* the sails, rigging and stores were afterwards disposed of in various lots. I suppose it will be impossible ever to float her off for there are great holes in her bottom through which the boys are creeping in and out all day long. (*Diary*).

Queen's window for the church. *Wednesday September 12.* Some new difficulties have arisen about our church works, especially concerning the Queen's window and the Earl of Buckingham's organ, detailed in my book about the church. I called on the Earl on the subject, *and* he was twice at my house afterwards during the day. (*Diary*). *In an attempt to impose a more 'rituralistic' arrangement within the church against the wishes of the majority of the parishioners, one of the Restoration Committee members had written to the Queen suggesting she donate a window in memory of her father who had died at Sidmouth in 1820, to which she assented. As the only suitable window was the western one, this artful scheme would mean that the organ, then in the course of erection in front of it, would have to be moved to the eastern end of the church after all.* Not long afterwards I found out the authors and contrivers of this scheme and the writer of the application. As I am mercifully disposed I will withhold their names, but my contempt remains the same. (*History of Sidmouth IV*, 76). *Over the following few days Hutchinson and the Earl, outraged at such underhand dealing, considered their next move.*

Osborne House to see the Queen. *Wednesday September 19.* Left Sidmouth for Osborne House, Isle of Wight, where the Queen is staying for a few days, having with me a memorandum referring to some curious proceedings about our church from the Earl of Buckinghamshire, which Her Majesty ought to know. Up at half past five, breakfasted at six and on the coach at half past six for Honiton. Took the new rail recently opened from Honiton via Sherborne to Salisbury and Southampton. Got immediately into a steamer and arrived at Cowes about 3.00 PM. At the hotel I immediately changed into my uniform and found the use of it. Sentries presented arms and the Queen's gatekeeper

60/9/19. *A little princess, Osborne House.* (Hist. of Sid. IV, 77)

threw the portal open wide as he saw me approach. As I walked through the Park, a pony carriage with a girl of six or eight years old in it, led by a groom in the royal livery, crossed the road about a hundred yards ahead of me. It was one of the little princesses. *Hutchinson here gives a short description of Osborne House before continuing:* My uniform had the same effect at the House, *as* the footman did not wait till I had knocked. I had a long talk with Major Elphinstone, tutor to Prince Arthur, and I am to call again tomorrow. Returned to West Cowes and got something to eat and drink, for I now had a right to feel hungry having had nothing for exactly twelve hours and travelled a few miles into the bargain. (*Diary*).

Petition presented. *Thursday September 20.* A fine morning *and* at eleven I girt on my sword and walked out again. Was nearly an hour with Major Elphinstone (whose father and family reside near Sidmouth) and pen and ink having been brought to me by one of the footmen, I wrote a note to Col. the Hon. Sir Charles Phillips, Her Majesty's Secretary, enclosing the petition to the Queen which I had brought with me. The prayer of the petition asks for *an* enquiry into some of our church matters and I was informed that it would be acted upon. Having therefore performed the object of my mission, I prepared to return. Awaiting the steamboat, I took a walk about Cowes and admired the many pretty yachts on the water. (*Diary*). *On returning to Sidmouth, Hutchinson immediately reported to the Earl.*

Further discussions. *Saturday September 22.* The Earl surprised me at ten this morning to talk over my recent mission and arrange future plans. The Rev. H. Gibbs, incumbent of All Saints, likewise was with me, the Earl having admitted him into his confidence. My other book on the *Restoration of Sidmouth Church* contains some other particulars about this business. (*Diary*). *The errand was successful, the Queen rescinding her grant of a window 'until the disputes respecting it are settled', and the restoration could now proceed as originally planned. Despite routing the other members of the Building Committee, Hutchinson's troubles were by no means over yet (see February 9, 1861 and April 10, 1862). The Queen's window was eventually installed at the west end of the church some five years later by removing the gallery and lowering the organ out of the way to the floor beneath.*

Sword play. *Wednesday November 14.* Today the drill sergeant was giving me my lesson in sword practise and we were cutting away pretty hard when my sword snapped in two in the middle. (*Diary*).

1861

New Years Day. *Tuesday January 1.* Accounts reach us of the unusual severity of the weather all over the country. On Christmas Day the thermometer seems to have fallen lower than on any other day this winter so far. At Sidmouth it was 23 degrees, in Hertfordshire zero, at Cheadle in Staffordshire 10 below zero, or 42 below freezing. It was 26 in my bedroom and everything frozen hard - jug, water bottle and toothbrushes. I broke the ice in my jug and sponged myself with water and then dressed. This is nothing to do if one does it quickly, the moment one jumps out of bed. I sleep under fifteen blankets – some are doubled but it is fifteen thicknesses at all events. (*Diary*).

Disagreeable visitor. *Saturday February 9.* This morning Colonel Hamilton, brother of the vicar, called on me in a very excited state on the subject of our parish affairs (of which he knows nothing), and on the subject of a letter I have written to his mother, regretting that circumstances over which I had no control should have placed me in opposition to her son the vicar. The vicar has just exchanged parishes with the vicar of Combe St. Nicholas, and he has done so because Sidmouth has become too hot for him. In my letter I remarked that he had been driven from his parish by adhering to bad advice and the Col. took exception to this expression. He said 'he would make me pay for it if I did not mind what I was about etc.,etc.' I told him he was a comparative stranger here and knew nothing of our parish affairs, that he had better let them alone *and* that I knew what I was about, etc. (*Diary*).

Sunday March 24. The Rev. H.J.Hamilton, the vicar, who has exchanged his living with the vicar of Chard, preached his farewell sermon this afternoon at the parish church. (*Diary*).

Twenty-one gun salute. *Monday March 25.* This being the day appointed for the funeral of the Queen's mother, we artillery men turned out in the Fort Field and fired twenty-one minute guns from our 24-pounders. One of the guns missed fire, 'the tube was blown' as they technically say. However, I had a spare tube in my hand and the moment the gun missed I rushed between the men, put the tube in the vent and fired. Everybody was struck with astonishment fancy-ing some accident had happened, but I was anxious the time should be well kept because people sometimes time us with their watches. And curiously enough, Mr. Heineken (who was at home at the time) afterwards meeting the Captain said 'You kept your time very well. I had my watch in my hand and every gun went off almost to the second'. (*Diary*). *The friction tube produced the spark to ignite the charge.*

Stranding of Clementina. *April. There is no mention in the Diary of the stranding of the schooner Clementina on Sidmouth beach, shown in the sketch.* She was afterwards unrigged, righted and floated off. (*Sketchbook E*).

Aylesbeare Hill and Belbury Castle. *Friday May 31.* Started with Mr. Heineken for an antiquarian expedition to Aylesbeare Hill, etc., and to look for Belbury Castle, for which we have been enquiring for a dozen years . . . On the top of Aylesbeare Hill we again made sympiesometer observations. We also pitched

61/3/25. *Friction tube.*
(Dairy)

153

61/4/?. *The schooner 'Clementina' driven on shore at Sidmouth April 1861. She was afterwards unrigged, righted and floated off.* (DRO, Z19/2/8E/125)

the water level, a useful instrument for rough purposes. It is merely two bottles connected together by a tin tube and placed on a pole. The fluid is water coloured with some ink or indigo in it. By looking along the edges of the bottles at distant objects, their relative levels can be seen. We then examined a number of very curious pits on the open heath, of which we had before heard but never seen. They lie some three or four hundred yards north of the two clumps of fir trees. They are called the 'Soldier's Pits' *and* tradition says they were made by soldiers once encamped on this hill. We mean to come another day expressly to examine them (see June 14).

We then steered north and on Venn Ottery Hill measured a ridge or earthwork in the form of an S for three hundred paces. Thence we proceeded to look for Belbury Castle. After some trouble, we found its site near 'Brick House', between two and three miles south-west of Ottery, or near the schools. On the flank of the hill in the plantation, there is a very remarkable sunken road. From Belbury Castle it can be traced all the way north to Streetway Head. Before the land was enclosed it was perfect but even now is visible. All our doubts were set at rest on falling in with an old man of seventy-nine called Samuel White, who lives at Castle Farm.

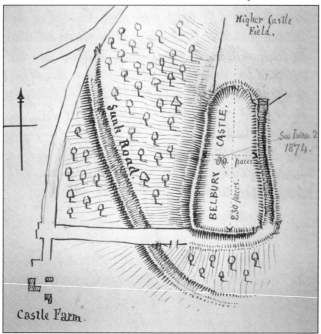

61/5/31-1. *Plan of Belbury Castle.* (Diary)

61/5/31-2. *Water level.* (Dairy)

He told us that seventy years ago when he was a boy the land was wild heath, that he and his father assisted in levelling the earthworks round the camp, that they raised the earth in the middle of the camp from what they got from the banks around it, that there was a great ditch all round outside the bank, that the present road round the south and east sides occupies the bottom of the former ditch, that he never heard of any coins or weapons or other relics ever having been found in the camp, that the camp was called Belbury or Belsbury Castle and that the field is known as Castle Field. He also told us he had traced the sunken road all the way to Streetway Head, and could point out many portions of it even now (see June 2, 1874). (*Diary*).

'Soldier's Pits', Aylesbeare Hill. *Friday June 14.* Started with Mr. Heineken to examine the 'Soldier's Pits on Aylesbeare Hill. They lie some three to four hundred yards north and north-east of the two tumuli planted with fir trees, on the top of the hill between Newton Poppleford and the Halfway House. They consist mostly of pits dug in the ground with the earth used to make the walls. The pits were evidently residences *for* a gap or door appears in each. They are six feet by eight *or* twelve and some *are* larger, *and* mostly extend like a street in two parallel rows for more than half a mile. There are also several circular trenches, perhaps gutters cut round tents to prevent the wet getting into them. We also found two ridges in the form of circles, one sixty feet across, the other larger. Between one of these and a long square pit, we found some pavement

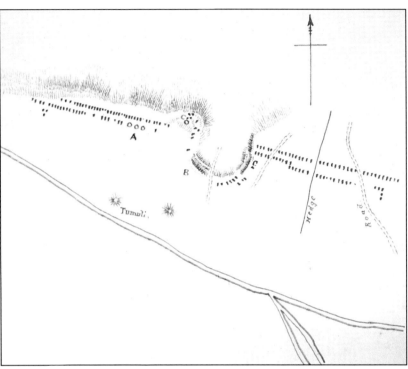

61/6/14. *Soldier's pits on Aylesbear Hill.* (Hist. of Sid. I,115)

made of the pebbles found on the hill, *and* we had been told that many *similar* patches existed in different places, *though* some had been destroyed by men cutting turf. On the north there are many curious earthworks, *including* a tumulus. That all these were pits where soldiers made their camp fires, as tradition says, must be incorrect. If they are not the remains of an ancient village, some suppose they may have been made about 1799 when a French invasion was expected, or in 1803 when Lieut. Gen. Simcoe had his forces on Woodbury Hill and perhaps sent a portion of them here. The accompanying fancy sketch may give some idea of their position. (*Diary*).

Mound near Blackbury Gate. *Wednesday July 3.* Mr. Heineken and myself went over to examine the earthworks behind the Three Horseshoes on the Lyme road. The bank looks very like the west side of a square Roman camp, with the north-west corner rounded. What I have got to say about this place I shall embody in my paper to be read before the Archaeological Association in Exeter next August. Mr. Chick in another carriage, assisting us, took over a man with tools. Him we set to work to examine the large mound in a field some three hundred yards south-east of Blackbury Gate, where tradition says the dead were buried after some desperate battle in the valley. A hole was sunk to ten feet perpendicular in the crown, but it was nothing but fine yellow sand all the way down which, from the water marks, had evidently never been disturbed since nature deposited it there. This is, therefore, a natural hill and not a tumulus. By chance we heard of some trenches on a hill in the parish of Branscombe. We must go soon. (*Diary*).

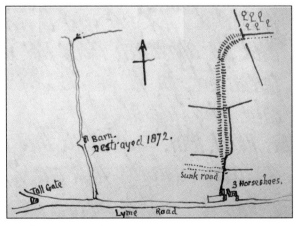

61/7/3. *Earthwork near the Three Horseshoes.* (Diary)

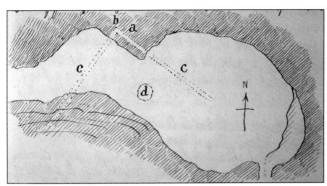

61/7/9. *Chalk quarry,*
Branscombe. (Diary)

Branscombe quarry. *Tuesday July 9.* We carried out our determination. We passed the Three Horseshoes and took the first road to the right, which brought us to the top of one of the Branscombe valleys where the view is beautiful. We were directed to the chalk quarry. From Mr. Daw, who rents the land, we learnt that in excavating the quarry they opened the ends of two trenches in the face of the cliff, and from time to time they came upon bones and crockery, either black or stone-coloured. This happened some fifteen years ago *and n*one has been saved. In the plan, the white is the part excavated; **a** - all that remains of the trench, but full of loose flints. It turns at an angle at **b**. **cc** - direction of the trenches over the quarry before *being* dug away; **d** - tumulus within the trench, dug away. In or near this tumulus was found a slab of stone, about three feet by two by nine inches thick, *and* under it were bones in a cavity. This stone now forms the floor of the 'eye' of the lower kiln close by. The spot is called 'Castle Close' and possibly these trenches may have formed two sides of a Roman camp. Bury Camp is visible on the cliff about a mile south-west by south. (*Diary*).

Gun sold. *Friday July 26.* Sold my 3 lb. gun, limber and side arms to Mr. B. Sampson of Great Wood near Penryn *and* Falmouth. I advertised it once in Woolmer's Exeter Gazette a fortnight ago and it got me a purchaser. I asked £20 and he gave me my price. The limber and gun were yoked to the carrier's wagon *whilst* I went in by coach. I met it at the station and saw it safe. (*Diary*).

School feast. *Wednesday August 7.* All Saint's Church School feast, held in the field opposite Coburg Terrace. I threw open my premises but afterwards regretted that I did, for the children trampled over everything. Their curiosity to see the 'Old Chancel' was intense. A few entered *and* I followed to see that my curiosities were not hurt, *then* the others crowded in, till at last we were as tight as – as – as – anchovies in a bottle. (*Diary*).

Exeter meeting of the Archaeological Association. *Monday August 19. There was* a meeting of the Archaeological Association in Exeter *and* I went in to join them, taking my paper on 'The Hill Fortresses, Tumuli and some other Antiquities of Eastern Devon' and some of my illustrations. The papers will be read and a temporary museum formed in the ballroom close to the New London Inn. Went there and saw all my objects of antiquity and drawings safe. Took the rail down to Dawlish, after visiting some parts of Exeter with the Associates, witnessing their reception by the mayor at the Guildhall and listening to Sir Stafford Northcote's introductory speech. (*Diary*).

Ram's head. *Saturday October 12.* Gilt with leaf, gold, the pedestal on which I am mounting the three humming birds given me by the Earl of Buckinghamshire. By the bye, the Earl sent me this morning the head of a ram carved in white marble brought from Cyrene (where excavations are going on) by his son, Capt. The Hon. Augustus Hobart RN. Unfortunately the face is injured. Called this afternoon at Richmond Lodge, Elysian Fields, to thank him. He read me a letter about his son's sojourn at Cyrene and some account of the discoveries, many things being sent to the British Museum, and then kept me talking for an hour and a half. The head is in the Old Chancel. (*Diary*). *He donated it to Exeter Museum in 1892 (letter to Perceval September 1893).*

Second sight. *Friday October 17.* At eight o'clock in the evening of the 17th of October 1861, I took to spectacles, being fifty years old and eleven months to a day. For the last two or three years I have not seen small print so clearly as heretofore, but before then no one ever had better eyes, either for the closest or the longest distances. But even now, I can see through some of my neighbours without spectacles. (*Diary*).

Further exploration of Lovehayne Farm tumulus. *Thursday October 24.* Mr. Heineken and myself went over to the barrow on Lovehayne Farm, as we had been informed by the present tenant, Mr. J. Dawe of Branscombe, that it was being removed for the sake of the stone (*see September 19, 1859*). As it turned out a wet day, no workmen were there but a man with a cart who had come to take away *the* stones. We arranged to come again next Tuesday. (*Diary*).

Tuesday October 29, 1861. And we went. They had cruelly destroyed the barrow and were carrying away the stone to build a barn or outhouse at Lovehayne Farm. We now discovered that at some former period a trench had been cut from the south into the centre of the barrow for the purpose of examination, and we inferred that the urn of which we had found pieces had been broken at this time. The trench had been filled in with earth and stones, a good section of which remained. We paid the workmen to dig *and* the following articles were found, which I have: Two pieces of bone, one about the size of a bean *being* a part of some joint, the other a piece of a left lower human jaw bone with holes for three teeth. Second, a piece of a coarse, rude urn of clay, apparently not kiln baked, three-sixteenths of an inch thick, about two inches long and one and a half wide, but of very irregular shape. Third, a portion of another urn apparently of the form annexed when perfect. The clay is finer and there is some glaze on it *and* the thickness is nearly half an inch. It seems to have had a flat top, either for the purpose of covering with a tile or of inverting it on one. A flat stone with some charcoal on it was found, but unfortunately carted away before we arrived. Perhaps this urn had been inverted on it. Fourth, a good deal of charcoal in small pieces scattered among the earth. If all these fragments are genuine, this makes three distinct urns buried here. The fragments of the first we found in the centre, that of the second I think about three or four feet south of the centre, and number three above some eight or nine feet south of the centre and the flat stone near it. The bronze instruments said to have been found in this barrow may have been met with by those who cut the trench. One is said to have been sold for old metal at Colyton, the other, if in existence, we are trying to trace. (*Later note:* Found it! See November 22). (*Diary*).

61/10/24-1. *Lovehayne Farm tumulus section.* (Diary)

61/10/24-2. *Reconstructed pot, Lovehayne Farm tumulus.* (Diary)

Paper on hill fortresses. *Wednesday November 13.* Sent my paper on the hill fortresses etc. of South-East Devon to Mr. Pettigrew, Treasurer of the Archaeological Association and fifteen plans of camps, etc. They propose publishing portions in their journal next year. (*Diary*).

Ferns of Sidmouth. *Friday November 15.* Began making the illustrations for a book on the Ferns of Sidmouth. My plan is a novel one and not hitherto tried that I am aware of. I take a fern leaf and ink it with printer's ink. I then press it upon a piece of lithographic transfer paper which I send to the printers, to be transferred to the lithographic stone. The process however, requires much care, and each leaf must be first pressed once or twice to take off the superfluous ink. I propose having from twelve to twenty plates. (*Diary*).

Bronze Age celt from Lovehayne Farm tumulus. *Friday November 22.* Made a plaster cast of a bronze celt found about sixty years ago in the barrow in 'Stone Barrow Plot' (see October 29, 1861). It now belongs to Mr. Snook of Colyton, grandson of the first possessor. It is five and a quarter inches long and one and seven eighths wide at the cutting edge. (*Diary*).

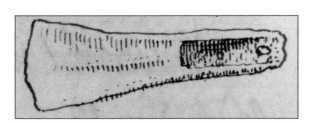

61/11/22. *Bronze celt from Lovehayne Farm tumulus.* (Diary)

1862

Oak mantelpiece. *Monday January 20.* Very busy for some days putting up an old oak mantelpiece in the Old Chancel. *The* oak panelling over it *is* made of old oak chests which I have bought in the cottages and villages near Sidmouth. (*Diary*).

Wreck of the Pandora. *March.* The Pandora brig was driven on shore in a gale near Salcombe mouth. (*History of Sidmouth V, 163*).

Vestry meeting. *Tuesday April 10.* The vestry meeting granted me for today came off. The statement I made in respect of the condition of the church was afterwards printed in the Exeter papers. Cuttings from those papers are pasted in the second book of my manuscript memorandums on the restoration of the church. (*Diary*). *Readers of the Exeter papers had long been entertained by the shenanigans surrounding the rebuilding of Sidmouth parish church and this latest article by Hutchinson made the front page. He reports that as no work had been carried out for over a year and there was no intention of doing more, he had been trying too wind up the Restoration Committee and hand back responsibility for the church to the parishioners. When he raised the issue at the previous Committee meeting, chaired by the ex-vicar Mr. Hamilton, he was 'rudely taunted' that 'he only wanted to hear himself speak'. The trouble was two-fold. The church was now in poor condition, the roof was badly insulated, the warming apparatus did not work properly, the external appearance was unsatisfactory, etc., and secondly there was a large deficit in the accounts which the vicar denied, wrongly, was the responsibility of the Committee. Hutchinson requested that he be permitted to pay his share of the debt and then be allowed to resign, but his offer was turned down. The parishioners, no doubt incensed by the years of discord for which they blamed the other members of the Committee, saw no reason to let them off payment and would only accept the church provided it was free from debt. (Exeter and Plymouth Gazette April 18, 1862). Eventually each Committee member's share was paid up, accounts were settled and the long-running saga of the church restoration was brought to a conclusion. Ironically, only sixteen years later the organ was quietly relocated at the west end of the church and a surpliced choir installed, with apparently little opposition from the parishioners (see December 15, 1878).*

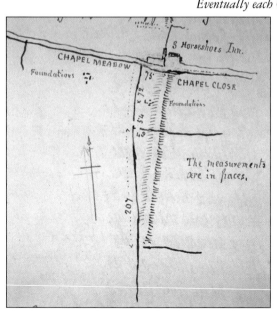

62/6/17. *Site of ruin near the Three Horseshoes.*
(Diary)

Labour in keeping diary. *Thursday May 1.* I have some notion of burning my diary. It gives some trouble and I do not see that it is of any use. (*Diary*).

Ruin near the Three Horseshoes. *Tuesday June 17.* Mr. Chick drove Mr. Heineken and myself over to a place near the Three Horseshoes to see some excavations in a field. It seems that in ploughing the field immediately south, or opposite the Inn, quantities of stone obstructed the plough. These were today partly cleared. They exposed apparently a wall running away north and east, the corner being as if the south-west angle of a building. As it was three feet thick, perhaps it was part of some chapel or cell once attached to a religious house. We also traced a low bank running south through this field and the next, *which* looks like a continuation of the great work on the north of the Inn (see July 3, 1861). (*Diary*).

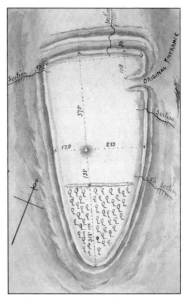

62/6/19-1. West side of Dumpdon and camp, as seen from the hills above Coombe Rawleigh. Sketched on the spot July 1865. (DRO, Z19/2/8E/179)

Dumpden Camp. *Thursday June 19.* Mr. Heineken and myself drove over to measure Dumpden Camp, a plan of which appears never to have been published. Started at 10.20 AM, went over Honiton Hill, through Honiton, passed over Longford Bridge and then made for the high ground via Shaugh Farm. Arrived in two hours and a half, left the carriage at the base of the cone, mounted and first discussed our dinner. In the accompanying plan the measurements are given in feet. The plantation at the south end is composed of beech trees. The mound in the middle was thrown up some years ago by the Ordnance surveyors as a point to take angles from, and is not a tumulus. This Camp is very like Hembury Fort in shape. *(Diary). A small excavation undertaken in 1990 suggested that the hillfort was unfinished and indeed had barely been occupied (Todd 1992). The accompanying sketch of the Camp is dated some three years later, though there is no mention of it in the Diary.*

62/6/19-2. Plan of Dumpden Camp. (Diary)

Stockland Camps. *Tuesday July 22, 1862.* Went with Mr. Heineken to examine two camps on Stockland Hill. We drove over Honiton Hill, through Honiton (where we saw the Town Clerk proclaiming the opening of the Fair with a large glove tied to the top of a pole), then over Cotleigh Hill, where we saw some gypsies intensely foreign in look, with black hair and eyes and brown or olive complexions. On ascending Stockland Hill we stopped at a public house kept by a man called Lane, to enquire about the camps. Here we were shown a gold coin, found with many others some years ago at a farm called Lower Cleave a mile and a half south by west. The coin was of fine gold about the size of half a sovereign but only half as thick. I easily made out the word 'Edward'. A man went with us to show us the camps. We ascended the hill, passed the main road and went down some lanes - down the lane represented at the top of the annexed plan. We discussed our sandwiches and then took the dimensions of the 'Little Castle', as it is called. It is nearly circular, measuring 371 feet one way and 331 the other. A small portion of the vallum on the north side is all that is perfect. The agger is eight or ten feet high and composed of earth and stones mixed, but on the inside it is made of dry stones piled up, in some places with tolerable regularity. Whether this dry wall is ancient work or more recently made when the land was first cleared and cultivated some thirty years ago, is a question for consideration. This camp is not laid down in the maps. We now proceeded to the 'Great Castle' half a mile south or south-west. We sent the carriage round as the man took us a short cut across the fields. This camp is nearly obliterated. The public road

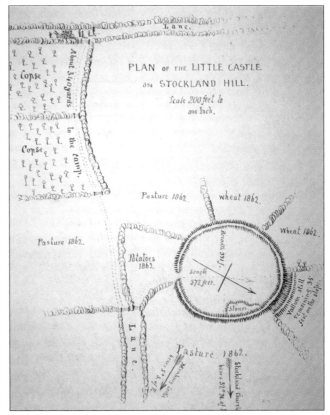

62/7/22. Plan of Stockland Little Castle. (Diary)

runs through the middle of it, east and west.   Both halves are now in wheat *so* we could not measure them, but we took the road through the camp from one side to the other and it was 810 feet.   All round the south side the vallum has been destroyed, only a hedge remaining, but round the north it is perfect.   It is thirty-eight feet on the slope.   Late in the autumn measurements might be taken.   This camp is laid down on the Ordnance map.   Tradition says that the Saxons were posted here when the Danes entered the Axe, and were severely beaten at the Battle of Brunenburg.

In returning home, we varied the route by going south through the village of Wilmington, then by Copleston's Tower and along Farway Hill to Roncombe Gate.   We descended the steep hill of Roncombe and so on to Sand. On this hill the iron tyre of the off-fore wheel came off and we expected the wheel to go to pieces, *but* the driver led the carriage quietly into Sidbury where we got it fixed, *and then* drove home at a slapping pace.   (*Diary*).

Alphington Cross. *Thursday July 31.* It was this evening I sketched Alphington Cross.   (*Diary*).   This cross, which is of grey granite, stands on the right hand side of the road going from Exeter to Alphington.   At some former period it was broken across near the top, but has been refixed.   (*Sketchbook E*).   *Hutchinson was in Exeter for a week, summoned as a juror to attend Exeter Assizes.*

62/7/31. Alphington Cross near Exeter, from a sketch taken July 30, 1862. (DRO, Z19/2/8E/129)

Resignation from the Corps. *Wednesday August 13.* A combination of circum-stances have for some time weighed upon the Artillery Corps.   It has never been properly supported by the inhabitants.   A meeting of the officers and non-commissioned officers took place at Salcombe Mount, the Captain's residence, this afternoon.   The Captain reviewed the past and present position of the Corps and then told us he would write to Lieut. Col. Sir Warwick H. Tonkin at Teignmouth tomorrow and tender his resignation. (*Diary*).

Saturday August 16. In the present state of the Corps, *its* funds and two or three other considerations, it is not likely that I would take responsibility *for it* upon my own shoulders. I therefore sent, for transmission to the proper authorities, a note tendering my resignation. (*Diary*). *So ends Hutchinson's military career. With both Captain Smith and Lieutenant Hutchinson resigning, J.B.Lousada of Peak House took over as Captain of the Corps.*

Iron Pits near Dunkeswell. *Friday October 10.* About the beginning of October a friend and myself determined to try and find the 'Iron Pits', as they are called, on the Blackdown Hills. Tradition says that the ancients at some unknown era used to dig for iron there *but* I confess my doubt about this, scarcely comprehending how iron ore could be found in so unlikely a place, or if found how in sufficient quantities. Another opinion supposes they may be the remains of a British village. I scarcely know what to say to this notion, but where there is mystery, speculation and conjecture will always be alive. However, we determined to find some of them if possible. We inferred we must look on Blackdown near Hembercomb, Downlands and above Sainthill near Punchy Down. When we were within the area of Hembury Fort with our gig, we met Mr. Venn, the owner of all the land thereabout, whom I had known

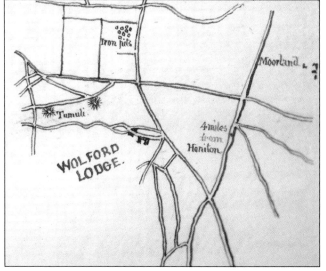

62/10/10. *Site of the Iron Pits near Wolford Lodge.* (Hist. of Sid. I,112)

before. He said he had passed them fifty or sixty years ago when he was a young man and directed us to go by the road to the north of Wolford Lodge and at the Four Crossways turn towards Dunkeswell. When near the place we were directed to an enclosure nearly a quarter of a mile north of the Crossways. The spot is still covered with furze, heath and ferns. I got over the gate and had a search, for owing to the state of the ground nothing was visible from the road, *and* about a hundred yards in I found them. We then opened the gate and got in the gig. The excavations have not been made continuously, like one great gravel pit, but the pits and hollows seem to have been made separately, at all events for the most part, and this is why some have thought they may have been the foundations of ancient dwellings. To me however, they have not got the regularity of dwellings when compared with the undoubted remains of villages on Dartmoor. If they were really iron pits, in or near which smelting may have taken place, we thought it would be well to dig to the bottom of one or two. Our tools however were not sufficiently strong. In one we dug down nearly two feet but found nothing but fine mould which the rains of many years had washed down from the sides. Perhaps it would be necessary to descend three or four feet before finding the original bottom of the pit. Possibly cinders or scoria may be found there. About half a mile or a mile eastwards, near Moorland, we were told that another group of pits existed but we had not time to go. We returned *the* fourteen miles to Sidmouth, resolving to come again. (*Diary*).

Lusus naturae. *Saturday November 8.* Amongst the pears from the tree at the north corner of the garden, a lusus naturae has manifested itself. The lower half of the fruit is like the ordinary type, but the pear stops short in the middle and the upper half consists of something between a pear and a branch covered with small leaves. I have two of them, both exactly alike. (*Diary*).

Christmas Ball. *Friday December 19.* Went to the Christmas Ball at half past nine this evening at the London Inn, Sidmouth, gentlemen's tickets 7/6. Tea, refreshments and supper difficult to get at and uncomfortable to take. What is most remarkable in the present day, and equally absurd, is the size of the ladies dresses, *for* their crinoline petticoats extended with steel hoops have attained dimensions quite ridiculous. Because it is the fashion it is tolerated but even the

62/11/8. *Lusus naturae.* (Diary)

ladies admit the absurdity, and wish the Empress of the French (who makes and maintains fashion for the whole world) would be so good as to reduce the size. I remarked one young lady seated on a row of chairs *whose* dress covered three chairs and a half. And as they are as unnecessarily long as they are wide, sweeping the ground as they go, it is most difficult to walk near them or after them without stepping on their skirts and flounces. Very laughable were the jams and collisions that often took place in the rapid, too rapid, twirling of the waltzes. Sometimes one was suddenly enveloped in sundry huge clouds of muslin or silk by the meeting together of several of these spinning couples inadvertently converging, and then off they were again in an instant to the four corners of the room. Towards the latter part of the evening it was amusing to see strips of blue, red or white muslin or shreds of silk which had been torn off by collisions lying on the floor or driven about by the whirlwind of these fleet revolvers. Quadrilles, Lancers and polkas were the other dances. I got home at a quarter to four. (*Diary*).

Ancient races. *Monday December 22.* Read some interesting articles on ancient human skulls in the 1861 volume of the 'Natural History Revue', suggested by my recent reading of Bateman's book (*Ten Years Digging*). It is here shown that there is strong evidence to prove that the earliest of the human race co-existed with the hyena, rhinoceros, elephant and bear, the bones of which are found in caverns among the diluvium of the late geological period, being animals among the extinct genera. Drawings are given in the illustrative plates by which we see that the skulls differ very little from those of the gorilla and the chimpanzee. There is no fixing a date to the ancient races to which these belonged, *but* their evidence seems to throw us entirely out in respect of our chronology of the duration of the human race, or the era to be assigned to Adam. But the most humiliating point is that it is hard to say where the monkey ends and man begins. These ancient races must have been as brutal, debased and as savage as the brute beasts themselves. (*Diary*). *Hutchinson was much influenced by Bateman's book describing the results of ten years of barrow excavation in the midlands, copying some of his conclusions and illustrations into his Diary. Though he does not mention reading 'The Origin of Species' published three years earlier, Hutchinson seems by now to have accepted the possibility of human evolution.*

Peruvian gift. *Wednesday December 31.* Spent the evening with Mr. and Mrs. Melhuish of Greenmount. They gave me two antique clay bottles from Guayaquil in Peru. (*Diary*).

1863

New Years Day 1863. *Thursday January 1.* New Years Day. Mild and drizzly weather. (*Diary*).

Wedding of the Prince of Wales. *Tuesday March 10.* Today Edward Albert, Prince of Wales, was married to the Princess Alexandra of Denmark *and* great preparations to celebrate this event loyally have taken place all over the country. At Sidmouth, the Volunteer Artillery began by firing a royal salute of twenty-one guns at the Battery under Peak Hill. When they came back a procession was formed at the top of Fort Field, headed by the Artillery Corps with their drum and fife band. Gentlemen and tradesmen then fell in and walked two and two, and finally the schoolchildren numbering several hundreds. The immense number of these juveniles excited the astonishment of everybody. They carried plenty of flags, and the long string was very amusing to look at. Dinners, tea-drinkings and balls took place afterwards. A general wish had been expressed throughout the country that every person should wear a rosette or favour of Coventry ribbon, in order to do some good to the trade of that town, which has lately been much depressed, *and* the wish seems to have been complied with. Mine cost a shilling. It is of white silk ribbon with the Prince of Wales's badge in crimson. (*Diary*).

Stockland Great Castle. *Tuesday April 14.* Went with Mr. Heineken to examine Stockland Great Castle, which we had been unable to do on the 22nd of last July (which see) because the corn was on the ground. We took the same route, via Sidbury, Honiton and Cotleigh Hill. We had measured the camp before through its east and west diameter along the road and made it 810 feet.

63/3/10. *Coventry ribbon.* (*Diary*)

63/4/14-2. *Sling stone from Stockland Great Castle.* (*Diary*)

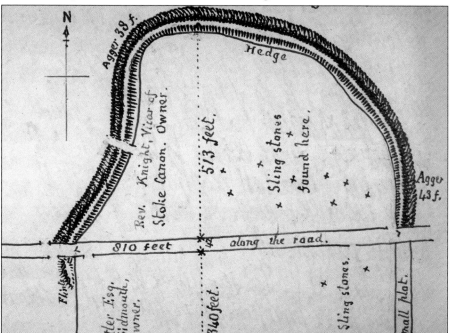

63/4/14-3. *Flint found at Stockland Great Castle on April 14, 1863.* (Hist. of Sid. I,52a)

63/4/14-1. *Plan of Stockland Great Castle.* (*Diary*)

63/4/15. Sidmouth Church plate. All in silver. Taken April 15, 1863.
(DRO, Z19/2/8E/131)

63/6/23-1. Clerestory window, Ottery Church: the south-west window. Some suppose these windows are not the original ancient ones.
(DRO, Z19/2/8E/137a)

63/6/23-2. From south transept of Ottery Church, outside. June 1863.
(DRO, Z19/2/8E/137b)

We now examined the north and south halves, being two large fields, and took the dimensions according to the plan. The vallum is perfect all round the northern half *and* I made the slope of the agger at the east side to be 43 feet. Writers say that a quantity of sling stones have at different times been found within the area, and that a vase or earthen pot was once dug up full of them. The ground was being ploughed, so we had every facility for examining it. We entered at the east corner and had not walked far before we picked up the objects in question, at the places where I have put crosses xx. These stones are so totally different in their form and nature from anything to be found among the natural soil of the hill, which is of the Greensand formation with angular stones, as to be easily detected the moment they are seen. The sling stones are flint or chert pebbles, more or less oviform *and* about the bigness of a bantam's egg, not unlike the sketch *annexed*. They have been picked up from some beach, possibly at Seaton, for they have all been rounded by the action of the sea. We brought away a few as specimens but left many that we saw lying on the ground. They are most abundant in the northern half of the camp and towards its eastern or lower side. We saw some in the southern half, but not so many. Davidson says that the camp contains twelve acres of ground, and that it shows indications of having been enlarged subsequent to its original formation. The northern half is of very irregular form. We did not see any elevated spot on the north side which may have been the place of the commander's tent, as mentioned by Davidson (*Notes on the Antiquities of Devonshire*). The vallum on the southern side has been totally destroyed. There is nothing but a common hedge, *though* there is a small narrow plot at the eastern end where the old vallum ran. The length of the camp east and west along the road is 810 feet, and north and south 340 + 42 + 513 = 895 feet.

We left to return home at five o'clock, taking the route via Wilmington, Coplestone's Tower, Farway Castle, Putt's Corner and Sidbury. We had not gone far however, before our horse began to give in, so that at last he was scarcely able to put one leg before the other. He was not well and ought not to have been sent out. He dragged us on as far as Sidbury, but as he was five hours taking us little more than ten miles, it was ten o'clock at night before we arrived there. Seeing no hope of improvement but rather the contrary, we got out and, leaving the driver to bring the horse and carriage on the best way he could, we walked the last three miles to Sidmouth not much pleased with such a termination to our day's labours. (*Diary*).

Sidmouth Church plate. *Wednesday April 15.* It was on the 15th of April that I examined the plate at the residence of the Clerk. It consisted of eight pieces, and does so still. (*History of Sidmouth IV, 144*).

Visit from Sir Henry Dryden. *Friday June 19.* Sir Henry Dryden of Canons Ashby, co. Northampton, Bart., came to see me. I used to be much at his house in the autumn of 1857. (*Diary*). *Hutchinson entertained his old friend for a week, taking him to various places of interest in the district.*

Sketching at Ottery St. Mary. *Tuesday June 23.* Drove to Ottery to examine the church, which of course was not new to me. Sir Henry began a coloured drawing from the south-west, after having first looked inside and out, *whilst* I made a coloured sketch of the recumbent male figure said to be Bishop Grandisson's father or brother. There are no flying buttresses though the roof is of stone. The side aisles are narrow and massive and may answer the purpose below, but the clerestory has no support outside. Returned by half past six. (*Diary*). *The two effigies sketched by Hutchinson are those of Grandisson's younger brother Otho and his wife Lady Beatrix.*

Return to Ottery. *Wednesday June 24.* To Ottery again. Sir Henry finished his drawing whilst I made a sketch of the recumbent female figure *and* afterwards took one or two windows for him. We then went up on the north tower, which carries a steeple of beams covered with lead, *where* we examined the construction of the building between the roofs and other parts. Having finished here we drove

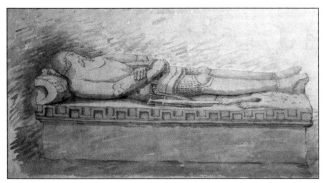

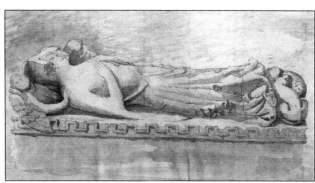

63/6/23-3. Ottery Church, supposed Bishop Grandisson's father, June 1863. (DRO, Z19/2/8E/140)

63/6/24. Ottery Church, supposed Bishop Grandisson's mother. (Not dated) (DRO, Z19/2/8E/141)

a mile out to look at Cadhay House, where Captain Collins received us. The points most notable were the newel staircase on the left of the entrance, the quadrangle with the statues and inscriptions, the great stone trough, just the same shaped stone as the base of the Alphington Cross, the cast lead pipes, etc. The fishponds are ancient, I believe. Sir Henry took a sketch in a shower of rain *and* we got back to Sidmouth soon after six. (*Diary*).

Croquet. *Saturday July 4.* Had a game of croquet and drank tea at the Vanes. Croquet, I believe a French game introduced about three or four years ago, is now much in vogue and as it is an outdoor game, the fine weather gives it great encouragement. On the grass of a smooth lawn, eight bows of thick wire are pitched and a stick at each end painted in different colours according to the colours of the balls of each player. Starting from the nearest stick, each player knocks his ball through the wire arches with a sort of wooden hammer, *but* your adversary may 'croquet' your ball away and impede your progress if he gets near enough. There is not much in the game but it gives good facilities for chatting and flirtation. (*Diary*).

Ploughing match. *Wednesday September 30.* Went to the ploughing match got up for the parishes of Sidbury, Sidmouth and Salcombe. It was held near Cotford. It is the first thing of the kind held in this neighbourhood and is a step in the right direction. (*Diary*).

Apples on a branch. *Monday October 5. Hutchinson went to Dawlish for a month, returning to Sidmouth on November 2. Whilst there he did a considerable amount of walking along the cliffs and over the surrounding hills, and presumably did the accompanying sketch entitled: 'Bunch of 13 apples (12 visible) from Dawlish'. (The dates do not match).*

Shipwrecked sailors. Monday *October 12. The following event must have taken place whilst Hutchinson was staying in Dawlish.* New moon, gales and rain. The river was swollen and the wooden bridge at its mouth was washed away. At 10 PM there came ashore a boat from a wrecked vessel, the Richard Pearce of 150 tons, with seven men and a woman aboard. (*History of Sidmouth V, 164*). *The Richard Pearce, bound from Portland to Dublin, was abandoned by passengers and crew just before it sank twenty-one miles out in the Channel. Their life boat, holed in three places, was only about sixteen feet in length and they had been drifting about for many hours before seeing the lights of Sidmouth.* (*Lethaby's Sidmouth Journal and Directory, November 1863*).

Boat trip to the Parson. *Wednesday October 21.* Went in a boat with my cousins Marion and Fanny Jones to the Parson and Clerk Rocks, the sea being as calm as a pond. The girls and myself rowed the boat. We passed between the Parson Rock and the cliff, the space *being* only about six or seven feet. The water was rather deep *and* I could not reach the bottom with the oar. The cove just beyond was full of fish called 'brits' *and* the mackerel were darting after them and devouring them. We saw them carry them away in their mouths, the water was so transparent. (*Diary*).

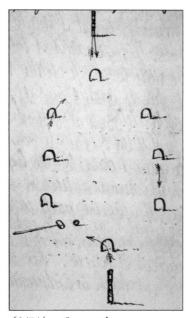

63/7/4. Croquet lawn. (Diary)

63/10/5. Bunch of 13 apples (12 visible) from Dawlish. September 1863. (DRO, Z19/2/8E/143)

Parson's head. *Thursday October 22.* Walked to the Holcombe new villas and then out to the cliff over the Parson Rock *where* I sat down to enjoy the view. The flagstaff that the railway people planted on the Parson's head some years ago still remains but is decaying, and the storms are doing their best to break it off. (*Diary*).

Long day. *Tuesday October 27.* Made a long expedition. Took the rail to Exeter to shop *and then* took the rail four miles to Topsham. Got out and walked a mile and a half to Ebford and called on General Lee, some of whose family I had seen at Sidmouth. The house is large and built of brick. The iron gates came from the Duke of Chandos's many years ago, and I believe the tall mantelpiece inside. There are some good old books in the library. Went and looked at the summer-house in the wood and examined the old chairs. One bears the name 'Shillebeer', with a coat of arms and the date 1685. Walked back to Topsham and visited the museum of the late Mr. Ross. This is a capital museum, especially for objects of natural history. The stuffed birds are admirably done *and t*here is a sword fish caught in the Exe. The sword is flat horizontally, not up and down, and not toothed but smooth. I saw Mr. Ross's drawing books, in which he has beautifully done drawings of birds, fish, zoophites, seaweeds, etc. This museum ought to be preserved.

The river was between me and Dawlish *so I* crossed on the ferry for Exminster. I was deposited on the marshes as night was coming on, and had to find my own way as I could. I should certainly have been benighted and lost had I not called to a man who was fetching some sheep at a distance. These flat meadows are traversed by ditches, which are crossed by planks wholly invisible except to those who know where to find them. By his directions, scarcely audible at the distance, I got across and reached the station in the dark. Waited for the train and then got to Dawlish. (*Diary*).

Parson and Clerk Rocks. *Thursday October 29.* Had another go at the Parson and Clerk, this time geological. I have been collecting specimens of all the different kinds of rock in the red conglomerate, which is here very coarse. Visited new ground today by going to the Teignmouth side of the said Parson. Being low water, spring tide, I found I could get as near as the cove in which we saw the fish. The rocks are very bold here, and the Clerk standing off at sea, very picturesque. (*Diary*).

Two medlars. *Thursday November 5. Hutchinson did the accompanying sketch of two medlars.*

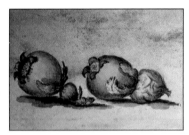

63/11/5. *Two medlars gathered at Camden, Sidmouth, Nov. 5, 1863.* (DRO, Z19/2/8E/145)

63/12/15. *The re-erected Old Chancel, Sidmouth, before additions.* (Soc. of Antiq. Ms. 250)

Awliscombe church window. *Tuesday December 15.* Went over to Awliscombe to look over an old church window. Ever since I erected the 'Old Chancel' I have contemplated adding to it in the same antique style and thereby converting the whole affair into a residence. Took coach to Honiton, nine miles, and then walked out two further to the village. The large window of the south transept has been taken out . . . and the pieces were lying in the south-east corner of the churchyard.

Wanting to see the churchwarden Mr. Banfield about the window, I walked a mile further to Wadhay. Banfield's father desired to be buried in a field close to the house, and there is his grave sure enough, enclosed within an iron railing. Mr. Banfied told me he understood the old window was worth £6 but that I might have it for £5. Did not then conclude any bargain. (*Diary*).

Monday December 28. Mr. Wm. Banfield, churchwarden of Awliscombe, came over on business and called on me at 9 AM. He had breakfast with me *and* we concluded our bargain about the church window. I gave him £4 and conditionally one more if worth it.

A shark was brought me this morning to look at. It ran ashore near the Chit Rocks yesterday and was caught. I found it seven feet three inches long on measuring it *and* from its colour and shape, I suspect it to be the Blue Shark or Squalus glaucus. (*Diary*).

Tuesday December 29. John White the carrier, with his wagon and two horses, went over to Awliscombe and brought over about half of the great stone window. (*Diary*).

Wednesday December 30. The wagon was unloaded in the back yard. (*Diary*).

1864

Family business. *Monday January 25. Hutchinson went to London to see the Earl of Donoughmore, a distant family connection, about pedigrees and other family matters, returning to Sidmouth on February 20.*

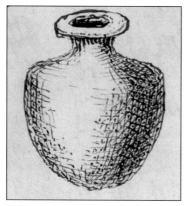

64/3/28-1. *Old glazed jar.* (Diary)

64/3/28-2. *Coin of Antoninus Pius.* (Hist. of Sid. I,97)

Sidbury Castle. *Monday March 28.* Went to examine Sidbury Castle, as men are now working on its stones preparatory to bringing the land into cultivation. Found men there and asked them whether they had not met with any old coins or other antiquities? They replied no, but that they had found a cave or hole full of round pebbles. They had dug down and dispersed the pebbles, but on going to the spot at the west end of the inner agger on the south side of the Camp, I found a considerable space strewed with them. They were beach pebbles, totally different from the angular flints of the hill and resembling the sling-stones of Stockland Great Camp, as mentioned on April 14, 1863. They varied in size from a pigeon's egg to that of a small hen's, *and* I put half a dozen in my pocket. They had probably come from Sidmouth beach and there is no doubt what they are. Wrote a fuller account when I got home and sent it to the Exeter and Plymouth Gazette, which may appear next Saturday. *Apart from Sidbury and Stockland Great Castle, caches of sling stones have also been found at Hembury Fort and Blackbury Castle.*

On returning to Sidmouth, I made a circuit to Sidford and down the fields to Seed. Here a man whom I had known before, Parkhouse, told me he had some antiquities he would sell me. He produced an old jar with a round base and some green glaze about the mouth made of clay, *which* the children had unfortunately cracked. He said it was brought from Yarcombe but he knew nothing of its history. He also produced a Roman coin of Antoninus Pius which he had dug up at Seed some time ago. These I bought and have put in the Old Chancel. (*Later note:* Now in Exeter Museum). (*Diary*). Mr. Parkhouse more recently tells me that his wife found the Roman coin many years ago in a cottage garden at Yarcombe. (*History of Sidmouth I, 97*).

Branscombe and Seaton church bells. *Thursday April 7 or 14.* The Rev. H.T. Ellacombe and myself went to examine some churches. We started about half past nine AM and drove to Steven's Cross and up Trow Hill, passed Slade and entered Branscombe by the Dean. We stopped at the church *and* noticed the Norman features outside – the square tower, corbel table and round turret. Some of the windows are Decorated and some Perpendicular. Outside the south front is an old dial over a former doorway without the gnomon. Inside is *an* Early English arch and tops of three clustered columns in the north transept. Made a rubbing of the slate slab, or blue lias slab, in *the* south transept. There is a good oak chair of the seventeenth century near *the* altar. Ascended the tower. The newel staircase is arched over. The mortar overhead shows that a number of small pieces of wood were used to turn the arch on, and continually shifted. The marks of the tool still remain on the newel. The bells were all set. They were rung for a wedding yesterday and have not been lowered *so* we therefore moved between them carefully. The tenor or large bell measured 41 inches in diameter and by that size ought to weigh 13 cwts 3 qtrs. It bore the letters TP EXON 1671. The 4th bell is said to have been recast in the churchyard or on the ground adjoining. Bell founders used to recast bells on the spot to save heavy carriage. It bears the words T.WROTH FECIT 1747.

We then went on to Beer, walking up the steep hill. There is a chapel here but nothing to detain us, so we proceeded to Seaton. On the road I learnt that the tradition of a former plague is remembered (I believe in 1646) and that the dead were buried on Chapel Hill and several other places. Seaton church has traces of Decorated work. Inside there is a large squint on *the* north side of the chancel arch and a small one on *the* south side in *the* corner of *the* chancel aisle. Piscina with basin and small hole in bottom *and t*races of another piscina in south aisle of chancel. There are two pieces of old glass in *the* head of *the* north window of the chancel, one piece a yellow bird with wings expanded. The steps of *the* tower turret are much worn. There are five bells. The clappers of the bells are hung in the old-fashioned plan with the 'baldrick' or rawhide hinge. In some old churchwardens accounts may be found – *soluta pro baldrickis* (or *baulderiks*) *pro tympanis*, etc. The 3rd bell bears IP EXON 1663. The tenor measures 41^1/2 inches in diameter. We took rubbings of the inscriptions, which Mr. Ellacombe has. Two or three of the bells are old *and* some of the inscriptions are faulty. We got back to Sidmouth by six PM. (*Diary*). *Rev H.T. Ellacombe, author of numerous works on campanology including 'The Church Bells of Devon', was the greatest living authority on church bells. A previous query directed to Hutchinson concerning the old bell at Beer elicited a rather light-hearted reply in a letter dated September 21, 1863:* Rev. and Dear Sir. Beer is rather out of my line – I mean the place, not the liquor. I was within reach of the liquor at dinner time, but as for the place, I have not been near it for several years. I was not aware there was an old bell there. I scarcely know how to promise I will go there on purpose, but I will bear it in mind. If, in any of my rambles, I can manage to get there, I will do all I can in the way of rubbings or anything else. . . . (*British Library Add. Ms. 33 206*). *They examined it together on September 21, 1864.*

Addition to the Old Chancel. *Tuesday April 19.* Mr. Piper and his men laid the first stone of the first addition to the Old Chancel, being a small room on the north side. This will use up some of the materials of Awlescombe Church, bought last January. When I can procure more old church materials perhaps I may go on with further designs of the house. (*Diary*).

Hayes Farm. *Wednesday April 20.* Went with Arthur Church over to Budleigh to see Hayes Farm, where Sir Walter Raleigh was born. The house is being renovated and, I am sorry to see, in some degree modernised with lime wash and partly red brick chimneys. The old outbuildings are soon to be pulled down to give place to new. We went up to Sir Walter's room, which is on the first floor of the left wing on entering, *but* there are no remains of antiquities here. We took our sandwiches and walked out to wild moors of Woodbury Hill, where we discussed

64/4/20. Hayes Farm, East Budleigh, Devon, the house where Sir Walter Rawley was born. Taken on the spot April 1864. (DRO, Z19/2/8E/149)

them. Lady Rolle of Bicton, with her coach and four and outrider, drove by whilst we were there. Returned to Hayes, got out our carriage, drove to Budleigh and through Collaton Raleigh to Harpford to see some friends, and then home. (*Diary*). *This picturesque sixteenth century farmhouse remains much as Hutchinson depicts it.*

Sidbury Castle revisited. *Thursday April 21.* Drove with Mr. Heineken to Sidbury Castle, Mr. Chick accompanying us on his horse, they being desirous of seeing the sling-stones on the spot (see March 28, 1864). We traversed the Camp in various directions, which we had often done before, and the quantity of sling-stones much surprised them. Leaving this we went to Ottery East Hill where we found one of the plantations on fire, the furze and heather being very dry and the wind very strong. It was not without some difficulty that we plunged through the smoke close to the flames. We went down to Cold Harbour, an ancient name of disputed origin, hoping to find something, *but* there was nothing but a miserable little cottage and no traditions. Something led the wife of the man living there to mention methaglin, that ancient British drink made of honey, *and* I said something that made her bring me out a glass of it. It is sweet in taste with a flavour of spirit, and in colour it is yellow like cider only not so clear or transparent. We returned over the hill, *where* the fire had nearly burnt out, and then came down the lane on the north side of Core Hill near Manstone Farm towards Sidmouth. (*Diary*).

House let. *Sunday June 1.* Let my house, No. 4 Coburg Terrace, to Mrs. Maitland, a widow lady. Her term for one year begins today. (*Diary*).

64/8/29. *Remains of an old granite cross outside the east entrance of Dawlish churchyard, Devon. Sketched on the spot August 1864.*
(DRO, Z19/2/8E/151)

To Dawlish. *Monday August 29.* I went over to Dawlish to see my cousin Mary Roberton at Belmont Villa. I walked to Budleigh Salterton, six miles, took the omnibus to Exmouth, four miles, hired a boat to Starcross and then took the rail. This is a varied and pleasant trip in fine weather, and the weather was charming. (*Diary*). *Hutchinson stayed three days in Dawlish but there is no mention of his making this sketch of the cross-shaft on its plinth outside St. Gregory's Church. Probably the figure was added later as the stump is barely a metre high. He spent much of the next five months away from Sidmouth, going first to London, to Lichfield in October and then returning to stay with his cousin in Dawlish until March 1865.*

Church bells again. *Wednesday September 21.* Examined the bells in four church towers today with the Rev. H.T. Ellacombe of St. George's Clyst. On looking up under the bells of Sidmouth church tower, I saw that all had baldrics to the clappers except the last or smallest of 1824, by which I mean that the clappers are hung with a leather strap instead of a metal hinge as is the custom now. *They now go on to Branscombe to examine the bells in more detail (see April 7 or 14, 1864).* After copying the inscriptions on all the bells and measuring their sizes etc., we drove on to Beer, to look at the bell there. This chapel of ease to Seaton exhibits Decorated features at the east end, but the building has been sadly marred by 'Churchwardens Gothic' at various times. We took off our coats and managed to get up to the bell turret. The bell is ancient. It bears the words A ve MA RI A in old letters, divided or distributed on several cartouches round the bell. *Hutchinson and Ellacombe finish up in Sidbury church tower before returning to Sidmouth.* Mr. Ellacombe and self had tea in the Old Chancel before he joined his party to return to Clyst St. George. (*Diary*)

Offwell, Widworthy and the Wilmington stones. *Saturday April 22.* Accompanied Mr. Heineken and his nephew Mr. Thomas Horsfall of Hornby Grange, Yorkshire, to Offwell and Widworthy. Sketched the holy water stoup in the south porch of Offwell Church. *There is* old oak carving of The Last Supper on *the* reading desk *and also* at *the* west end of *the* north aisle, brought from London. *I* observed that the floor descends from *the* west door down to *the* east end. There is, near the schools, a large square granite pillar on a pedestal covered with runic patterns, on *which* are the words 'Crocker, Crwys and Coplestone, when the Conqueror came, were found at home'. This was erected by Bishop Coplestone.

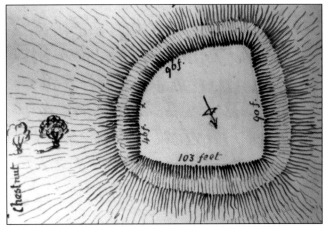

65/4/22-1. *Plan of Castle Wood, Widworthy.* (Diary)

On Widworthy Hill south of the church, in a plantation, is a circular enclosure 90 paces north and south and 92 the other way. It may be called a circle 225 feet in diameter, allowing 2 foot 6 inches to a step. We then went down and measured Castle Wood at Widworthy *(see plan)*, and also the girth of one of the Spanish chestnuts on east side and made it 20 foot 6 inches. (*Diary*). Castle Wood is looked upon as having been an outpost commanding the valley, and perhaps connected with Widworthy Camp on the hill above. No plan of this has been published. (*Soc. of Antiq. Ms. 250*). Then to *Widworthy* church, where there is a fine yew tree at the west door. Over the tower door there is a shield bearing three locks *(as sketched) and* over the south door there is an old dial without style. Inside there are monuments to the Tuckers, Marwoods, etc., and a recumbent figure in the north transept. Returning home, I made sketches of 'Grey Stone' and 'Drummer Stone'. (*Diary*).

Grey Stone is a mass of stone about four feet high, supposed to have been either a milestone or a boundary stone. It stands on the north side of the road about half a mile west of Wilmington, on the Icknild, nearly opposite the entrance to Widworthy Court, the seat of Sir Edward Elton, Bt. The stone is close against the hedge, with the bushes hanging over it. In his *British and Roman Remains in the vicinity of Axminster,* p.59, Mr. Davidson speaks of the Icknild as passing 'through the village of Wilmington and past the horestones called 'The Grey Stone' and 'Drummer's Stone' to Mount Pleasant'. The 'Drummer's Stone' is only part of a larger mass, being now little more than eighteen inches out of the ground. It is not on the Icknild but is 50 yards up Drummer's Stone Lane near the left hedge. Drummer's Stone Lane leaves the Icknild more than half a mile west of

65/4/22-3. *Drummer Stone.* (Hist. of Sid. I,120)

65/4/22-4. *Shield over Widworthy church door.* (Diary)

65/4/22-5. *Gray Stone.* (Hist. of Sid. I,120)

65/4/22-2. *Gray Stone, half a mile west of Wilmington. Sketched on the spot April 22, 1865.* (DRO, Z19/2/8E/177)

65/4/22-7. *Holy water stoup, partly mutilated, in the south porch of Offwell church, Devon. It was made out of a block of stone inserted in the wall in the corner. Sketched on the spot Saturday April 22, 1865.* (DRO, Z19/2/8E/173)

65/4/22-6. *Drummer Stone, 50 yards on the left up Drummer Stone Lane. Sketched on the spot April 22, 1865.* (DRO, Z19/2/8E/177)

Wilmington and goes north. Tradition says that a drummer boy died near this stone and hence the name, but this designation is of course modern. (*History of Sidmouth, I, 126*). *Neither stone is now visible.*

Hawkesdown hillfort and Axmouth Church. *Thursday April 27.* Went as before to Hawkesdown Hill camp. Proceeded via Trow Hill and along the level till we descended to Colyford, *then* crossed Axe bridge and turned south to the foot of the hill. *Here we* eat our sandwiches and then mounted, and a rather stiff pull *it was* on a warm and sunny day. The chasm on the north side of the upper part is natural but it serves the purpose of an immense fosse. The Camp appears to have been surrounded by two aggers with a fosse between them. The work is most perfect on the east, where the slope of the agger is fifty feet. The interior area is 852 feet long, 466 wide at the east end and 420 two thirds towards the west. About 200 feet east of the east end, a hedge crosses the ridge of the hill, *and* it may be a question whether this was an outwork. I think not however, as there is no fosse. The west point of the camp rises above the River Axe and commands an extensive view. We found many sling stones in the interior, beach pebbles like those at Stockland and Sidbury Castle. *Interestingly, five Roman lead sling-shot were picked up in the area between the eastern rampart and the outwork in 1987, suggesting the possibility of an attack on the hillfort by the Roman army during the invasion of the West Country.* No excavations have been carried out on the site (*Holbrook 1989*).

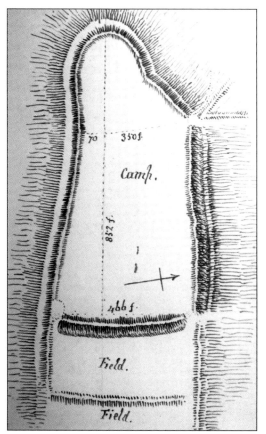

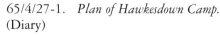

65/4/27-1. *Plan of Hawkesdown Camp.*
(*Diary*)

65/4/27-2. *Norman doorway, north porch, Axmouth church.   The north porch has been converted into a vestry.   Sketched on the spot April 27, 1865.   (DRO, Z19/2/8E/175)*

We descended and visited Axmouth church which wants restoring (*where Hutchinson did the accompanying sketch of the north porch*) *and* did not get home till after nine. (*Diary*).

American papers.   *Wednesday May 3. Following the death of his cousin the Rev. Canon Hutchinson at Lichfield, Hutchinson travelled up to his funeral on April 29. Whilst there he spent* Nearly all day helping to look over, preserve and cancel old letters, papers, etc. The accumulation of more than forty years is something enormous.   The American papers, I am sorry to say, are given to me.   I look upon them as belonging to all the descendants of Governor Hutchinson and that whoever has custody of them is keeping them for others as well as for himself. (*Diary*).   *He returned to Sidmouth via London and Southampton, stopping off to search for flints on the eastern side of Southampton Water where some flint arrowheads had recently been found.*

Honeyditches.   *Monday May 22.*   Went with Mr. Heineken to explore Honey Ditches or Honeyditches, an earthwork only recently known to us on Seaton Down.   We were guided by Mr. Cawley of Seaton Hill Farm.   The works consist of a fosse and vallum drawn across the hill from east to west, with fosse on the south indicating that the enemy was expected on that side.   The fosse is 19 feet on the slope *and* the two together *measure* 33 feet.   This work is 770 feet long and dips some distance down the slope of the hill on each side.   At 466 feet north of this, there is a short piece of similar construction but only 130 feet long, running about WNW and ESE, *which* looks unfinished.   Perhaps the enemy removed and it was not necessary to complete it, or its constructors may have been driven out. These works in construction somewhat resemble those that remain across the hill behind and before the Three Horseshoes.   From the fosse being on the south side, in the short piece as well as the long, it may be inferred that they were intended to defend the road coming up from Colyford, as if the enemy were in the valley of Seaton.   They may have been thrown up either in British or Saxon times.   If the former, they were a defence against the Romans whose galleys may have entered

65/5/22-1. *Location of Seaton Down and Honeyditches.* (Hist. of Sid. I,59)

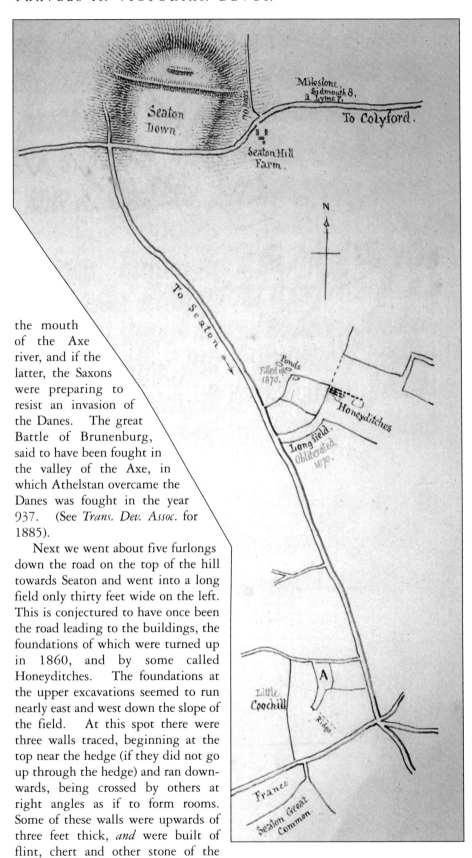

the mouth of the Axe river, and if the latter, the Saxons were preparing to resist an invasion of the Danes. The great Battle of Brunenburg, said to have been fought in the valley of the Axe, in which Athelstan overcame the Danes was fought in the year 937. (See *Trans. Dev. Assoc.* for 1885).

Next we went about five furlongs down the road on the top of the hill towards Seaton and went into a long field only thirty feet wide on the left. This is conjectured to have once been the road leading to the buildings, the foundations of which were turned up in 1860, and by some called Honeyditches. The foundations at the upper excavations seemed to run nearly east and west down the slope of the field. At this spot there were three walls traced, beginning at the top near the hedge (if they did not go up through the hedge) and ran downwards, being crossed by others at right angles as if to form rooms. Some of these walls were upwards of three feet thick, *and* were built of flint, chert and other stone of the neighbourhood. A great quantity of red tile was turned up, some having patterns on them. Mr. Cawley gave us a piece of one, but Sir William Trevellian saved some of the best, the land belonging to him. Axmouth church bore about east from this spot and the mouth of the river SE half E. On grubbing about, we turned up pieces of brick, tile and slate, and also some beach pebbles like sling stones, but from the apparent nature of this place, perhaps the fact of their being sling stones may be questionable. The piece of tile given us by Mr. Cawley has letters on it medieval in character.

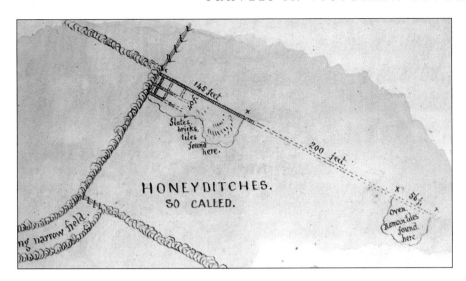

65/5/22-2. *Plan of Honeyditches.* (Hist. of Sid. I,59)

About 200 feet lower down the field and apparently connected with it by a stout wall and a ditch or gutter outside, other foundations with much rubbish were found. The area over which they were met with we found to be about forty-eight feet by fifty-six. Tiles rather more than an inch thick, eleven inches one way but of uncertain dimensions the other, as those we saw were broken, were dug up here. They had been broken off all round the edge underneath by the workman when he laid them. Fragments of pounded brick had been mixed with the mortar, an indication of Roman work. From the presence of charcoal, it was inferred that this may have been the remains of a fireplace, oven or furnace attached to a bath suite or sudatorium. We were allowed to take away some of the pieces that lay on the surface. (*See September 1865*).

Returning home, we went into the fields in front of the Three Horseshoes to see whether we could trace the earthworks further south than the second field, but though we went into the field on the south-west towards which they pointed, we could not be sure of anything. (*Diary*).

Unsolicited appointment. *Tuesday June 20.* On the 27th of last month I received a letter from the Society of Antiquaries of London asking me to become a Local Secretary for Devonshire. Not knowing what it might involve, I replied rather indecisively, implying (after tendering my thanks for the honour) a desire for further information. Today, however, without another word, I received a 'diploma' signed by Earl Stanhope, President, and C. Knight Watson, Secretary, conferring the appointment. (*Diary*). *Despite his surprise Hutchinson must have promptly set to work, for by November the following note appears in the Proceedings of the Society. 'The Secretary called attention to the very valuable communication on the antiquities at and near Sidmouth, copiously illustrated by drawings, which had been sent to the society by P. O. Hutchinson Esq., Local Secretary for Devonshire' (Proc. Soc. Antiq. III, 163). The 'communication' was a substantial manuscript (number 309) not only describing numerous ancient and historical monuments in the vicinity of the town but illustrated with drawings copied from the Diary.*

Hemyock and Dunkeswell. *Monday July 24.* Went with Mr. Heineken to Castle Hill, over Hemyock, to look for a camp. Left at 9.5 A.M., *and* passed over Honiton Hill, through Honiton and Coombe Rawleigh towards Woodford Lodge. Owing to an alteration in the road, I did not recognise the proper turning and advised the wrong one. We went too much to the east and then were obliged to go by the Abbey Mill to Hemyock, which we had not intended to do. This however, gave us the opportunity of again examining the ruins of the castle. We thought that the remains did not look in as good a condition as at our last visit some thirteen or fourteen years ago. *We* turned back towards Honiton, up to the top of Castle Hill *where* we examined part of the summit, but not all. We could get no tidings of any old camp whatever and we are now inclined to think that the hill may bear its name from Hemyock Castle, to the south of which it rises though a mile off. We then pushed on for Dunkeswell and then to the 'iron pits', which

I had visited before (in October 1862) but which Mr. Heineken had not. Several had been examined by the Rev. Mr. Simcoe, the owner, at my instigation after my visit *and* we saw where the bottom of three or four had been tried. The remains of fires had been found in some *and* on grubbing about I found a few pieces of iron stone in one of them. From making enquiries along the road, we learnt the following; that similar pits occur at Moorland a mile east and on many parts of the Blackdown Hills, that there is a large patch of cinders in a field near Tudborough between Hemyock and Culmstock in which the plough always turns up scoria, and that at Bowerhayes Farm between Dunkeswell and Dunkeswell Abbey there is an immense heap and great quantities scattered about, as if smelting works had been there. A blacksmith to whom we were talking took up a 'clinker' from his forge and said they were exactly like that, only that some were as large as his head. We then turned home, stopping only in Combe Rawleigh to take a hasty look at the outside of the church, and in Honiton to give the horse a bottle of ale. We did not reach Sidmouth till half past ten. (*Diary*).

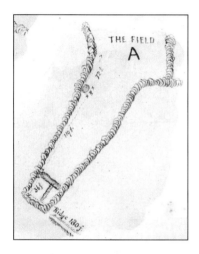

Model soldiers. *Wednesday July 26.* Today a bazaar was held in aid of the funds for the Artillery Volunteer Corps. I finished up my little model of a field-piece with limber complete and two artillery men in uniform. The whole stood on a plank covered with green velvet to represent grass and covered with a glass shade. It was raffled for, and won by Mr. Barrow, a brother-in-law of Mr. Lousada. The bazaar was held in the grounds of Peak House. (*Diary*).

Concert. *Wednesday September 6.* Played the French horn part in the overture of *La Dame Blanche* and *Tancredi*, at a concert given at the London Hotel by Mr. Pinney the organist. Mr. Heineken played double bass there and Captain Hooper flute. (*Diary*).

Encore. *Thursday September 7.* Went over to Honiton with a party and played the same again – the concert being repeated. (*Diary*).

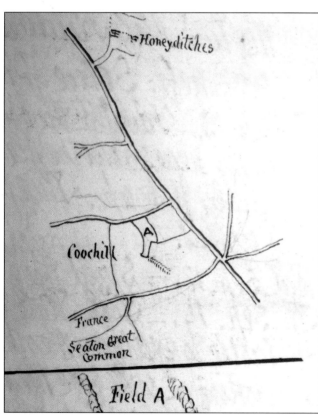

65/5/22-3. *Plan of Coochill.*
(Hist. of Sid. I,59)

Honeyditches again. *September.* Mr. Heineken and myself went again to explore Honeyditches, and try to verify some of the statements made by the old writers about this place (*Diary*). Stukeley, quoted in Camden, says Honeyditches was an oblong moated camp, Lysons that much wrought stone had been dug up there, Davidson that it was nearly circular, and people living on the spot all call Honeyditches the Roman Villa (*Soc. of Antiq. Ms. 250*). These conflicting statements lead to the conclusion that there is a jumble of more places than one mixed up together. Some speak of wrought stone as having been dug up. This does not imply either a British, Saxon or Danish camp. From the stout stone walls found there and the tiles of various types, this should seem to have been a Roman villa as originally constructed, but occupied in subsequent times – the times of the Edwards and Henrys - possibly as an ecclesiastical establishment. Perhaps the field on the north-north-east called Hermitage Close and the other on the east named the Vineyard may lead to the notion that some chapel with buildings used by the monks existed here. And in the fields some hundred yards or more on the west or higher side of the remains, we came upon what we had not seen before, namely two pits in one field on the north and *one* full of water on the south-east in another. These look very much as if they had been fish ponds. We dug for an hour at Honeyditches but our tools were too small *and* we turned up only several lumps of mortar full of pounded brick, which we brought away. Some supposed Roman tiles lying in the field we buried to preserve them from the frost, marking the spot.

Not thinking that any camp could have been placed here, we mounted to the top of Coochill, or Little Coochill, where there are traces of earthworks. A man called Robins of Seaton told us he had been employed there about two years ago digging stone, at the top or south end of field A, that the stone lay in the ground in lines, as if thrown into trenches and covered over, and that they took away scores of cartloads. From the position of this hill, commanding as it does the estuary of the Axe and the whole valley up to Axminster, this looks as if it had been a station, and perhaps one seized by the Danes on their landing in 937, previous to the Battle of Brunenburg. The trenches on Seaton Down look as if the Saxons had been posted there watching them. (*Diary*). *Despite several excavations in the vicinity of Honeyditches over the past century, revealing traces of a number of buildings including a bath house and trackways, the precise nature of Roman settlement at Seaton remains unclear. There may have been a mansio or villa here and possibly a Roman fort on Couchill. (Holbrook 1987).*

Decorating the ceiling. *Wednesday September 27.* *Since the beginning of the year, Hutchinson had been supervising the additions he was making to the Old Chancel.* I have now begun to decorate the panels of the ceiling of my new room on the north side of the Old chancel. By means of a stage upon which I lie on my back, with my head and shoulders supported with hassocks and pillows, I can get on pretty well, though it is rather slow work. The chief parts of my patterns (all taken from ancient examples) are done by means of stencil plates, the minor parts, or finishing touches, by hand. (*Diary*).

Another medlar. *Thursday October 27.* *Hutchinson did another sketch of a medlar from Camden (see November 5, 1863).*

65/10/27. *Medlar from Camden, Sidmouth. October 27, 1865.* (DRO, Z19/2/8E/181)

Burnt in effigy. *Monday November 6.* Sidmouth is in a little uproar. Mr. Lethaby, the publisher of the Sidmouth Journal, has incautiously quizzed the races held lately, and spoken too plainly (though perhaps not too truthfully) of one or two other things; so this evening, instead of burning Guy Fawkes or the Pope, they burnt him in effigy. (*Diary*).

Vestry meeting. *Thursday November 16.* Attended a vestry meeting convened by our new vicar, but old friend, Mr. Clements. (*Diary*). *The meeting was held to reconsider that sensitive subject, the position of the organ inconveniently sited in front of the west window of the church. It was agreed to lower it to floor level.*

Wreck in Ladram Bay. *Saturday November 25.* Another gale from the south, as violent as before. About three this afternoon, a barque said to be partly laden with grain and with an Italian crew, drove into Ladram Bay and soon became a wreck. She struck against the isolated rock just west of the Arch, when the crew got into a boat and came ashore. The front door of the Old Chancel is made of her outside timbers. (*Diary*). *The vessel was the Clorinda, an Italian ship built about 1857 on passage from Nicolieff on the Black Sea to Falmouth. Not for the first time Exmouth was mistaken for Falmouth, and whilst the Captain dallied offshore waiting for a pilot to come out, the gale drove the vessel landwards until disaster was unavoidable. The cargo of migio (a seed for mixing with maize before milling) and all the personal belongings of the crew were lost along with the ship. (Lethaby's Sidmouth Journal and Directory, Dec. 1865).*

Sunday November 26. Again calm and fine, the wind having shifted to the northwest. In the afternoon I waked over Peak Hill to Ladram Bay, some two miles west. There were a great many people there from Sidmouth, Otterton and all the neighbourhood. The vessel was a complete smash, lying just inside the isolated rock near the embouchure of the road leading down to the bay. One half or one side of her lay just inside the rock, *whilst* the bow with the windlass, anchors and a mass of ropes and spars all tangled together and half buried in gravel was driven higher up nearer the cliff. All the beach eastwards to the Natural Arch was covered with planks and fragments. (*Diary*).

1866

To Belmont Villa. *Thursday February 1.* Left Sidmouth for a few weeks went down to Belmont Villa, Dawlish, on a visit to my cousin Mary Roberton. Mrs. Kersteman, formerly Frances Bingham (*another cousin*) was there. (*Diary*).

66/2/9-1. *Teignmouth harbour from Haldon Hill.* (Not dated) (DRO, Z19/2/8D/27)

Walk to Teignmouth. *Friday February 9.* Made a geological view of the cliffs each side of Dawlish, from the Bishop's Parlour on the south-west to Langstone Point on the north-east. Walked to Teignmouth and back. I went first to see the new villas at Holcombe, which are now all occupied, and then down what used to be a romantic gully called 'The Smuggler's Path' to the beach *where I* mounted the railway wall and so to Teignmouth. Returned over Teignmouth Hill by the road all the way. I find great changes since I was this way last, not the least of which is the great nunnery on the high ground, recently built. Report says that the priests and the young ladies amuse themselves during the fine weather by playing croquet on the lawn. (*Diary*). *The two earlier but undated sketches of Teignmouth, viewed from the north and north-east, were probably done about 1847.*

Walk to Little Haldon. *Monday February 12, 1866.* Walked to the top of Little Haldon and back for the purpose of examining the camp. Every part was so wet with the recent rains that I could do little. I hunted about for any chance arrowhead but hunted in vain. (*Diary*).

Shipwrecks in Torbay. *Monday February 26.* The recent dreadful wrecks in Torbay have given rise to some absurd rumours. It is said that the authorities (whoever they are) have forbidden the sale of fish because so many drowned persons have not yet been found. Again, that the divers who have been employed to examine the wrecks, when examining one ship underwater, saw some ladies sitting in a cabin reading. And again, that a

66/2/9-2 *Teignmouth, Devon, from the East Cliff.* (Not dated) (DRO, Z19/2/8D/31)

woman who recently bought a hake found three gold rings inside it. (*Diary*). *Torbay's worst maritime disaster occurred on the night of January 10, 1866, as seventy-four vessels were sheltering in the bay from severe south-westerly gales. When the wind shifted to the north-east and increased to hurricane force, some fifty vessels were sunk or driven ashore and around seventy-seven sailors lost their lives. The rumours arose from the fact that many of the bodies were never recovered.* (Illustrated London News January 27, 1866).

Luscombe Chapel. *Wednesday March 7.* Today was set apart in Dawlish as a day of prayer and humiliation, mainly on account of the cattle plague now raging in many parts of the country, attacking them by hundreds. I got leave to go to the private chapel attached to the house at Luscombe Park. The little building is a beautiful specimen of architecture and no expense has been spared. The walls inside are buff-colour sandstone well put together, the arched roof the same and groined. A good effect is produced in the roof by the insertion of bands of darker colour stone. There is a small north aisle *with* and organ in it. The east end of the nave is a sort of circular apse, not railed off *but with* five single light windows in it. The style of architecture, I need scarcely say, is late Early English or early Decorated, for nine architects out of ten now-a-days build nothing else. The columns, of various sizes, are of finely polished vari-coloured Devonshire marble, as well as a band of the same let in flush with the surface of the wall all round about, four feet from the floor. Minton's tiles cover the floor. The seats are very good – some being of oak, some apparently birch and some deal, all unpolished. At the north-west corner there is a space measuring about six feet by eight, railed in by high filligree work, coloured and gilt and made of iron. I am told that when Mr. Hoare is at home he sits there. The present chaplain is the Rev. Kingdon. (*Diary*).

Exeter, Gandy Street cross-shaft. *Tuesday March 13. Hutchinson left Dawlish for Sidmouth, going via Exeter.* Whilst in Exeter, made a sketch of the block of granite at the corner of High Street and Gandy Street, which is supposed to be part of the shaft of an old cross. (*Diary*). The stone, which is of Dartmoor granite, was discovered among the masonry of old Exe Bridge in 1774. It was bought by Mr. W. Nation for a guinea and placed against the corner of his house. It is supposed to have been part of a cross, perhaps from St. Nicholas Priory, as materials from the Priory were formerly used on the Bridge. (*Sketchbook E*).

Fire in Westerntown. *Friday May 25.* At eleven this evening a fire broke out in Westerntown. The alarm was sounded and the Yeomanry turned out, *who* exerted themselves well and did good service. Four houses burnt. (*Diary*).

66/3/13. *Block of stone at the corner of High Street and Gandy Street, Exeter. Sketched on the spot Tuesday March 13, 1866.* (DRO, Z19/2/8E/183)

Architectural Society meeting. *Thursday June 7.* Went to Exeter to attend a quarterly meeting of the Exeter Diocesan Architectural Society. I have belonged to this Society for five or six years but owing to the distance and the inconvenience of getting to and from Exeter, I have never been till now. The meetings are held in the College Hall, a large room on the east side of South Street, some fifty to a hundred yards from the Carfoix. This is a good specimen of a Gothic chamber, panelled in the 'napkin pattern' *up to* about six or seven feet. Three or four feet above that is Jacobean or later scroll patterns in raised work *and* the rest to the arched ceiling being the wall. There is a fine carved oak table in the middle of the room. The Rev. H. T. Ellacombe, Rector of Clyst St. George, read a paper on all the church bells of Devon - very interesting. I think he said he had mounted 420 church towers during the course of his researches, *and* in one or two of his expeditions I accompanied him. (*Diary*). *See April 7 or 14, 1864 and September 21, 1864 for their investigations into the church bells near Sidmouth. The Hall of the College of Vicars Choral was destroyed in 1942 during the Blitz.*

Budleigh Salterton pebble bed and East Budleigh Church. *Tuesday June 19.* Looked round Budleigh Salterton and made a sketch of the pebble bed cropping out of the cliff west of the town. (*Diary*). Though rather beyond my limits (*of the History of Sidmouth*) I cannot refrain from alluding here to the Budleigh pebble bed. It crops out close to the beach in the sea face of the cliff a few score yards to the west of Budleigh Salterton. The pebbles are more disposed to be flat than spherical, like muffins or cakes, from a slightly schistose nature in the rock of which they are composed. They are water worn and smooth. This vast amount of material from an ancient sea beach extends all across England from this spot on the south and in width several miles in some places. Near Sidmouth the width is from the River Otter on the east to the Clyst on the west. Indeed they make their appearance on the east in the village of Harpford. These pebbles have hitherto been a puzzle to geologists. That they contained fossils is only a recent discovery, but these belong to the Devonian or Silurian formation, although found in the New Red. (*History of Sidmouth 1,15*).

Started back for East Budleigh. Took a hasty look around the church *and* noticed they are re-seating it using the beautiful old bench ends again, *though* I am sorry they are using deal instead of oak. They have misplaced the carved end of the Rawley seat with the date 1537 on it. I miss the tomb of Radulphus Node (who broke his neck trying to fly from the tower) near the south gate of the churchyard. (*Diary*).

66/6/19. Outcrop of the Budleigh Pebble Bed in the sea face of the cliff, 300 yards west of Budleigh Salterton. (Not dated) (DRO, Z19/2/8D/189)

66/8/24-1 *Squint cut roughly through the wall, Aylesbeare Church, Devon. August 24, 1866.*
(DRO, Z19/2/8E/185)

66/8/24-2. *Half of base of granite cross, Aylesbear.* (Diary)

66/8/24-3. *Rockbere church, chancel boss.* (Diary)

66/8/24-4. *Tablet over door of the Windmill Tower, Broadclyst Heath.* (Diary)

Camps on Broadclist Heath. *Friday August 24.* Went with Mr. Heineken to examine Broadclist Heath where the old camp used to be. We proceeded through Newton Poppleford (Pebbleford) to the top of Aylesbeare Hill and to the Halfway House. Here we turned off to Aylesbeare . . . to examine the church. It is all third pointed. The east window is one of five lights and square-headed, the west gallery *is* carved oak (if oak it be) of seventeenth century style *and* the arch into *the* east end of the north aisle *has* panelling under a broad soffit. Diagonally through the square support of the west end of this arch, a squint or hagioscope has been somewhat roughly cut, subsequent to the completion of the church. *There are* five bells in the tower. Outside the east entrance of the churchyard, against a house, lies half the base of an old granite cross, *of the* same pattern as those at Alphington and at Dawlish. It is three feet long, twelve inches wide and sixteen inches high. The sexton's wife could not give us any account of other portions.

We also stopped at Rockbere to see the church. The chancel is under repair *but* the new chancel arch is a miserable affair *and* the east window was entirely out, a new one being in preparation. The north aisle has a wagon ceiling divided into squares by ribs, the intersections being set off with rude wooden bosses painted yellow and red, like in the sketch. The windows are Third Pointed. The west doorway (blocked up) is the gem of the building *and* Mr. Heineken took two photographs of it. It is a good arch, with square headed moulding over. The label over the square head descends on each side to the springing of the arch, *but* there are no bosses at the lower ends, *as* the mouldings make a turn and run into the wall.

On leaving this and getting into the Honiton and Exeter road we proceeded westwards and turned north over the rail at the Broadclist Station. On Broadclist Heath we hunted in vain for a small camp which Mr. Heineken remembers to have looked at more than thirty years ago. But the land about here has been enclosed and cultivated and we could not identify localities. We then mounted the hill to where the remains of the windmill stand. A well-known ancient camp once crowned this hill, as is recorded in county history, but the camp is entirely obliterated and the whole district is now cultivated fields. The windmill tower stands near the middle of a large field, at the north-west corner of a garden of about fifty or sixty yards square, sloping towards the south-east in full view of Woodbury Castle, Hembury Fort, etc. (*Hutchinson copied the inscription over the door to the tower*). After due examination we felt persuaded, in default of other evidence, that this garden occupies the area of the camp itself, and that the enclosing hedge is no other than the old agger. A small farmhouse stands at the lower corner of the garden. I sketched the tablet over the doorway to the tower.

On proceeding home we altered our course. We went along the great road, then by Streetway Head to Ottery, where we observed that the Ottery people are beginning to clear away the ruins of the fire and to rebuild. And so to Sidmouth, where we arrived by nine. (*Diary*).

Farway and Northleigh Churches. *Monday August 27.* Mr. Heineken and myself made an expedition to Farway and Northleigh, commonly pronounced Norleigh by the country people. In Sidford we saw a bent sixpence of William III, dug up where they are now erecting the new church at the lower end of the village, and heard of some copper coins which we could not see. Passed Sidbury and Sand farm and stopped a few minutes at Roncombe farmhouse and admired

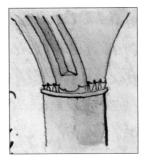

66/8/27-3. *Farway church column.* (Diary)

66/8/27-1. *Tablet in north aisle of Farway Church. Sketched on the spot August 27, 1866.*
(DRO, Z19/2/8E/187)

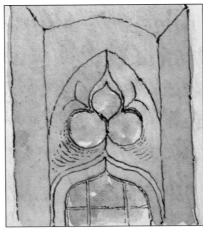

66/8/27-2. *Farway church, east window.* (Diary)

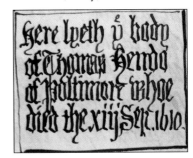

66/8/27-4. *Farway church, Thomas Hendo's tablet.* (Diary)

66/8/27-5. *Northleigh church font.* (Diary)

66/8/27-6. *Northleigh church, upper border of screen.* (Diary)

66/8/27-7. *Northleigh church, Norman capital at east side of south door.* (Diary)

the splendid view down the valley looking towards Sidmouth. The road is very steep here *so* we got out of the carriage and walked. *Noticed* patches of Lady fern on the left and Asplenium trichomanes on the right, neither *of which are* found very near Sidmouth, *and* collected horsetail for polishing. On reaching the top of the hill, we drove northwards and turned down to Farway at a place called Money-acre-corner, *and* visited Farway church. The columns down the nave are Norman surmounted by pointed arches, the soffits of *which* consist of plain chamfer of two orders. Tradition says that this church was built by a maiden lady of a certain age called Mallock, who had a great dislike of the male sex and desired that she might be buried on the left of the porch where the men did not go. Perhaps this was on the left of the west entrance, which would place her on the north side of the church. Possibly the sexes may have been separated in this church during divine service. And we were told in the village that her coffin was to be placed upright, so that no man should walk over it. Another tradition says that at Money-acre-corner a crock of gold was found, on the top of which was written the words 'Do good with this', and that the finder therewith built the north aisle of the church. It may however be observed, that the north aisle should be as old as the nave of the church itself, as shown by the arcade of Norman columns. And it may be further remarked, that on the north wall of this aisle there is a tablet bearing the effigy of one Humphrey Hutchins *and* the date 1628, who 'new built' this part of the church. Perhaps he rebuilt the north aisle. On the north side of the chancel is a slab recording the death in black letter of George Haydon, 1558. The name is obliterated but it is preserved in Lyson's *Devon, II, 239.* At the north-east corner of the north aisle are two recumbent figures. The upper one represents the first Sir Edmund Prideaux in his lawyer's robes, the other is in armour with his head resting on a helmet decorated with a plume. The windows are Perpendicular, except the east window, which is Decorated with some old glass in the top light. Many of the supports under the seats have remains of carving. South door decorated. In the church-yard a few yards south of the church there is an altar tomb, on the north side of which is the tablet of Thomas Hendo, *which I give.*

We proceeded to Netherton Hall, the seat of Sir Edmund Prideaux, Bart., the external appearance of which disappointed us for the building has been much repaired and modernised during the time of the present baronet. I have been told by Farway people that after the present baronet's mother had been more than forty years in her coffin, she was removed to a new one as the old coffin was much decayed. The body was very perfect and the flesh but little decayed, and the only accident that occurred during the operation was the loosening of a nail of one of the great toes, which caused it to come off. She was a farmer's daughter of the neighbourhood.

66/8/27-8. *Northleigh church,*
upper part of north aisle screen.
(Diary)

66/8/27-9. *Northleigh church,*
lower border of north aisle screen.
(Diary)

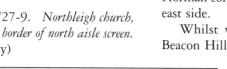

We then pushed on to Northleigh and went into the church. There are the remains of a good deal of oak carving here, *such* as the screen in the nave, being columns supporting half-round fan groining, which possibly once supported a rood loft, the panels of the groining being carved in low relief.   There is a good open border above.   The pulpit is of oak carved in late seventeenth century work, *and* there are a number of good bench ends *also* of carved oak.   At the east end of the north aisle there is an open screen, *which has* two bands of leaf work along the top, carved, painted and much undercut *which* are especially noteworthy.   The font is Norman, a square block of stone with engaged columns at the corners.   The south door, covered by the porch, was once flanked by Norman columns, the capitals still remaining.   The sketch represents that on the east side.

Whilst we were in the village of Northleigh, we made every enquiry for Beacon Hill and Northleigh Beacon, mentioned by Davidson and other writers.   We could get no information, but enough to encourage us to come again.   On reaching the top of Farway Hill, we cut across the Common towards Putt's Corner and descended Honiton Hill. *(Diary)*.

St. Michael's Church, Honiton. *Tuesday September 26.   Hutchinson travelled to Sherborne to stay with an old friend, Rev. Edward Harston.*   I missed the Sherborne train in Honiton so I went and looked at the parish church, which curiously enough lies half a mile out of the town up a hill.   To account for this, Honiton people have a tradition that the church was built before the town existed, and that there was once another and an older town, though small it may have been, clus-

West
Doorway,
Honiton Parish Church,

66/9/26. *Carving over west*
doorway, Honiton parish church.
(Diary)

tered near the church which fell to decay when the new town was built.   There is an avenue of yew trees leading across the churchyard to the north door of the church.   The present church is in the Perpendicular style, *and* the tower has a square stair turret at the south-east corner and five bells.   *There is* a good oak screen inside but miserably painted to resemble grey marble.   Also looked at the new church in the town, built to resemble Norman.   The foundation stone *was* laid in October 1835 and the church *was* consecrated in April 1838. *There are* two coloured windows to Mules on the south side of the chancel and one on *the* north side to someone else. There are six bells. *(Diary). Hutchinson returned to Sidmouth on September 29.*

Guy Fawkes Day 1866. *Monday November 5.*   The weather is mild and agreeable, and has been mostly so for some time.   A disposition manifested itself in Sidmouth to keep the usual fifth of November celebrations with unabated vigour. *(Diary).   These were not quite as violent as on some previous occasions and Hutchinson sent an account of them to the Tiverton Gazette:* Licence indeed there was, for squibs and crackers were freely let off in the town and troops of disguised persons paraded, swinging those brilliant but dangerous meteors called fireballs round their heads. The practise for troops of boys and men to disguise themselves by putting on masks and covering themselves with fantastic costume, and even of dressing themselves in the gowns and petticoats of women, is, comparatively speaking, only of recent introduction in Sidmouth.   These mountebanks do not seem to have committed any assault.   It is well of course for the general public to give them a wide berth, for a blow on the back with one of these balls will go far to destroy a coat, either with flames or hot pitch . . . These fireballs are also a recent introduction, comparatively speaking.   They are in a great degree superseding the time-honoured tar barrel. *(Tiverton Gazette, extract).*

Meteor shower. *Tuesday and Wednesday November 13 and 14.*   Astronomers had foretold an unusually numerous display of the periodical meteors at this period, as the cycle of rather more than thirty-three years is now completed.   Mr. Samuel

Chick having some time ago erected a small observatory at the back of his house, Mr. Heineken and myself, together with Mr. Chick's eldest son and Mr. Bray, proceeded there before eleven o'clock PM on Tuesday the 13th. Occasional shooting stars showed themselves but it was not until after midnight that we began to keep regular count, nor was it until past one AM on Wednesday morning that they appeared in their greatest numbers. From midnight to 12.50 (when it became cloudy) we counted 457. From 1.00 to 1.10, namely in the space of ten minutes, we noted 130. About this period they became too numerous to count, *but* by 2.00 AM they had very much lessened in numbers. From 3.10 to 3.20 AM, namely another space of ten minutes, we only registered 31. Perhaps one of the largest of the night was the one represented *here.* It appeared at 1.8.10 AM on Wednesday. After it had burnt out, it left a train on the sky where it had passed looking like bright vapour or smoke. This we saw for upwards of six minutes *but* other people out of doors declare they saw it for much longer. This train gradually collapsed, or folded up, and slowly drifted away to the south-east.

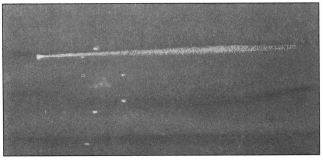

66/11/13-1. *One of the largest meteors.* (Diary)

After midnight, when the constellation of Leo had risen, nearly all the meteors seemed to emanate from that point, as is shown in the *second* sketch here annexed. Another large meteor, perhaps large from its nearness, showed itself at 1.27.20, the light, or vapour, or smoke of which was visible for three or four minutes afterwards. In colour some variety appeared. The burning head of some were ruddy, in some yellow, and some had almost a white light. The tails were green or bluish-green. None exploded, *though* one seemed to scintillate as if an explosion of its brilliant head was immanent. (*Diary*).

Cowey Stakes. *Tuesday November 27.* Read the account of Caesar's attack on Britain in an old book of my late father's, entitled *Commentaries of Julius Caesar, with Observations thereupon etc.,* by Clement Edmonds, London 1655. My reason for turning to this again was to see

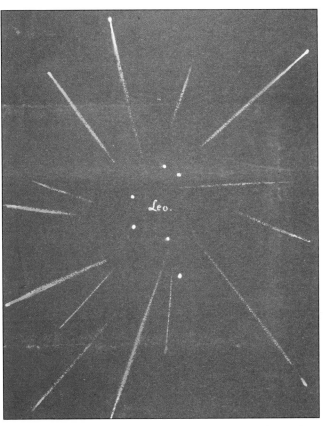

66/11/13-2. *Constellation of Leo.* (Diary)

what it said about the Cowey Stakes and the ford somewhere above London where Caesar and his army passed the Thames in the face of the whole army of Cassivilaunus and despite all opposition. All the researches of modern times have failed to discover the place of the ford . . . *and therefore* the Cowey Stakes. When I was in New York in 1837, I went one day to see Peel's Museum as it was then called, though I believe it has been called by different names since, for this museum was one of the sights, nominally (supposing all the curiosities genuine) worth visiting. In a case in one of the upstairs rooms I saw a bit of old wood about as long as one's forefinger and nearly as thick, labelled 'piece of one of the Cowey Stakes found in the River Thames near London' or words to that effect. Having just come over from London and knowing something of the controversy respecting the disputed site of the ford, I confess I was somewhat staggered. On coming down stairs I told one of the attendants what I had seen, and then added that the Cowey Stakes had never yet been discovered – at which he looked very foolish. I mention this as one instance of American veracity. (*Diary*).

1867

New Years Day 1867. *Tuesday January 1.* Today the wind got round to the northward, the thermometer rapidly dropped and the first snow fell. *(Diary).*

Death of Mrs. Webber. *Monday January 21.* My old servant Mrs. Webber succumbed to the cold. She died quietly soon after four this afternoon owing to benumbed circulation in the lower extremities. *(Diary). Hutchinson and his old servant Mrs. Webber had moved into the Old Chancel the previous year. The last few weeks had been particularly cold and it may have been that the discomforts of the Old Chancel contributed to Mrs. Webber's demise.*

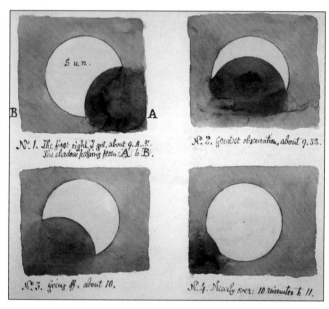

67/3/6. *Eclipse of the sun.* (Diary)

Eclipse of the sun. *Wednesday March 6.* Ash Wednesday. This forenoon there was an eclipse of the sun, *though* unfortunately there were many passing clouds so that I only got some occasional glimpses. I observed it from the library or Oak Room of the Old Chancel where I breakfasted, the sun being directly opposite the window. *(Diary).*

Dartmoor antiquities. *Thursday March 7. Hutchinson's continued concern for the fate of the antiquities on Dartmoor is shown in a letter to C. Knight Watson, Secretary of the Society of Antiquaries.* Dear Sir. Nothing in the way of ancient remains has come to light recently but my anxieties are constantly wandering towards Dartmoor. You are aware that this is not only a very extensive district but that it is full of highly interesting traces of British or Roman or other occupation. I know from good authority that the tenants on the Duchy are no so careful of the ancient remains as they ought to be and that a great deal of destruction has taken place. The late Dr. Crocker of Bovey Tracey has assured me over and over again of this, and has pointed out the objects destroyed. He was very jealous and drew up a very practical Guide to the Eastern Escarpment of Dartmoor. Several persons desiring to arrest the evil if possible, mooted the question of a memorial to the late Prince Consort about ten years ago, and in order that this idea should not end in talk I sketched out one myself and sent it to Dr. Crocker. He got it signed by several gentlemen round Dartmoor and in Exeter, as I did in Sidmouth, and it was forwarded for presentation to the Prince. Whether it reached him or not, the answer was not very encouraging. They would not allow that any mischief had been done at all. To Dr. Crocker this answer was monstrous, as he could point out several Druidic circles, monoliths, etc., which had been broken up within his own memory and under his own observation. The Society of Antiquaries as a body, or the Earl Stanhope as its President, would have great influence with the Prince of Wales. Considerable tracts on Dartmoor have recently been advertised to be let and destruction is sure to follow unless the tenants are bound in their leases to respect these monuments of antiquity. I sincerely hope that something can be done to preserve so interesting a locality from further injury. I remain Dear Sir, etc. Peter Orlando Hutchinson. *(Letter preserved in the Library of the Society of Antiquaries). At their next meeting the Council of the Society of Antiquaries resolved to consider the 'important subject' raised by*

'their zealous and learned Local Secretary for Devonshire' (Proc. Soc. Antiq., IV, 452-3),
and on March 19 the Council instructed the Secretary to write to Lord Portman, Chairman
of the Duchy of Cornwall, 'expressing the earnest hope that his Lordship would use his best
endeavours to give effect to Mr. Hutchinson's suggestions' (Proc. Soc. Antiq., IV, 455). (See
April 18, 1867).

Queen's window in Sidmouth church. *Saturday March 9.* The vicar of
Sidmouth, Mr. Clements, called on me at the Old Chancel and brought me a very
pretty present, a photograph in a gilt frame of the Queen's window in Sidmouth
parish church. It measures ten and a half inches by fifteen *and* I have hung it up
in the Oak Room opposite the fire. This is an acceptable present, *as* I have suffered
enough for this window first and last. When on the church building committee
six years ago, I could not sanction the dishonest mode of trying to get a window
from the Queen, not to honour Her Majesty but for the purpose of promoting a
party quarrel and of defeating an existing agreement between the Earl of
Buckinghamshire and the parishioners relating to the proposed position of the
organ. With the Earl's sanction I took a petition to Osborne House, praying Her
Majesty for an enquiry. The gift of the window was withheld for a time but has
recently been given, and now that we have got it honestly and openly we may be
proud of it. *(Diary).*

67/3/9. *The Queen's window.*
(Illustrated London News,
16.3.1867)

Proposed survey of Dartmoor. *Thursday April 18.* *Following his letter to the*
Society of Antiquaries referring to the destruction of Dartmoor antiquities (March 7,
1867) it seems that a proposal was made to Hutchinson that he should carry out a survey
of the Moor. Letter to C. Knight Watson: My Dear Sir. I am afraid Lord Portman
imposes upon me a history, a survey and a topographical account of all Dartmoor.
I forget the exact extent but I think somewhere about 130 000 acres or so. Yet I
would willingly please his Lordship if one pair of hands could do so much work
and one life was long enough. It is apparent from the late Rev. S. Rowe's
Perambulation, Dr. Crocker's little (but practical) *Guide to the Eastern Escarpment of*
Dartmoor, Mr. Davidson's *Notes on the Antiquities of Devon* and Sir Gardner
Wilkinson's papers on the *British Remains on Dartmoor* in the 1862 volume of the
Journal of the Archaeological Association, that every part of the vast extent of this
wild expanse is more or less rich in interesting remains left by the Romans,
Greeks, Britons and even the Phoenicians. To enumerate all the ancient monu-
ments on Dartmoor would fill a volume, to note down only the larger would be
but useless and incomplete, as the value of a relic is not measured by its mere size.
Perhaps it would be difficult to enclose a square plot of nine acres anywhere in that
region without taking in something of archaeological account worthy of preservation. Pretty profuse may be found hut circles, Druidic circles, traces of mining
and tin works, monoliths, sacred avenues, cromlechs, British villages and so on.
Many such I am informed have been destroyed within recent times and the blocks
of stone broken up to make or mend roads. I should be sorry to interfere in the
remotest way, even by implication or suggestion, in affairs that do not concern me,
but your letter emboldens me to make a remark in reference to Dartmoor which I
hope may not be deemed too much steeped in presumption. If the Moor is too
vast and the remains scattered about it too numerous or varied in character to be
noted down and described within convenient time, I venture to think that the
object may be forwarded in a classified and simplified way by taking portions at
a time. We may suppose that the open moor not in the hands of tenants will
continue with its monuments unmolested in time to come, as they have done in
time past, but it is the parts which are threatened with enclosure and cultivation
that are in danger. If it were proposed to take in and let a plot, some person who
had received the authority might first visit it and note down on the spot for the
information of the Council of the Duchy such objects as were worthy of care.
Possessed of this information, in granting a lease it would be easy to insert a clause
warning the tenant that such relics of antiquity must on no account be interfered
with. In proceeding with other parcels the same process repeated would conduce
to the same end. As to the qualifications of this archaeological pioneer, he would
do if he were a man of good general education, some historical knowledge and a
love of his subject. He ought to be able to draw in order to sketch anything on

the ground for the better information of the Council. Such a gentleman could easily be found, probably among the present staff of the Council, for clever fellows nowadays are as plenty as blackberries. Surely these ancient relics in their original positions on Dartmoor are as worthy of care by the nation as all those relics collected into the British Museum. I remain Dear Sir, Yours Faithfully, P. O. Hutchinson. (*Letter dated April 18, 1867, to the Soc. of Antiq.*). *Hutchinson's efforts to preserve the prehistoric remains on the Moor seem to have been partially successful, for later complaints about their destruction add comparatively few further examples to the list until well into the twentieth century. Nevertheless he was still worried about their fate some two decades later:* I am more concerned about Dartmoor than about any district I know in the south-west of England, for I do now and then hear that another hut circle has been cleared to enlarge a potato field, or another megalith has been overturned and broken up to mend a road or build a pigsty. But the greater part of Dartmoor belongs to the Duchy and is private property and hard to meddle with, and if the owners of an estate don't look after these things and don't lay down stringent regulations upon their tenants warning them against doing any injury to objects of antiquity under heavy penalties, very little I fear can be done by outsiders. The members of the Duchy court who regulate all the affairs of the Duchy for the Prince of Wales, and of whom Viscount Portman is President, would seem to be the responsible parties, but if they are too indifferent to the care of these things, it isn't for you or me to call them to account, though I think they ought to be by somebody. (*Letter to Perceval dated October 23, 1888*).

Book burning. *Thursday April 25.* It is a pity that a man should be employed the latter half of his life in correcting, or undoing, or destroying the works of the earlier half. Or rather, it is a pity that he should have so much misdirected his talents or his time as to think that he had better undo what once he had the labour of doing. In turning out the contents of a closet this morning, I came upon the manuscript of a small book entitled '*Busts and Burial in Poet's Corner*'. It was written in 1845 and originated in a discussion in the House of Lords on the propriety of admitting Thorwaldsen's statue of Lord Byron into Westminster Abbey. After skimming parts of it I put it into the fire, and then sent '*Terence Crosbie*' into the flames after it. This last was a five-act play written about the same time. (*Diary*).

Beating the bounds. *Tuesday May 30.* Beating the bounds, or Perambulation, of the parish of Sidmouth gone through today. Owing to the unsatisfactory state of the affairs of the Manor, this has not been properly done for about forty years. I walked the entire route, and a good fag it was. I furnished the report for the papers, which I shall cut out and put away among my Sidmouth historical memorandums (in my ms. *Hist. of Sidmouth*). (*Diary*).

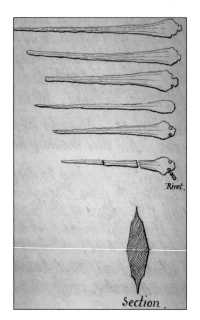

67/6/24. Bronze hoard. (Diary)

Bronze weapons. *Monday June 24.* Got on the Exeter coach but stopped short of *the city.* Got down at Liverydole, in Heavitree, and called on Mr. Charles Tucker, who has the custody of some bronze weapons recently found by men digging trenches for drainage purposes at Larkbere, on the line of the ancient road from Streetway or Straightway Head to Hembury Fort. As they are to be engraved and described in the *Journal of the Archaeological Association* I did not take careful drawings of them, but I subjoin sketches of them from memory. They are six in number, the length of the largest about two feet, or perhaps a trifle more. The smallest, which has a detached rivet, is broken. They are broad and thin where the handle was and the holes of the rivets are decayed out. Their name, or mode of use, or shape of the handle has not yet been ascertained. I think he said that none, or only one, had hitherto been found in England, but several in Ireland. He showed me an Irish one, with the rivet holes and rivets perfect but no haft. Some have hazarded the conjecture that the handles may have been of horn.

He told me of a lady now in London (whose name he could not remember) whose late father found, or became possessed of, a mould in which such weapons were cast. I think he said this mould was found at Salcombe or Kingsbridge or thereabouts in this county. Before his death her father had made the remark that the mould would make her fortune if she sold it. From this observation, she has

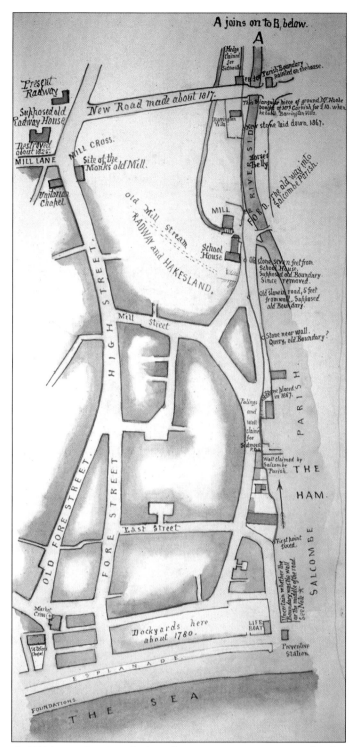

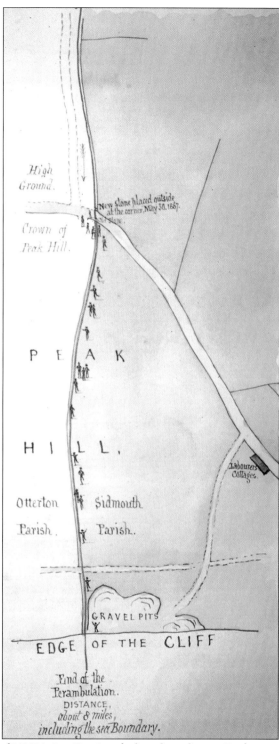

67/5/30-1. *Beating the bounds, starting point.* (Hist. of Sid. II,86)

67/5/30-2. *Beating the bounds, ending on Peak Hill.* (Hist. of Sid. II,86)

taken up the idea that it is worth some fabulous sum. She has offered to sell it to the British Museum and has demanded five hundred pounds as the price, *but* this has been rejected so she still retains the article. I believe it is the only mould of the kind that has ever been met with. (*Diary*).

Unexpected legacy. *September 9. Hutchinson received a pleasant surprise. A letter informed him that he was due a legacy of a hundred pounds from a Miss Dawson of Audley, 'as a testimony of her admiration of his unflinching adherence to truth, through good and evil report, throughout the church disturbances in Sidmouth'. The disturbances were of course the acrimonious disputes that arose during the rebuilding of the church.*

1868

68/1/27-1. *Round tower, St. Mary Major, Exeter.* (Diary)

68/1/27-2 *Parson and Clerk Rock, from the cliff above. February 1868.* (DRO, Z19/2/8D/346A)

68/2/4. *Recumbent female figure, Powderham Church. Sketched on the spot February 3, 1868.* (DRO, Z19/2/8E/189)

Exeter, Church of St. Mary Major. *Monday January 27.* Went from the Old Chancel, Sidmouth, to Belmont Villa, Dawlish. Took the omnibus to Ottery Road Station and the railroad to Exeter. Went and looked at St. Mary Major's new church in the Cathedral Yard which is now approaching completion. Some people in Exeter think the old church need never have been pulled down, and certainly I much regretted its destruction. I have heard it said that there was some ancient Roman work about it but I do not know whether this was really true. A curious and interesting feature was a sort of round turret at the north-east corner covered I think by a cone. There was also near it, as in the sketch, a figure of St. Lawrence who I think is said to have suffered martyrdom on a grid-iron, *though* I do not know whether this piece of ancient sculpture has been preserved. (*Diary*). *The slab depicting St. Lawrence's martyrdom was rescued from its position near the east porch and was reset within the new church on the west wall. (Cresswell 1908). When this church was in turn demolished in 1971 after barely a hundred years, the slab was again rescued and is now displayed in the south quire-aisle of Exeter Cathedral. Hutchinson stayed in Dawlish for a month and whilst there did the annexed sketch of the Parson and Clerk.*

Powderham Church. *Tuesday February 4.* Went to see the annual coursing in Powderham Park. Took the rail to Starcross and walked to the Castle through the Park. The weather was beautiful and an immense number of people were there. I then walked to Powderham church. The only monument in it is a white stone recumbent female figure in the south transept, which I copied. There is a good carved oak screen, I was told old, *and* the north transept is divided off by a new open carved oak screen by Gush of Exeter. The Earl of Devon's family sit there. The organ is at the south-west corner of the church *but* a new *one* is in contemplation. The west. window is by Beer of Exeter, the other coloured glass by makers from a distance. (*Diary*). *The monument is probably a cenotaph to Elizabeth, daughter of Edward 1 and Countess of Devon who died in 1316 and was buried at Walden Abbey, Essex. (Rogers 1880, Sepulchral Effigies).*

Bone discovery. *Thursday March 19.* Human bones *have been* found behind the site of St. Peter's Chapel near the Market Place. (*Diary*). A deep drain was being cut through the narrow lane at the back of Marlborough Place when the men came upon a large deposit of human bones lying promiscuously. They were considered as marking the burial place of the Chapel and lay at the depth of about six feet. I have the bones of the left arm, sound and in good preservation though they must be at least some centuries old, and the sub-joined is a rough pen and ink sketch of

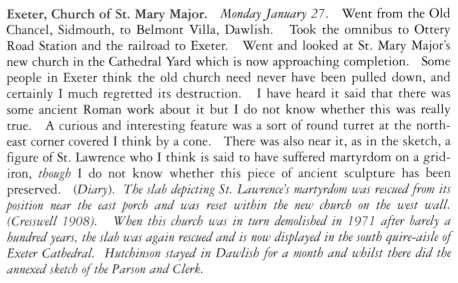

them. The humerus measures thirteen and a half inches long but I regret that one of the workmen broke it across the middle after it had been extracted from the ground. I do not think that the two small bones belonged to the larger one as they do not fit well enough at the elbow joint. After keeping these bones for a dozen years I gave them to Dr. Pullin. (*History of Sidmouth IV, 148a-149*).

Colaton Rawley Church. *Tuesday April 7.* Mr. Heineken and myself took a trip to Colaton Rawley and neighbourhood. We proceeded via Bulverton and

190

Newton Poppleford Hill, turned to the left, or south, and stopped to look at Dotton or Datton, spelled Donitone in Domesday Book. Under a limewash floor at the mill, towards the latter half of the last century, a gold or silver-gilt cup was found, which was given to Mr. Duke of Otterton who then owned the property. It may have been a sacramental cup as a chapel is said to have existed here. Somewhere about 1855 William Cornish found some old copper coins near the bank in the bed of the river one day when he was fishing. Neither he nor his father, C. Cornish of Salcombe House near Sidmouth, could tell me any more of them, *as* a few that he brought home had been mislaid or lost. It was near the ford and the wooden bridge over the Otter. They were said to have been Roman.

We now proceeded to Colaton Rawley and examined the church. The windows are Perpendicular except the east window of the nave, which has traces of late Decorated. The stonework however, seems to have been renewed. *There is a* small window on the south side, the lower ends of the dripstone of which end without bosses, knees or returns, *and there is* the same sort of label ends to the windows on the north side of the old house *to be* mentioned presently. Over the south porch is a sundial with three faces. The gnomon of the west face is the only one remaining, *but* from the pattern and character of the stonework this dial is not very ancient. There is something in it rather Jacobean. The west door of the tower is good. A man's and a woman's head terminate the hoodmoulding *and* may represent benefactors of the church. The horned head-dress adorns the woman, *similar to one* at the west door of Clyst St. George. The deep hollow in the middle of the mouldings round the door produces a fine effect. Annexed is a sketch of the font in the church, perhaps made a trifle high for the width, though I am not sure. The church is a nave and north aisle, contemporary, and at the north-eastern corner an addition apparently of the Third Pointed period, partly against the north aisle and projecting several feet eastward of it. The floor is about eighteen inches above the church *and* the connection is by a large arch. A hole nearly two feet square has been cut at right angles through the north wall of the nave near the communion table, as if to make a sort of squint to those who occupied this chamber during the service. The columns down the nave are massive, circular Norman, the arches are pointed *and* the mouldings a plain chamfer of two orders. The easternmost column of the series, though of the same pattern, is less massive than the others and is plainly not so old. *The* wagon roof of *the* nave, divided by wood ribs into squares, *has* good timber bosses at the intersections, once coloured. The bosses in the north aisle are finer and better cut. Along the cornice, flowers and coats of arms *are* intermixed. I saw one of three torteaux and a label of three points for Courtenay occurring twice, and also one with three cinquefoils, two and one, on another shield. Both the two great east windows are too close to each other and consequently not under the points of the gables. The tower has three bells, but they are out of order, *and* a turret at the south-east corner *without* buttresses.

A hundred or two hundred yards west of the church is an old house called 'Place', *possibly* a contraction of Palace as the Abbots of Dunkeswell once had a residence here, *and* the rural palace of the Bishops of Exeter just below Chudleigh is *also* called 'Place'. The Dean of Exeter had a rectory in this parish, *so* could this house have been the Dean's rectory? Traditional says that Sir Walter Rawley

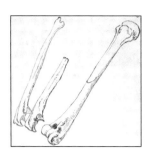
68/3/19-2. *Arm bones from Marlborough Place.* (Hist. of Sid. IV,148a)

68/3/19-1. *Colaton Rawley church, sundial over south porch.* (Diary)

68/3/19-3. *Colaton Rawley church, font.* (Diary)

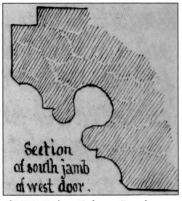
68/3/19-4. *Colaton Rawley church, section.* (Diary)

68/3/19-2. *Colaton Rawley church, west door.* (Diary)

68/3/19-5. *Colaton Rawley church, horned headress, west door hood moulding.* (Diary)

68/3/19-6. *Colaton Rawley church, nave column.* (Diary)

68/3/19-7. *Colaton Rawley church, piscina.* (Diary)

lived here at the time the property belonged to his family, *and* the gardener pointed out a spot on the north side of the house where Sir Walter is said to have first grown potatoes. The house is built with the red stone of the neighbourhood, except where patched with brick in more recent times. Over the entrance porch on the east is a little chapel. There is a piscina *with* two holes on the south side and a two-light window blocked up. The entrance to it is from a bedroom on the north side, and also a single light window on this side blocked up. At its east end is a two-light window with quatrefoil in head, of a Decorated character. At its west end is a splayed hole, blocked up, about two feet square and about eighteen inches from the floor. It is on a level with the floor of the room on the other side of the wall at the top of the stairs. *Its* use *is* a mystery. Mr. Cutler of Sidmouth owns this house. (*Diary*).

May Day in Dawlish. *Friday May 1.* May Day. At Sidmouth on May Day the children carry about boughs of trees decorated with ribbons, flowers, etc., and call at the houses for pence. At Dawlish the girls bring about what they call a May Doll, which I have never seen before. The one I saw was a doll about fourteen inches long laid in a basket and surrounded with flowers. Sometimes a little cradle is used instead of a basket. (*Diary*).

Elephant Rock 1. *Monday May 4.* Walked out to Langstone Point and finished a coloured drawing of the 'Elephant rock'. The face of the cliff on the eastern or Exmouth side of the Point, near the railway wall, has been shaped out by the action of the waves at high water into the form of an immense elephant. It is certainly very like. The legs have been disengaged by caverns which run into the cliff. As the rock is not very hard, perhaps it will not endure many years. I have often been through the caverns and passages, in one side and out the other, but I think I can remember before they were formed. (*Diary*).

68/5/4. *'The Elephant Rock', east side of Langstone Point near Dawlish, Devon. It is only apparent at one point on the railway wall. Coloured there May 4, 1868.*
(DRO, Z19/2/8E/193)

Wreck on Chit Rocks. *May.* Schooner driven on shore against the cliff above the Chit Rocks. (*Sketchbook E*). *There are no further details of the grounded vessel shown in the sketch either in the Diary or in the local newspapers, so it was probably floated off. Later in the year, on the night of August 21, the Providence of Lyme Regis was driven ashore and broken up below Salcombe Hill cliffs (Lethaby's Journal for September 1868) and an October gale caused the total loss of the Scottish Maid, also on Chit Rocks (see September 24, 1868).*

Otterton Cartulary. *Thursday May 7.* After breakfast, went into the church. After that I called on Sir John Coleridge about the Otterton Cartulary, which had been lent to me for historical purposes some years ago by some of his relations, now dead. He did not know where it was now kept or who had it *and* I told him it ought to be in the British Museum. Got to Sidmouth about noon. (*Diary*). *The Cartulary is now kept in the Devon Record Office.*

68/5/?. Schooner driven on shore against the cliff above the Chit Rocks. May 1868. (DRO, Z19/2/8E/195)

Jury service. *Tuesday June 23.* Summoned to Exeter. Formerly they used to put me on the special juries at the Assizes, when I got a guinea a trial but was kept

68/7/31-1. *Barrow 53, section.*
(Hist. of Sid. I,73)

68/7/31-2. *Cup from Seven-barrow Field.* (Hist. of Sid. I,73)

68/7/31-3. *Barrow 54, section.* (Hist. of Sid. I,73)

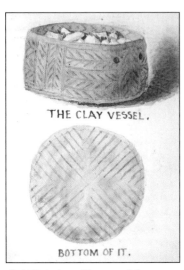

THE CLAY VESSEL.

BOTTOM OF IT.

68/7/31-4. *Clay vessel from barrow 54, side and bottom view.* (Hist. of Sid. I,73)

in Exeter the whole week. But a few years ago the County Magistrates made some alteration, so that now I am on the grand jury at the General Sessions, when I get nothing but am only required for one day. The sessions begin today but I am not required till tomorrow so I went on to Dawlish. (*Diary*).

Bacon monument, St. Thomas's Church. *Tuesday June 25.* Came in today to attend one of the quarterly meetings of the Exeter Diocesan Architectural Society, held at College Hall in South Street. Some good papers were read. Went down to St. Thomas's *and* visited the church for the purpose of seeing the monument to the memory of Mrs. Medley, formerly one of the Miss Bacons of Sid Cliff, near Sidmouth. Her father, the sculptor (the younger Bacon) executed the recumbent figure of his daughter. The monument is on the north side of the chancel within the communion rails. It *has* a fuller face and fatter hands than most of the Miss Bacons had, *but* the countenance is extremely pleasing. Most of them died young. They were as fair and delicate as wax dolls to look at. *I then* returned to Dawlish. (*Diary*).

Seventh annual meeting of the Devonshire Association. *Tuesday July 29.* The Devonshire Association foe the Advancement of Science met in Honiton *and* I went over to read a paper on the *Hill Fortresses, Sling Stones and Some Other Antiquities of South-eastern Devon.* Attended the meetings according to the programme. (*Diary*). *Although the Devonshire Association first met in 1862, Hutchinson did not become a member till this year, possibly because of the difficulties involved in getting to the meetings.*

Barrow excavations near Roncombe Gate. *Friday July 31.* By way of a pleasant wind up, an expedition to the tumuli near Roncombe Gate on Honiton Hill was planned. Today was a very agreeable one, though it would have been better if thc labourers who were employed to dig had been more closely looked after. (*Diary*). *The members were invited out to see the excavations into three large barrows in Seven-barrow Field (Barrow Report numbers 52-54) and another across the road on the open moor (BR no. 57). The excavations were supervised by Rev. Kirwan and his report appears in Trans. Dev. Assoc. II, 619-649. Nothing was found in Barrow 52 (which Kirwan refrains from mentioning), but Barrow 53 produced the Kimmeridge shale Farway cup, 'a little masterpiece of Bronze Age craftsmanship' (Allen and Timms 1996). Hutchinson was present and his more scientific account of the proceedings in the Second Report of the Barrow Committee was rather critical of Kirwan's management. Referring to Barrow 54:* Unfortunately that gentleman was so very much occupied in Honiton at the time of the meeting there that he was unable to be with the labourers whom he had set to work to make the excavations... . Mr. Blackmore, a gentleman from Torquay, was walking over the newly-turned out earth on the eastern flank of the barrow when he espied and picked up the cylindrical clay vessel full of calcined bones in the illustration... . Now it may be assumed as a certainty that as this vessel was picked up unsullied by any clay, dirt or earth, but fresh and clean, it must have been enclosed within some other and larger urn, which the ignorant workmen must have broken to pieces with their tools and never saw... . This shows the necessity of never leaving workmen for a moment when they are engaged in such researches, for no one knows what the next spadefull of earth may reveal. (*Second Report of the Barrow Committee*). *Hutchinson also assisted in the excavation of Barrow 57, drawing the section and some of the pottery found.*

Wreck of the Scottish Maid. *September 24.* The Scottish Maid, a coal vessel of 150 tons, was driven by a gale onto Chit Rocks. (*History of Sidmouth V, 165*). *A trim and well-fitted vessel of about 120 tons belonging to Captain Adams of Sidmouth, it brought a cargo of coal for Mr. Ellis' gas works, the unloading being finished at a late hour on Thursday September 24. Towards morning a storm beat upon the empty ship and drove* *her upon Chit Rocks. And there she has remained, stripped of her sails and everything portable and daily threatened to be ripped asunder by the angry waters. (Lethaby's Sidmouth Journal and Directory, October 1868, extract).*

Meteor. *Monday November 9.* Looking out at the back of the Old Chancel at about half past seven this evening, I saw a meteor passing over the zenith. It went from NNE to SSW rather slowly *and* had a short tail which waved like the tail of a fish swimming. When it got behind the chimneys of my house, No.4 Coburg Terrace, I rushed from the back to the front out upon the gravel, where I caught sight of it again. I have sent an account of it, with a coloured sketch, to the Astronomer Royal. *(Diary).*

68/7/31-5. *Barrow 57, section.* (Hist. of Sid. I,74)

Diary gloom, etc. *Saturday November 14.* A long, long interval and no entry in my diary, and it was likely to have been longer for I have often thought of dropping it altogether and throwing the whole into the fire. *Cui bono?* What is the good of jotting down memorandums which I may never require to refer to as long as I live and which nobody may care to refer to after I am dead? If I had a wife and children, I might wish to leave something after me for their amusement or instruction, because men 'live in their children'. When the ladies sometimes joke me or reproach me for continuing single so long, I generally tell them not to hurry me, and that I mean to look out as soon as I come to the marrying age.

Before I burn this book, I may as well note down in reference to the Devonshire Association, that I made several expeditions in August and September to the top of Honiton Hill, to assist in the excavations of some of the tumuli near Roncombe Gurt on Broad Down. I found two flint arrow heads one day, a flint flake, pieces of ruddle or red ochre with which the Ancient Britons coloured their faces to look terrible in war, and other things which I handed over to Mr. Kirwan, the Secretary, for the Exeter or British Museum.

It is a notable fact that the new Reform Bill has divided the county into three parts instead of two as before, that Sidmouth is in the eastern division and that this town has become a polling place *for* the parishes of Salcombe Regis, Branscombe, Sidbury, Harpford and Sidmouth. I am sorry politics have come so near our doors, *as* we shall derive no benefit and a bone of contention has been thrown into the place. *I* voted for Lord Courtenay, *the* first time I ever took the trouble to vote for anybody.

Shortly before my cousin died, he requested that the Hutchinson papers might be handed over to me. After his funeral (May 2, 1865) I brought them with me to Sidmouth but have only recently found time to look them over. For two or three months, at odd times, I have been examining, reading *and* arranging them, making indices, notes, memoranda and a catalogue.

I sat up last night till about two in the morning, most of the time walking up and down on the gravel, to look for the November meteors (see November 13, 1866). They were only few and far between, so at two I went to bed. *(Diary).*

68/7/31-6. *Pottery fragment from barrow 57 and supposed reconstruction.* (Hist. of Sid. I,74)

68/7/31-7. *Fragment of second vessel found in barrow 57.* (Hist. of Sid. I,75)

68/11/9. *Meteor.* (Diary)

1869

Early man. *Wednesday February 13.* I have just read a book in which I am much interested, entitled *'Pre-Glacial Man'*. It is by J. Scott Moore, whose uncle, now residing in Sidmouth, lent it to me. The antiquity of the human race on earth, the glacial periods, the periodical changes in climate, the causes of those great changes and the endeavours to convert geological periods into ascertained time are among the many great questions now occupying the attention of learned men. (*Diary*).

Garden well. *Tuesday February 23.* Had a well dug in the corner of the field behind the Old Chancel. The soil in this part of the valley of Sidmouth is a deposit of alluvium, consisting of gravel, sand and clay lying on the red rock of the New Red Sandstone. They sank a shaft four feet in diameter. For the first four feet down they had fine mould hardening to a clay, then about five feet of gravel with some clay and stones of various sizes up to the bigness of two fists with the corners rounded off, then a bed of finer gravel some eight or ten inches thick, then coarser gravel as before with very little clay for about two feet, then a thin bed of peat or mould like 'old dead leaves' (as the men said), and lastly gravel and stones partly water-worn as before down to fifteen feet, below which they could not go as the water came in so fast. As the season has been excessively wet for some time, water was probably found sooner than it otherwise would have been. The well was bricked up, somewhat contracted at the top, with a hole left nearly two feet in diameter, and this sealed down with a flagstone. The charge for digging is a shilling a foot the first ten feet, eighteen pence the second ten, two shillings the third ten and so on. The bricking up (not including the cost of the bricks) is the same, the lowest work being the dearest. (*Diary*).

69/2/23. *Section of well.*
(Diary)

69/3/19. *Elephant's tooth dredged up off Sidmouth.* (Hist. of Sid. I,23a)

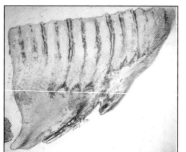

Further additions to the Old Chancel. *Monday March 14.* Men came and began to dig trenches for foundations for some additions I wish to make to the Old Chancel. I hope now to build an entrance hall, two rooms and a bedroom over the hall. (*Diary*). *Hutchinson now started to embark on a second series of additions to his house.*

First fossil elephant's tooth. *Friday March 19.* A Sidmouth sailor brought me a fossil elephant's tooth. They often bring me curiosities or coins for sale which they find on the beach. He told me he found it at low water, spring tides, at the latter part of last month (full moon was on the 26th of February) amongst the rocks far out, at about a mile and a quarter west of Sidmouth. This is at the commencement of the reef approaching High Peak Hill and opposite 'Wind-gate', as they call the gap between Peak and High Peak Hills. Though a little sceptical at first, I examined it and gave him five shillings for it. It occurred to me that

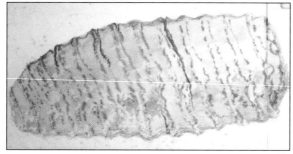

in the Torquay Museum there is a tooth of an extinct mammal, and it therefore would be worth securing. If this turns out to be valuable on enquiry, it will do either for the Exeter or for the British

196

Museum. In the Torquay Museum there is the last lower left side molar of a mammoth, dredged up from the bottom of Torbay at no great distance from the shore, *which* probably belonged to one of the elephant tribe that once roamed through the submerged forest along that coast. It had not laid long at the bottom of the sea, being devoid of any incrustation of marine polyzoa. Mine however, has some slight incrustations (see June 2, 1869). *(Diary). This tooth, along with one found on Sidmouth beach on January 18, 1873 (see Diary entry) is now on display in Sidmouth Museum.*

Thorn Farm, Blackbury Castle and Southleigh Church. *Tuesday April 27.* Mr. Heineken and myself went out for a day's excursion according to the plan we have followed for the last twenty years, by which we have amused ourselves in looking up the antiquities in the neighbourhood of Sidmouth. Getting into a carriage after breakfast, together with sandwiches, beer, bread and cheese, cakes etc., maps, books, sketch books, memorandum books, photographic camera, pickaxe, spade, measuring rod, tape, probing iron, and sometimes other things if we were likely to require them, we started and went up Salcombe Hill. Left Salcombe on our right, stopped at Thorn Farm *and* went and looked at the hall ceiling, panelled work with moulded oak beams. Since we were last here the hall is divided into a parlour and a passage. The lower round moulding of the cross-beams is covered in a pattern like the annexed. There used to be a picturesque old well arched over with stone in the orchard on the north side *of the building, but* it seems to have been removed *as* we could not find it. It was like this *sketch.* We observed the Ordnance mark on the pound and went on to Trow. There used to be (and still is) a tradition that a man called Trump found a crock of gold many years ago when ploughing in a field between the pound and Trow, but his nephew some decime or duodecime of years ago laughed at the story when I told him that I had heard so, and assured me his uncle made his money in other ways. From the Lyme road, we turned north and passed the farm called Long Chimney, after the road called Longue Cheminee, I suppose, by the Normans. We crossed Rakeway or Rakeway Head bridge and turned east at the foot of Broad Down. *Here we* stopped and looked again at the Lovehayne tumulus (see October 29, 1861). Nearly one half of the tumulus still remains, about five feet high and sixty broad. Walking over it, we picked up a flint flake and a piece of ruddle or red oxide of iron, used as war paint, *and* coming back to the road we found some flakes and apparently a core of flint in the intervening field

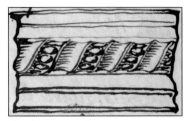

69/4/27-1. *Thorn Farm, moulding.* (Diary)

69/4/27-2. *Thorn Farm, well covering.* (Diary)

69/4/27-3. *Fire beacon.* (Diary)

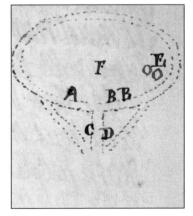

69/4/27-4. *Sketch plan of Blackbury Castle.* (Diary)

We went on to Blackbury Castle where we had often been before, *but* this time we wished to examine for sling stones and calcined flints. On digging in several places round the ramparts we met with them on the south side at A, more at BB, some at C but most at D. It was from about D that seventy cartloads were taken away some fifty years ago to make mortar for the new Wiscombe House, as a man called Mutter, who did it, once told us in the camp. The ramparts seem to have been heightened and repaired with these calcined flints, *but* whence came they? For some time a feeling has been growing upon me that perhaps there was a beacon in this camp built of stone, like the still perfect one on Culmstock Hill which I examined and sketched on August 7, 1851. I believe there was a similar one on Shute Hill and the same over Harpford, near Sidmouth. Such a beacon consists of a circular wall about ten or twelve feet in diameter and six or seven high covered with a dome roof having a large hole in the top. If wood were put in at the doorway and lighted, the draught would send out a great flame at the top. If such a beacon were built of flints, the great heat of the flames against the sides of the interior must necessarily calcine and split them, and these splinters would accumulate in a heap on the floor. It would be requisite from time to time to clear them out, and they would be thrown on the ramparts. I cannot believe that partial, or ephemeral, or the accidental burning of the woods could have produced such quantities of flint splinters, as some writers have supposed, nor could fires burning on the level ground have done it, for fire has very little effect downwards. It must have been the result of long-continued action under favourable conditions.

We then traversed the field on the south in various directions. Mr. Heineken found nine egg-shaped beach pebbles scattered over a space thirty or forty yards in front of the entrance at D, whilst I walked away towards the sides of the fields

69/4/27-6. *Southleigh church, coats of arms on Robert Drake's tomb.* (Diary)

69/4/27-5. *Southleigh church, string course around tower.* (Diary)

69/4/27-7. *Southleigh church font.* (Diary)

and into the field below. But I discovered nothing until I came back and crossed the region where he had been successful, when I soon picked up two. It is rather strange that they should have abounded only at that spot, unless we imagine that they had been used in a fight which took place before the entrance. He afterwards found one at F in the camp, but as the ground in the interior is not tilled we could not make any special examination. There are two low mounds at E near the east end of the interior, like tumuli, which owing to the bushes and brambles we had not noticed in our former visits. We sat on the north agger and eat our dinner. *The Camp was partly excavated by the Devon Archaeological Exploration Society in 1952-4, confirming Hutchinson's observations. The palisade revetment at the entrance proved to have been destroyed by fire perhaps explaining the calcined flints, and of over 1200 sling stones recovered from around the Camp 'by far the greatest number came from the entrance'. (Young and Richardson 1953).*

Like giants refreshed, we arose and proceeded to Southleigh. At the Belvedere, a quarter of a mile from the Camp, we stopped. This hexagonal tower was inhabited when we were here before but it is now shut up and is falling to ruin. We got a view of Wiscombe House in the valley, a very ugly house indeed, the seat of Charles Gordon Esq., J.P. His late father, whom I well remember, was a stout athletic man of whose surpassing strength many anecdotes are current in the neighbourhood. One of his feats was to take a bull by the horns, and by giving him a jerk he would fling the animal upon his side to the ground. He was the first of Wiscombe, and owed his existence, as common report says, to the error of some Scotch lord.

We could not learn that there were any antiquities in the neighbourhood of Southleigh *but* we walked round the church. There is a string course of good effect (annexed) round the tower, but nearly all gone. New windows of Beer stone, at the expense of Miss Gordon of Wiscombe, were being put in in, of the Decorated style. The tower is square with angular buttresses *but* no turret, the staircase *being* built out over on the north side and in again. *There are* four bells, one of them 'crazed', I suppose cracked, *and* three Early English lancet windows at the east end not older than about 1855. The font formerly stood in the tower, with a small stone bracket over it in the north wall, *but though* the bracket remains, the font is now in the church. Unfortunately, it has recently been tooled all over. When will modern improvers be modest enough to learn discretion? When Sidmouth Church was pulled down in 1859, some fragments of a Norman font of a similar pattern were dug out of the walls and sent to my premises when I bought the old materials of the old chancel and had them re-erected. The fragments of the font I have just had built into the buttresses of the hall on each side of the door. The church inside was partly rebuilt about 1855, that is, the chancel. On the north side of the latter there is a Jacobean monument to Robert Drake . . . The five coats of arms *annexed* are sculptured on the tomb, the first and last look*ing* more modern than the others. The Royal arms are on the north wall of the church. There is an old copy of Josephus *and* over the south door there is a large oil painting of the Adoration of the Magi, once at the east end. There is a large old lock in the south door in good order, enclosed in a piece of oak fixed across the door, thickest at the lock end and thin at the hinge end. Mr. Heineken took a photograph of the outside of the tower and church. The window over the tower door is Perpendicular. (Photograph failed).

We returned home by the same route we had come. *(Diary).*

Funeral procession. *Friday May 14.* Went to the funeral of an old lady and wore a hat band and scarf of black silk and black kid gloves which are given to persons invited. Mr. Buttemer (pronounced Butter-meer) of the Elms was walking before me.   It was very windy *and* we had not walked far when the pin which should have held his scarf better on the shoulder gave way and his scarf slipped down, unconsciously to himself.   It had descended by the wind with the motion of walking as far as his waist and was beginning to look very ridiculous on a solemn occasion, when I thought it better to step forward and give him a friendly hint.   However, before I did this, it slid down about his ankles until it nearly tripped him up.   Then hastily making an effort to replace it, he pushed the tails of his coat up behind his head, which was even more absurd.   Not long after these things had been set right, the wind loosened the pins and blew round our hatbands.   The tail of mine was twisted round until it hung over my right shoulder, but Mr. Buttemer's was turned round in front and hung over his face. (*Diary*).

Report on fossil tooth.   *Wednesday June 2.*   Professor Owen, in a letter dated yesterday at the British Museum, informs me (judging from a coloured rubbing I sent him) that the fossil tooth found at low water last February near Sidmouth appears to be that of Elephas indicus (see March 19, 1869). (*Diary*).

Miss Hooper's oratory.   *Wednesday June 16.*   Miss Geraldine Hooper that was and Mrs. Denning that is, came over with her husband to give a religious address at the London Hotel.   They live on an estate called Pitt near Ottery where he has some five hundred acres of his own.   As Miss Geraldine Hooper I have heard of her wonderful powers of extempore speaking and zeal for religion, *and* I was not disappointed.   Her rapidity and clearness of enunciation were very striking and as she is a gentlewoman of good birth and education, she is perfectly ladylike even in her most vehement sentences.   As Mr. Denning has a similar turn they are well matched. (*Diary*).

Stonework in Sidmouth Church.   *Wednesday June 23.*   Finished carving the capital of the column in the middle of the arch between the vestry and the church, or rather the side next the church for there is wood panelling next the vestry.   I hope to do the vestry side some day.   Also carved the flowers and leaves of the arches above.   I have however, not been so much accustomed to carve stone as to carve oak.   The stonework of this archway has been recently put in, but the well-meant attempt of the mason at the ornamental work was so displeasing to the vicar and the churchwarden, that they allowed me to cut it all out and do it again. The glass is expected soon. (*Diary*).

Old glass in Sidmouth Church.   *Thursday June 24.* Took a rubbing of and partly coloured the piece of old glass in the vestry, formerly in the east window of the church.   If I had not been very vigilant nine years ago when the church was re-built, this piece of glass would have been stolen by a dishonest workman. I wish to send a copy to the Exeter Diocesan Architectural Society, of which I have for some years been a member. (*Diary*). The specimen of old glass is the last remnant probably of an entire window.   It is Pre-Reformation in date and highly interesting as a work of art.   Under the form of a heraldic shield it bears the kite-shaped figure in red, round at the top and pointed below, representing the Five Wounds of Christ running drops of blood.   Each *is* surmounted by a crown yellow, outlined in brown, over each of which is a yellow table bearing a brown inscription.   Unknown to the Committee, the Clerk-of-the-Works took this piece of glass from the head of the window by means of a ladder (the window now in the Old Chancel), but the Committee never showed any anxiety for its recovery nor even troubled their heads about it.   I was determined however, it should not be lost, *and* during the several months that elapsed between

69/5/14.   *Funeral dress.* (Diary)

69/6/23.   *Screen between the church and the vestry.*   (Hist. of Sid. IV,94)

69/6/24. *Old glass formerly in east window, Sidmouth parish church.* (Hist. of Sid. IV,62)

the pulling down and rebuilding of the church, I spoke of it more than once to *him*, to let him know that I had not forgotten it. When the new windows were being put in I required it to be produced. On getting possession of it, I at once employed a glazier to make the window for the vestry and set this old glass in the middle of it, and further secured it by having a wire netting placed outside. I never had any doubt in my own mind what was intended. (*History of Sidmouth IV, 63*). *The glass has since been moved again, to the head of one of the windows in the Lady Chapel.*

Lydes of Sid House. *Wednesday June 30, 1869.* So Mr. Lyde has been killed on the railroad at the Clapham Junction, and in a very dreadful way. I knew him well some twenty-five years ago when he was practising the law in Sidmouth, and I can just remember his father, an old Captain in the Navy, being drawn about in a three-wheeled chair. They own a good deal of scattered property in this neighbourhood, with Sid House and adjoining land in Salcombe parish . . . It seems that *he* was standing on the platform reading the paper when he was seen to reel and lose his balance just as a train was coming in. He fell off down upon the rails and the train went over him. His body was picked up, but dreadfully mutilated, with I think one arm and one leg cut off. He was not dead and even survived an hour or two in that state. He revived a little once, and said 'What's the matter?' From this it is supposed he had fallen in a fit and was ignorant of what had happened to him. I think he married a baronet's daughter and has left a family. (*Diary*).

Sid House, a red brick building out on the Salcombe Hill side of the road, was raised in about 1818 by the *elder* Mr. Lyde, *the father of the Captain.* The name of Lyde was known in Sidmouth long before this period and several tombstones belonging to the family are under the east window of the church outside, and two tablets in the north porch. After Mr. Lyde died, the place was 'troubled' as the country people phrased it. According to the popular story long current in the neighbourhood, and which I have heard from several mouths, his hazy and supernatural form used to come back and haunt the premises to the terror of the living. *He* had a strange habit of sitting on the gate of the field opposite the house, so that few had the courage to pass up or down the road and none through the gate. The thoroughfare being thus barred and obstructed to the great inconvenience of the public, the clergy undertook to lay the ghost. I forget just at this moment how many persons had a hand in this important ceremony, whether it was three or seven, but at all events I believe that the vicars of Sidmouth, Sidbury and Salcombe were present. I cannot describe what they did, but the rustics told me that 'they spirited him away'. The exorcism succeeded for he has not appeared since. (*History of Sidmouth III, 141*).

Velocipedes. *Wednesday July 8.* Velocipedes are all the fashion again at the present time. I am not sure they have not been revived in France but the youth of England are warm in the pursuit. But instead of 'pedestrian hobby-horses', 'dandy horses' or 'velocipedes', such names as bicycle and tricycle, according as to whether they have two or three wheels, have found general acceptance. As a child I can remember them before they went out *of fashion.* I remember seeing two gentlemen coming slowly down Teignmouth Hill, when my father lived near East Teignmouth Church, when the first ran over a dog and was overturned and the other immedi-

69/6/30. *Exorcism of Mr. Lyde.* (Hist. of Sid. III,141)

ately ran over them *both* and was capsized too. Velocipedes, men and dog were all in the road together *and* this circumstance made an impression on a young mind. The rider forced himself forwards by touching the ground with his feet. It was said that this strained the loins and caused rupture, which was partly the cause of them going out. By the modern contrivance, the knees are gathered up and the feet are placed on the arms of a crank affixed to the axle of the front wheel, which they turn. This plan however is rather laborious. (*Diary*).

Church restoration at Salcombe Regis. *Tuesday July 13.* They are at present engaged in rebuilding the chancel of the parish church of Salcombe Regis *and* Mr. Heineken and myself went over to see what they were doing. They have taken off the roof (which by the way was pushing the north and south walls outwards) and they offered me the old oak timbers if I would buy them, but I do not see that I could in any way work them up for the Old Chancel. The north wall is still standing but they had knocked a hole through the middle where there are traces apparently of an old doorway. The east end with its windows is to remain untouched and the Norman patterns under the window and the cross above are not to be meddled with. The south wall is down except one piece about six or eight feet long sustaining part of the arch and the shaft below of a Norman doorway. It is intended to push this mass of masonry upright without disturbing it.

In the angle of the south side, the pulling down has revealed an old squint, which had been walled up from the side of the church. I do not know whether these walls are all of the original work *but* I did not think much of the mortar, nor of the putting together. *The* chalk lime and the sand of the district are not calculated to make good mortar. What I am now using for my entrance hall and other additions to the Old Chancel is Babbacombe limestone burnt at Budleigh Salterton (there having been no limekilns at Sidmouth since the kilns over Chit Rocks fell into the sea about 1855 and the sloping road from them to the beach was washed away) and coarse sea sand with the salt washed out. This makes strong mortar. At Salcombe Regis however, I believe they are going to use blue lias limestone from Yarcombe, which is *also* very good. I give a section of the south jamb of the west door, taken only by eye, also of the bold moulding forming *the* square head over *the* pointed west doorway, and also a section *of one of the mouldings* of *the* tower arch, by eye only. There is an old, massive lock behind the west door. The soffit of the tower arch is about seventeen feet ten inches above the floor *and* on the south side of *it* is a quatrefoil opening from the tower stairs into the church. On the west side of the pier on the south of the nave, there is a small shallow niche about a foot high. In the floor there is an old slab to the memory of Henry Grig *and* in the south aisle there is a slab recording the death of George Drake, 1645, with arms similar to those at Southleigh, as mentioned April 27 last. At the north-east end of the nave there is a mural tablet to the Mitchels, with the Mitchel arms impaling ? The oldest tomb in the churchyard is an altar tomb to the same family, nearly in front of the west door, of 1611.

In the south-east corner of the north aisle there is a niche or piscina. The easternmost window of the north side of this aisle is peculiar. The escoincon arch is circular over a pointed window head and the jambs have columns with circular capitals and octagonal bases, very rude and the bases perhaps not original. The window is new, the stonework made by a Sidmouth tradesman who evidently knew nothing of architecture. The painted glass is to the memory of Colonel Grey who, I think, died at Sidmouth. At the west end of the north aisle is the vestry, and beyond it, further west, is a dead house, or place where the sexton keeps his tools, etc. This dead house, or whatever it be, is entered from the churchyard at the west end by an arched doorway, and when a man told us it was generally called the 'Old Chapel', Mr. Heineken started the idea that this adjunct to the church was perhaps a chapel of St. Clement and St. Mary Magdalene mentioned by Lysons, as being in the parish of Salcombe, though without any indication as to where. The idea is new to me but I think it is worthy of consideration. The timbers of the roof are moulded, like the annexed section. From an examination of the whole north wall, it looks as if the whole north aisle formed the chapel though *now* a portion of the church, and the peculiarity of the window mentioned above and apparently a piscina in the proper place for a chapel, unusual in the aisle

69/7/13-1. *Salcombe Regis church, Norman column south wall.* (Diary)

69/7/13-2. *Salcombe Regis church, old hagioscope.* (Diary)

69/7/13-3/4 *Salcombe Regis church, section of south jamb, west door, and section of moulding over west doorway.* (Diary)

69/7/13-5. *Salcombe Regis church, section of moulding of tower arch.* (Diary)

69/7/13-6. *Salcombe Regis church, arms of (1) George Drake and (2) Mitchel and ?* (Diary)

69/7/13-8. *Salcombe Regis church, view of west end.* (Diary)

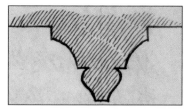

69/7/13-9. *Salcombe Regis church, section of roof timber.* (Diary)

69/7/20-1. *Remains of Harpford Beacon.* (Diary)

69/7/20-2. *Micrometer measurement.* (Diary)

of a church, altogether tend in the same direction. . It must however be observed that there is a break in the wall and that the roofs are not the same level. I have been informed that there were formerly the ruins of a building supposed to have been a chapel somewhere in the fields to the north of Trow turnpike gate. What could these have been? Could the chapel in question have been situated there? I suspect the ruins of Chelson Chapel were alluded to, *which* were removed about 1850. They were at the head of the Packham valley about two and a half miles north-east of Salcombe (see May 1, 1874).

(*Later note,* March 3, 1890. I read in the *Newberry House Magazine, II, 231*, that Commissioners visited Salcombe Regis in 1301 to examine the state of the church, and reported that 'the Chapel of the Blessed Mary Magdalene at the west end of the church was in ruins, having been crushed by the falling of an ash tree'. This identifies the chapel and says nothing about St. Clement). (*Diary*).

Harpford Beacon. *Tuesday July 20.* The weather being beautiful, we went to explore Harpford Beacon where neither of us had been for many years. Today I ought to have started for Dartmouth to attend the meeting of the Devonshire Association and be there all week, but I could not leave the workmen at the Old Chancel so long. I intended to have produced the fossil tooth found here last February, but failing in this I sent a coloured rubbing with a description to Mr. Edward Vivian of Torquay, and he kindly undertook to communicate the facts to the members. We drove to Sidford, along High Street (the old Roman road) and then up the long lane all along the north flank of Core Hill from *which* we had a fine view of Sidbury Castle. The last pinch of the hill rises one in five, as we found by levelling . . . Beacon Hill is about 764 feet high. The remains of the beacon consist of a circular wall, the diameter outside being fourteen feet, the thickness of the wall two and the height of the wall outside five feet. The whole is in a state of decay and it is nearly concealed by the three hedges converging on it. I could not find any decidedly calcined flints within it, as at Blackbury Castle, though one piece looked like it, but it would take a great deal of digging to examine thoroughly. For the purpose of experimenting with the micrometer, Mr. Heineken requested me to measure a notice board on the hillside, *and we then* measured a fir tree thirty-eight feet high with Mr. Heineken's apomecometer, a little instrument recently invented by him, though since pirated by others (see *Student* April 1869).

We then drove away northwards along the ridge of Ottery East Hill, enjoying the splendid views over the valley of the River Otter, until we came to a tumulus at the four cross-way cut into a star with four points (see October 21, 1854) where we turned back again. In so doing, we observed something very like a tumulus or barrow over the hedge in the plantation on the left and, wishing to ascertain its position, we determined to measure from it to the lane leading down to Sidbury Castle, where we were going. We made a chalk mark on the box of the hind wheel and I counted the number of revolutions as we drove on, and made them 244. The circumference of the wheel is nine feet six inches so *by calculation the distance was* 782.2 yards, or nearly half a mile. We had often measured in this manner before. (*Diary*).

Pin Beacon. *Thursday July 29.* Mr. Heineken and myself drove to Pin Beacon, where we had not been since 1855. We took the road by the cliff up Peak Hill. The gradient just above the cottage on the left, where it is steepest, is 1 in 5. On the top of the hill we turned to the right over the open heath, and making a circuit round the head of the valley, made to the south-west point covered with fir trees. We found men at work felling timber. They told us that the mound at the south point of the ridge or promontory was called the 'Old Beacon', the trees around which are about sixty years old, and the mound at a hundred paces north, the 'New Beacon', where they are from forty to forty-five years growth. Were it not for the trees the views would be splendid and most extensive, commanding all the country towards the south, west and north. Towards the east, it is shut in by the Honiton and Sidmouth ranges. At about sixty paces north of the 'Old Beacon', a hedge with a ditch on each side has been drawn across the ridge of the hill, running down on each side till it meets modern hedges. On reconsidering this I started the idea, which was adopted by my companion, that this has not got the appearance of a modern hedge at all, but wears more the appearance of an ancient work constructed to protect the 'Old Beacon' from being interfered with by an enemy.

North of the 'New Beacon' there is a field through which we passed which forms a third and newer plantation, having been planted only two seasons *ago* with little trees, which at first I did not discover amongst the grass. Here, clear of the *plantation*, we could see Blackstone Rock near Moretonhampstead, under which in a line towards us Haldon Belvidere *was visible,* and a little to the north of the line and nearer us, Woodbury Castle. We then proceeded north-east over the heath towards Salter's Cross and were surprised to see how much Mr. Balfour, our recent Lord of the Manor, has enclosed and brought into cultivation of the greater part of Bulverton Hill and the flank of Peak Hill near Mutter's Moor. We descended *via* Broadway to the town, passing the new lodge of Mr. Thornton's place at Knowle. (*Diary*).

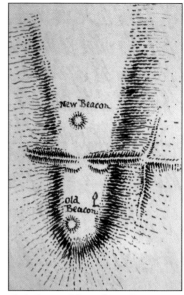

69/7/29. *Plan of Pin Beacon.* (Diary)

Barrow excavations on Gittisham Hill. *Monday August 16.* Went to the top of Gittisham Hill to watch the opening of two tumuli for the Secretary. They lie nearly three hundred yards eastwards from the sixth milestone from Sidmouth and three from Honiton. Some members of the British Association for the Advancement of Science, now assembling in Exeter, are coming out on Saturday. A thunder shower drenched me and the men, *though* I held a bundle of fern on my shoulder between me and the storm. (*Diary*).

Thursday August 19. Up on the hill again. Only met with a few flint flakes, a sling stone like those at Sidbury Castle, a large beach pebble nearly as big as a fist, spherical but flattish, probably a hammer, and some scattered pieces of red ochre. (*Diary*).

Saturday August 21. There again. Some tents were pitched in the field on the west of the milestone where we had a splendid collation, I sat with the Bayleys of Cotford, *and then* we went out on the open heath. The rector of Gittisham stood on the nearest barrow, number 1 *in the sketch (B.R.No. 27) and the* first opened, and gave an address on barrow and other antiquities of a like nature. The afternoon was quiet, warm and delightful and some two hundred or more people sat in groups on the heath. They have opened two others. Number 1 consisted of dark peat earth laid in strata, which I am inclined to think had not been disturbed, though some thought otherwise. This was capped with a layer of loose flints about a foot thick which extended over the top and south-west side only. Above this was a thin stratum of soil. Number 2 (*B.R.No.28*), about a hundred yards south-east, consisted of a circle of large rough flints from twelve to eighteen inches long, inside which was apparently a heap of earth covered by a layer of flints, again covered with earth. Number 3 (*B.R.No. 29*) was a circular patch of fern (Pteris aquilina) in the midst of the open heath and furze. Perhaps a barrow had once been there, but removed. Number 4 (*B.R.No.25*) near the great tumulus covered with trees, was of a dark peat earth. It was opened by a tunnel or trench from the south to the centre, where a heap of large stones was uncovered, as if a kistvaen was there, but there was not time on the day of the meeting to proceed further.

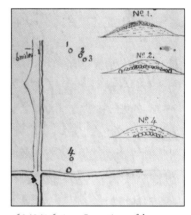

69/8/16-1. *Location of barrows on Gittisham Hill.* (Diary)

69/8/16-2. *Section of barrow 27.* (Hist. of Sid. I,70)

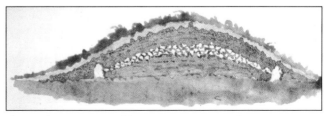

69/8/16-3. *Section of barrow 28.* (Hist. of Sid. I,70)

(Diary). Hutchinson later explained the reason for this in the Barrow Report. So large a slice of the afternoon was consumed in the splendid collation in the tent near the six-mile stone, together with many other slices of a variety of good things, that there was no time left to complete the examination of the barrow, or even to open the kist-vaen... . It had been intended to open *it* in the presence of the visitors but they did not even visit the spot. The earth was afterwards thrown in and the trench filled up as before, and to the best of my belief the kistvaen still remains intact and undisturbed. *(Second Report of the Barrow Committee). Kirwan's account of these excavations appears in Trans. Dev. Assoc., IV, 297-300. Hutchinson's sections of these and other tumuli, 'redrawn by R. H. Worth' but unacknowledged, have frequently been used to illustrate the burial mounds of east Devon.*

Torquay croquet tournament. *Monday September 13. Hutchinson left for Sidmouth once more on the eleventh, caught the wrong train again 'by some error' and was carried back to Dawlish.* My recent visit to Torquay has been very agreeable. Croquet is now becoming one of the institutions of the country, almost as much so as the constitution of Parliament or the Circuits of the judges. Went to the croquet tournament, open to all England. The game is played very differently from what it used to be *and* the best players proceed with all the caution of a player at chess. I soon discovered that my mallet was too light *and that* a heavy mallet is a great advantage. The play began on Monday the 6th and continued till Thursday the 9th inclusive. The last day I won a sweepstake of sixteen shillings.

On Friday I went to look at Paignton and called on some friends. It is a dreary-looking place. The peculiar petrifactions called Beekites are found in this neighbourhood *but* I had not time to search in the cliffs. There is a harbour enclosed by a pier on the north side of Roundham Head *and* near the church there is a square tower covered with ivy standing by itself, very pretty and picturesque. I believe it is the remains of a former bishop's palace. *(Diary).*

Death of Bishop Phillpotts. *Friday September 24.* So Harry Phillpotts, Bishop of Exeter, has gone the way of all bishops at last. He died at his residence, Bishopstowe in Torquay, last Saturday the 18th, aged 91. By talent and pugnacity he raised himself from a low origin to the mitre. His father was a wholesale brickmaker in Bridgewater who afterwards kept the Bell Inn at Gloucester. Amongst his many controversies, his refusal to install the Rev. G. C. Gorham to the vicarage at Bramford Speke near Exeter (but which the Archbishop of Canterbury compelled him to do) on the grounds that his belief in the efficacy of baptismal regeneration was defective, was not one of the least. As it must be now some sixteen or seventeen years ago I forget the particulars, but I recollect sympathising with Mr. Gorham at the time and thinking he was an ill-used man. *(Diary).*

Lifeboat for Sidmouth. *Saturday September 25.* A Mrs. Remington has given a lifeboat which is to be stationed at Sidmouth, *and* amid great demonstrations it was today drawn through the town and launched. It has a crew of twelve men, ten being at the oars. The new crew in the new boat were exercised in rowing, then sailing and afterwards in capsizing the boat, the distance being about a quarter of a mile from the shore.. They all stood on the starboard gunwale and by repeated efforts at rocking, they at last compelled her to make a somersault. She rolled quite round, down one side and up the other *and* of course the men were all thrown into the water but one or two unable to extricate themselves, who were shut in under the boat and went round with her. One or two boats were near her in case of accident and the men had their cork jackets on. It was a novel and amusing sight and Sidmouth beach was crowded with people. *(Diary).*

69/10/4. Inscription hidden in the Old Chancel. (Diary)

1869.
PETER ORLANDO HUTCHINSON NAT. WINTON. NOV. 17. 1810. BAP.
HEAVITREE 1811. FIL. ANDREÆ ET ANNE (PARKER) FIL.
THOMÆ ET SARAH (OLIVER) FIL. THOMÆ ET MARGARETÆ (SANFORD)
FIL. THOMÆ ET SARAH (FOSTER) FIL. ELISHÆ ET HANNAH (HAWKINS)
FIL. EDWARDI ET CATHERINE (HANBY) FIL. GULIELMI ET
ANNE (MARBURY) FIL. EDWARDI HUTCHINSON ET SUSANNA
DE ALFORD IN COM. LINC. ... FIERI FECIT. 1869.
SIDMOUTH IN COM. DEV. 1869.
In 1859 and 1860 the Old Chancel proper was erected on my ground

Hidden inscription. *Monday October 4.* Today I hid away the accompanying genealogical and absurd inscription in the masonry of the Old Chancel. In 1859 and 1860 the Old Chancel proper was erected on my grounds out of the materials of the old chancel of the parish church, when the church was rebuilt. In 1864 I built the Oak Room on to the north side of it with connecting walls, the window being part of the south transept window of Awliscombe church, near Honiton, soon after carving the mantel shelf and brackets in oak, the bookcase behind the door, the cornice over the window, and painting, carving and gilding the gothic heraldic ceiling containing the coats of arms of the Lords of the Manor of Sidmouth. Now I am going to make the place habitable by adding an entrance hall with some lower and upper rooms, though not to complete the whole design. The above whimsical inscription I punched with steel letters on a piece of sheet lead measuring about six inches by four, and put it behind the top stone of the left hand buttress going into the entrance hall. I am now engaged in carving the corbels in the four corners of the hall from which the vaulted ceiling springs, and the four corbels of the small vaulted ceiling of the short passage inside the hall. It has occupied me a great deal. (*Diary*).

Sanskrit writing. *Tuesday October 19.* Mr. A. Burnell, at present residing with his parents at Claremont (House, so called, near Broadway) who has been much in India, gave me *some* impressions of Sanskrit writing engraved on copper plate. He has also brought home quantities of manuscripts written on palm leaves, the leaves being long strips, pierced near each end with holes and strung on cords, each outside being a piece of wood to form the cover. Such a package constitutes a book. The writing on palm leaves is done with a steel pen or style, like *the illustration*. The writing is from left to right, like English and not like Hebrew. The style is held as in the annexed sketch, and its point is steadied by being pushed against the left thumb. The writing is indented or scratched in the leaf and then fine charcoal is rubbed in. In modern days, naphtha is sometimes applied to prevent insects attacking the leaves. (*Diary*).

Guy Fawkes Day 1869. *Friday November 5.* 'Old Pope Day' as it used to be called. The Tractarians, Pewseyites, High Church party or those who have Romanising tendencies are trying to discourage this annual demonstration, and I suppose they have in some degree succeeded. For the first time since my earliest recollection there were no stuffed figures of Guy Fawkes with his lantern and matches carried about by the children this morning. After dark in the evening however, there were plenty of fireworks and a large bonfire down on the beach. The fire was made on the shingle at the end of Fore Street *and* lit up the waves beautifully. (*Diary*).

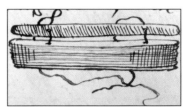

69/10/19-1. *Sanskrit 'book'.* (Diary)

69/10/19-2. *Style.* (Diary)

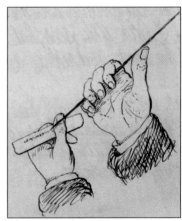

69/10/19-3. *Writing on palm leaf.* (Diary)

1870

70/3/15. *Old cracked jug.*
(Diary)

Dr. Temple's enthronement. *Monday January 3.* The papers describe the enthronization of Dr. Temple, the new Bishop of the diocese, which took place in Exeter Cathedral last Wednesday. He is the author of a paper called *The Education of the World,* bound up with others in a book known as *Essays and Revues.* Most of these have been strongly condemned for their materialistic views and tendencies towards infidelity. I have recently read the volume. If Dr. Temple's contribution to the book is not the worst of the essays, it is certainly found in very bad company. Great opposition both by clergy and laity has been made to his appointment but when the nomination has once taken place, no power apparently can arrest the course of events. (*Diary*).

Belzoni's widow. *Monday February 7.* Engaged all the morning carving the stone boss to go up in the arched ceiling between the hall and the staircase in the Old Chancel. The papers record the death of Belzoni's widow aged 88, *who* had a pension of £200 a year from government. Belzoni's travels in Egypt were my delight as a child. (*Diary*).

Exceptionally cold weather. *Monday February 14.* 'Please sir, the beer barrel is frozen and I can't draw any beer for dinner'. So I had a glass of hot brandy and water. (*Diary*).

Tuesday February 15. 'Please sir, the pump is frozen'. What next? It was thawed with a kettle of hot water. (*Diary*).

Old cracked jug. *Tuesday March 15.* Mrs. Willey, a fisherman's widow, brought an old cracked jug for me to buy. I said it was not worth sixpence it was so injured, for sum she gave it up. Its probable age and whether Dutch or English, I may find out some day. (*Diary*).

70/3/22. *Exotic weapons.*
(Diary)

Exotic weapons. *Tuesday March 22.* I have an elegant weapon, steel blade, chased and ornamented in gold, long handle, hollow, with a knife or dagger screwed in at the end, given me by Mr. Shaw, who brought it back from India. He told me it came from Nepal, but he did not know its name or its use. A short sword two feet two inches long has *also* just been given me, silver mounted with shagreen hilt, scabbard of leather *and* silver mounted. (*Diary*).

Walk to Harpford. *Thursday April 7.* Walked this afternoon to Harpford to call at the vicarage. Took the lanes via Cotmaton to Jenny Pine's Corner, along Bulverton Lane having Bulverton Hill on my left and then down Newton Poppleford Hill. I only saw Mr. Gattey, Mrs. Gattey being unwell and Annie was preparing for her wedding very shortly. Took a walk around the churchyard *and examined the* octagonal stair turret at the north-east corner of the tower. The farmhouse just below the churchyard towards the river, I believe occupies the site of the old building which some silly writers in old books said was the county gaol, *before* they then transferred *it* to Bicton. In my manuscript *History of Sidmouth* I have shown that it was always at Exeter. Walked home over Bulverton Hill via Salter's Cross and Mutter's Moor, *the* weather clear and dry and sun very hot. (*Diary*). *Whilst in the churchyard, Hutchinson sketched the remains of an old granite cross. This battered fragment has since been incorporated into a new one erected in memory of Augustus Toplady, vicar of Harpford for two years from 1766 and author of such fine hymns as 'Rock of Ages'.*

Dinner with G.W.Ormerod.

Friday April 15. Good Friday. At the parish church. Mr. G.W.Ormerod, now of Teignmouth but for seventeen years of Chagford, came over and dined with me. He is the son of the historian of Cheshire and himself a geologist and scientific man. He came to examine the cliffs all the way along *and I gave him several geological sections and drawings which I have recently made for him. (Diary).*

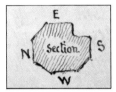

70/4/7. Shaft of Harpford Cross. (Diary)

Beer Church.

Wednesday April 20. Went to Beer with Mr. Heineken. Drove over Salcombe Hill, passed the pond and observed the Ordnance mark *and* got on the Lyme road at Trow. *We* stopped at the Three Horseshoes and took another look at the earthworks or cross-dyke on the north side, and noted especially the sunken road or remains of an entrenchment in the field next the road and parallel *with it. We* drove on, passed Hangman's Stone and Bovey House and stopped at Court Barton, a farmhouse, descending the hill to Beer. Passing this way on former occasions, our attention had been attracted by the remains of a building in the farmyard having somewhat the appearance of a church. I think I can remember the nave and chancel, dilapidated and altered, *with* a gable in the middle like *that* of a transept, and the tracery of a pointed window knocked out and the hollow filled in with boards. To our dismay we found everything bright and new. Two or three years ago, the old place was all pulled down and rebuilt *and* with respect to the old building we could learn nothing definite. They told me that the pulling down revealed many little chambers, passages and loopholes, but they never knew what the building had been. Much disappointed we continued down to the end of the street near the sea and saw a new boathouse covered with corrugated metal. We mounted the high chalk hill on the opposite side, lay down on the grass, eat our sandwiches and enjoyed the view. Our driver, who carried up the hamper, slipped and broke a bottle of ale *and* soon after, the bright sun being very hot, the cork of another bottle flew out with the report of a pistol and we lost half the contents. But as we had a jar of sweet cider, we did very well. *We could see* the cemetery and the new cemetery chapel (built about three years ago) from where we stood, but did not go there. *We* descended the hill and visited the old church or chapel, the remains of the architecture *being* of the Decorated period. *It has* one bell on a small turret. A tablet at the east end records the existence of the plague in 1646. I have heard that Beer was nearly depopulated and that dead were mostly buried on the left hand side of the road leading from Beer to Seaton at a spot on the crown of the hill. Another tablet on the east side of the chancel arch records that Edward Wood, late a fisherman, left twenty pounds in trust for the use of the poor. He died November 7, 1804. The chancel arch is the best feature. Outside, it looks as if the church had three transepts *but* it is merely that the north and south aisles are covered by three gables. The west door is plain. The two small doors of the aisles at the west end are of the annexed pattern.

A fine spring of water rushes down through the street and over it are built two conduits of stone and an iron fountain supplied with water from a reservoir. I once saw a son of Jack Rattenbury, the great smuggler, here but I forgot to ask for him today. The evening being rather cold, we got home soon after six to a good tea, always very refreshing. (*Diary*).

70/4/20-1. Beer church, tablet recording the plague. (Diary)

70/4/20-2. Beer church, aisle door at west end. (Diary)

Sword and dagger.

Monday April 25. A woman from Sidbury brought me a dagger which she begged I would buy for half a crown as she wanted to pay the coach fare to go and see a sick relation, so I bought it. She said that her son and a man were working in an old house in Sidbury, nearly opposite the church, *and whilst* they were engaged in pulling down the roof, they found a sword and dagger

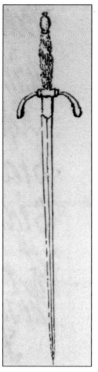

70/4/25. *Dagger from Sidbury.*
(Diary)

of antique pattern amongst the thatch. They had perhaps been hid there by some former owner who had died, and the circumstance died with him. The man took the sword and the boy the dagger. I must enquire what the sword is like, *but* the dagger I give in the *illustration.* It is fifteen inches and five eighths long, blade and hilt together, *and* the blade is thick with a lozenge section. (*Diary*).

Exeter Museum. *Tuesday April 26.* The paper says that on Friday last the 22nd inst., the Exeter Museum in Queen Street was formally transferred to the custody of the Mayor and Council of Exeter to hold as their property as trustees for the public. The Museum was also declared to be open free, *whereas* hitherto we have paid a penny. I believe it will be supported by a rate. (*Diary*).

Scandal. *Monday May 16.* Walked to the Holcombe Villas and out to the top of the Parson and Clerk Rocks. Returned part way near the cliff. There is a very pretty schooner yacht anchored off, called the 'Florence'. She belongs to the Duke of Leeds (Osborne) and the noble owner comes on shore and stays with a family called Holt, sometimes for weeks at a time. Mr. Holt generally goes away. It causes a great scandal in the place. There are three daughters and one son. Young Mr. Cann married one of the daughters a year or two ago. They were married by the Duke's chaplain, which caused some talk. (*Diary*).

Dancing bears. *Wednesday May 18. On May 10, Hutchinson had gone to Dawlish for a week, walking, visiting friends, etc.* Returned to Sidmouth. The morning I left home I saw two bears with their keepers near the market place. They are rarely brought about now-a-days. There is a story going that they have since eaten a boy and have been killed. I have not seen the story in the paper. (*Diary*).

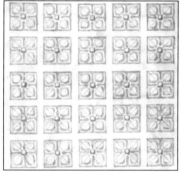

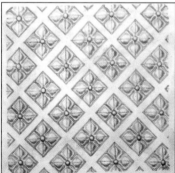

70/6/27. *Decorative plasterwork in Sidmouth church.* (Hist. of Sid. IV,117)

Plaster work in the parish church. *Monday June 27.* Began doing some diaper work in the parish church as an experiment, similar to what I have been doing in the Old Chancel, *over an area* about six feet high and three wide on the two flat piers near the transept. Today it was only preparation. (*Diary*).

The diaper pattern subjoined originated in the Old Chancel. When I was engaged on that building, it occurred to me that a good effect in wall decoration would be produced by quatrefoils or other Gothic forms in low relief, similar to the enrichments employed by architects in the Middle Ages, and I recalled to memory the effect of diapering cut in the stonework of the spandrels over the arches in Westminster Abbey. In my own case, as my walls were to be plastered, I had to stamp the patterns in the soft mortar to produce the same effect. I made the experiment in the passage beyond the hall at the Old Chancel with stamps of two sizes I carved for the purpose, and some time afterwards when thoroughly dry, coloured and gilt them. The vicar, seeing these, thought that some parts of the church might be much improved by similar work only without the colour, so I said I would try my hand. The three or four specimens in the transepts and chancel I did at different times in 1870. The square pattern is by far the easiest to do, the diamond being much more troublesome to measure and lay off on wet mortar, which must not be handled. I employed masons to take off the old mortar, had zinc lath nails driven into the joints in the stonework with the heads slightly out to hold the new mortar, the wall wetted and the new coat laid on. A day or two after, the second was laid on and smoothed, and further smoothed the next morning when the surface was drier. The mortar I used was Babbacombe lime and clean sand. It may now be dry enough for work. Having completed the measurements, the stamp should be driven in gently with a mallet. All the wet mortar must be impressed in one day as it would probably be too hard in twenty-four hours. Cracks in drying can be closed by pressure or with a dinner knife or trowel. (*History of Sidmouth IV, 117*).

Tuesday June 28. The plaster being ready, I impressed the stamps. (*Diary*).

Wednesday June 29. Finished the two piers but the work will require a thin coat of limewash when dry to fill up the cracks. The pattern is in diamonds. (*Diary*). *Hutchinson's work can still be seen decorating the two piers facing the chancel.*

Broad Down barrow excavations 1870.
Monday July 18. There is no Diary record of Hutchinson attending Kirwan's latest barrow excavations on Broad Down, but a full account of the Exeter Field Naturalists visit when barrow 62 and two others were opened is published in the Exeter and Plymouth Gazette for July 22, 1870. Kirwan excavated Barrows 61 and 60 over the next few days. The following extracts are taken from Hutchinson's Second Barrow Report and the coloured sketches from his History of Sidmouth. Kirwan's account can be found in Trans. Dev. Assoc. IV, 1870.

70/7/18-1. *Section of barrow 62.* (Hist. of Sid. I,76)

Broad Down Barrow No. 62. *Mr. Kirwan* asked me to come up when *this barrow* was opened and meet the Field Naturalists who were to be there, but I was prevented on that day. Mr. Heineken and myself were there immediately after whilst the trench and the kist-vaen were still open. It was a large mound of earth with the kist-vaen built up of rough stones in the centre. Many traces of charcoal were mixed with the earth. I sketched the open kist-vaen stone for stone, standing at the north end of the trench looking towards the south... . I then went down on my knees and thrusting my arm and hand in as far as I could reach, felt about the dark corners for another cup. 'Perhaps there's a snake in there', said Mr. Heineken. Didn't I pull my hand back! I felt nothing but fine soft black mould, and I regretted I had not got a trowel or a hand-digger to search more thoroughly. Something has always been forgotten. The calcined bones of an adult and those of an infant had already been removed, and Mr. Kirwan gives an engraving of what he terms a 'bone bead' from the same place (*Trans. Dev. Assoc IV, pl. II, fig. 2*), but this does not resemble the objects in the Museum and which I give in the *sketch*. The fine socketed celt was met with in the earth.

Broad Down Barrow No. 61. Seven feet high and 120 in diameter. Opened in 1870 by a trench from the south to the centre. Surrounded by a shallow fosse and a ring of large detached stones. There was a cairn of flints covered with three or more feet of earth *and* the kist-vaen had fallen in. Within it were found burnt bones on the bark of a tree and the fragmentary remains of a bronze spearhead, or perhaps a dagger, and also a rivet. Three feet from these a Kimmeridge coal cup was found, somewhat resembling that in No. 53. This tumulus was opened by Mr. *Kirwan and* I was unable to be present. He has given an engraving of the cup in its perfect state *and* I give one as I saw it in the Museum. Unlike the other, which resembles dark brown wood, this one looks cracked and fragile and very like charcoal.

Broad Down Barrow No. 60. A mound of flints covered with peat and clay. Opened in 1870 by a trench four or five feet wide from the south to the centre. Diameter nearly ninety feet and elevation about six. Burnt bones in the centre, and near them traces of a bronze quite gone to decay. (*Second Report of the Barrow Committee 1880*).

70/7/18-2. *Celt from barrow 62.* (Hist. of Sid. I,76)

70/7/18-3. *Bone objects from barrow 62.* (Hist. of Sid. I,76)

70/7/18-4. *Kist-vaen in barrow 62.* (Hist. of Sid. I,76)

70/7/18-5. *Section of barrow 61.* (Hist. of Sid. I,76)

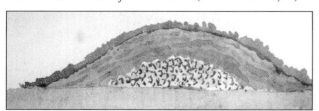

70/7/18-7. *Section of barrow 60.* (Hist. of Sid. I,76)

BRONZE SPEAR HEAD.   THE CUP.

70/7/18-6. *Cup and bronze spearhead from barrow 61.* (Hist. of Sid. I,76)

Further research in London. *Monday August 8.* Went to London, chiefly to verify some dates and look up some further historical facts for my *History of Sidmouth*, which has stood over too long, having been busy about other matters. To make a fair copy of the whole will occupy the winter evenings. I put up at the Charing Cross hotel. *(Diary). In London much of Hutchinson's time was spent in the British Museum Library and the Record Office, now moved to Chancery Lane, but he also made a short trip out to Ware to see his cousin , Rev. Oliver. He returned to Sidmouth on August 22 but was back in London again on October 13 for a further week's research.*

Belmont House, Sidmouth. *Friday September 30.* Called on Mr. Haycock at Belmont. He bought a lease last year and has much improved the house and grounds. *(Diary). Hutchinson's sketch depicts Belmont House in 1836.*

70/9/30. *Belmont House, Sidmouth,   May 14, 1836.* (DRO, Z19/2/8A/117)

Brother's death and a Communion Cup. *Tuesday October 18.* Having recently heard of the death of my brother in Australia, I wished to see my cousin the Rev. Wm. Oliver, Rector of Stapleford, Herts., who is my executor in England. Took the rail from King's Cross *and* changed trains at Hatfield, where I caught a glimpse of the Marquis of Salisbury's mansion. Got to Hertford *and* walked between three and four miles to Stapleford. My brother died of apoplexy on the 3rd of August at his seat Beaudesert in Hindmarsh Valley near Port Elliot, South Australia. He was my parent's oldest child (I was the fourth). His first name Young he had from an intimate friend of my father's. His second, Bingham, from Admiral Bingham who married one of my mother's sisters, daughters of Vice-Admiral Sir Wm. Parker of Harburn, co. Warwick, Bt. He was educated at Tiverton School, went some years into the Royal Navy *and then* accompanied the first Governor, Sir John Hindmarsh in 1836 to found the Colony of South Australia. He bought about 1000 acres of land mostly near Port Elliot and Goolwa, returned to England in 1851 to marry Miss Augusta Kingdon at Heavitree and returned that year to Australia. His wife and four children survive him.

I made a coloured sketch (in one of my sketchbooks) of an old silver cup or tankard just rescued from America. It was given to the second church in Boston, Massachusetts, by Thomas Hutchinson, my great-great-grand-

70/10/18-1. *Silver tankard.* (Diary)

70/10/18-2. *Silver tankard with the H. arms on it, once the drinking cup of my great-great-grandfather. (Not dated).* (DRO, Z19/2/8E/201)

father (father of the Governor) for the communion wine. The plate has been sold, fetch*ing* 63.70 dollars. It holds near three pints and a half *and* the Hutchinson arms are on it. (*Diary*). My cousin, the Rev. W.H., vicar of Blurton, co. Staffs., bought it back for about £13. (*Sketchbook E*).

History of Sidmouth. *Tuesday November 1.* Began transcribing my *History of Sidmouth* into two quarto volumes bound in green vellum which I have had made on purpose. This is the third time of transcribing. The first draft consisted of mere notes, with copies of old charters, deeds, etc. The second was pretty fairly written *and* the third, if I live to complete it, will be an improvement on the second. (*Diary*).

Guy Fawkes Day, 1870. *Saturday November 5.* I was up at the top of the church tower during the greater part of the day, superintending putting up a sham pinnacle on the north-west corner of the tower. It is proposed to put up four stone pinnacles (as there probably once were) to give the tower height and lightness. This is the more needed since the roof of the church has been raised when it was re-built. This scheme has always been mine since the re-building ten years ago. This experimental pinnacle is merely a framework of wood covered with canvas.

This evening there was a great rioting in the town. Under the plea of celebrating the fifth of November, a low mob of idle and dissolute fellows disguised in masks and some in women's clothes, placed a tar barrel all on fire against the shop of a saddler called Bennet living about the middle of the south side of New Street east of the market place. They also forced in the shutters, broke the glass and then threw fire into the house, *so that* it was with great difficulty the house was saved from being burnt. He had had a dispute with his apprentice boy and this was a piece of revenge. Several other persons had been threatened. (*Diary*).

70/12/10-1. *Man of God Rock, with Sidmouth beyond.* (Hist. of Sid. I,16)

Lord Courtenay's debts. *Thursday November 10.* Some more particulars of Lord Courtenay's bankruptcy have recently appeared. He owes £215 292 to unsecured creditors and £502 362 to creditors secured on the Devonshire estates. This seems to imply utter ruin to himself, to his relations and to all those who may come after him. How could any man not in a madhouse have been such an intense ass as to have got into such a gigantic predicament. (*Diary*).

Sixtieth birthday. *Thursday November 17.* My birthday. I am sixty but I feel as young and active as thirty. I was born in Winchester November 17, 1810, my father then being physician to Winchester Hospital. I believe he had previously been physician to Exeter Hospital. I was baptised at Heavitree in 1811, at the time, I have heard, that my father's only sister Mary married Captain Oliver RN, but I never examined the register. (*Diary*).

70/12/10-2. *Tortoiseshell Rock and Man of God Rock, looking south.* (Hist. of Sid. I,16)

More plaster work. *Friday November 18.* Finished some more diaper work in the church, this time in rectangular or square pattern on the north and south aisle sides of the flat piers before treated. (*Diary*). *Hutchinson continued his decorative plaster work in the church on and off over the next few months.*

Coastal changes. *Saturday December 10.* Walked to Ladram Bay and back, *as* I wanted to look at old scenes for the use of the geological chapter of my *History of Sidmouth*, not having been there for several years. I am surprised to see how many falls of the cliff there have been in many places and how much some features of some points in the coast have been thereby altered. Took sketchbooks and revised some of my old sketches of the 'Tortoiseshell

70/12/10-3. *Great Picket Rock, Otterton Point beyond.* (Hist. of Sid. I,16)

Rock' (so called) and others. The point of rock between Sandy Cove and Hern Rock Cove has been entirely detached from the mainland since my last visit by the falling away of the soft cliff at the neck of the promontory (as I may call it) so that the end has now become a complete island or separate mass of rock. Went through Ladram Bay arch, *a beautiful arch which* must go like the rest some day. The tide was not low enough to let me get into Ladram Bay, so I turned about and walked back the same way. It is rather a fagging walk, slipping and sliding over seaweed, springing over pools of water, short steps, long steps, high steps, low steps, over a great block of stone, then carefully across some stepping stones, *etc.* The sun was bright but the air very cold, and though the 'conkerbells', as they are pleased to term icicles in Devonshire, fringed the cliff, I was frequently in a good perspiration. Started at 11 AM and got back at 3 PM. (*Diary*).

Another solar eclipse. *Thursday December 22.* An eclipse of the sun is now going on *and* though the light is considerably lessened it is not so dark as I expected. The moon came on the west side of the sun's disc, passed below the centre and went off to the east. At the greatest obscuration about one fifth of the upper part of the sun was uncovered. There was a peculiar and beautiful bluish subdued light over the landscape, like looking through tinted grey glass. (*Diary*).

70/12/22. *The sun at its greatest obscuration.* (Diary)

End of Volume One – Diary continues in Volume Two.
Index and Bibliography appear in Volume Two.

BOOKS AND ARTICLES
BY P.O. HUTCHINSON

1836. *A Pedestrian Tour of One Thousand Three Hundred and Forty Seven Miles through Wales and England, by Pedestres and Sir Clavileno Woodenpeg, Knight of Snowden,* London.

1840. *A Guide to the Landslip near Axmouth, Devonshire.* Sidmouth: John Harvey.

1843. *The Geology of Sidmouth and of South-eastern Devon, illustrated with engravings on copper and wood.* Sidmouth: John Harvey.

1844. *The Chronicles of Gretna Green. Two Vols.* London: Bentley.

1849. *'A Dissertation on the Site of Moridunum, on the South Coast of Devonshire'.* Gentleman's Magazine, Vol. 31, 137-46.

1854. *'Singed Vellum'.* Notes and Gleanings, First Series. Number 249. Vol. X, 106.

1857. *A New Guide to Sidmouth and its Neighbourhood.* (Several editions). Sidmouth: Thomas Perry.

1860. *A History of the Restoration of Sidmouth Parish Church.* Sidmouth: Thomas Perry.

1860. *Rifled shot in smooth-bore guns.* Sidmouth: John Harvey.

1862. *The Ferns of Sidmouth: Illustrated with impressions from the ferns themselves.* Sidmouth: John Harvey.

1867. *A General Account of the Public Charities of Sidmouth.* Sidmouth: Richard Lethaby.

1868. *'On the opening of Tumuli at Farway'.* Proceedings of the Society of Antiquaries, Vol. 4, 159-161.

1868. *'On Hill Fortresses, Sling-stones, and Other Antiquities in South-eastern Devon'.* Report and Transactions of the Devonshire Association, Vol. 2, 372-382.

1869. *'Fossil Elephant's Tooth'.* Report and Transactions of the Devonshire Association, Vol. 3, 143.

1871. *'On a second Fossil Tooth found at Sidmouth'.* Report and Transactions of the Devonshire Association, Vol. 4, 455.

1872. *'Fossil Teeth at Sidmouth'.* Report and Transactions of the Devonshire Association, Vol. 5, 39-40.

1872. *'Iron Pits'.* Report and Transactions of the Devonshire Association, Vol. 5, 47-50.

1872. *'Bronze Celt found near Sidmouth'.* Report and Transactions of the Devonshire Association, Vol. 5, 82-3.

1873. *'Submerged Forest and Mammoth Teeth at Sidmouth'.* Report and Transactions of the Devonshire Association, Vol. 6, 232-5.

1875. *'The population of Sidmouth from 1260 to the Present Time'.* Report and Transactions of the Devonshire Association, Vol. 7, 203-8.

1876. *'Jar found at Musbury'.* Report and Transactions of the Devonshire Association, Vol. 8, 535-6.

1876. *'On some antiquities found in Devonshire'.* Proceedings of the Society of Antiquaries, Vol. 7, 37-41.

1877. *'A Scheme for a History of Devonshire'.* Report and Transactions of the Devonshire Association, Vol. 9, 292-5.

1879. *'Marriage amongst Birds'.* Animal World, October issue.

1879. *'Fossil Plant discovered near Sidmouth'.* Report and Transactions of the Devonshire Association, Vol. 11, 383-5

1879. *'On some circular patches of turf near Sidmouth'.* Proceedings of the Society of Antiquaries, Second Series, Vol. 8, 209-210.

1880. *'Second Report of the Barrow Committee'.* Report and Transactions of the Devonshire Association, Vol. 12, 119-151.

1880. Exhibits cast of steelyard weight found at Ashmore (Dorset). Proceedings of the Society of Antiquaries, Second Series, Vol. 8, 359-360.

1881. *'Second Report of the Committee to Obtain Information as to Peculiar Tenures of Land'.* Report and Transactions of the Devonshire Association, Vol. 13, 103-5.

1881. *'On the decay of Ancient Buildings'.* Proceedings of the Society of Antiquaries, Second Series, Vol. 8, 483-490.

1882. *'The Site of Moridunum'.* Report and Transactions of the Devonshire Association, Vol. 14, 516-24.

1884/6 *The Diaries and Letters of His Excellency Thomas Hutchinson, Esq., B.A., (Harvard) LLD (Oxon).* Two Vols. Boston: Houghton, Mifflin & Co.

1885. *'Honeyditches'.* Report and Transactions of the Devonshire Association, Vol. 17, 277-48.

1885. *'Sidmouth'* in *'Rate of Erosion of the Sea-Coasts of England and Wales'.* British Association for the Advancement of Science 417-422.

1886. Exhibits drawing of a saint in painted glass. Proceedings of the Society of Antiquaries, Vol. 11, 156-157.

1888. *'An Old Spring-gun'.* Notes and Gleanings, Vol. 1, 41-42.

1888. *'The Cartulary of the Priory of Otterton and Sidmouth'.* Notes and Gleanings, Vol. 1, 88-90, 106-107, 117-119, 139-142, 168-171, 187-190.

1890. *The Subsidy Rolls'.* Notes and Gleanings, Vol. 3, 118-119.

1890. *'The Subsidy Rolls, Second Series'.* Notes and Gleanings Vol. 3, 156-158.

1891. *'Joanna Southcott'.* Notes and Gleanings, Vol. 5, 9-13.

Not all of Hutchinson's literary output is listed here. Apart from his contribution to the Devonshire Association's version of Domesday Book, a novel 'Branscombe Cliffs' appeared in print and various plays, poems and fiction mentioned in his autobiography at the beginning of this volume remained unpublished.

Newspaper articles

Hutchinson's numerous articles on a great variety of subjects, often of considerable length, regularly appeared in both the regional and the national newspapers. He did not trouble to record them all but those few he thought worth preserving were cut out and pasted into the Diaries. Mentioned in this edition but not quoted from include:
'*A dissertation on the Site of Moridunum, on the South Coast of Devonshire*'. Harvey's Sidmouth Directory January 3 and 17, 1850.
'*Notes on Sidmouth*'. Harvey's Sidmouth Directory, No. 1 October 10, 1850 – No.XXI May 4, 1853. (A series of articles on the history of Sidmouth and neighbourhood).
Book revue of 'Claude' reprinted from Woolmer's Gazette, in Harvey's Sidmouth Directory December 19, 1850.

Manuscripts

In the West Country Studies Library, Exeter.
1870 – 1881. *History of Sidmouth*. Five quarto volumes bound in green vellum. A good photocopy is available for inspection.

In the Devon Record Office, Exeter.
1833 – 1893. *Sketchbooks*. Six volumes.
c. 1849 – 1894. *Diaries*. Five volumes. Also includes a number of letters, newspaper cuttings, etc.

In the Devon and Exeter Institution, Exeter.
1850 to *A History of the Town, Parish and Manor of Sidmouth in the County of Devon. Second Transcription.* Not illu
1860s strated except for a few small maps. The Institution also holds *Sidmouth Harbour Documents,* Hutchinson's bound collection of railway and harbour Acts relating to Sidmouth, letters on the same subject, etc.

In the Library of the Society of Antiquaries, London.
1865. *Antiquities of Sidmouth, Devon.* Soc. of Antiq. Ms. No. 250. (This volume is a 'list of antiquities existing near Sidmouth, and of antiques found either in the place or neighbourhood'. As well as brief descriptions and illustrations taken from the Diary, together with a few others not to be found there, it has bound in a number of letters on archaeological subjects written by Hutchinson to the Society of Antiquaries).
1886. *Report on the Court Rolls and Other Documents Relating to the Manor of Sidmouth in the County of Devon.* Soc. of Antiq. Ms. No. 309. (A bound volume containing the transcribed version of the Otterton Cartulary and other early documents relating to Sidmouth).
Four coloured sketches of the Zitherixon clay-pit discoveries numbered 46 and 47 contained in brown Devon folder.
Four loose letters in correspondence files for 1865, 1867 and 1888.

In the British Library, London.
Add. Ms. 46 650. Bentley papers, Vol. XCI. *Letter number 260.*
1863, 1867. Add. Ms. 33 206. Ellacombe Correspondence. *Letters, numbers 60 and 123.*
1876-1896. Add. Ms. 41 494. Correspondence of S.G.Perceval, Vol. 1. *Contains 96 letters written by Hutchinson.*
Add. Ms. 56 304. Dawson Correspondence. *Letter and circular 366 to Mr. Keily.*
Various dates. Eg. Ms. 2660. Correspondence of Governor Hutchinson, Vol. 2. *Contains letters by Hutchinson relating to the editing of the Governor's Diary. (See also Vol.1, ms. 2659; Letter Book of Gov. Hutchinson, ms. 2661; Diary of Gov. Hutchinson – four vols., mss. 2662-2665; Memorandum book of Gov. Hutchinson, ms.2666).*

SUBSCRIBERS

Dr N. W. Alcock, Leamington Spa

Countess of Arran

John Balderson, Colyford, Devon

Caroline Belam, Ludgate, West Buckfastleigh

Stephen Benson, Heasley Mill

Brian and Lorraine Bewsher, Buckfastleigh

John D. Bewsher, Paignton, Devon

Allan Bissett, Roborough, Winkleigh, Devon

Stuart and Shirley Blaylock, Cullompton, Devon

B. Bolt, Exeter, Devon

C. H. Bolton, Kilmington, Axminster

John Bosanko, Paignton

J. E. Bottom, East Budleigh, Devon

Joan Breach, Widdicombe, Kingsbridge, Devon

Collin W. Brewer,

Willemina Brice-Smith, Spreyton

T. C. Bryant, Llwyngwril, Wales

Martin Burdick, Shaldon, Devon

Peter Burdick, Topsham

K. J. Burrow, Bucks Cross, Devon

The Right Reverend R. F. Cartwright, Exeter, Devon

Roger and Paula Chapple, Barnstaple

Roy F. Chapple, Colyford, Devon

Sarah Child, Rackenford, Devon

Yvonne Cleave, Exeter, Devon

Robert Crayford, Orpington, Kent

Mrs B. J. Davison

Count Charles de Salis, Somerset

Mrs M. Down,

John Elliot, Bournemouth

Anne Everest-Phillips, The Old Chancel, Sidmouth

Max Everest-Phillips, Chelsea

John F. Finlay, Exeter, Devon

Miriam Fitter, Dolton, Devon

Mr and Mrs W. Foster, Tavistock, Devon

Dr Mary Freeman, Tavistock, Devon

Sarah Fulford, Exeter, Devon

Rhoda M. Gill, Turnchapel, Devon

J. H. S. Gillespie,

Dr T. and Mrs E. Greeves, Tavistock, Devon

Mr P. Hamilton Leggett B.S.C., Tavistock, Devon

M. J. Harris, Exminster, Devon

S. A. Harris, Newton Abbot, Devon

William Hart, Lower Knowle, Lustleigh, Devon

Johnathan and Susan Hassell, Torquay, Devon

P. Brian Hicks

Priscilla Hull, Budleigh Salterton, Devon

Christopher P. Humphries, Launceston, Cornwall

Fiona Hutton

Derek Jackson, Exeter

Andrew R. Janes, Taunton, Somerset

Elizabeth Jarrold, Ash, Dartmouth, Devon

Stephen and Janet Jenkins, Dunsford, Exeter, Devon

Ruth Kidson, Nigeria

Mr I. C. King, Northlew, Devon

John Laithwaite, Seaton, Devon

Brian Le Messurier, Exeter, Devon

Miss J. Lee, Tavistock, Devon

Philippa Luard, Barnstaple, Devon

Phillip Marchant, Exeter, Devon

Elsie Mayo, Branscombe

Ross C. McGinn, Teignmouth, Devon

Dr Roger Meyrick, Peter Tavy, Devon

Dr Roger Meyrick, Peter Tavy, Devon

Quentin and Helen Morgan Edwards, Glebe House, South Courtenay, Devon

Dr S. A. Mucklejohn, Wigston Magna, Leicestershire

Edward Murch, Dousland, Devon

David and Elizabeth Neill, Ebford

Jennifer Norton, Exmouth, Devon

John A. M. Overholt, London

Mr and Mrs K. Owen, Tavistock, Devon

Mrs R. I. Payton, Exeter, Devon

Bruce R. Peeke, Sidmouth, Devon

John W. Perkins, Babbacombe, Torquay, Devon

Angela Perkins, Sandford

Professor John Perrin, Ashburton, Devon

The Revd Dr Douglas E. Pett, Truro

Miss R. Pitts, Exeter, Devon

Mr John Anthony Pook, Teignmouth

Frank Potter, Exeter, Devon

Brenda Powell,

Audrey Prizeman, Plymouth, Devon

Anthony Pugh-Thomas, Somerset

Graham C. Pyke, Appledore, Devon

Bill Ransom, Ilsington

Adrian Reed, Uffculme, Devon

James and Margaret Richards, Abbotskerswell, Devon

G.H. Robertson-Owen, Ilsington

Mr and Mrs Rolfe, Tamerton Foliot, Plymouth, Devon

Kenneth Rowe, Topsham, Devon

Royal Institution of Cornwall, Truro, Cornwall

Muriel Sawtell, Winchcombe, Glos.

W. and A. Scarratt, Kingston, Kingsbridge, Devon

Margaret Sheppard, Hemyock Castle, Devon

Roger B. Slape, Bovey Tracey, Devon

Marjorie F. Snetzler, Buckland Brewer, Devon

Barbara Softly, Sidbury

Jeffrey Stanyer, Exeter, Devon

D.I. Stirk FRCS, Barnstaple, Devon

Dr Jeremy Stone, Dublin

Richard C. Stone, London

C. P. Stone, Exeter, Devon

Sarah Taylor, Cleveland, Ohio, USA

Mrs P. Theobald, Haslemere, Surrey

Graham Thorne, Maldon, Essex

Dr Martin Tingle, Creaton, Northants

John Tremlett, Bickham, Exeter, Devon

Marguerite Tunnicliffe, Barnstaple

Ms M. A. Turner

John F. W. Walling, Newton Abbot, Devon

Arthur H. Way, Seaton, Devon

Mr C. J. Webb, Winchester

Christine M. Weller, Exmouth, Devon

Mr and Mrs F. W. West, Dawlish, Devon

Mr P. D. Whitcomb, Whitcomb, Salisbury, Wilts.

Brenda Williams, Paignton

Mr John H. Wilsher, Sidmouth